Environmental Policy in the European Union

To our sons Gregory and Neil with our love and thanks for their patient understanding during the writing of this book.

Environmental Policy in the European Union

Pamela M. Barnes

Principal Lecturer specializing in EU Studies, University of Lincolnshire and Humberside, UK

Ian G. Barnes

Jean Monnet Professor of European Economic Integration and Professor of European Studies, University of Lincolnshire and Humberside, UK

Edward Elgar

Cheltenham, UK • Northampton, MA, USA

Published by
Edward Elgar Publishing Limited
Glensanda House
Montpellier Parade
Cheltenham
Glos GL50 1UA
UK

Edward Elgar Publishing, Inc.
136 West Suite 202
Northampton
Massachusetts 01060
USA

A catalogue record for this book is available from the British Library

Library of Congress Cataloguing in Publication Data
Barnes, Pamela M., 1950–
     Environmental policy in the European Union / Pamela M. Barnes, Ian
G. Barnes.
     Includes bibliographical references.
     1. Environmental policy—European Union countries. I. Barnes,
Ian, 1945–   . II. Title.
GE190.E85B37   1999
363.7'0094—dc21   99–15403
                                                                                                     CIP

Printed in the United Kingdom at the University Press, Cambridge

ISBN 1 85898 339 8 (cased)

10/01

Contents

List of figures

List of tables

Preface

This book examines the state of the European Union's environmental policy at the dawn of the twenty-first century. The authors of the book can only pass comment on a limited number of areas because of the vast array of legislation and policy initiatives that have been adopted by the national governments of the EU since the policy was launched in 1972. The focus of the analysis presented has as a result been on the period since the EU's Fifth Environmental Action Programme was published in 1992. An early evaluation of the impact of this programme would have been premature, given the political processes which need to be gone through to make policy statements a reality. Now it may be possible to come to a tentative view about progress, but of course the authors realize that the context of the policy has moved on. The EU's environmental policy does not operate in a vacuum and is both influenced by and in turn influences global environmental policy. A disappointment of the 1990s has been the failure of the global community to rise to the challenges posed during the United Nations Conference on the Environment held in Rio in 1992 (the Rio 'Earth Summit'). Whilst the global environmental problems are recognized by all concerned, too many of the participating states at the United Nations Conference are environmental 'free-riders'.

The context of policy making within the EU has also changed significantly. The Treaty on European Union has been adopted, and the Amsterdam Treaty has been agreed. The significance of these treaty changes is an important underlying theme of the book. At the same time the challenges facing the EU have increased. Its membership has increased from 12 to 15 member states with the inclusion of Austria, Finland and Sweden in 1995. This is seen by many as a positive move, given the commitment of the governments of these states to higher environmental standards. Further enlargement of the EU to Central and Eastern Europe is impending. The scale of environmental degradation in Central and Eastern Europe is only now becoming clear. The EU is facing the prospect of sharing the burden of this problem, while at the same time operating within a decision-making mechanism which is not up to the task.

There have been some successes with respect to several aspects of environmental policy. Some of these can be attributed to the efforts of the EU, others have been brought about by the intervention of the member states, or have been due to an increasingly responsive industrial and commercial sector. The continued demands of interested citizens and groups within society have also made a contribution to areas where there have been successes. However, it is apparent that some aspects of environmental degradation have worsened. The national governments of the EU continue to fail in their application of the negotiated and agreed treaty-based commitments. This lack of commitment ignores the economic and political costs this is imposing on the European Union. The economic cost lies in the waste of resources and costs of clean-up which the national economies face. The political costs lie in the impact that the national lack of commitment has on the process of European integration. This is particularly disappointing, as environmental issues have become of greater interest to the citizens of the EU.

Analysis of the EU's environmental policy provides an insight into the problems of reconciling differing national interests even in an area where there is agreement on the importance of developing an effective policy. The purposes of this book are therefore:

- to investigate the effectiveness of the policy at the end of the twentieth century;
- to present a critical appraisal of the impact of developments and proposals for the future; and
- to propose a number of alternative scenarios which would ensure the effectiveness of the EU's policy on the environment in the future.

The underlying argument being presented in this book is that more radical measures are not required for an effective environmental policy within the EU. What is required is that the opportunity be given for the measures already in place to be effectively implemented.

PMB
IGB

Acknowledgements

The authors of this book would like to thank Karen Blanchard for lending us her technical expertise in the compilation of figures and tables. Our thanks also go to the anonymous reviewer for some perceptive comments which were of great assistance.

Abbreviations

ACEA	European Automobile Manufacturers' Association
ACP	African, Caribbean and Pacific countries
ALTENER	Programme for the Promotion of Renewable Energy Sources
BAT	Best available technique/technologies
BATNEC	Best available technology not exceeding cost
BOD	Biochemical oxygen demand
CAP	Common agricultural policy
CEC	Commission of the European Communities
CEE	Central and Eastern European countries
CEP	Common energy policy
CEST	Centre for Environmental Studies
CFC	Chlorofluorocarbon
CFSP	Common foreign and security policy
CoM	Council of Ministers
CoR	Committee of the Regions
COREPER	Committee of Permanent Representatives
CORINE	Community Information System on the State of the Environment and on Natural Resources
CSCE	Conference on Security and Cooperation with Europe
CTE	Committee on Trade and Environment
DG	Directorate-General of the European Commission
DoE	Department of the Environment (UK)
DTI	Department of Trade and Industry (UK)
EAGGF	European Guidance and Guarantee Fund
EAP	Environmental action programme
EC	European Community
ECHO	European Community Humanitarian Office
ECJ	European Court of Justice
ECOFIN	Meetings of ministers with responsibility for finance and economic affairs
ECOSOC	Economic and Social Committee
ECSC	European Coal and Steel Community
ECU	European Currency Units
EEA	European Environment Agency

EEB	European Environmental Bureau
EEC	European Economic Community
EIA	Environmental Impact Assessment
EIB	European Investment Bank
EMAS	Environmental Management and Audit Scheme
EMIT	Environmental Measures and International Trade
EMU	Economic and monetary union
ENDS	Environmental Data Services Limited
ENTEC-UK	Environmental consultancy company (UK)
ENVIREG	Programme to finance environmental projects in less developed regions of the EU
EP	European Parliament
EQS	Environmental Quality Standard
ERDF	European Regional Development Fund
ESF	European Social Fund
EU	European Union
Euratom	European Atomic Energy Community
EUROPEN	European Organization for Packaging and the Environment
FAO	Food and Agriculture Organization (UN)
FEOGA	European Agricultural Guidance and Guarantee Fund
GATT	General Agreement on Tariffs and Trade
GMO	Genetically modified organism
HELCOM	Commission of the Helsinki Convention on the Baltic Sea Environment
ICLEI	International Council for Local Environmental Initiatives
IEEP	Institute for European Environmental Policy
IEM	Internal energy market
IGC	Intergovernmental Conference
IIT	Inter-industry trade
IMPEL	Informal Network for Implementation and Enforcement of Community Law
IPC	Integrated pollution prevention and control
IPCC	International Panel on Climate Change
ISPA	Instrument for Structural Policies for Pre-Accession
IT	Information technology
JHA	Justice and Home Affairs
kgoe	kilograms of oil equivalent
LFA	Less favoured areas
LIFE	Financial Instrument for the Environment
MAST	Marine Science and Technology Programme
MB	Marginal benefit
MEA	Multilateral environmental agreements

MEPs	Members of the European Parliament
MPC	Marginal private cost
MSC	Marginal social cost
NACCB	National Accreditation Council for Certification Bodies (UK)
NCC	National Consumer Council (UK)
N_2O	Nitrous oxide
NGOs	Non-governmental organizations
NIS	Newly independent states
NO_x	Nitrogen oxides
NTB	Non-tariff barriers
OBDS	On board diagnostic systems
OECD	Organization for Economic Cooperation and Development
OPET	Organization for the Promotion of Energy Technology
PCP	Pentachlorophenol
PHARE	Programme of Assistance for economic reform in Central and Eastern Europe
PPP	Polluter pays principle
QMV	Qualified majority voting in the Council of Ministers
RES	Renewable energy resources
RIIA	Royal Institute for International Affairs
RTD	Research and technological development
SAVE	Specific Actions for Vigorous Energy Efficiency
SEA	Single European Act (1987)
SEM	Single European market
SFs	Structural Funds
SMAP	Short and Medium-term Priority Environmental Action Programme
SME	Small and medium-sized enterprises
TEC	Treaty of the European Community
TENs	Trans-European networks
TEN-T	Trans-European Transport Network
TEU	Treaty on European Union
THERMIE	Energy Technology Support Programme
toe	tonnes of oil equivalent
UCLAF	Unité de co-ordination de la lutte anti-fraude (EU's anti-fraud unit)
UN	United Nations
UNCED	United Nations Conference on Environment and Development
UNEP	United Nations Environment Programme
UNFCCC	United Nations Framework Convention on Climate Change
UNICE	Union of Industrial and Employers' Confederations in Europe
WCED	World Commission on Environment and Development
WHO	World Health Organization
WTO	World Trade Organization

1 Introduction: the rationale for a European Union policy on the environment

INTRODUCTION

The environmental debate gained a new prominence on the political agendas of all governments during the 1970s. Industrial production processes and the increased use of chemicals were widely recognized as the source of severe problems of environmental degradation. As the member states of the European Union (EU) began to develop national policies to control growing pollution problems from various sources, the danger grew that trade might be distorted by these measures. In 1972 the EU[1] launched the first of a series of environmental action programmes (EAPs). The main concentration of the action programmes was on harmonization of national environmental policies to ensure that new barriers to trade did not emerge. Whilst this was the primary concern of the EU's environmental actions, other considerations were also met. Wide-ranging measures were introduced which included legislation covering the areas of water and air pollution, waste management, controls on the chemical industry, environmental impact assessment, protection of wildlife and human health, and incentives to stimulate research and development of eco-technology. By the mid-1980s the number of measures introduced by the EU meant that it was possible to conclude that EU action had become the single most significant factor affecting the development of the national environmental legislation of the member states.

The late 1990s marked an important stage in the development of environmental policy for a number of reasons:

1. There was a recognition that the environmental problems and challenges had increased. The sources and consequences of the impact of pollution on climate change had become the single most important of these concerns.
2. A framework of environmental legislation was in place within the EU and the number of pieces of legislation introduced began to slow down. As a result the question of effective implementation and enforcement became more important, in order to avoid the danger that the EU's environmental policy might become fragmented and therefore ineffective.

3. Attention had switched to other types of action to ensure that the objectives of the policy were achieved.
4. The requirement to apply the principle of subsidiarity to environmental actions had brought greater scrutiny of legislation and careful consideration of how the policy was to be managed.
5. The search for a policy which would achieve the longer term objectives of sustainable development had given new opportunities for the public to participate in the policy-making process.
6. The changed geopolitical structure of Europe brought both environmental challenges and opportunities for the European Union in the twenty-first century. See Table 1.1.

Table 1.1   From European Community to European Union

Date	Treaties and membership
1951 (April)	The Treaty of Paris signed by France, Germany, Italy, Belgium, the Netherlands and Luxembourg to form the European Coal and Steel Community
1957 (March)	Treaties of Rome signed by France, Germany, Italy, Belgium, the Netherlands and Luxembourg to form the European Economic Community and Euratom
1973 (January)	Accession of UK, Ireland and Denmark
1981 (January)	Accession of Greece
1986 (January)	Accession of Spain and Portugal
1987 (July)	Single European Act ratified
1990 (October)	Unification of Germany admits the former German Democratic Republic to the EU
1992 (February)	Treaty on European Union (Maastricht) signed by the Heads of Government of the member states
1993 (November)	Treaty on European Union ratified
1995 (January)	Accession of Finland, Sweden and Austria
1996 (March)	Member States begin to negotiate to revise the Treaty
1997 (October)	Heads of Government sign the revised Treaty (Amsterdam)
1998 (March)	Identification of the states which are to hold negotiations with the EU for 'fast-track' accession – Poland, Hungary, Czech Republic, Slovenia, Estonia and Cyprus
1998/1999	Germany first country to ratify the Treaty of Amsterdam, followed by the other member states
1999 (May)	Treaty of Amsterdam ratified

THE IMPACT OF THE EU'S ENVIRONMENTAL POLICY

Since the launch of the European Union's environmental policy in 1972 wide-ranging measures have been introduced which focus not just on pollution control but also on the protection of human health and the preservation of the environment. Standards have been set in relation to air and water quality, transport pollution, and chemical emissions, and outline waste management procedures have been introduced. These measures have acted as an important stimulus to action in some of the member states where environmental standards may have been lower than in others. The danger of a legislative gap emerging between the member states has been reduced, with the EU's legal measures increasingly setting the pace of environmental legislation for member states as well as for other countries (Kramer 1995: 160). The EU's environmental policy would therefore appear to have had a positive impact, especially if its success is measured by the number of legislative acts which have been adopted within the European Union since 1972.[2]

FAILURE OF THE POLICY

If the measure of success used is the degree of environmental 'clean-up' which has resulted, the conclusion is less certain, as shown in the Dobris Assessment of the state of the European environment (Stanners and Bourdeau 1995). The Dobris Assessment confirmed the poor quality of the environment in Europe. Whilst the most serious problems were found to be in Central and Eastern Europe, serious stresses on the environment, natural resources and human health were evident across the whole of Europe. The second report on the state of Europe's environment (European Environment Agency 1998) was presented at the meeting of the Environment Ministers of all European Countries Conference held in Aarhus, Denmark in June 1998. The 12 key environmental problems identified in the first Dobris Assessment were reviewed. See Table 1.2.

The analysis in the 1998 report showed that some of the pressures on the environment had been reduced but that there had not been an overall improvement in the quality of the European environment. Whilst it was possible to attribute some of this to natural time delays in the build-up of the effectiveness of policy measures, many of the measures have been too limited to deal with the problems. Transport, energy and agriculture were highlighted in the report as the sectors most damaging to the environment and as those where least progress had been made. In the manufacturing and energy sectors there had been more progress as there was a longer history of concentrated environmental policy in these two areas.

Table 1.2   Summary of progress on environmental problems, 1993–98

Key environmental problem	Progress on policies	Progress on state of the environment
Climate change	+/–	–
Stratospheric ozone depletion	+	–
Acidification	+	+/–
Tropospheric ozone	+/–	–
Chemicals	+/–	–
Waste	–	–
Biodiversity	+/–	–
Inland waters	+/–	+/–
Marine and coastal environment	+/–	–
Soil degradation	–	–
Urban environment	+/–	+/–
Technological and natural hazards	+	+

Notes:
+   Positive development with regard to policies or the state of the environment.
+/–   Some policy development but insufficient to deal with the full problem (including geographical coverage).
     Can also indicate uncertain or varying developments in the various areas.
–   Little development of policies or unfavourable development of the state of the environment. Can also indicate continuing high pressure or poor state of the environment.

Source: European Environment Agency (1998).

An equally uncertain conclusion about the success of the EU's environmental policy comes from a consideration of the record of the national governments of the member states on the incorporation of the EU's environmental legislation into their national laws. The lack of action taken to enforce the EU's environmental measures by the national governments undermines the operation of the policy. Initial policy failure has often been attributed to the fact that the EU's environmental policy was not one of the common policies adopted by the founder member states of the European Economic Community (EEC) in March 1957. This has frequently been identified as the reason for the poor record of some national governments on the implementation of legislation. However, since environmental policy was given a firm legal basis in 1987, that view has been without validity for more than a decade. Furthermore, it was never sufficient to explain why some areas have been particularly subject to lack of effectiveness in the policy of the EU. The basis of that failure is more fundamental and wide-ranging. It has its origin in both political and economic failure.

The EU is a unique organization with many more policy tools at its disposal than any of the other groupings of nations in international environmental agreements. However, difficulties remain in reconciling national and specialist interests. The seeming lack of political commitment of the national governments to environmental policy is posing a number of challenges as well as obstacles to the functioning of the policy. The progress report on the implementation of the Fifth Environmental Action Programme published by the Commission in 1996 concluded that 'what is lacking is the attitude changes and the political will to make the quantum leap to make the necessary progress to move towards sustainability ... ' (CEC 1996p: 3). As the development of the EU continues, it will become more problematic to achieve a reconciliation of the different national interests. The reasons for this political failure will be discussed in Chapters 3 and 4, which evaluate the role of the actors in the policy process from decision making to policy enforcement. The impact of the political failure will be investigated in each of the sectoral chapters.

All environmental policy is characterized by the economic failure to internalize the costs of environmental degradation into the policy process. This failure has consistently led to inappropriate policy making. The full and true costs of environmental degradation have not been taken into account in the formulation of policy by all tiers of government. These costs are considerable and are an often-unacknowledged drain on the national resources. This economic failure of the EU's environmental policy will be analysed in Chapter 5 with an evaluation of the new policy instruments that have been introduced within the EU to overcome the problem. Examples of the impact of the failure to internalize the cost of the policy will be discussed in the chapters dealing with the different sectors of economic activity.

The above criticisms of lack of commitment and failure to acknowledge the costs of environmental degradation may be levelled at all governments and policy makers. Within the unique organization of cooperation and collaboration of the EU, additional pressures are evident. They originate from two sources. First, the framework of the policy is based on shared responsibility for environmental matters at both the national and supranational levels of government. The success of sharing the responsibility for environmental protection will depend on the member states of the European Union having the same priorities and value systems. Everyone would acknowledge that there is a need to protect the environment, but differences exist among the national governments about how this is to be achieved.

The differences in the national policies are the result of differences in the physical geography of the member states; differences in resource endowment and economic activity, differences in the priorities given to the allocation of resources for environmental protection, and differences in national values. The national differences in approach to environmental policy are demonstrated most clearly in the concern in some states to ensure that environmental measures produce high standards of environmental protection in order to preserve the national resource base. As a result, states such as Denmark, Germany, Austria, Sweden, Finland and the Netherlands have gained a reputation as 'leaders' (Sbragia in Wallace and Wallace 1996: 235) or 'pioneers' (Andersen and Liefferink 1998) in environmental protection. In other states environmental issues are considered to be of lesser importance to the resolution of problems of unemployment or poverty. Among this group of 'laggards' are states such as Portugal, Greece, Italy, Spain, Ireland and Belgium.

The second source of criticism which may be made relates to the objectives of the EU's environmental policy. On the one hand the EU's policy is concerned with ensuring that trade within the European market is not distorted. On the other hand the policy is an attempt to meet the wide-ranging and increasing problems of environmental degradation in Europe. These policy objectives are frequently seen as contradictory to one another. Policy measures may therefore be seen as unsatisfactory to a number of the interested parties as they appear neither to fully address the problems of the market nor environmental protection.

WHY AN EU POLICY ON THE ENVIRONMENT?

It is possible to identify physical, economic, political and social rationales for concerted action to be taken in this area of EU policy. The European Union encompasses in a relatively limited geographical area a very wide range of physical regions. There are therefore many examples of the problems of trans-border pollution. The very diverse physical environments within the European Union generate numerous problems in relation to providing them with what might be considered an adequate level of environmental protection. Concerted action within the framework of the European Union offers many additional opportunities for these problems to be dealt with in a more effective manner than through the separate national environmental policies of the member states.

The member states of the European Union occupy a geographical region which stretches from beyond the Arctic Circle to the northern shores of the Mediterranean Sea. The states are in very close proximity to one another, sharing many of the same physical and geological features, for example the River Rhine, the Ardennes Plateau, the Fenno-Scandinavian Shield, and the North Sea and Mediterranean Sea coastlines. The prevailing winds are westerly across the geographical region. Of the four main geographical areas it is possible to identify within the European Union, the North European Plain has been the centre of the densest population for a long time in the history of Europe. See Table 1.3.

Table 1.3   Population profile of the member states of the EU

Member state	Total area km²	Population, 000s (1996)	Population density (1996)	Population increase, 1960–93 (%)	GDP per capita, 1996 (ECU at current prices)
Austria	83 860	8 054.8	96	13	21 553
Belgium	30 518	10 143.0	332	11	20 455
Denmark	43 093	5 251.0	121	13	26 100
Finland	338 150	5 116.8	15	14	22 763
France	549 096	58 265.3	106	26	20 610
Germany	356 947	81 538.6	228	12	22 763
Greece	131 957	10 474.5	79	25	9 132
Ireland	70 285	3 591.2	51	26	15 509
Italy	301 311	57 333.0	190	14	16 353
Luxem.	2 586	412.8	159	26	32 942
Netherl.	41 480	15 493.9	373	33	19 892
Portugal	91 986	9 920.8	107	11	8 481
Spain	504 759	39 241.9	77	28	11 720
Sweden	449 960	8 837.5	19	16	22 567
UK	244 138	58 697.3	240	11	15 297
EU 15	3 240 153	369 715	114	17	18 088

Source: Compiled from *Europe*, 20 January 1997, p. 2, CEC (1996e: 8).

The North German Plain's natural and resource advantages made it the focus of developments in manufacturing and population growth during the Industrial Revolution. In the late 1990s this historical legacy, combined with modern processes, has produced an area which is characterized by declining industry, intensive farming, urban sprawl and heavy traffic congestion, with all the associated environmental problems. The other regions of the EU include upland areas such as the Central and Southern European Highlands, for example the Spanish Sierra Nevada mountains, the Pyrenees and the Alps, which are less densely populated. In the northern states of the EU the Fenno-Scandinavian Shield, the Scandinavian Highlands, and the northern and western areas of Ireland are also sparsely populated. However, as many of these areas have fragile ecosystems, environmental protection is a no less urgent priority here than in the densely populated regions. In addition, the countries of the EU have a combined coastline of more than 89 000 km, which brings other issues to the top of the environmental policy agenda.

The distribution of agricultural land, wooded areas, and other land in the EU is not uniform. See Table 1.4. Of the total area of the EU, 27 per cent is arable land, 35 per cent is wooded and 18 per cent is grassland. The average forested cover in the EU states is 20 per cent: however some states have considerably more forested areas than others (Finland 69 per cent, Sweden 62 per cent) and some have relatively small areas (Ireland 5 per cent, the Netherlands 8 per cent). Ireland has the most extensive agricultural usage at 80 per cent of the country's total land mass.

Table 1.4   Distribution of agricultural land, wooded areas and other land in the EU (figures in km²)

	Agric. land – crop land[1]	Agric. land – meadows[2]	Wooded areas	Other land	Total area
Austria	15 060	199 860	32 100	16 700	83 860
Belgium	8 270	5 280	6 170	10 798	30 518
Denmark	25 480	2 080	4 450	11 083	43 093
Finland	25 130	1 200	232 220	79 600	338 150
France	192 500	111 040	148 720	96 826	549 096
Germany	119 100	52 430	104 120	81 297	356 947
Greece	39 050	52 550	26 200	14 157	131 957
Ireland	9 230	46 900	3 200	10 955	70 285
Italy	119 700	48 750	67 680	65 181	301 311
Luxembourg	560	696	890	446	2 586
Netherlands	9 220	10 640	3 500	18 120	41 480
Portugal	31 730	8 380	33 000	18 876	91 986
Spain	199 460	102 600	159 150	43 585	504 759
Sweden	27 680	5 520	280 200	136 560	449 960
UK	65 910	111 090	24 250	42 880	244 138
EU 15	888 080	579 010	1,125 930	647 133	3,240 153

[1] Arable land and permanent crops
[2] Permanent meadows and pastures

Source: CEC (1996e).

The EU also encompasses five diverse types of climate zone. A maritime climate prevails along the western fringe of the EU, including the UK and Eire. This climatic type is characterized by mild winters, cool summers, and constant humidity. The semi-continental climate characterized by cold dry winters and hot stormy summers is found further inland and becomes most extreme where the EU borders the states of Poland, the Czech Republic, Slovakia and Hungary. The Mediterranean climate prevails in the coastal areas of the southern states and is characterized by mild, wet winters and hot dry summers. The mountainous and upland regions have a climate which is affected by the altitude and exposure to wind, sun and rain. Extremes of cold are found in the regions close to the Arctic Circle in the states of Finland and Sweden.

The differences in climate and physical geography of the member states give rise to a considerable diversity of the ecosystem within the geographical region of the EU. This raises many problems for the protection of these areas. The geographical regions do not coincide with the political divisions of Europe into nation states. The development of an EU policy enables a more coherent approach to be adopted to the protection of physical regions which cross national boundaries. It provides a firm basis for pollution controls to avoid the problems of damage which originates in one state but affects another, for example wind-borne sulphur deposition.

Following the enlargement of the EU in 1995 to include Finland, Sweden and Austria, its population increased to 370 million (see Table 1.3), equalling 6.5 per cent of the total world population. The enlargement of the EU to include the states of Central and Eastern Europe[3] will create an EU of nearly 500 million people. At the same time it is apparent that the rate of natural increase of the population is slowing within the EU and that by 2020 the population is projected to equal only 4.2 per cent of the world total (CEC 1996c; 1996e: 8). From the point of view of environmental policy developments, it is not absolute numbers of people that are of concern but their location and concentration. The concentrations of population and the current levels of urbanization are unlikely to be radically altered by the process of demographic change which is taking place.

The EU has the most concentrated population in the world after monsoon Asia and this has given rise to many environmental problems. The population in each of the member states of the EU varies from the very densely populated Netherlands (373 per km^2) to the sparsely populated Nordic states of Finland and Sweden. The highest densities of population are to be found in the so-called 'hot banana' (describing the geographical shape of the area) formed by drawing a diagonal line from the north west of England to the north of Italy, including Belgium, the Netherlands and the industrialized regions of the Ruhr in Germany (see Table 1.3). Industrial developments, large-scale urban concentrations, intensity of farming techniques and increasingly complex transportation networks accompany high densities of population in the EU. Of the most polluting activities within modern industrial societies, many are associated with the way in which transport and industry operate. The developments of the EU's environmental policy in these two sectors are analysed in Chapters 7 and 10.

The link between the increased economic integration of the evolving market and the type of environmental policy which would be required to counterbalance its impact was the impetus for the First Environmental Action Programme (EAP) in 1972. The objective was to avoid barriers to trade between the member states created by the existence of national environmental policies. The view was that within an integrated market the trade distortion effects of national environmental measures would be greater and the damage to economic growth from persistent trade barriers would be intensified. Whilst there is no simple answer to the question of whether differing national environmental policies will prove to distort trade, the potential does exist. Barriers are evident from two areas of national action: the maintenance of national product standards which are set with environmental criteria as their basis, and the additional costs incurred by companies operating within the integrated market but subject to differing national regulations. The objective of the EU's evolving action has therefore been to harmonize the national policies so that these distortions to the operation of the market did not occur. See Chapter 5.

The 1980s global debate about the means by which the objectives of sustainable development might be achieved focused attention on the need to develop an environmental policy which ensures integration and balance between the liberalization of trade, environmental protection and economic development. The response of the EU was to lay the foundations in the Fifth Environmental Action Programme for the strategy by which this was to be achieved (see Chapter 2). The Fifth EAP outlined the measures which were to be considered by the national governments within the EU as well as the role which the EU was to adopt in the global forums determining policy.

In the late 1990s the unemployment rate within the EU had risen to over 10 per cent of the labour force. The potential of environmental policy to influence employment creation provides a linkage of the economic and the social rationales for the EU to take action. In 1997 the Organization for Economic Cooperation and Development (OECD) presented the following conclusions in its report on environmental policies and employment (OECD 1997b: 10): first, that there are direct linkages between the environment and employment creation; second, that rather than destroying jobs as some industrialists claim, the net impact of environmental policies is positive; and third, that it is possible to coordinate environmental and employment concerns. What the OECD findings seemed to uphold was that although environmental and employment policies are not strictly complementary, they may be compatible.

The heavy burden on the national economies of the EU in the late 1990s was the result of the high levels of unemployment combined with an inability of the respective governments to create employment (see Chapter 7). If the advantages outlined in the OECD report were to be gained within the EU, then two issues had to be taken into account. The first was the importance of ensuring that any environmental actions being taken by the EU did not have a harmful impact on existing employment opportunities. The second was that environmental measures should not stifle job creation initiatives within the EU. The pressure for EU-level action on unemployment led to the addition of a chapter on employment to the Amsterdam Treaty and initiatives to ensure that the protection of the environment and creation of employment began to be seen as linked (see Chapter 7).

Whilst the primary focus of the European Union's environmental policy has been to prevent distortion of trade, the policy has developed and become, for the general public, one of the most readily identifiable areas of activity within the EU. As the nature of the EU's policy has widened to include more issues which are of environmental interest rather than being narrowly economically focused, the opportunities for the EU to gain support and a positive 'popular face' have grown. This interest remains at a high level. The policy is based on a sharing of responsibility between the national and supranational tiers of government within the EU. The opportunity exists for public participation in the policy-making and monitoring process, encouraged through a number of initiatives which have been proposed by the European Commission. The interest and support for the policy area by the Members of the European Parliament (MEPs) reflect this public awareness and concern.

In 1992 the Maastricht Treaty included a commitment to the promotion of sustainable growth respecting the environment. This was coupled with the aim of achieving a policy which was based on a high level of environmental protection, with environmental considerations being taken into account in the drawing up and implementation of other EU policies. Expectations of action to protect the environment were therefore raised, but there was little time to evaluate the likely outcome of the changes before the round of treaty revision began in 1996.

Action that would respond clearly to the concerns of citizens about environmental protection was given a high priority in the mandate for the Intergovernmental Conference (IGC) presented to the Turin European Council in 1996. The European Commission's opinion paper on the IGC (CEC 1996u) proposed that the right to a healthy environment and the duty to ensure it should be included in the provisions of the Treaty on Union citizenship. This view was reinforced by the Swedish, Dutch, Italian and Finnish governments, in their position papers at the beginning of the Intergovernmental Conference. However, the 1997 treaty amendments did not include this requirement. What was done in the Treaty of Amsterdam was to re-emphasize the commitment to a high level of environmental protection and the necessity to integrate environmental requirements in all the polices and activities of the Community: article 6 TEC (3c TEC).[4]

Ensuring that the integration of environmental requirements into policy is carried out will give rise to much controversy for the policy makers. It will also be a difficult requirement for the European Court of Justice to rule on. Measures and mechanisms will have to be put in place so that it is possible to evaluate how far the measures are matching the commitment. In June 1998 the Commission presented a procedural document outlining ways in which it could be done (CEC 1998d). In addition, the recommendations made by the Commission on implementation of policy, discussed in Chapter 4, provide a means by which the integration of the environmental requirements in policy may be monitored.

THE ENVIRONMENTAL PROBLEM

Environmental degradation in Europe is continuing to increase. The EU has identified a number of concerns on which to concentrate its efforts. Since the adoption of the Fifth Environmental Action Programme in 1992 the European Commission has been required to present regular evaluations of the progress that has been made in fulfilling the environmental objectives of the programme. When the first of the progress reports from the European Commission on the implementation of the Fifth Environmental Action Programme was published in 1996 (CEC 1996p), it was accompanied by a comprehensive and wide-ranging report on the state of the environment from the European Environment Agency (EEA) (Wieringa 1996). The overall picture which emerged from the EEA assessment was that the European Union was making progress in reducing certain pressures on the environment, but that this was not enough to improve the general quality of the environment and even less sufficient to progress towards sustainability.

This conclusion is disappointing for a number of reasons. The active approach which the EU has adopted towards the development of environmental policy since 1972 is demonstrated by the extent of the legislative framework which has been established. Recognition that funding is important to assist with innovative approaches to the protection of the environment has come since 1991 through the Financial Instrument for the Environment (LIFE) initiative, the Cohesion Fund and revisions to the regulations for the Structural Funds in 1993 and 1999. Support for other mechanisms of environmental protection, such as the use of environmental taxation and voluntary agreements with industry, has grown within the EU. The dilemma which the EU has to resolve is how to ensure that the rhetoric of environmental policy does not overwhelm the action and leave environmental damage as a drain on the economic resources and economic growth of the EU.

THE ENVIRONMENTAL DILEMMA

	HIGH LEVEL OF COMPLIANCE	LOW LEVEL OF COMPLIANCE
HIGH LEVEL OF PROTECTION	Box 1 The Ideal World. The ideal environmental protection standard High cost of implementation High risk of failure	Box 2 Policy drowned in rhetoric. Good for rhetoric but in the long term lacks credibility Low level of environmental protection Low commitment to implementation Poor for the internal market as trade distortion is possible
REALISTIC* LEVEL OF PROTECTION	Box 4 Realism and Progress. Achievable, therefore raises commitment and confidence Allows for progressive increase of standards in the future Good for trade High risk politically, as not good for rhetoric	Box 3 The Compromise Candidate. Current situation within the EU Standards which are a compromise Implementation left to the member states High-risk strategy for the environment as the member states may not be committed to the environmental measures Poor for trade as it allows distortion to emerge

*Must answer three questions: Is the measure needed? Are resources available? Is it politically acceptable?

Source: Adapted from Barnes (1996a: 3).

Figure 1.1   The European Union's environmental dilemma

Figure 1.1 shows a number of possible scenarios which might characterize the future development of an effective EU environmental policy. The ideal-world scenario shown in Box 1 identifies the most effective environmental protection policy which would result if stringent measures and high standards were coupled with a high level of compliance. The ideal-world scenario presupposes that the policy which is being developed is based on rational and informed choices made between possible policy options. As such, this scenario is not one that is deliverable by the EU or indeed by any other tier of government! (See Chapter 3.)

Environmental policy makers in the EU are subject to many constraints which limit the nature of the decisions which are made. These include the constraint of the requirement for a sharing of the responsibility for environmental actions between the supranational and national tiers of government. Other constraints are the result of the existence of differing values and expectations amongst the individual actors in the policy process. The organizational structures within which the policy makers are operating also act as a constraint on the type of action which may be introduced. Inevitably the costs of action will limit what may be done. Policy makers are also constrained by limits imposed because of past influences and developments in the policy process. In addition to these constraints, the EU has to overcome the problem that the introduction of stringent measures would not necessarily be accompanied by high levels of compliance because of the lack of willingness of the national governments of the member states to implement the policy measures.

The scenario shown in Box 2 of Figure 1.1 is a more minimalist approach: stringent measures and high standards coupled with low levels of compliance. Aspects of the EU's environmental policy are characterized by this approach. Little environmental improvement results. The rhetoric of the approach therefore destroys the long-term credibility of the policy. The German government has long been considered to be the 'lead' state within the EU with regard to environmental protection. Some evidence began to emerge in the late 1990s that under the twin pressures of environmental degradation of the eastern *Länder* and rising levels of unemployment, this position was being undermined (Boehmer-Christiansen 1998; Cremer and Fisahn 1998). On some issues the German position has become closer to the scenario of Box 2. It is obvious that there is still strong support in German opinion polls for the development of environmental measures.[5] The emphasis among the general public has, however, moved to support action designed to reach a balance between environmental protection and employment provision.

The compromise option of Box 3 in Figure 1.1 is a reflection of the current situation in the majority of the member states. The danger of continuing with this approach is that environmental policy will become fragmented and concentrated at the national level as the European Union enlarges. The consequences of that would be that the harmonization of national policies becomes impossible and the integrated market subject to distortion. The overall impact would also be to slow any progress being made on preventing continued degradation of the environment. At the end of the 1990s, therefore, the EU is faced by some difficult choices with regard to the future development of its environmental policy.

Box 4, the realistic scenario, outlines a scenario which would enable progress to be made. It does not necessitate a radical difference being made to the policy instruments which the EU has at its disposal in the environmental area. It is a scenario which is deliverable by the European Union as the tools to support it are already in place. What is clear is the importance of a greater concentration on the search for the means of effective implementation. To aid this process three questions must be posed and answered before decisions are taken about environmental measures.

- Is it needed?
- Is it politically acceptable?
- Is it affordable?

The responses to these questions should be made more readily available to the electorates of the member states. Because environmental policy is of great interest to the general public, the provision of information is important to enable them to participate actively in the implementation process. Information provision is also crucial so that the institutions of the EU may play an enhanced role in the monitoring and management of the policy. And information is the key to enabling the European Parliament, as the elected representatives of the citizens of the EU, to perform its role in the democratization of the policy. Finally, information is essential if the EU's ambition to make environmental policy more accountable and transparent to the electorates of the member states is to be achieved.

Monitoring and management of the policy have also gained a new prominence for a number of reasons:

1. The increased simplification of the legislation and introduction of framework legislation.
2. The need of the developing policy for more a more flexible, more holistic and integrated approach.
3. The use of new methods of environmental protection.

The role and work of the European Commission will be altered by these developments. There are two main reasons for providing additional measures to enable the European Commission to perform the role of monitoring policy more effectively: first, to ensure that all interests are able to participate actively in the policy-making process; and second, to ensure that there is an opportunity for information to be widely disseminated to national electorates to stimulate support for the adoption of stricter environmental measures.

An important part of the monitoring and management process will concern the attempts of states with more stringent environmental protection measures to maintain them. It would be politically unacceptable to the electorates of those member states that any lowering of environmental protection should occur. It would also be environmentally unacceptable. On the other hand the member states which are reluctant to implement environmental protection measures must be encouraged to take action. If the effectiveness of the policy can be guaranteed, then long-term commitment of the national governments, no matter what the reservations, will be ensured. Modest objectives may be exceeded, but those that are too high may never be achieved by some!

Environmental policy since 1992 has been firmly grounded on the application of the principles of shared responsibility and subsidiarity (see Chapter 12). The consequence has been a slowing down of the introduction of legislation and an increased use of framework directives in line with these principles. A strengthened management role for the European Commission would not undermine the application of the principle of subsidiarity as it would not increase the involvement of the European Commission in the decision-making process. The European Commission has been engaged in reviewing legislation since 1992 to ensure that the principle of subsidiarity is being applied. Equally a decrease in the number of legislative acts does not indicate a lack of willingness on the part of the European Commission to introduce measures. However, as the number of legislative acts decreases there must be a mechanism by which the agreed objectives of the Treaty and the legislation are achieved.

It is not possible for the EU to abandon the centralized regulatory approach which characterized the policy until the adoption of the Fifth Environmental Action Programme in 1992. The various types of economic instrument, including subsidies, taxes and voluntary agreements do carry with them certain disadvantages, and legislation is necessary to counterbalance these. It must also be recognized that legislation has been instrumental in delivering environmental objectives in areas where the national governments or the targeted groups might otherwise have been slow or reluctant to act. A combination of legislation, economic instruments and additional finance as advocated in the Fifth EAP is an obvious requirement for effective environmental policy.

THE CHALLENGES FOR THE FUTURE

The EU's environmental policy has been developed in a series of environmental action programmes (EAPs) produced since 1972. The adoption of the Fifth EAP by the member states of the European Union in February 1993 changed the agenda of the EU's environmental policy for the end of the twentieth century and put into place the foundations for the policy of the twenty-first century. It was a move away from the highly programmatic nature of environmental policy. This action programme established a long-term strategy for the European Union which was intended to achieve the objectives of sustainable development. The challenge which was set for the EU in the Fifth EAP was to find a way to operationalize its proposals so that measures were found which would combine economic progress with environmental protection and conservation of resources for future development. The Fifth EAP also provided the basis for actions which were to be taken within the EU in its contribution to the global objective of sustainable development.

The Maastricht Treaty which was ratified in November 1993 raised the profile of environmental policy within the EU with its use of the term 'policy' rather than 'actions to protect the environment'. It also introduced changes to the roles of the institutions of the EU in the decision-making process. The most far-reaching of these, which had an impact on the development of environmental policy, was the introduction of increased powers for the European Parliament. The EP is often considered the 'greenest' of the institutions of the EU and the Members of the European Parliament have used their powers with great effect in the area of environmental policy. See Chapter 3. The European Court of Justice (ECJ) was also given the right to impose fines on the national governments of the member states which continue to fail to implement environmental legislation. This was a major step forward to support the implementation process. The Treaty, however, made few other changes which could be used to strengthen the effectiveness of policy measures once they were adopted.

The deliberations of the 1996/97 Intergovernmental Conference produced only minimal changes to the text of the treaty articles on the environment. The most important were to establish a legal basis for actions to achieve sustainable development and to extend the use of qualified majority voting to more areas of environmental action. Many of the remaining concerns about ineffective implementation were left unresolved by the 1997 treaty revisions. This is not surprising as the revisions to the Treaty are aimed to enable a legislative framework to be put into place, not to provide the detail of how the policy is to be run. However, the search for an appropriate mechanism of ensuring implementation of policy is crucial to its effectiveness.

A number of pressures combined in the late 1990s to make the search for a strategy that would ensure effective implementation more urgent. Within the European Union the progress towards the completion of the internal market and then economic and monetary union (EMU) dominated the work of the policy makers. Aspects of the internal market programme had not been completed and in June 1997 the European Commission introduced an action plan to improve its operation. Concerns about the impact of unemployment on the economies of Germany and France during 1997 and 1998 threatened to undermine the progress towards the introduction of the single currency in January 1999. The urgency of finding an environmental policy that would be compatible with economic growth and not be perceived to hinder competitiveness therefore grew.

The impact on environmental issues of the fourth enlargement of the EU to include Austria, Finland and Sweden was still being assessed in the late 1990s. The conclusion was mixed and in some respects disappointing to groups within the EU that were looking to the Nordic states and Austria to combine as a bloc within the EU and push for a radical policy agenda on the environment. The electorates of the three states had demonstrated considerable concern about pressure to introduce less strict environmental measures which might follow membership of the EU. However, the three states have their own individual national environmental priorities, which undermined their opportunities to act in a concerted way within the EU.

A number of special derogations were agreed on some of the EU's environmental legislation during the accession negotiations with the Nordic states and Austria in 1994. The derogations were in response to specific national environmental interests. For example, before accession to the EU the Austrian government had imposed stricter controls on emissions from heavy goods vehicles. The Swedish national environmental policy included more stringent controls on the use and marketing of dangerous substances. The Finnish government had targeted the sulphur content of some fuels for stricter control. The intention of the derogations from the EU's legislation in these areas was to enable a four-year period of transition to be put into effect before the controversial legislation had to be transposed. During this period the European Commission reviewed the relevant legislation in order to prevent any lowering of the environmental protection in the new member states.

The deadline for the derogations was 1 January 1999. It was apparent during 1997 and 1998 that this would not be an easy issue to resolve. The review by the European Commission depended on the flow of information from the national governments about the transposition of the environmental measures. All three governments of Austria, Finland and Sweden were slow to provide the necessary information. The Swedish government was the slowest. There seemed to be some evidence of a rather reluctant and hesitant approach which the new member states had initially towards their membership of the EU (Liefferink 1996, quoted in Andersen and Liefferink 1998: 23). On one issue, however – that of acid rainfall – the Swedish government did take an active stance. As a result of the pressure and leadership of the Swedish government a major revision of the large-scale combustion plant directive[6] was carried out.

The leadership of the Nordic states and Austria as a group was apparent on the issue of maintenance of environmental standards during the late 1990s. The introduction of the so-called 'environmental guarantee' to the Treaty of Amsterdam which gave the member states the opportunity to maintain and introduce more stringent national environmental measures was the result of pressure from the governments of the three states. The acceptance of this proviso in article 95 TEC (100a TEC) by the other national governments was clearly an attempt to avoid the untidy compromises and opt-outs which had been introduced to ensure the ratification of the Maastricht Treaty. It was considered to be of importance as the means of defusing any concerns which might be reflected by the Danish public in their referendum on the Treaty in mid-1998.

For the southern Mediterranean states of Spain, Portugal and Greece, the membership of the EU of the Nordic states and Austria was seen as a 'threat'. The cost implication for the national governments and industries of the pressure for a stricter approach to environmental protection was seen as a major cause for concern. The governments of the Mediterranean member states were reluctant to accept measures which might impose costs, as they were dealing with the twin problems of economic and monetary union and high levels of unemployment at the end of the 1990s. Article 95 TEC (100a TEC) includes the proviso that the introduction of higher national environmental standards must be based on new scientific evidence. However, this has not completely allayed the concerns which the southern states have about how the policy will develop in the future.

The physical environment of the Nordic states and Austria is very different from that of the physical environments of the other member states. The 1995 enlargement therefore brought other concerns about how the physical environment of the new member states might be accommodated within the existing priorities of the EU (see Table 1.4). Questions were raised about whether the EU's environmental actions were appropriate to support the balance in these states between economic activity and environmental protection. For example, the 1995 enlargement brought a dramatic increase in the total forested area of the EU. The production of pulp for the paper industry is an important economic activity in these areas. There is a heavy reliance on the use of chemicals in this industry. In many regions of the new member states where tourism is an important part of economic development, the natural environment is very sensitive to degradation as a result of acid rainfall. Controls on possible increased levels of traffic movement in such regions was therefore considered to be a high priority following accession.

The Nordic states have Baltic Sea coastlines. The high levels of pollution in the Baltic Sea have, as a result of the accession of the Nordic states, become of greater interest to the EU. An opportunity has been created for the European Commission to play a more important role in the international forums on the protection of the Baltic Sea (see Chapters 2 and 12). The environmentally damaging procedures during the Communist era meant that the Baltic Sea was considered to be in danger of ecological death by the turn of the century unless action were taken. More than 132 environmental 'hot spots' were identified within the Sea. In 1992 the Helsinki Convention on the Baltic Sea Environment was established. The EU is a signatory of this convention and as a result the European Commission has had a role in the holding of the rotating presidency of the commission (HELCOM) set up to administer this convention. In June 1996 HELCOM published a report on the 132 environmental 'hot spots'. Its main conclusion was that only 1 in 10 were showing any improvement. In addition, the potential danger of increased transport of oil by water in the area was growing.

The changing nature of the geopolitical structure of Europe during the late 1980s and throughout the 1990s brought a new dimension to the environmental debate. By the beginning of the 1996/97 Intergovernmental Conference the number of applicant states for membership of the EU from Central and Eastern Europe almost equalled the actual membership.[7] Following the closure of the Intergovernmental Conference in July 1997 the European Commission presented its Opinion on the applicant states (CEC 1997p). All were deemed to have economic difficulties but the European Commission supported the opening of negotiations with Poland, Hungary, the Czech Republic, Estonia, Slovenia and Cyprus. The problems of environmental degradation in these applicant states were initially given a lower priority than concerns about the impact of these states on the EU's common agricultural policy or the Structural Funds.

In a report on the challenges facing the EU's applicants in April 1997 the World Bank highlighted the costs of the problems of environmental degradation in Poland. The conclusions reached in the report suggested that the Polish government would have to invest between ECU 35 and 40 billion to bring its industrial practices up to date. In the agricultural sector the major concerns were associated with the damage being done to both water and air quality. Whilst the commitment was made by the EU not to allow the environmental problems to undermine the enlargement process, the negotiations for accession had to include discussion of costs as well as the transposition of EU environmental legislation to national law in the applicant states (see Chapters 2 and 12).

The relationship between environmental protection and the promotion of global security and stability is beginning to occupy a central place within foreign policy debates. The division of the world between two great powers has gone. The end of the cold war and the bipolar world has brought the beginning of a period characterized by multipolarity. Certain features are becoming universally acceptable within this new world order. They are the establishment of democratic systems of government, the acknowledgement of and support for the rule of law, and development of free market economies. Different groupings of states have emerged to protect different types of interests. Among the changing perceptions and theories of international relations has been the development of an environmental security agenda. Environmental degradation was identified as an area of cause and effect of conflict in the Brundtland Report: 'Environmental stress is both a cause and effect of political tension and military conflict' (WCED 1987: 290). The primary reason for this conflict lies in the decline of resources which, in the increasingly interdependent world, is pushing national governments to take extreme action. The Gulf War of the early 1990s highlighted the lengths to which states are prepared to go to protect needed natural resources.

The European Union continues to be a politically weak organization, but its interests lie in fostering the new international environmental security order for a number of reasons. These are to:

1. Ensure that its access to the natural resources on which its economic development is based is safeguarded. 'Global environmental threats will increase as a result of rising poverty and over-consumption, atmospheric and water pollution are expected to increase, the degradation of the marine environment and the soil to continue, tropical forests to disappear and bio-diversity to be substantially increased' (CEC 1997z: 13).
2. Enable the EU to play an active role on behalf of the member states in the multilateral organizations that promote trade and finance and monetary relations.
3. Promote peace, stability and development in the wider European region which is the main geopolitical interest of the EU.
4. Enable coherent policy developments in agricultural, trade and development policies to take place within the EU.

The role that environmental policy has to play in the newly emerging security order both globally and in the regional context of Europe has implications for the development of the EU's common foreign and security policy. Adding an environmental dimension to the EU's common and foreign security policy did not feature in the negotiations during the 1996/97 IGC. Environmental policy is outside the third pillar[8] of the European Union. However, by implication and commitment the environment is part of the economic and development policies referred to in article 3 TEU (C TEU). This article commits the EU to consistency of external activities in the context of external relations, security, economic and development policies. Article 174 TEC (130r SEA) adds the promotion of measures at an international level to deal with regional or worldwide environmental problems to the task of the European Community. The inclusion in the Treaty of the phrase 'sustainable development' carries with it a number of implications for the policy makers. The consequence of the implied commitment of the EU to an environmental security agenda is that a policy may be adopted which enables the EU to act as a promoter of support for global environmental measures. This was demonstrated by the EU's attempts to gain support for increased global action against carbon emissions (see Chapter 5).

The EU has many connections with countries of the developing world. These ties are based on former colonial relationships between the states. The Lomé Conventions have been the main tool by which the EU has formalized these relationships. There has been a great deal of criticism of the unequal partnership which has emerged between the EU and the former colonies. The source of the unequal nature of the relationship is the number of the countries with which agreements have been made and their different needs. Also the difficulties of resolving the differences in the political agendas of the member states of the EU with regard to the developing states have made consensus hard to achieve. The EU has an opportunity to increase its support for the developing world through action on the environment, although this may be regarded by the recipients as an attempt to promote a form of environmental 'imperialism'.

CONCLUSIONS

The issues surrounding the question of how to protect the environment have led the European Union into a number of new areas of priority for policy. Some of the issues require the EU to take a more positive stance in global environmental agreements. Others have more relevance to the development of the EU's environmental policy within a European context. The period of the late 1990s has been one of major economic and environmental change for the EU. The introduction of the single currency and the rising levels of unemployment have acted as a constraint and as a catalyst for the changes within the EU. Environmental degradation is continuing throughout the whole of the European region. The enlargement of the EU to include Central and Eastern European states will bring a considerable increase of degraded areas into the EU. Difficult questions are therefore being posed to the EU's policy makers about how to reconcile conflicting and increasingly complex issues.

NOTES

1. European Community or European Union? Environmental policy within the European Union has been developed under the 'economic pillar' of the European Union. Initially the legal basis of the policy was provided by an interpretation of three articles of the European Economic Community Treaty of 1957. Later the legal basis of action was provided in the addition of a title to the Treaty in the Single European Act (SEA) in 1987. The policy was then reaffirmed in the Treaty of European Union (the Maastricht Treaty) in 1993 and the revisions in 1997 (the Amsterdam Treaty). For convenience the term European Union will be used throughout this book unless specific references and measures are being highlighted.
2. A total of 320 legislative acts of various types had been adopted by the EU by the end of 1998.
3. For candidate states for membership of the EU see Table 1.1, note 7 below and Chapter 12.
4. Following the Treaty of Amsterdam a consolidation of the treaty texts was carried out, resulting in renumbering of the treaty articles. The authors of this book will use the new treaty article numbers unless specific references are being made to the actual wording of the text. The old numbers will be shown in parentheses alongside. The abbreviation TEU refers to the articles of the Treaty on European Union. The abbreviation TEC will be used for the articles of the consolidated Treaty establishing the European Community.
5. Opinion poll evidence must always be viewed with caution, as there is a tendency among the general public to give 'politically correct' answers. In responding to questions about environ-

mental protection, people think that they should say 'yes' to the introduction of strong regulations.

6. Council Directive 88/609/EEC on the limitations of emissions of pollutants into the air from large-scale combustion plants, OJL 336, 7 December 1988.

7. Applicant states: Turkey, Cyprus, Malta (withdrawn by Maltese government in 1996, later revived by new Maltese administration in September 1998), Poland, Hungary, Czech and Slovak Republics, Bulgaria, Romania, Slovenia, Estonia, Latvia and Lithuania.

8. The first pillar of the Union is economic affairs, the second pillar is justice and home affairs and the third pillar is common foreign and security policy.

2 Developing the EU's environmental perspective

INTRODUCTION

The Treaty of Rome, which established the European Economic Community (EEC) in 1957, did not include any articles which made specific reference to the creation of an environmental policy. Indeed the Treaty inadvertently created obstacles to future environmental policy developments. Environmental concerns were not high on the political agendas of the member states of the EEC (see Table 1.2) and as a result environmental issues were not among those which were considered to be important for supranational action. The six member states of the European Economic Community were preoccupied with ensuring that economic recovery continued following the devastation of the Second World War. Measures were introduced by the national governments to deal with health-related issues which in some instances had a beneficial impact on the environment. For example, national restrictions on the emissions from coal-fired power stations and domestic fires were introduced in the 1950s with the primary objective of preventing damage to human health, not to prevent atmospheric pollution. Despite growing evidence that faster rates of economic growth were causing increased levels of pollution in the European region, public awareness of environmental problems had not been raised. It appeared that 'the issue-area of the environment did not exist per se' (Hildebrand 1993: 20).

Early legislation was based on an interpretation of a number of differing articles of the Treaty. Unanimous voting in the Council of Ministers was required for the pieces of legislation which were introduced. It was not until the inclusion of the environment chapter in the Single European Act (SEA) in 1987 that the EU's environmental policy was recognized as a legitimate area for supranational action and given a firm legal basis. The Maastricht and Amsterdam revisions of the Treaty reaffirmed and reinforced that legal basis. The purpose of this chapter is to chart the growth of the support which is shown in the European Union for the development of environmental policy through the environmental action programmes and the revisions to the Treaty which have taken place since 1972.

1957–72 – LIMITED ACTION

The lack of commitment to joint action on the environment resulted in early policy measures which were little more than harmonization measures to prevent differing national environmental standards from being barriers to trade. Between 1957 and 1972 only nine directives and one regulation were adopted. The impetus for the legislation was not environmental protection; rather it came from a need to deal with trade- or safety-related trading issues. Taken together, these limited measures did not represent the development of a coherent approach to protection of the environment. They were a very disparate set of measures which represented nothing more than reactions to specific trade-related problems.

As all the directives which were introduced used article 94 TEC (100 EEC) of the Treaty, the economic imperative for the legislation was emphasized. 'The Council shall acting unanimously on a proposal from the Commission, issue directives for the approximation of such provisions laid down by law, regulation or administrative action in the Member States as directly affect the establishment or functioning of the common market' (article 94 TEC (100 EEC)). Regulation 729/70 dealt with the financing of agricultural protection in less favoured areas. Unlike the directives, it was based on articles 36 TEC (42 EEC) and 37 TEC (43 EEC) of the European Economic Communities Treaty which authorized the granting of aid within the framework of economic development programmes. Although this regulation had an environmental consequence as a result of the programmes to which it applied, it did not have an overtly environmental objective.

GROWTH OF PUBLIC AWARENESS OF ENVIRONMEN-TAL PROBLEMS

The action which promoted the development of a more coherent approach to EU environmental policy in 1972 was not unique to the countries which formed the then European Economic Community. It came as a result of global environmental activity. Public interest in and awareness of the increasing problems of environmental damage and degradation began to grow during the 1960s, led by the findings of US scientists. Rachel Carson was the first of a number of very influential writers who used the increasing body of scientific evidence to raise the levels of public interest (Carson 1962). She identified the human health problems associated with the growing use of synthetic pesticides. Her work was important as it showed that the problems being caused to human health would only be overcome if the underlying environmental issues were dealt with first. This was a marked switch of emphasis which had an impact on the public and the policy makers. During the period between 1965 and 1970 public opinion polls in the US showed a tripling of the interest in environmental problems.

In 1968 Garrett Hardin used the phrase the 'tragedy of the commons' to identify the growing environmental problems as of international concern and not just for individual national governments to try to solve on their own (Hardin 1968). This view, expressed in Hardin's writings, influenced the development of legislation in the US. When the US National Environmental Policy Act of 1969 was adopted, the federal authorities were given a mandate to become involved in international collaboration in order to prevent a decline in the quality of the global environment.

Other influential reports added to the groundswell of demand for action. In 1972 a group of international businessmen, scientists and politicians, known collectively as the Club of Rome, commissioned a study by researchers at the Massachusetts Institute of Technology (MIT). A computer model was devised to investigate the long-term causes and consequences of growth in population, industrial capital, food production, resource consumption and pollution. The main findings of the study were that:

- at present (1972) rates of consumption of resources, the limits to growth on the earth would be reached within 100 years;
- it was possible to alter the present situation and establish economic and ecological stability;
- if this stability was what was wanted, then the sooner changes were made the better (Meadows et al. 1972).

The long history of economic activity in Europe had given rise to problems of air, soil and water pollution which were more severe than those of the US. Scientific evidence pointed to the worsening of these problems during the 1950s and 1960s as a result of the rapid growth and reconstruction of the European economies which took place following the Second World War. Sweden was among the European states where most concern was registered. Problems grew for successive Swedish governments during the 1960s as the national electorate became more aware of the damage being done by acid rainfall. Swedish scientists found that between 1962 and 1966 the wind-borne pollutants had increased the acidity of rainfall by a factor of eight. Swedish soil is low in calcium and as a result the Swedish ecosystem was particularly sensitive to acidification, with much damage being done to forests, lakes and rivers. Throughout Sweden the 'critical load' or quantitative estimate of the exposure to one or more pollutants at harmful levels was exceeded during the 1960s in these regions.

Sulphur dioxide from power stations and nitrogen oxides from traffic exhausts and stationary combustion plants were identified as the main causes of the pollution. The damage done to Sweden's environment was generated by only a limited amount of domestic pollution. The Swedish government took action against the domestic producers by banning the burning of high-sulphur oils in 1969. However, evidence accumulated that wind-borne sulphur dioxide and nitrogen oxide could be carried over long distances. As a consequence of the prevailing wind direction, the source of much of the pollution affecting Sweden came primarily from the UK, Germany and Poland. The problem therefore had a considerable international dimension and from 1967 the Swedish government began to mobilize support, especially from the US, for global action.

The combination of international political support, scientific evidence and raised public awareness led to the United Nations Conference on the Human Environment in Stockholm in 1972. The predominant theme of the 1972 conference was the linkage of environmental issues and international economic relations. A total of 114 states were represented at the conference, with the exclusion of the Soviet bloc states. Twenty-six broad principles for the management of the global environment were included in the conference's concluding declaration. Based on these principles an action plan was drawn up which included 199 recommendations for international cooperation on the environment. It was assumed that in the international arena the United Nations would take the lead on action and in December 1972 the UN General Assembly created the United Nations Environment Programme (UNEP).

The United Nations Conference was a catalyst for global international action but it remained characterized by a number of major constraints. The declaration at the end of the conference had asserted that it was 'the sovereign right of nation states to "exploit their own resources, pursuant to their own environmental policies" qualified only by a "moral duty" not to cause damage to others' (Aldous 1986: 462). The signatories had therefore made a commitment to environmental protection, but the pre-eminence of national economic interests was still apparent.

1972–86 – LAUNCHING THE EUROPEAN UNION'S ENVIRONMENTAL POLICY

The first major break point in the development of the EU's environmental policy came in 1972. The EU took its first formal step towards the development of a coherent approach to the protection of the environment during the Paris Summit meeting of the Heads of the Governments of the EU on 19 and 20 October 1972. This was the beginning of the EU response to the issues raised at the Stockholm Conference. It both reflected the individual concerns of the states of the EU about the specific problems of the region and laid the foundation of the cooperative approach which the EU has taken in other international groupings.

At the end of the Paris Summit the Heads of Government clearly stated:

> Economic expansion is not an end in itself: its first aim should be to enable disparities in living conditions to be reduced. It must take place with the participation of all social partners. It should result in an improvement of the quality of life as well as in standards of living. As befits the genius of Europe, particular attention will be given to intangible values and to protecting the environment so that progress may readily be put at the service of mankind. (Paris Summit declaration, (CoM 1973, Part 1: 5)).

Nevertheless the main focus of the EU's policy was to coordinate and harmonize the progress of national environmental policies without interfering with national-level activity. At the same time national-level activity was not to jeopardize the operation of the European market. Whilst the economic imperative remained the primary concern, the beginning of a recognition that environmental degradation was also a social issue marked a major readjustment of view on environmental policy. As a consequence the policy which was launched may be broadly characterized as a socioeconomic policy.

Following the Paris Summit meeting, a memorandum from the Council of Ministers was forwarded to the European Commission requesting the preparation of an environmental action programme (EAP) including an outline timetable for action. The action programme was adopted in November 1973 (CoM 1973: 1–53). Action programmes do not need a treaty basis, nor are they required for legal implementation of policy, and no amendment was made to the Treaty at that time. The failure of the national governments to revise the Treaty in 1972 showed their willingness to respond to pressure to develop an environmental policy but not to establish the legal framework which hindered its effective operation.

The First Environmental Action Programme was adopted in the form of a declaration of the Council of the European Communities and of the representatives of the governments of the member states meeting in the Council. This was important as it was an acknowledgement that actions should be carried out at the national or the supranational level of government, depending on the action in question. It thereby provided 'an early example, in fact if not in name, of the importance it attached to the application of what would later come to be called the subsidiarity principle to the field of the environment' (Johnson and Corcelle 1995: 13). All the action programmes contain a general framework to be developed during the period of the programme and also some examples of specific activity to be undertaken. Both elements of the First EAP were approved in the Council Declaration. However, with the subsequent programmes only the general guidelines have been adopted by the Council in the form of a Council Resolution and this has slowed the progress on some of the specific measures which have been identified in the action programmes.

Much criticism of modern environmental policy may be made as a consequence of the attitude demonstrated in 1972 and remaining prevalent in the late 1990s. The national governments of the EU continue to be reluctant to give complete support for environmental measures. This is despite the fact that the legal basis for environmental policy is now firmly established. The conclusion drawn by the European Commission in the first progress report on the implementation of the Fifth Environmental Action Programme was that 'what is lacking is the attitude changes and the political will to make the quantum leap to make the necessary progress to move towards sustainability' (CEC 1996p: 3).

The environmental action programmes have had different priorities. Analysis of the aims and objectives of each programme shows the focus of attention at the different stages of growth of the EU's environmental policy. It is also possible to identify a number of themes common to all the action programmes. Among these is the commitment to joint action. The following review of the programmes highlights the way in which this commitment has evolved. However, the practical difficulties of mobilizing the national governments to joint action on issues within the EU and to joint negotiating positions in the international arena remain.

THE FIRST ENVIRONMENTAL ACTION PROGRAMME, 1973–76 – DEFINITION OF BASIC PRINCIPLES (see Figures 2.1 and 2.2)

The First Environmental Action Programme was adopted on 22 November 1973 (CoM 1973). It contained limited priorities for the following two to three years. Its importance lay in the progress which was made to establish the framework for the future EU environmental policy. The principle of shared responsibility for environmental actions between the national and supranational tiers of government was clearly set out in the preamble to the First EAP:

> The Council of the European Communities and the Representatives of the governments of the Member States ... note that the projects to which this programme will give rise should in some cases be carried out at Community level and in others be carried out by the Member States. (CoM 1973: 1)

It was further stated that where the member states did carry out the projects it was for the Council to exercise the coordinating powers as laid down in the Treaties.

1. Prevention of pollution is better than curing the problem after it has happened. (To support this approach all available technology developments used should produce a policy which will improve the quality of life at the lowest cost. This will ensure that the policy will be compatible with economic and social development.)
2. Environmental impacts should be taken into account at an early stage in the planning and decision-making process.
3. Overexploitation of resources should be avoided.[1]
4. Scientific knowledge should be used to assist in the conserving and improvement of the environment and in pollution control.
5. Polluters should pay for their environmental damage (with certain exemptions to take into account the need to eliminate regional disparities).
6. The transboundary impact of pollution should be controlled.
7. The problems of developing countries should be taken into account.
8. The European Community (EC) should take on the role as international actor in the environmental area, especially in the context of regional cooperation and globally to support the work of the United Nations.
9. The EC should assume a role in the dissemination of information and education of the population about environmental problems.
10. The EC should decide the appropriate level at which action should be taken.
11. Harmonization of national environmental policies is the goal.

[1] In combination the first three principles provide an early commitment by the European Union to the ideas beginning to grow which were articulated in the 1987 Brundtland Report definition of sustainable development. 'Sustainable development is development that meets the needs of the present without compromising the ability of future generations to meet their own needs' (WCED 1987: 43).

Figure 2.1   Principles for environmental actions established in the First EAP

The policy objectives of the First EAP should be achieved by:

1. Application of the appropriate provisions of the Treaties.
2. Implementation of this action programme and any which follow in the future.
3. Implementation of an environmental information procedure.

Figure 2.2   Achieving the policy objectives of the First EAP

In order to ensure that the sharing of responsibility be done in the most effective manner, decisions about environmental action were also to be based on an application of the principle of subsidiarity, that is, that action be taken at the most appropriate level of government. Definition of the political principle of subsidiarity has been difficult to reach in the EU (see Chapter 12). It was not formally included in the Treaty as the way in which decisions should be made until the Single European Act (SEA) in 1987. The revisions made to the Treaty in Maastricht in 1993 and a protocol added in Amsterdam in 1997 strengthened the legal position of the principle but did little to clarify its meaning. During the British presidency in the first half of 1998 the issue of determination of the principle was again turned to, but with limited success.

The commitment that there should be no separation of environmental protection and objectives of economic growth was made in a strongly worded opening statement to the action programme:

> Whereas ... the task of the European Economic Community is to promote ... a harmonious development of economic activities and a continued and balanced expansion which cannot now be imagined in the absence of an effective campaign to combat pollution ... and an improvement in the ... quality of the environment. (CoM 1973: 1)

It was not until 1997 and the revisions of the Treaty made by the Heads of Government in Amsterdam that the goal of sustainable development was specified in the Treaty articles (articles 2 TEU, 2 TEC).

The desirability of integrating environmental objectives into other policy areas was stressed from the First EAP: 'the activities of the Communities in the different sectors in which they operate in agriculture policy, social policy, regional policy, industrial policy, energy policy ... must take account of concern for the protection and improvement of the environment' (CoM 1973: 11). Identification of the environmental problems affecting the EU was an important starting-point before integration could occur. The First EAP therefore contained an outline of necessary studies of problems of water scarcity and raw material supply and utilization. Lack of coordination in the development of regional and urban policies was also considered to have a major impact on levels of environmental degradation.

Integration of environmental objectives into agricultural policy was highlighted as an important prerequisite for safeguarding the natural environment. Mountain and upland farmers were identified as those who would be most affected by any measures introduced. Early legislation which came as a result of the First EAP authorized the national governments to introduce a special system of aid for specified less favoured areas to ensure that there would be continuity of farming in the regions and conservation of the countryside (Directive 75/268/EC on mountain and hill farming and farming in less favoured regions). This did not mean that the directive was an environmental measure. Any environmental impact which was achieved through the legislation came as a by-product and not as a primary objective (Haigh 1989: 316). Indeed, the lack of progress on the integration of environmental requirements into agricultural policy was responsible for the pressure which came from some national governments for the inclusion of an environmental objective in Article 33 TEC (39 EEC) during the 1996/97 Intergovernmental Conference.[1] The objectives set out in article 33 TEC for the common agricultural policy (CAP) were not changed but article 6 TEC (3c EEC) did extend the integration requirement to agriculture.

Whilst the rationale for the integration of environmental requirements into other areas of policy received early recognition from the national governments of the EU's member states, the reality of this objective proved to be much more difficult to achieve. The early lack of a legal basis for the policy objective was probably the most significant constraint on the integration of the environmental requirement into other policies. The continued failure of the national governments to implement the EU's environmental policy effectively demonstrates that the need for the integration of environmental requirements into policy remains (see Chapters 4 and 12). Furthermore, difficulties also remain about how rulings of the European Court of Justice (ECJ) may be made on this requirement.

The socioeconomic nature of the evolving policy was seen in the commitment made in the First EAP to improving working conditions through the drawing up of a social programme. The creation of the European Foundation for the Improvement of Living and Working Conditions supported research and publications which assisted in the improvement of working conditions. The Foundation continues to help to promote public awareness of environmental problems which is important if the sharing of responsibility for environmental measures is to be achieved.

Part II of the action programme gave fuller details of the limited priorities for action which were to be achieved in the following two-year period. The primary concern was to gather as much information as quickly as possible in order to establish the Community criteria for action. The information required varied from pollutant to the polluted target, but the importance of gathering objective and readily accessible information was repeatedly stressed throughout the programme. The pollutants chosen for study were those considered the most damaging on the grounds of toxicity given the state of scientific knowledge at the time. Among the pollutants targeted in the first group were lead and lead compounds, organic and organic phosphorus compounds and hydrocarbons with known or probable carcinogenic effects. Pollutants which caused acid rainfall were also targeted, including nitrogen oxides (NO_x) and carbon monoxide. Photochemical oxidants, asbestos and vanadium were considered to be a less important threat to the environment, but action was begun to standardize measuring methods for these pollutants.

In the case of noise pollution the First EAP attempted to identify where criteria were needed in order to establish noise levels and nuisance indices for various intensities of noise. This required the harmonization of the specifications of the polluting products. The legislation which followed during the 1970s[2] was focused on preventing barriers to trade. The legislation did not bind the national governments to set limits equal to those in the legislation but did place the obligation on the governments to ensure that, if more stringent national measures were introduced, they did not act as barriers to trade.

The control of water pollution has been a dominant theme of all the Action Programmes. As the first stage in the control of water pollution a number of pollutants were identified in the First EAP for urgent investigation to determine emission standards for effluents into water. Guidelines established by the World Health Organization (WHO) formed the basis of these investigations and provided the measure for the environmental quality standards (EQS) which were set. However, the opportunity remained for the member states to introduce stricter national requirements than those being introduced through the EU's environmental quality standards.

Other measures contained in the First EAP targeted specific products. These products had been included in a programme to eliminate technical barriers to trade adopted by the Council in 1969. Directives on lead content in fuel and crockery, the toxicity of detergents and the composition of paint were included in this programme. A number of industries were also specifically targeted where production practices were seen as particularly harmful to the environment (the chemical, food, metallurgical and textile industries).

The First EAP included a section on measures to control the damaging nature of energy production. The preamble to the section pointed to the extent of the concern about all forms of energy production as a source of various types of pollution. Specific concerns were identified because of the levels of air pollution from combustible plants, domestic heating, and internal combustion engines, the waste water discharged as cooling water and the thermal pollution of water and air by electricity-generating stations. However, the problems of pollution from energy use and production were not considered as important as the problems of marine pollution. The First EAP adopted an apocalyptic note in its description of the problems of marine pollution within the EU. 'Of all the different forms of pollution, marine pollution constitutes now and to an even greater extent in the long term, one of the most dangerous, because of the effects it has on the fundamental biological and ecological balances governing life on our planet' (CoM 1973, chapter 6, section 1:a: 23).

The attempts of the EU to overcome the problems of marine pollution demonstrate the ways in which the member states may work together in international environmental agreements, for example, by ensuring that the rules of the international conventions on marine pollution were implemented within the

EU through the introduction of the necessary legislation. In the early 1970s two international agreements had been adopted – the Oslo Convention on the control of deliberate discharge of particularly dangerous waste to the seas of the North East Atlantic and the North Sea, and the London Convention which concerned all the seas of the world. A third was under discussion which covered the western Mediterranean. The European Commission was given observer status at the meetings of these conventions as the first stage in the EU becoming a signatory to them. In addition, member states could give the lead in carrying out projects which would help combat land-based pollution affecting the coastline of the EU, which would also require other international support.

The importance given to the pollution problems of the River Rhine was signalled by the fact that a separate chapter was devoted to actions concerned with the protection of the whole river basin from pollution. The Rhine is a major artery for communications within Europe. It is navigable by barges as far as the Swiss city of Basle. Because the river is used as a corridor for transport within a densely populated region and with a concentration of heavily polluting industries, action was already being taken by the states through which it flowed to control the environmental damage. A number of the states of the then EEC were signatories to the Berne Convention on the Protection of the Rhine against Pollution. When the first ministerial conference of the Berne Convention was held in the Hague in 1972 an observer from the European Commission was present. Following this conference the European Commission proposed the initiation of an emergency programme for the cleaning of the Rhine water. As a result of the initiatives to remedy the transfrontier impact of water pollution, the possibility of joint action by the member states of the EU was accepted both within the EU itself and in the international conventions.[3]

The First Environmental Action Programme laid the basis for a potentially far-reaching environmental policy which would have an impact on all aspects of life. Measures were aimed not just at pollution control but also at the protection of human health and the preservation of the environment. Overall it represented a statement of commitment to an ambitious attempt to achieve a coherent management plan for the protection of the environment within the geographical region occupied by the EEC.

The actions which followed did not match the ambition. A number of directives were agreed following the adoption of the programme. They were broadly in two categories, adopted under either article 94 TEC (100 EEC) or 308 TEC (235 EEC) of the Treaty. Those directives which related directly to the functioning of the market, that is, the removal of trade barriers by the setting of emission standards, were adopted using article 94 TEC (100 EEC). They were limited in number and scope as they dealt with very specific issues, for example emissions from motor vehicles. Standards contained in the directives were low and represented little more than a limited attempt to harmonize product standards to prevent market distortion. Those directives that were adopted using article 308 TEC (235 EEC) were more far-reaching, but many did not require direct action. The result was slow adoption and patchy implementation of these directives. Overall the approach to environmental policy during the 1970s was based on measures which were either directly related to trade interests or restricted to very general provisions which did not target the main sources of pollution.

THE SECOND ENVIRONMENTAL ACTION PROGRAMME, 1977–81 – CONTINUITY OF EFFORT

The primary focus of this programme, adopted on May 1977 (CoM 1977), was to enable projects and measures begun during the First EAP to be updated and continued. The objectives of the First EAP were therefore restated. Within the EU there should be:

- improvement of the quality of life and protection of the natural environment as 'fundamental tasks of the Community and it is therefore necessary to implement a Community environment policy' (CoM 1977: 1);
- particular attention paid to non-damaging use and rational management of land, environment and natural resources;
- measures to encourage the growth of public awareness and personal responsibility for environmental protection.

An important recommendation of the Second EAP was that preventive action was to be the basis of measures. Special attention was given in the programme to proposals of the German and Italian governments on protection and rational management of space, the environment and natural resources. Priority was given to reduction of pollution of water (both sea and fresh water), the atmosphere and noise. The policy of cooperation among the states of the EU in the growing number of international conventions on the environment was supported for the future.

What was new in the Second EAP were sections dealing with monitoring and assessment of the policy, protection of flora and fauna, the use of environmental impact assessments (EIAs) and the development of environment labels. Measures to implement these sections have been slow to materialize. Monitoring and assessment of policy continues to constrain its effectiveness. The progress on the protection of wildlife has been more significant than that on the protection of the countryside (see Chapter 8). The requirement for EIAs developed a firm legal basis in Directive 85/337/EC on the assessment of the effects of certain public and private projects on the environment. This directive is, however, one which the national governments have continued to fail to implement (CEC 1996n: 83; 1997g: 97; 1998c). It was amended in 1996 (CEC 1996i) in an attempt to remove some of the discrepancies which existed, as some of the national governments were applying the assessment to all projects and others only to those listed in annex 1 of the directive. The inclusion of a declaration in the Treaty of Amsterdam which authorizes the Commission to prepare environmental impact assessments when proposals are likely to have a significant environmental implication has the potential to overcome the problems of national governments' failure to implement the directive (Declaration no. 12, Treaty of Amsterdam).

The introduction of environment labels was advocated in the Second EAP as an important initiative which would change the behaviour of consumers by giving them more information about products. The objective was to encourage consumers to buy products which occasioned a minimum of pollution and wastage during the production process as well as in their usage. The rationale for supranational action lay in the concern that developments in national environment labelling would distort trade in the labelled products within the integrated market. Despite the early support for this initiative the regulation establishing the eco-labelling scheme was not adopted until 1993. It has not met with the success which was hoped for (see Chapter 7).

THE THIRD ENVIRONMENTAL ACTION PROGRAMME, 1982–87 – PREVENTION RATHER THAN CURE

The Third EAP, adopted on 7 February 1983 (CoM 1983), was different in tone from the two earlier programmes.[4] The action which had been taken as a result of the First and Second EAPs was considered a success. The objective of the Third EAP was to move the harmonization of the national policies forward to 'make the most economic use possible of the natural resources offered by the environment' (CoM 1983: preamble). This was despite the questioning which was apparent in the action programme itself of whether priority should be given to environmental issues, as the member states were experiencing increased economic difficulties. A response to the question was also given clearly in the EAP: 'environment policy is a structural policy which must be carried out without regard to the short term fluctuations in cyclical conditions' (CoM 1983: annex: point 5). The emphasis in the programme was on the need to prevent national governments adopting different measures which were likely to result in market distortion. The Third EAP gave a new focus on the commitment to the integration of this area of action into the other sectoral policies of the EU. This was to help to strengthen environmental policy as the European Union faced the twin challenges of the Mediterranean enlargement[5] and the completion of the programme to integrate the market.[6] Another important consideration was the possibility that if environmental and economic considerations could be integrated, then the EU's environmental policy could contribute to lowering the increasingly high levels of European unemployment.

A decisive factor in the development of environmental policy outlined in the Third EAP was the support for the introduction of measures to ensure that polluters paid for the pollution they produced. The normal method envisaged for the polluter pays principle (PPP) to be applied was through the setting of standards in legislation and/or charges to be imposed for exceeding these standards. As such it was to be the chief way of bringing market forces to bear to achieve optimum restructuring within the market economy and, at the same time, pollution control. The national governments retained the opportunity to grant state aid to finance the investments required to reduce pollution in some regions if it was needed to protect nature and their landscape.

Among the other directions for the development of future policy outlined in the Third EAP was the commitment to reduction of pollution at source. There are a number of ways to deal with pollution control. In some instances measures designed to curb pollution close to source have been introduced in national legislation. Often these measures are considered costly and they have had little support. Some national governments have taken an approach based on leaving problems until urgent action is needed, on the basis of cost-saving. This reactive approach was what the First EAP had attempted to change. In the Third EAP support for a more proactive approach to environmental protection was reiterated. Linked with this objective was the development of new environmental technologies. The introduction of eco-technology was seen as a way of fulfilling several objectives, including providing the basis for early pollution control and employment creation.

The Third EAP hinted at the changes which were later made by the introduction of the environment chapter into the Treaty in the Single European Act (SEA 1987). For example, the commitment to the application of the principle of subsidiarity was present as it was noted in the EAP 'that the Commission intends to be guided, as in the past by ... the desirability of action at Community level' (CoM 1983: preamble). The programme preamble also stressed that the following three principles should guide any decisions about action:

1. Each type of action must be applied at the most appropriate level.
2. Prevention rather than cure should be the rule.
3. Attempts at restoration following damage must be made wherever possible.

There are limits to a policy which does not carry with it financial backing. The economic difficulties of some of the areas of the European Union put financing environmental protection low on national policy agendas. In recognition of this, the European Commission proposed that a financial instrument for the environment should be set up to be both an incentive to and a catalyst for action. Progress on this proposal was slow. The budget of the European Communities for 1982 included what was regarded as a 'symbolic amount' of resources to be specifically set aside for environmental purposes. Initially some funding was given through the EU's Structural Funds (SFs),[7] but it was limited in nature and the procedures for obtaining it were bureaucratic. It was not until the introduction of the Financial Instrument for the Environment (LIFE) in 1991 (see Chapter 4) that some coherence was given to funding for environmental measures. The revisions of the regulations for the Structural Funds during the late 1980s and 1990s also increased the opportunities for funding for environmental projects as part of the national regional development plans. The introduction of the Cohesion Fund in 1993 to assist with the development of the transport and environmental infrastructure in the poorest states of the EU has been the subject of criticism (see Chapter 4) but does add to the resources which are available to fund the EU's environmental policy.

THE FOURTH ENVIRONMENTAL ACTION PROGRAMME, 1987–92) – THE SINGLE MARKET IMPERATIVE

The mid-1980s was an important period for the development of the EU's environmental policy. The Fourth EAP, adopted on 19 October 1987 (CoM 1987), was scheduled to run at the same time as the programme to complete the internal market. The issues identified for action in the programme therefore reflected the concern to ensure that economic development and environmental protection were seen as compatible. The Fourth EAP did not replace the earlier programmes but was an extension of actions which had been taken as a result of their adoption. In contrast to the earlier three programmes, the Fourth EAP did attempt to introduce a more holistic approach to environmental protection. The view that increased economic integration would lead almost inevitably to environmental degradation caused a change in the framework of the programme. Examples of the problems which would result from the removal of the border controls were identified. These included increased movements of hazardous waste, and increased numbers of road vehicles and aircraft.

The European Commission established a task force to investigate the environmental impact of the single market. The task force was headed by a European

Commission official and drew together a number of experts from throughout the EU. Their findings highlighted the impact of transport and electricity generation as the most important problems to be faced. Together the two produce 60 per cent of the sulphur dioxide, 80 per cent of the nitrous oxide, 55 per cent of the carbon dioxide and 40 per cent of the non-methane hydrocarbons in the EU. The estimates which the task force used were based on an increase in transfrontier lorry movement of 30–50 per cent which would cause a rise in emissions of sulphur dioxide of 8 or 9 per cent and nitrous oxide of as much as 12 to 14 per cent (CEC 1990). In the 1996 report on the operation of the single market, the conclusion was reached that 'It is still too early to make a definitive assessment and to quantify the environmental static or dynamic impact of the Single Market in order to validate or disqualify those estimates' (CEC 1996s: 99).

The importance of two developments was noted in the introduction to the programme. First, the legal basis of the policy had been clarified by the inclusion of the 'Environment Title' to treaty articles in the Single European Act. Second, environmental protection was identified as having a positive role to play in the process of job creation and for that reason had to be considered as an essential element of any economic policies introduced within the EU (see Chapter 7).

> Environmental measures are an integral component of the Community's economic activity because environmental protection improves the quality of life, safeguards natural resources, thus permitting the full realisation of the benefits of economic activity in the form of better patterns of economic growth and employment. (OJL 175 (1997): 14, para 2.4.1)

A number of the principles already identified in earlier programmes were reiterated. They included, first, the principle of shared competence for action between the national and the supranational tiers of government and, second, that any action taken to protect the environment was not to distort the market. The Fourth EAP was influenced by the broader debate taking place in environmental circles about the most effective means of environmental protection. The recognition of the failure of attempts made to that date to curb environmental degradation by a predominantly sectoral and issue-specific approach was leading to a search for alternative means of protecting the environment. Among the ideas put forward in the Fourth EAP were multi-media pollution controls, substance-oriented controls, and source-oriented controls.

The approach used by the EU in its environmental legislation was based on setting emission standards or environmental quality standards for a single medium, for example air, water, or land. Where there were problems caused by emissions of pollutants from a number of sources into one medium with little cross-over effect into others, this approach was appropriate. The advantage of adopting a multi-media approach was that where protection of one medium, for example the land, results unintentionally in pressures on another, for example the air, the environmental measures are already in place to take account of this. The success of a multi-media approach depends on the introduction of stringent measures. One of the main priorities of the Fourth EAP was therefore that there should be a tightening of environmental standards which had not been sufficiently strict in the past.

The chemicals sector was identified as an appropriate target for the introduction of substance-oriented controls. The European chemical industry is a very diverse sector because of the differences in the production, transport, distribution and end uses of the substances involved. Within the EU there are more than 100 000 chemical substances and several million chemical preparations which may be moved freely in the single European market. The advantage of introducing substance-oriented controls specifically for the sector came from the feasibility of targeting pollution no matter what its origin. It was also possible to target individual industries within the sector or a group which together posed a significant threat to the environment. The use of the approach made it possible to introduce integrated risk assessment procedures which took into account the different ways in which people and the environment were exposed to pollution. The choice of pollution control measures available to support substance-oriented control was broader than that available for media-based control measures, but it required more information to make it effective. The role and the work of the European Environment Agency (EEA) (see Chapter 4) as the providers of the appropriate level of information were crucial to the development of substance-oriented policy measures.

Other priorities identified for action in the Fourth EAP included complete and effective implementation of environmental measures by all the national governments and the integration of environmental considerations into other Community policies. Integration was to be carried out at three levels: initially at the level of the Community's own policies and then at the level of the policies being implemented by the national governments; and finally in a more generalized way so that all economic and social developments by either the public or the private sector would have the environmental requirements included in both the planning and the execution of the proposals. The Fourth EAP also advocated instituting an effective education and information policy to make the policy-making process more transparent and to involve a larger number of people. This was to be accomplished in three ways: first, by the adoption of Directive 92/313/EEC on 'freedom of access to environmental information'; second, the designation of 1987 as the European Year of the Environment was intended to raise public awareness of the importance of environmental issues; third, the development of the Community Information System on the State of the Environment and on Natural Resources (CORINE) was to be a means of providing objective information for policy makers.

THE FIFTH ENVIRONMENTAL ACTION PROGRAMME, 1992 ONWARDS – STRATEGY FOR SUSTAINABLE DEVELOPMENT

The conclusion reached in the Fifth EAP (CEC 1992a) when it was adopted in March 1992[8] was that the previous four programmes had successfully put into place a considerable number of measures and achieved certain environmental improvements. However, the full effects of the measures had not been felt:

- Many of the measures were still in progress and it was therefore difficult to evaluate their final impact.
- Many of the measures had not been fully implemented.
- Most of the measures which had been introduced were not adequate to meet the additional environmental damage which would result from the integration of the market.

The Fifth EAP therefore differed from its predecessors as it was a response to the search for new instruments to use to protect the environment, in addition to those which already existed. This search was not unique to the European Union. The global recognition of the need to find ways of combining economic development and protection of the environment led to the report of the World Commission on Environment and Development (WCED) in 1987, the 'Brundtland Report'.[9] The Fifth EAP combined the EU's own concerns about the development of its environmental policy and its response to the issues which had been debated in the global context.

The Brundtland Report had defined sustainable development as 'development which meets the needs of the present without compromising the ability of future generations to meet their own needs' (WCED 1987: 43). This seemingly neat definition led to much controversy about the meaning of the concept and how its objectives might be achieved. The commonly accepted view has come to be that sustainable development has a number of dimensions – social, economic and environmental. It reflects a more optimistic view than that taken in the 1960s when the environmental problems began to gain prominence on political agendas. Sustainable development is based on an idea that something is possible, in contrast to the view of the 1960s which was that economic growth led inevitably to environmental degradation. In the Brundtland Report the definition is prefixed by the comment that 'Humanity has the ability to make development sustainable ... '

The definition of sustainable development used in the Fifth EAP contains the three dimensions of the concept. Sustainable development is 'intended to reflect a policy and a strategy for continued economic and social development without detriment to the environment and the natural resources on the quality of which human activity and further development depend' (CEC 1992a: 3). Providing policy solutions which will enable this to happen is difficult and requires the development of a long-term strategy. At the same time sustainable development is a dynamic process, the objectives and outcomes of which are subject to constant change. The implications for the policy makers of adopting this view are that the policy measures taken must be flexible enough to provide the means to manage the process of change. The policy measures must ensure that a balance is maintained between demands made on natural resources and their usage. Any policy which is an attempt to achieve sustainable development will inevitably be a trade-off between the economic, social and environmental dimensions which underlie the concept.

The Fifth EAP was devised as the EU's long-term approach to achieving the objectives of sustainable development. It was the only EAP to have a title – 'Towards Sustainability' – and was designed to cover a longer period of time than the others. It was the first to use a targeted approach, identifying specific sectors of economic activity which were the heaviest actual and potential polluters (see Figures 2.3, 2.4 and 2.5).

• Industry	• Energy
• Transport	
• Agriculture	• Tourism

Figure 2.3   Five target sectors of the Fifth EAP

• Climate change	• Waste management
• Acidification and air quality	• Management of water resources
• Urban environment	• Protection of nature and bio-diversity
• Coastal zones	

Figure 2.4   Seven themes in the Fifth EAP

In order to balance the sharing of resources and economic development and to protect the environment, the approach advocated in the Fifth EAP was one of sharing the responsibilities and active participation by a large number of groups which would be the target of any policy measures introduced. Three networks were established to enable a dialogue to take place between the policy makers and the various interested parties. The 'Green Forum' was first established as a consultative forum on the environment and had 32 members from representatives of consumers, unions, professional organizations, non-governmental organizations (NGOs) and businesses. This group began its meetings in 1993 in a series of consultations about the environmental aspects of the White Paper on Growth, Competitiveness and Employment (CEC 1993g). At the end of 1996 the value of the work of the Forum as a body reviewing initiatives and making recommendations to the European Commission was recognized. It was retitled the European Consultative Forum on the Environment and Sustainable Development, and given a wider remit. The appointment of Thorvald Stoltenberg[10] as the Chair of the Forum was another indicator of the importance which the European Commission attached to the feedback which came from the reports of the members.

• Improvement of environmental data	• Public information and education
• Scientific research and technological development	• Financial support mechanisms
	• Professional education and training
• Sectoral and spatial planning	• Economic approach – getting the prices right

Figure 2.5   Types of policy instruments identified

During the 1993 UK presidency of the Council of Ministers the Chester Network of Enforcement Authorities began to meet. It was an informal network of the national authorities which were involved in practical implementation of legislation, and formed the basis for the development of the second initiative – the Network for Implementation and Enforcement of Community Law (IMPEL). IMPEL brings together the representatives of the relevant national authorities involved in the practical implementation of legislation and the officials of DG XI (Environment, Nuclear Safety and Civil Protection). The objective of this network is to ensure an exchange of 'best practice' on aspects of practical implementation and also that the policy makers are made aware of the practical problems encountered (see Chapter 4).

The third initiative, the Environment Policy Review Group, includes officials of the European Commission and the national governments at Director-General level (see Chapter 3). The discussions within this group have concentrated on the target sectors of the Fifth EAP. Part of their responsibility is to keep the implementation of environmental policy under review through the publication of regular reports on implementation of environmental measures which was required following the Maastricht Treaty. The first of these reports was presented in 1994 and informed the debate leading to the publication of the progress report on the implementation of the Fifth EAP (CEC 1996p).

The Fourth EAP had questioned the effectiveness of the implementation of the environmental measures. The importance of finding measures which would overcome this problem was highlighted again in the Fifth EAP. The approach advocated in the Fifth EAP was to identify participants within the policy-making and implementation process to share the responsibility for environmental measures (see Chapters 3 and 4). There are a number of constraints to this approach. Without careful management and commitment to shared aims and objectives, the participants in the policy process may find ways to leave the responsibility to others and as a consequence policy may become fragmented. In order to overcome the possibility of lack of commitment to shared responsibility for environmental measures the Fifth EAP contained proposals for the use of a variety of instruments in addition to the legislation which had given the main thrust to environmental policy in the past.

The underlying principle of the proposals in the Fifth EAP was that measures should be introduced which modified behaviour by making use of market forces. In order to do that environmental costs have to be internalized through economic and fiscal incentives and penalties, including the use of taxes, subsidies, tradable permits, extending the use of techniques of environmental impact assessment and environmental accounting. Market-based solutions may help to solve the problems of environmental degradation, but this is not guaranteed (see Chapter 7). Other measures are required including funding to support the introduction of new policy instruments. The importance of increasing the levels of available funding was recognized in the Fifth EAP particularly through the Financial Instrument for the Environment (LIFE) which was established in 1991.

During the mid- and late 1990s there was a disappointing lack of progress on some aspects of the Fifth EAP. In January 1996 the Commission proposed a draft decision to the European Parliament (EP) and the Council of Ministers on the first progress report on the implementation of the Fifth EAP (CEC 1996p). In this draft decision a number of priorities were identified which would assist the development of a targeted sustainable development policy. They included:

1. Improved integration of the environmental objectives into the areas of sectoral policy
2. Use of wider range of policy instruments

3. Additional measures to ensure that information was made available to the public
4. Reinforcing of the EU's role as an international environmental actor.

The EP raised a number of criticisms of the draft decision and proposed a total of 28 amendments. The Council of Ministers was slow to accept the suggestions made by the EP and asked that the conciliation procedures should be followed (ENDS 20/05/98). It was not until May 1998 that an agreement was reached in informal discussions between the representatives of the institutions which was presented to the Conciliation Committee and accepted in June 1998 (see Chapter 4).

The outcome of the agreement was that the EP's view that the Fifth EAP should be recognized as the starting-point of a process of change to achieve sustainable development rather than the ultimate goal was recognized. The main areas which had been the sticking points in the discussions centred on how the integration of the environmental objectives into policy was to be achieved and the rights of national governments to maintain higher environmental standards. Both of these requirements had been strengthened in the text of the Amsterdam Treaty and this paved the way for the agreement on the progress report. This reconciliation of the different views of the institutions of the EU on the European Commission's proposals to strengthen the process of implementation of the Fifth EAP had to be achieved before any action could be taken.

As the Fifth EAP was increasingly accepted as the starting-point for sustainable development policy within the EU, the main question to be resolved at the end of the 1990s was how the process was to be taken forward. To introduce another EAP required agreement from the whole of the European Commission to any proposals adopted before the programme could be presented to the Council of Ministers. There are difficulties in establishing agreement within the College of the Commissioners (see Chapter 3) on many environmental issues. Enlargement to include Central and Eastern Europe began to dominate the agenda of the EU, which made the questions of reform of the institutions more urgent during 1998 and 1999. This included reform of the European Commission. It was therefore considered to be too difficult to introduce a new EAP before the appointment of the European Commission in the year 2000 (see Table 3.3). Whilst the treaty changes made during the 1996/97 Intergovernmental Conference were relatively minor, they did provide the legal basis and opportunities for wide-ranging development in environmental policy. The next stage of that development was to prepare a Sixth EAP which contained a more structured sustainable development plan for the EU to build on the achievements of the Fifth EAP after the year 2000.

THE PROVISION OF A LEGAL BASIS FOR ENVIRON-MENTAL POLICY

Before 1993 all actions taken in the environmental area were as described as part of 'environmental policy'. However, the first attempt to bring coherence to the policy did not come until the First EAP, and the legal basis was not provided until the Single European Act (SEA). Legislation on environmental issues adopted before the SEA was possible because of the interpretation of several articles of the EEC Treaty.

- Article 2 TEC (2 EEC) 'The Community shall have as its task ... to promote ... a harmonious development of economic activities, a continuous and balanced expansion, an increase of stability, and accelerated raising of the standard of living ... '
- Article 30 TEC (36 EEC) detailed the allowable prohibitions which could be imposed on trading activities within the integrated European market. 'The provisions of articles 28 TEC (30 EEC) to 29 TEC (34 EEC) shall not preclude prohibitions, or restrictions on imports, exports, or goods in transit justified on grounds of public morality, public policy or public security; the protection of health and life of humans, animals or plants ...'
- Article 30 TEC (36 EEC) implied environmental protection in terms such as 'protection of health and the life of humans, animals or plants ...'
- Article 94 TEC (100 EEC) gave an opportunity for the adoption of directives which would help with the functioning of the market.
- Article 308 TEC (235 EEC) included the opportunity for appropriate measures to be taken on the basis of a unanimous vote in the Council of Ministers if the Treaty had not provided the necessary powers to fulfil one of the objectives of the Community in the operation of the common market.

These treaty articles gave some support for the introduction of environmental measures, but they were seen in the context of the needs of the integrated market. Article 94 TEC (100 EEC) and article 308 TEC (235 EEC) were in fact crucial to the development of early environmental policy since they allowed for actions to be taken which were not specified in the original Treaty. Whilst these articles were important and provided a link between environmental and economic policies, they contain no clear statement about the necessity for environmental protection measures. Ambiguity therefore remained about the nature of the actions that could be taken at the supranational level. The commitment to the linkage between economic development and environmental protection was very tenuous.

Lack of clarity in the legal underpinning to proposed measures had the effect of allowing member states to circumvent the policy. As the legislation was subject to unanimity in voting in the Council of Ministers, actions being taken were not always the most environmentally effective but represented political compromises. Attempts to harmonize the environmental policies of the national governments were much more problematic than the attempts to harmonize national policies to create the integrated market. There was a fundamental failure to acknowledge the impossibility of separating economic development and environmental protection, and the emphasis on economic development was clear. This attitude continues to undermine modern environmental policy.

The first major revision of the founding Treaty of the European Union was undertaken in 1986. Minor amendments had been made to the Treaty to allow the accession of the UK, Ireland, Denmark, Greece, Spain and Portugal (see Table 1.1). However, by the mid-1980s a number of pressures were combining which led to more fundamental and far-reaching changes. The focus of attention was the commitment to the completion of the internal market. Environmental degradation had increased in Europe during the 1980s. National policies to deal with environmental issues were developing. Increased economic integration was seen as carrying with it twin threats for the environment: first, more economic activity might result from the completion of the market and in turn create further environmental degradation, and second, the development of national environmental policies had the potential to distort the market. The Danish government led the pressure for the inclusion of a chapter on the environment in the treaty revision, the Single European Act (SEA) in 1987. The SEA marked the single most influential step forward in the history of the development of the EU's environmental policy. It has been described as the result of a 'tacit bargain' between the northern and southern states of the EU, identifying what the basis of future cooperation should be (Weale 1996: 597). The northern states of the EU agreed to make regional and social funds available to the southern states in return for agreement to higher environmental standards and the completion of the internal market.

In addition to giving a legal basis for the policy, the SEA also introduced the principle of qualified majority voting (QMV)[11] for measures introduced under article 94 TEC (100 EEC) on the harmonization of policy relating to the market. The proviso was added that if a harmonization measure was introduced that would lower the existing national standards, then it was possible for a national government to 'opt out' of the measure. The European Commission had, however, to be satisfied that there would be no distortion of trade (article 176 TEC (130t SEA)). This proviso gave member states with higher national standards of environmental protection the opportunity to maintain them. In his evaluation of the impact of the SEA in the early 1990s Pinder concluded that 'The provision ... has not so far led to any fragmentation of the market, because harmonisation has set high enough standards to avoid it' (Pinder 1991: 109). This did not prevent frequent expression of concern about the potential for trade distortion, especially during the negotiations with the Nordic states and Austria before their accession to the EU in 1994. The existence and strengthening of this provision in the Treaty of Amsterdam have renewed the concerns about its future use (see Chapter 6).

The Single European Act incorporated the objectives of the environmental policy as it had developed in the EAPs since 1972. The commitment was made to preserve, protect and improve the quality of the environment, to contribute towards protecting human health and to ensure a prudent and rational utilization of natural resources (article 174 TEC (130r SEA)). The framework which it provided was for a policy based on the following principles:

- Priority should be given to preventive action and remedying of damage at source.
- The polluter should pay for pollution caused.
- Scientific and technical data should be taken into account in the framing of measures.
- The various environmental conditions which existed in the differing regions of the EU should be considered.
- Some view of the potential cost and benefits of the measures is desirable.

Underlying all measures, however, was a commitment to the economic and social development of the whole of the EU. Article 175 TEC (130s SEA) also detailed the decision-making procedures to be used and the roles of the institutional actors in the making of environmental policy (see Chapter 3).

During the period between the ratification of the Single European Act in July 1987 and the opening of the negotiations to revise the Treaty in 1991 a new global agenda was set for environmental protection and economic development. This was as a result of the publication of the work of the World Commission on Environment and Development in 1987 – the Brundtland Report. The Brundtland Report emphasized the need to find a strategy of sustainability which would bring continued economic and social development without detriment to the environment. At the same time as the Fifth EAP was being negotiated, changes were also made in the Maastricht Treaty to the chapter on the environment. These changes had a mixed impact on environmental protection. The rhetoric of the commitment to environmental protection was strengthened in amendments made to article 2 TEC (2 TEC) of the Treaty. The Fifth EAP provided the basis of the EU's environmental policy to the year 2000 and beyond. It did not contain a definitive list of environmental laws which the European Union was going to introduce. Instead it was an outline of a long-term strategy of environmental protection. To achieve its goals, laws had to be combined with the introduction of other measures such as eco-taxes, subsidies, tradable permits, and financial assistance for environmental projects. The legal basis for this wider range of environmental protection measures was strengthened by the use of the term 'policy' rather than 'action on the environment' in the Maastricht Treaty.

The powers of the European Parliament in the decision-making process of the EU were extended by the Treaty revision. The European Parliament is considered to be the most environmentally concerned of the institutions of the European Union. The changes to the powers and the role of the EP have had a positive impact on the environmental protection policies of the EU (see Chapter 3). The use of qualified majority voting in the Council of Ministers was extended to decisions about environmental legislation. The extension of QMV was seen as a way of ensuring that one national government could not hold back the passage of legislation. Other aims for environmental policy which were reiterated in the Maastricht Treaty included the principles that prevention is better than cure, damage should be rectified at its source, and that the polluter should pay to remedy damage. The Single European Act had included the principle that environmental requirements were to be included in all other areas of EU policy. The Maastricht Treaty left this unchanged.

Two developments as a result of the Maastricht Treaty changes threatened to undermine environmental policy. First, in a number of key areas, such as decisions about energy choice by the member states and the use of fiscal instruments to protect the environment, the use of unanimous voting procedures in the Council of Ministers remained. Second, the principle of subsidiarity was extended and no longer applied solely to the environment chapter of the Treaty. Extending the application of the principle of subsidiarity in this way emphasized the underlying decentralizing tendency of the principle (see Chapter 12). This left opportunities for the member states to 'claw back' the responsibility for environmental protection from the EU and also led to a lack of clarity about how the sharing of the competence for environmental policy was to be achieved.

The problem of ineffective implementation of environmental policy was not resolved by the Maastricht Treaty. The Fifth EAP included details of how the implementation process could be improved, but the treaty revisions did little to support them through the legal process. It is not of course the purpose of treaty amendments to resolve problems of implementation; that is left to the European Commission and the national governments. However there were calls for the Treaty to incorporate measures which would support the work of the European Commission and enable the EP to exercise greater scrutiny of the policy.

Specific tasks had been included in the Maastricht Treaty for the 1996 Inter-governmental Conference in articles 1 TEU (A TEU), 2 TEU (B TEU) and article

N (2) TEU.[12] They centred on the promotion of economic and social progress, economic and social cohesion, the establishing of economic and monetary union including the single currency, the implementation of a common foreign and security policy including defence policy, the introduction of a citizenship of the Union and the development of cooperation on justice and home affairs. Some of this agenda was altered as a result of a number of changes within the EU which took place between 1993 and 1996. It was a period marked by renewed dynamism within the EU. By 1995 it was apparent that the first deadline for the introduction of the single currency was not going to be possible, but this renewed the commitment to ensure that the 1999 deadline was met. Enlargement of the EU to include Sweden, Finland and Austria was accomplished in 1995. As the negotiations on the treaty revisions proceeded through the Italian and Luxembourg presidencies of 1996, among other issues dominating the agenda were worsening unemployment, the problems of the national economies as they moved to create economic and monetary union and the strengthened commitment to enlargement to include Central and Eastern Europe. Reform of the institutions of the EU was also recognized as an essential element of the enlargement process.

As a result, environmental policy was not initially on the agenda for the IGC. Major reform of the environment chapter which had been included in the Treaty in 1987 was not considered necessary. However, a commitment was made in the Turin Council Summit which opened the IGC in March 1996 to find ways to meet the fundamental challenge of providing a healthy and sustainable environment for the citizens of the EU (*Europe* 1996; CEC 1996u: 11). By the beginning of the Dutch presidency in 1997 the negotiations on how this could be achieved were centred on three issues.

The first of these was the inclusion in the Treaty of the objective of sustainable development. This was something that had been discussed in the negotiations for the Maastricht Treaty revisions but ambiguity remained in the treaty articles. The Maastricht Treaty had been the outcome of two IGCs (one focusing on monetary union, the other on political union) which had proceeded during 1991. The monetary union deliberations had been concerned with the economic issues and the problem of inflation in particular. The political union debate included the idea of policies which would result in sustainable development. The final drafting of the Treaty during the Dutch presidency in 1991 was an attempt to bring together ideas from both sets of deliberations. The result was unsatisfactory. When it was translated, the wording of the article led to a weakening of the commitment to sustainable development (Haigh 1995: 2). In English the article read 'sustainable growth respecting the environment', in German 'continuous and non-inflationary growth' and in French 'lasting growth respecting the environment'.

Support had existed since the 1980s for commitment to sustainable development within the EU. At the end of the Greek presidency of the Council of Ministers in December 1988 a declaration was adopted by the European Council which included commitments to 'sustained growth and a better quality of life' and stated that 'Sustainable development must be one of the overriding objectives of all Community policies'. This was reflected in the Fifth EAP, which had been subtitled 'Towards Sustainability'. The EU was committed to achieving the objectives which were implied, but the legal basis for actions was not in place. The primary concern was therefore to ensure that the ambiguities were removed and the Amsterdam Treaty made a clear statement of commitment to sustainable development. Changes were made to article 2 TEU (B TEU) of the Treaty on European Union. 'The Union shall set itself the objective ... to achieve balanced and sustainable development' and article 2 TEC (2 TEC) of the Treaty establishing the European Community: 'The Community shall have as its task ... balanced and sustainable development of economic activities'.

The second issue was strengthening the statement that environmental requirements should be taken into account in other policy areas, which had been introduced in the Single European Act. In the SEA the policies to which this was to apply had not been clearly specified. In order to support sustainable development it was necessary to identify the objective in those sectoral policies that had the most potential for damage to the environment, for example transport, energy and agriculture. Article 6 TEC (3c TEC) specified that environmental protection requirements had to be integrated into the definition and implementation of Community policies and activities referred to in article 3 TEC (3 TEC) which included all of these areas. A minor modification was also made to article 174 TEC (130r (2) SEA) to support and clarify the integration requirement.

In June 1998 the European Commission presented a proposal for a strategy for meeting this integration requirement to the Cardiff Council Summit which ended the 1998 British presidency (CEC 1998d). The strategy concentrated on a number of issues, the most important of which was that new proposals should be properly assessed to identify their environmental implications. As a first stage in demonstrating that there would be commitment from the national governments, the Commission asked the Council to use the Agenda 2000 reforms (CEC 1997o) and the EU's strategy for implementing the Kyoto Protocol (CEC 1997v) as test cases.

The third major area of change was to reinforce the 'environmental guarantee' in article 95 TEC (100a TEC). Changes were made to paragraphs 3, 4 and 5 of the article and additional paragraphs added. The amendments gave national governments the opportunity to maintain national provisions if they were based on new scientific evidence in order to protect the environment (article 95 (4) TEC (100a TEC)). After the harmonization measure was adopted, the national governments had the opportunity to introduce national provisions if the problem was one considered specific to the individual state (article 95 (5) TEC (100a TEC)). The objective of these changes was clearly to enable countries which had higher national environmental standards both to maintain them and to introduce higher standards in the future. A number of conditions were attached to article 95 TEC (100a TEC). Paragraph 3 stipulated that any new developments had to be based on scientific facts and take as a base a high level of protection. The national governments had to notify the European Commission of measures being taken and justify their adoption (para. 4). The Commission was entrusted with the task of verifying the national provisions, establishing whether they would constitute a barrier to trade and approving or rejecting the measure within six months of notification (paras. 4, 5 and 6). In cases where new scientific evidence was presented, the European Commission was required to reassess the original harmonization measure (para. 8).

These changes to article 95 TEC (100a TEC) carry advantages and disadvantages. They reaffirm the commitment to working constantly to improve environmental protection within the EU by means of the requirement for changes to be based on new scientific data and the reassessment proviso. This reinforces the general application of the precautionary principle in article 174 TEC (130r TEC). On the other hand, the changes appear to open the way for fragmentation of the policy. The amendments to the Treaty were made following pressure from the Nordic states and Austria where there were concerns about a lowering of environmental standards before their accession to the EU in 1995. The Mediterranean states of the EU on the other hand saw this as a threat which carried the potential to undermine the competitiveness of their companies and add to industries' costs (see Chapter 5 for discussion of competition among rules).

The Central and Eastern European applicant states for membership of the EU included some areas with severe problems of environmental degradation. In May 1998 the European Commission asked for the applicant states to provide detailed plans of how the governments intended to implement the environmental 'acquis'[13] (ENDS 25/05/98). At the same time there was an acknowledgement that none of the applicants would be able fully to comply with the environmental legislation before accession. Derogations from some legislation and readjustment of deadlines for each state for specific pieces of legislation appeared to be the only way forward. The changes to article 95 TEC (100a TEC) may bring further weakening of the policy, as some states introduce stricter national measures, others ignore the legislation because of lack of commitment, and yet others have negotiated longer and individual schedules for introduction of the measures. The danger also exists that some national governments could use the amendments as a new form of protectionism and create a barrier to trade within the integrated market (see Chapter 6).

The Treaty of Amsterdam also made some amendments to the decision-making process and the role of the European Parliament in the development of environmental policy. The co-decision procedure was both simplified and extended (article 175 TEC (130s SEA)). As a result of pressure from the German government, the use of qualified majority voting in the Council of Ministers was not extended to this provision. The involvement of the EP in decision making about environmental taxation, planning, the management of water resources and energy supply therefore remained limited (see Chapter 3).

What is clear is that commitment to the protection of the environment has been increased, putting it on to a basis equivalent to that of economic development, but questions remain about the implementation, monitoring and enforcement of the policy. In addition to the legal basis established for the policy, a number of other initiatives were developed during the mid- and late 1990s in an attempt to overcome some of these concerns. The Fifth EAP advocated the use of a number of market-based and voluntary measures to support the legislation. There have also been calls for the European Commission to review and simplify the legislation which has been adopted.

Two areas of policy in particular were identified where a more global approach to the legislation could result from an overhaul of the existing legislation – water quality and air quality. The introduction of framework directives as the form of legislation for these two issues is important for a number of reasons. First, it is an attempt to bring coherence and clarity into both water policy and air policy, areas which have been the focus of EU attention since the First EAP. Second, the introduction of framework legislation fulfils the commitment to the application of the principle of subsidiarity and the sharing of the competence for legislation. It is a form of legislation which is designed to be a flexible instrument to take into account wide regional differences in air and water conditions across the EU. The use of framework legislation marks the beginning of a new phase in environmental policy, using as it does an approach which concentrates on the medium which is being affected and less on the individual sectors or factors which are causing the damage. It is an attempt at a more holistic approach which will require careful management and monitoring to ensure effective implementation.

The proposal for a framework directive for water was introduced by the Commission of the European Communities in February 1997 (CEC 1997n). The framework directive replaced six directives on water quality – on surface water, on measurement and sampling frequencies, exchange of information on fresh water quality, fish water, shellfish water and ground water. At the same time the framework directive was intended to complement other directives, for example on urban waste water treatment, nitrates pollution and integrated pollution prevention and control. However, there was no intention to include the drinking water and bathing water directives in this initiative. Initially the dangerous substances directive was also excluded from the terms of reference of the legislation, but with a view to repealing it once the other legislation was fully in place. The objective of the legislation is to ensure that 'a good status of waters should be pursued within the river basin ... ensuring that waters belong to the same ecological and hydrogeological systems are managed as a whole whether ... present as ground water or surface water' (CEC 1997n: preamble; para. 22). The intention was to ensure that the directive was in place by December 1999, but a number of amendments were introduced during 1998 which resulted in some delays to the timetable.

The framework directive on ambient air quality (Directive 96/62 EC) was adopted in 1996. The primary objectives of this legislation were to establish a common strategy for standards of ambient air quality: to avoid, prevent or reduce harmful effects on human health and the environment. It replaced a number of directives on quality standards for sulphur dioxide and particulates, lead and nitrogen oxide. Proposals were also made to introduce a number of daughter directives over a period of ten to fifteen years, setting optimal air quality limit values, margins of tolerance, assessment procedures, and reporting requirements for individual procedures. The intention was that the framework directive would act as a complement to the directives on control of emissions from motor vehicles and fuel combustion, limits on sulphur content in fuels and emissions from engines to be installed in mobile machinery.

These developments in the introduction of framework legislation have a number of implications. They require the effective support of commitments which have been made and introduced into the legislation on:

- use of the best available technologies (BAT) to achieve the stated objectives;
- ensuring that the precautionary principle is adopted in all the environmental measures used;
- integration of environmental requirement into other policies; and
- acceptance of available scientific information and technical data.

The flexibility introduced into the framework legislation to take account of the regional differences within the EU requires changes to the role of the European Commission, especially as monitor of the policy. The legislation will bring an added pressure to ensure that mechanisms are in place to strengthen the work of data collection by the European Environment Agency and the connection that the organization has with the European Commission. The most far-reaching implication of the adoption of framework legislation will, however, come from the opportunity for the national governments to maintain or introduce higher national standards, if doing so does not distort the market. Introducing a more flexible instrument must be linked to more effective implementation if the approach is to be extended to other issues without undermining the coherence which the legislation is attempting to bring to the policy.

CONCLUSIONS

It is possible to identify three important break points in the development of the EU's environmental policy. The first was the introduction of the First EAP in 1972, which signalled the response of the national governments to growing global awareness of environmental degradation and a recognition that joint action would result in benefits for the creation of the market and protection of the environment. The second came in the adoption of the Single European Act in 1987 and was crucial to the development of the policy. The SEA gave a firm legal basis to supranational action. It put in place the foundations for the move away from a policy based on *ad hoc* measures which attempted to address individual problems, and provided the basis for the introduction of an environmental policy founded on the principle of integration of environmental objectives into other areas of policy. The SEA also enabled the EU to play a more active role in global environmental agreements which were being negotiated.

The commitment to integrate environmental requirements into legislation in article 6 TEC of the Treaty of Amsterdam is the third of the major steps forward in the development of the policy, which has been frequently criticized for being high on rhetoric and low on reality. All legislation, not just that proposed by DG XI (Environment), has to take environmental impact into account. In addition, there is an explicit statement of the legitimacy of supranational actions to achieve a policy based on the principle of sustainable development. National environmental policies are also increasingly being built on the basis of a commitment to sustainable development. The EU's environmental policy is a catalyst for national action as well as being stimulated by developments at national level.

The problem does remain, however, of tension between the supranational and national tiers of government about where responsibility for the different actions should be placed. This tension underlies the criticism contained in the following chapters, which analyse the different aspects of environmental policy. Chapter 4 presents a critique of the methods which have been used to date to remove this tension and evaluates the proposals for the future. The introduction of the principle of subsidiarity into the Treaty has raised more questions than it has answered. Acceptance of a commitment to a policy which will lead to sustainable development is similarly surrounded by problems of definition. The challenges to future developments in the policy area are mounting in severity; they come from the political, economic, and social dimensions of EU action, but most of all from within the political system evolving within the EU. The dominance of national governments in the policy process has remained unchanged throughout the history of the EU. Events seem to be occurring which are reinforcing that dominance. There is a significant danger that the EU's environmental policy will become fragmented and unable to fulfil its twin objectives of environmental protection and support for a freely operating European market economy.

NOTES

1. The negotiations for the revision of the EU Treaty known as the 'Amsterdam Treaty' began on 29 March 1996 in Turin during the Italian presidency and were concluded in June 1997 in Amsterdam during the Dutch presidency. Both before and during these negotiations the idea of changing article 33 TEC (39 EEC) was discussed. The outcome of the negotiations fell short of what those pressing for change had hoped for. No specific reference to environmental objectives was added to Treaty article 33 TEC (39 EEC). Agriculture was, however, listed among the policies where environmental requirements should be taken into account in article 3 TEU (3b TEU).
2. Council Directive 70/157/EC on permissible sound level and the exhaust systems and its amendments in 1973, 1977, 1981, 1984 (2) and Directive 78/1015/EC on permissible sound level and exhaust systems of motorcycles.
3. The usual procedure for negotiation in international conventions is for the Council of Ministers to agree a common position to be adopted and then to authorize the European Commission to negotiate on behalf of the EU.
4. The legal basis for environmental action was provided in the revision of the Treaty – the Single European Act which came in 1987 as this programme was drawing to its close.
5. *The Mediterranean enlargement*

Applicant state	Application made	Negotiations begun	Treaty of Accession	Accession
Greece	June 1975	July 1976	May 1979	January 1981
Spain	July 1977	February 1979	June 1985	January 1986
Portugal	March 1977	October 1978	June 1985	January 1986

6. The single market programme, outlined in the Cockfield Report (CEC 1985), was launched during the Third EAP.
7. The EU's Structural Funds include the European Regional Development Fund (ERDF), the European Social Fund (ESF) and the Guidance element of the European Agricultural Guidance and Guarantee Fund (EAGGF).
8. Resolution of the Council of Ministers on a Community programme of policy and action in relation to the environment and sustainable development (5th EAP) OJC 138, 17 May 1993, Brussels.
9. The Report which followed the 1987 Commission has come to be commonly known by the name of the Chair of the Commission, the former Norwegian premier Gro Harlem Brundtland.
10. Thorvald Stoltenberg was the Norwegian ambassador to Denmark who had been a UN Special Peace Envoy to the former Yugoslavia.
11. *Qualified majority voting in the council of ministers*

Member state	Number of votes	Member state	Number of votes
UK	10	Portugal	5
France	10	Sweden	4

Italy	10	Austria	4
Germany	10	Denmark	3
Spain	8	Finland	3
Greece	5	Ireland	3
Belgium	5	Luxembourg	2
Netherlands	5		
		Total 87	QMV 62

Note: The system of weighting was introduced to help the development of the internal market. The number of votes allocated to each of the member states was to reflect the size of each state. A proposal is only agreed when 71 per cent of the available votes are cast in its favour.

12. This article was replaced in the Treaty of Amsterdam by article 48 which gave the legal basis for the convening of IGCs. It did not, however, specify any dates, as was done in the Maastricht Treaty.
13. 'Acquis communautaire' or the body of EU legislation, in this case environmental legislation.

3   The makers of environmental policy

INTRODUCTION

The European Union (EU) does not have the ideal organizational structure for the formulation of policy on the environment. The institutions involved in the decision-making process were established to provide a framework for negotiation and collaboration among six nations on economic issues. The twin pressures of moving forward the process of economic integration and an increasing concern about the negative consequences of economic growth pushed the development of policy on the environment on to the agenda in the early 1970s. However, there were no significant treaty changes to accommodate the needs of environmental policy until the adoption of the Single European Act (SEA) in 1987.

Despite the progress which has been made on the introduction of environmental protection measures, the economic imperative continues to provide the context in which policy is formulated. Furthermore, the EU's environmental policy has developed against a background of an increasingly crowded national policy space. It is a policy that has emerged from an often confrontational process of international negotiation and agreement. It has therefore proved to be difficult on occasion to alter the focus of the policy quickly. In addition, the formulation of policy has been constrained by the physical nature of the EU and the capacity of the natural environment to react to the problems of pollution and environmental degradation. Currently the need for reform of the institutions of the EU and simplification of the complex policy imposes limits on future action. This complexity is exacerbated by:

- the number of issues with which the Policy is attempting to deal;
- the existence of the principle of 'shared competence' for environmental policy;
- the way in which national issues may come to dominate the EU's environmental policy agenda;
- the multiplicity of environmental actors and interests in the EU and their influence on the policy-making process;
- the fragmentation of policy making; and
- the lack of coordination in the policy-making process.

The objective of this chapter is to present an analysis of the way in which environmental policy is made within the EU. The chapter concentrates on the issue of who decides on the actions to be adopted. As the policy-making process within the EU has been characterized as multi-layered (Puchala 1983: 406) and more recently as unstable and multi-dimensional (Mazey and Richardson 1993), the resolution of this question is problematic.

STRUCTURE OF THE POLICY PROCESS

The European Union is an organization with extensive powers and special legal status. It has a unique political and judicial system with an institutional framework within which decisions are made. This has a fundamental impact on the policy-making process. Within the EU, policy emerges from the complex negotiation which takes place within the institutional triangle of the Council of Ministers (CoM), the Commission of the European Communities (CEC) and the European Parliament (EP). The institutional framework for policy making is supported by the European Court of Justice (ECJ) which, whilst not part of the decision-making process, has had a significant impact on the development of policy through its rulings. Other institutional actors include the Economic and Social Committee (ECOSOC, established by the Treaty of the European Economic Communities in 1957) and the Committee of the Regions (CoR, established by the Maastricht Treaty changes in 1993). The relative roles which they play in the policy decision-making process are illustrated in Figure 3.1.

The three main tasks of government – the legislative, the judicial and the administrative – are shared between the four institutions. The Council of Ministers is the main source of EU legislation. Its legislative powers are, however, shared with both the Commission of the European Communities and the European Parliament. This is not always a harmonious arrangement. In describing the relationship between the Council of Ministers and the Commission in the policy-making process Cini concluded that it is one of mutual dependence between two sometimes competing institutions (Cini 1996: 131). As a consequence of the complex consultation and negotiation stages which characterize the decision-making process, the outcomes of policy may be unexpected and sometimes fall short of the objectives of any original proposals.

In addition, environmental policy making is open to the influence of interest groups, national government departments and agencies, industrial organizations and individuals. Table 3.1 identifies the roles of the actors in the making and implementation of environmental policy. The issues surrounding the implementation and enforcement of environmental policy, identified as phases 7–9, are discussed in detail in the following chapter.

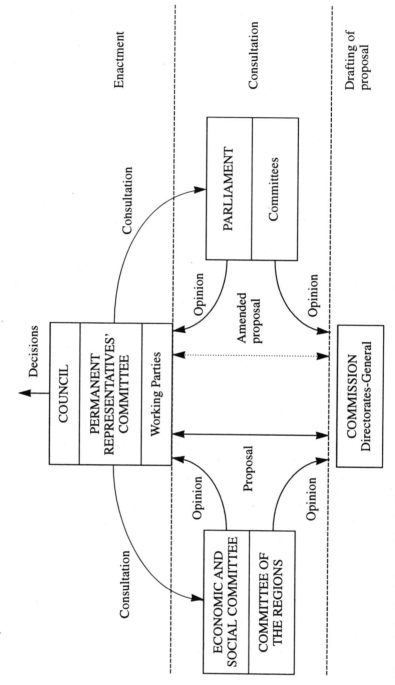

Figure 3.1   Decision making in the European Union

Table 3.1   Actors involved in making EU environmental policy

Policy phase	Actor	Comments
1. Defining the environmental problem in general terms	Multiple influences at national and EU level	Lobbying by interested groups at both national and supranational levels of government
2. Deciding how to apply the principle of subsidiarity	Council of Ministers, European Commission, Commission initiates the legislation	Lobbying of Commission, European Parliament
3. Setting the agenda	European Council, Council of Ministers. Influence of the Commission and the EP	Lobbying of the Commission and the European Parliament. Reflects the separate agendas of each actor
4. Teasing out the differing strands of the problem	Consultation phase, adding the European Parliament, the Economic and Social Committee and the Committee of the Regions	Lobbying done at this stage is already too late to have a significant impact on the legislation
5. Objectives setting and prioritization of the issues	Council of Ministers	Constraints emerge, placed by the national governments, especially if financial issues are identified
6. Identification of the preferred option	Council of Ministers	Outcome of negotiation and bargaining process – legislation adopted
7. Implementation, Monitoring, and control	National governments and the Commission; support of the European Court of Justice	Public participation as an important part of the process. Importance of the development of the role of the European Environment Agency
8. Evaluation and review	National governments, Commission. NGOs, individuals, industrial actors	Wide range of actors involved at this stage. Problems of control and monitoring emerge
9. Policy maintenance, succession and possible termination	Commission and national governments	Problems of control and monitoring emerge

CONSTRAINTS ON THE POLICY-MAKING PROCESS

Environmental policy was not mentioned when the European Economic Community Treaty was signed in 1957. The evident need for action at European level came from pressures during the 1960s from two directions. Within the broader international community there was an acknowledgement of the necessity to introduce polices which would promote environmental protection. Within the European Union the imperative for environmental policy grew from the increasing integration of the market. The existence of different national environmental measures might act as a barrier to trade and cause market distortion. The First EAP in 1972 was therefore not a common policy on the environment, but was an attempt to harmonize the policies of the member states. The inclusion of the environment chapter in the Single European Act (SEA) marked the beginning of a common policy on the environment. The legitimacy of the role of the EU in the development of environmental policy was formally recognized. However, the background from which the policy has emerged still influences the approach adopted in the legislation. This is seen nowhere more clearly than in the opportunity given to national governments to introduce and maintain higher environmental standards if there is no impact on the harmonization measures needed for the market to operate (article 95 TEC (100a TEC), paras 5 and 8).

The early opportunities for the European Union to become involved in the formulation of an environmental policy resulted from the existence of what may be described as a 'policy space' (Hogwood and Gunn 1984: 13). The role of the governments of the EU states in the development of national environmental policies in the late 1960s and early 1970s was limited, though the opportunities and the perceived need existed to introduce policy at the supranational level. It was unfortunate that, whilst the SEA marked the legitimacy of EU action on the environment, it came at a time when the policy space at the national level was increasingly filled with national initiatives. The EU's environmental policy in the 1980s and early 1990s assumed the characteristic features described by Hogwood and Gunn as a 'crowded' policy space, as more interventions by the national governments took place. The interactions between the national and supranational tiers of government have therefore become more complex.

The reports on the implementation of EU law, published annually by the European Commission, have all highlighted concerns about the commitment of the national governments to the EU's environmental policy. The European Commission has identified a lack of political will to enable the policy to function effectively (CEC 1996p: 3). As the national governments have come under increasing pressure from national industrial or environmental interests, the idea of an EU policy on the environment has become more difficult to achieve. The national governments have assumed the green mantle and begun to occupy the moral high ground on environmental issues. The demise of the green political parties across the EU in the late 1980s and early 1990s was the result of the green agenda becoming part of the mainstream of national politics. At the end of the 1990s the green political parties had still not been able to regain that ground.

The formulation of policy is constrained by the nature of the background from which it emerges. The European Union has fewer policy instruments to choose from than the national governments in order to achieve the objectives of environmental policy. The member states' governments have placed limits on the powers ceded to the EU. The EAPs provide the framework for the policy, but limited amounts of funding are available to support environmental initiatives. The increased discussion of issues through the publication of White and Green Papers has been an important development during the 1990s. The form these publications take has enabled discussion of concerns about legislation to be incorporated at an early stage in the formulation of policy. A number of directives and regulations have been adopted which extend the range of instruments which may be used to achieve environmental objectives. These include the environmental management and audit regulation, the eco-labelling regulation and the directive on landfill taxes. At the supranational level, however, environmental policy is framed against a background which is essentially programmatic and technocratic.

Although the concept of developing policy communities and networks was originally applied to the relationship between the central and local tiers of government in the UK in a period of policy stability it provides a valuable tool for understanding the way in which policy is formulated in the EU (Mazey and Richardson 1996). It is an attempt to explain the interactions which take place in a policy-making environment which includes a large number of actors. EU environmental policy is based on the concept of shared responsibility and this encourages the development of policy networks with many partners. The use of the policy networks approach provides an explanation of four major constraints which affect the actors in the EU's policy making process. These are:

- the differences in the values and expectations of the actors in the policy-making process;
- the formal limits imposed on the policy-making organizations by the roles given to them in the treaties;
- the cost constraints and financial dependences which may affect the policy makers;
- the situational constraints, that is, the influence of past developments in the policy area.

Two types of policy network are often identified at the opposite ends of a continuum. Policy communities are formed where there are shared common values within a small group which has a stable membership. It is possible to identify a group of states (Denmark, the Netherlands and Germany) with more stringent national environmental standards which show the characteristic form of a policy community in their commitment to promoting their higher standards at EU level. In the ongoing debate within the EU about the introduction of a carbon/energy tax, these states were joined by Austria, Belgium, Luxembourg, Finland and Sweden. The Mediterranean states (Spain, Greece and Portugal) often form the nucleus of an opposing coalition. In 1996 the two groups took very different viewpoints on a proposal made by the Italian government to combine the carbon/energy tax with the introduction of excise duties on mineral oils. The proposal was unsuccessful in bringing the two coalitions of states together.

The same core of environmentally 'progressive' states formed a coalition which regarded the directive on landfill standards as too weak. Again the opposing coalition comprised the Mediterranean states and in addition the UK. The objections of this group were however based on differing concerns. The UK government objected to the timetable which was set in the legislation. The poorer EU states objected to the proposals because of the burden which might be placed on more remote areas with smaller landfill facilities.

Issue networks on the other hand emerge to deal with specific pieces of policy and disband quickly once the issue is dealt with. There was general support from industrial groups for the introduction of the EU's eco-labelling regulation, but there were some groups which had reservations about how the scheme would operate. However, full support was given to the initiative by groups of industries which would not under other circumstances be found to have similar concerns, for example the European Association of the Textile Industry and the European Confederation of Paint Manufacturers.

With the growth in the number of issues covered by the EU's environmental policy has come the opportunity and necessity for groups within the EU to gain access to the policy-making process. DG XI (Environment) of the European Commission is actively pursuing measures to increase the involvement of various interests in the policy process, for example green interest groups, consumer groups and industrialists. The European Consultative Forum on the Environment and Sustainable Development, the 'Green Forum' (see Chapter 2) has an important role to play in this increasing pattern of openness, as has the Committee of the Regions and the Economic and Social Committee. Environmental measures carry with them significant benefits, but for some groups there are perceived to be enormous costs (see Chapter 7). There are therefore advantages to be gained by finding some way of influencing the policy-making process. Lobbying at the national level is an important way of mobilizing support for an issue, as existing national policies play a crucial role in the design of EU policies (Liefferink 1996: 189).

Mazey and Richardson conclude that those groups which can manage in a series of multi-level and shifting coalitions will be the most successful (Mazey and Richardson 1996: 214). Environmental interest groups can be effective lobbyists at both the national and supranational level.[1] As the European Parliament has gained in its powers, the environmental groups have made the MEPs targets for lobbying. However, much of the lobbying done on behalf of the industrialists by professional lobby organizations and business associations targets the European Commission. Lobbying at an early stage of the design of policy has the most successful outcome. Once the negotiation process begins within the Council of Ministers, any flexibility in the system is lost as the vested national interests of all the member states begin to be brought to bear on an issue.

PROBLEM IDENTIFICATION AND AGENDA SETTING

The identification of the problem and control of the agenda are vital aspects of the policy-making process. There are a large number of actors involved in identifying a problem and pushing the issue on to the policy agenda in the EU. The Commission has the formal right of initiation of legislation but is open to the influences of the Council of Ministers, the European Parliament and/or groups of lobbyists for the identification of problems. Problem identification takes place on a number of differing levels and involves different actors with differing results. Specific issues may be brought forward by national governments, interest groups or individuals and result in single measures being introduced. Commitment to environmental concerns as a priority for EU action rather than competition or agricultural policy measures may have a much greater and more wide-ranging impact on the overall policy agenda and the policy's future developments.

Within the institutional framework of the EU the importance of the role of the European Council in the agenda-setting process is crucial. No major development in the EU has occurred without having been discussed in summit meetings of the Heads of Government. Environmental policy emerged in 1972 as a result of decisions taken in a summit meeting of the Heads of Government in Paris in October. These summit meetings took place in the early history of the EU on an *ad hoc* basis. The institutional framework for the European Council became established following the Single European Act. The European Council meetings do not set the details of the legislation to be adopted but do provide the direction which is to be taken by the EU in its policy (see Table 3.2).

Public awareness of environmental degradation has helped to maintain the level of interest in the development of an environmental policy within the EU and its priority on the EU's policy agenda. This is the result of organized

Table 3.2 Key European Council declarations on the environment

Date, presidency	Declaration	Issue of concern	Action to be taken
1983, June, Stuttgart, Germany	Called for increased pollution control	Acid rainfall and impact on forests	Control on air pollution Reduction of lead in environment
1985, March, Brussels, Belgium	Preparations for the inclusion of environment in the treaty revisions – SEA	To integrate environmental objectives as essential to economic, industrial, agricultural, social policies	SEA chapter, designation of 1987 as the Year of the Environment
1988, June, Hanover, Germany	Need to ensure that the environmental objectives were integrated	Increased levels of pollution of water and air	
1988, December, Rhodes, Greece	Sustainable development had to become one of the objectives of the EU		
1990, June, Dublin, Ireland	'The Environmental Imperative' EU had a global role to play		Command-and-control approach had to be supplemented by other measures
1992, December, Edinburgh, UK	The outlining of the principle of subsidiarity	Air and water pollution	Simplify, consolidate and update legislation
1993, June Copenhagen, Denmark	Linkage between employment and environmental protection	Rising levels of unemployment within the EU and the opportunities which eco-technologies bring	White Paper on Growth, Competitiveness and Employment highlighted the benefits of eco-technologies in job creation in the EU
1996, March Turin, Italy	Environmental protection to be included on the IGC agenda	Necessity of improving implementation of policy; as a means of ensuring commitment of the citizens of the EU to the process of integration	Changes to treaty articles which included the addition of sustainable development and environmental objectives to sectoral policies
1997, June, Amsterdam, the Netherlands	Reaffirmation of the commitment to protect the environment; need for a concerted approach to the UN Conference on Climate Change in December 1997	Increasing levels of carbon dioxide pollution	Preparations on the approach to be adopted at Kyoto and decisions about the levels of emissions to be negotiated
1998, June, Cardiff, UK	Importance of integration of environmental requirements into other policies in order to achieve sustainable development	Costs of enlargement to Central and Eastern Europe	Detailed plans to be submitted by the governments of the CEE states by March 1999; introduction of national environmental audits

interests being focused on specific environmental issues, for example the chemical industry, the existence of highly motivated protest groups, and the commitment of various national governments and political party leaders. The media have played an important role in mobilizing public interest, often through the use of spectacular and sensational reporting.

THE ROLE AND POWERS OF THE COMMISSION OF THE EUROPEAN COMMUNITY

The Commission of the European Community is more than the EU's civil service. It has a vital role in the legislative process. In addition the Commission has to:

- ensure that the interests of the European Union are paramount and the integration process is advanced;
- initiate legislation and propose policy;
- act as the executor and administration for the Council and the European Parliament;
- manage the EU's financial resources;
- ensure that the legislation is implemented and enforced;
- act as external negotiator for the member states in a number of different international negotiations and treaties;
- act as mediator between the national governments.

As a consequence the Commission has the opportunity to play a major role in the formulation of the European Union's environmental policy. It is 'a truly supranational bureaucracy that can openly seek to influence the policies of its own members' (Porter and Welsh Brown 1991: 47)

COLLEGE OF THE COMMISSIONERS – THE POLITICAL 'ARM' OF THE EUROPEAN COMMISSION

The many roles which the Commission of the European Community is required to fulfil have created an institution that is very complex in structure. It is, however, possible to identify two broad 'arms' to the Commission – a political 'arm' and an administrative 'arm'. The political arm centres on the College of the Commissioners and the support mechanisms provided for the commissioners by their cabinets or private offices of advisers. Appointments to the Commission are made by the mutual agreement of the 15 governments of the member states and the Commission president for terms of office of five years. All the commissioners may have their appointments renewed by the national governments which nominated them. In practice this has meant that some commissioners have served several terms of office.[2] There are currently 20 commissioners forming the College of Commissioners, two from each of the larger states – France, Germany, Spain, Italy and the United Kingdom, and one from each of the other states. Each commissioner is nominally of equal importance within the College of the Commissioners.[3]

However, the individual who is president of the Commission is in a more prominent and somewhat ambivalent position. On the one hand the president is regarded as *primus inter pares* (first among equals) in relation to the other commissioners and may be outvoted by the other members of the College. On the other hand the choice of the president of the Commission is made by the heads of the national governments of the member states. The Commission president is an automatic member of the European Council (see the next section on the Council of Ministers) and represents the European Union in many international negotiations. As a result many of the individuals who have been chosen as presidents of the Commission have been former prime ministers or of equivalent standing.

The Amsterdam Treaty gave the president of the Commission the right to be involved in the choice of the other commissioners. This has increased the role of the Commission president and may as a result undermine the formal equality of the College of Commissioners. The addition of a clause to article 219 (article 163) TEC which stipulates that the Commission shall work under the political guidance of the Commission president will give that individual greater control over the Commission's agenda for action. In practice this will mean that future environmental developments will rely to an increasing extent on commitment to environmental issues from the individual appointed as president. At the same time the events surrounding the resignation of the European Commission in March 1999 (see the following discussion) have highlighted the need for the Commission president to look for commissioners who are of high standing and competent to perform their respective roles. The potential for confrontation within the College of Commissioners on the agenda for environmental policy may have been increased and not lessened as a result.

The president of the Commission is more easily identifiable as the 'public face' of the European Union than the head of state whose country holds the six-monthly rotating presidency (see Table 3.5). Some Commission presidents have striven to gain a high profile during their presidencies. This was particularly true of Jacques Delors who was president of the Commission between 1985 and 1994. Confrontation between the Commission president and the heads of the national governments may occur over the direction which EU policy should take. As a result the nomination of the individual to hold the position of president may be subject to a great deal of political controversy between the national governments. The appointment of Jacques Santer as Commission president in 1994 was a compromise following just such a controversy. The UK government exercised its right of veto of the French- and German-favoured candidate Jean-Luc Dehaene, the former Belgian prime minister.

Following the ratification of the Maastricht Treaty, changes were made to the consultation process about the nomination of the Commission president and the commissioners. Agreement is required amongst the national governments on the President's nomination and the appointment is subject to the approval of the European Parliament (article 214 TEC (article 158). The rights of the European Parliament to be consulted about the nominations for the president were also increased. These rights were first used in 1994 when Jacques Santer was nominated. The incoming Commission under Santer was required to present itself to the European Parliament at a series of hearings and was subject to a vote of approval by the EP. Also amongst the changes made as a result of the Maastricht Treaty was the extension of the commissioners' term in office to five years, to coincide with the terms of the European Parliament. This was to enable the EP to exercise its supervisory powers over the Commission.

The strengths of the EP's supervisory powers over the Commission president and the College of Commissioners began to be tested in 1997 and 1998. It was during this period that allegations about financial mismanagement by the European Commission and more specific irregularities by individual commissioners, which had been a concern since the beginning of the 1990s, began to increase in number and severity. As a result, the position of some of the commissioners began to be subject to question.

It is possible for individual commissioners to be compulsorily retired (article 215 (article 159) TEC) for misconduct or incapacity to fulfil their office following an application to the European Court of Justice by the Council or the Commission. The terms of article 215 had, however, been applied on only one prior occasion. In 1976 Commissioner Borschette had been replaced on the instruction of the European Court of Justice following a stroke. The EP does not have the right to compulsorily retire an individual commissioner. If the MEPs wish to take action, they have the right to dismiss the entire Commission following a vote of censure. Generally this right has been seen as such a radical step that it has not been seriously considered by the EP until the scandal of 1998/99.

In December 1998 an official in DG XX (financial control) Paul van Buitenen presented a dossier containing alleged and proven irregularities in the EU's programmes for tourism, humanitarian aid, nuclear safety, aid to countries bordering the Mediterranean Sea and research and youth training, to the European Parliament. Specific allegations were directed against Edith Cresson (commissioner responsible for science research and technology developments, human resources, education and youth and training) and Manuel Marin (Commission vice-president responsible for external relations). Despite the presentation of this information to the EP about the allegations of mismanagement, fraud, nepotism and cronyism, there was a great deal of reluctance within the EP to take action. When the van Butienen dossier was discussed in the EP in early 1999, fewer than a quarter of the MEPs were in favour of bringing pressure to bear on the other institutions to initiate the necessary proceedings to have the two named commissioners removed.

The Commission president, Jacques Santer, did not have the power to dismiss Commissioners Cresson and Marin himself. In any event the course of action which he decided to follow was to support their management of their policy portfolios and administrative departments. Neither Commissioner Cresson nor Marin opted to resign themselves. A vote of censure on the Commission's financial management was proposed in the EP, and held in the Parliament's plenary session on 14 January 1999 following an acrimonious debate. It failed to reach the two-thirds majority of the Parliament (article 201 (article 144) TEC) required for the vote to succeed and for the Commission to be subsequently dismissed. The vote was defeated by a narrow margin of 232 MEPs voting for the motion and 293 against. The party of European Socialists in the EP, which included the British Labour Party MEPs and the large French Socialist grouping, refused to vote in favour of the motion.

Although the vote of censure taken in January 1999 did not result in the removal of Commissioners Cresson and Marin, it did produce three outcomes considered by the European Parliamentarians to be positive. First, Jacques Santer made a commitment to introduce codes of conduct to govern the work of the College of Commissioners and Commission officials and the relations between the two. There was a second commitment from Jacques Santer to introduce a timetable by the end of January 1999 to modernize the administration and ensure that there would be consultation with the MEPs about what should be done. Complaints made by the MEPs that the Commission did not consult the EP in a broader sense were also answered in proposals by Jacques Santer for an inter-institutional agreement which would enable scrutiny of the Commission's financial management to take place. The third positive outcome was the formation of an advisory committee of independent experts – five 'wise men' under the auspices of the EP and the Commission. The committee was, however, to be impartial. Both the EP and the Commission agreed to support its work and respect the findings.

The mandate given to the committee was to examine the way in which the Commission detected and dealt with fraud, mismanagement and nepotism. The terms of reference of the committee were to 'establish to what extent the Commission, as a body, or Commissioners individually, bear specific responsibility for the recent examples of fraud, mismanagement or nepotism raised on

Parliamentary discussions, or in the allegations which have arisen in those discussions' (European Parliament 1999: para. 1.1.4). The subject of its first report was the actions taken by the College of Commissioners itself.

The committee of independent experts presented this report (European Parliament 1999) on the allegations of fraud, mismanagement and nepotism in the College of Commissioners on 15 March 1999. The committee had decided to concentrate on specific examples rather than to conduct an in-depth investigation of each case. This was a response to the time constraints the members faced and to avoid duplication of work which other investigations had already done, including work by the European Parliament's committee on budgetary control, the Commission's financial control department in DG XX and the anti-fraud unit UCLAF (Unité de co-ordination de la lutte anti-fraude).

The report was damning and upheld the allegations in a general sense against the whole of the Commission in addition to specific cases. In their defence to the committee the Commissioners had argued that they were not aware of what was happening in the administrative departments (directorates general) for which they had responsibility. The findings of the committee accepted that in many cases the individual commissioners had not been personally involved in the alleged cases of fraud or mismanagement. However, the committee concluded that 'the protestations of ignorance ... are tantamount to an admission of loss of control by the political authorities over the administration that they are supposed to be running. This loss of control implies at the outset a heavy responsibility for both the Commissioners individually and the Commission as a whole' (EP 1999: para. 9.2.2). The final concluding paragraph of the report stated that whilst 'Each individual [Commissioner] must feel accountable for the measures he or she manages ... It is becoming difficult to find anyone who has even the slightest sense of responsibility ... The temptation to deprive the concept of responsibility of all substance is a dangerous one. That concept is the ultimate manifestation of democracy' (EP 1999: para. 9.4.25).[4]

Following the publication of this report the whole of European Commission took the unprecedented action of resigning on 16 March following meetings held through the night of 15 March 1999. This action forestalled any initiatives that might have led to their compulsory retirement and left the opportunity open for the individual commissioners to be renominated by their national governments. The Santer Commission was due to 'step down' in the autumn of 1999 following the June Parliamentary elections in any case. Some of the commissioners, including Manuel Marin, had already indicated before these events that they did not intend to seek renomination by the national governments. In the case of Edith Cresson further evidence was presented to the EP that she had lied during the investigations into her financial management of programmes and there was no national support for her renomination. If the French government had proposed her renomination, this would have led inevitably to further controversy between the European Commission and the European Parliament. The commissioners were able to continue in a 'caretaker' role until September 1999 when the new Commission was appointed. Whilst there were calls from the EP and some of the national governments for the Commission to stand down immediately following the report, the caretaker role was in accordance with the provisions of the Treaty. Article 215 (article 159) TEC stated that whilst the duties of a commissioner ended upon resignation, he/she should remain in office until replaced, except in a case of compulsory retirement.

The procedures in the case of the Commission president differed slightly in that article 215 stipulated that the president should be replaced immediately upon resignation. Initially Jacques Santer indicated his intention to remain in a caretaker capacity as well, but the heads of the governments of the EU confirmed the appointment of Romano Prodi, the former centrist prime minister of Italy, as president of the Commission during the Berlin Summit of the Heads of Government held on 25 March 1999. Romano Prodi presented his intended policy agenda for his presidency to a hearing of the EP on 14 April 1999. The EP voted on his appointment in early May, just before the EP was dissolved in preparation for the June 1999 EP elections. During this formal ratification process Jacques Santer continued to perform the role of acting president of the Commission.

As the Commissioner for the Environment Ritt Bjerregaard was not named specifically in any section of the report, the impact of the Commission's resignation on the formation of the EU's environmental policy in the early years of the twenty-first century was indirect. Her own position was undermined as the Danish government showed some reluctance to renominate her. Her term of office had been controversial and included examples of disagreements between the Commissioner and both the Council of Ministers and her fellow commissioners. She had tried to push through some more radical measures than the Council of Ministers was prepared to accept, including an attempt to introduce a more stringent regime in response to international concerns about global warming. Early in the Santer presidency Commissioner Bjerregaard had caused some friction when she published unfavourable comments on her fellow commissioners in the Danish national press. The work which was begun in the late 1990s in the Directorate General for which she had responsibility (see the following section) on the replacement for the Fifth EAP was also delayed as a result of the uncertainty surrounding her position.

The outcome of the resignation of the whole of the College of the Commissioners is, however, potentially far-reaching in areas that will have a direct impact on the EU's environmental policy. In terms of the relationship between the institutions of the European Union, the EP demonstrated its concerns to bring greater transparency and openness to the institutions through more rigorous investigation of the management procedures of the European Commission. The urgency of institutional reform was reaffirmed and pushed to the top of the EU's political agenda. Questions began to emerge about the power of the EP to dismiss the Commission in its entirety and whether or not the EP should have the opportunity to compulsorily retire an individual commissioner. It was clear that a minor treaty amendment would be sufficient to accomplish this change if the national governments were in agreement.

The events of early 1999 seemed to support the view that the Commission should be made more accountable for its actions and that the EP should have a greater role to play through its increasing supervisory powers. However, the Commission's powerful right of initiation of policy measures remains intact. It may be that increased cooperation between these two institutions of the EU is the outcome of the resignation of the Santer Commission. The right given to the EP of scrutiny of the financial management of the commissioners enlarges the scope for future developments in environmental policy. The right of scrutiny carries with it the responsibility to take action when issues of concern are identified. The concerns in the report by the independent experts (EP: 1999) about the increased work load of the commissioners, the failures adequately to staff specific departments and programmes, and concerns about some individual budgets, are issues which the EP must respond to in cooperation with the Commission. As environmental protection measures are high on the political agenda of the European Parliament, the opportunities may have been enhanced as a result for support from within the EP for increased financing for environmental projects as well as support for more radical environmental proposals introduced by the Commission.

Changes to the role of the Commission president were included in the Amsterdam Treaty in article 214 (article 158) TEC so the Commission president had much more involvement in the choice of the individual commissioners. The Commission president was also given more opportunity to identify the portfolios of the individual commissioners, so that skills could be more easily matched to the requirements of the responsibilities. In the past the portfolios of individual commissioners had been allocated on the basis of political decisions made by the national governments. The existence of the new powers for the Commission president did not remove all political controversy amongst the national governments about the appointments of commissioners, but did give the Commission president increased opportunities to exert an influence on the national nominations.

Among the most urgent of the tasks for the new Commission of 2000–2005 was the introduction of a wide-ranging institutional reform programme in preparation for enlargement to Central and Eastern Europe. Institutional reform was also a high priority for the Commission president in order to ensure that similar problems of mismanagement did not occur again. In the short term this may undermine support for a radical environmental agenda within the Commission until these issues are dealt with.

Table 3.3 The Commission 2000–2005, (replaced the Santer Commission which was in office from 1995–1999)*

Commissioner	Responsibilities
Romano Prodi, President (It)	Horizontal services, CFSP, Monetary and institutional affairs
Neil Kinnock, Vice-President (UK)	EU administrative reform
Loyola de Palacio, Vice-President (Sp)	Transport and energy, relations with the European Parliament
Philippe Busquin (Bel)	Research
Mario Monti (It)	Competition
Viviane Reding (Lux)	Education and culture
Anna Diamantopoulou (Gr)	Social affairs
Erkki Liikanen (Fin)	Information Society and enterprise
Michaele Schreyer (Ger)	Budget and anti-fraud
Chris Patten (UK)	External relations
Franz Fischler (Aust)	Agriculture and Fisheries
Margo Waldstom (Sw)	**Environment (replaced Ritt Bjerregaard)**
Antonio Vitorino (Port)	Immigration, JHA, Anti-fraud, ombudsman
Poul Nielson (Den)	Development and Humanitarian Aid
Pascal Lamy (Fr)	Trade
Pedro Solbes Mira (Sp)	Economic and monetary affairs
Michel Barnier (Fr)	Regional Policy and funding (also ad personam Inter-governmental Conferences)
David Byrne (Ire)	Consumer affairs and health
Frits Bolkstein (Fin)	Internal Market and Taxation
Gunter Verheugen (Ger)	EU enlargement

* The Santer Commission resigned in its entirely on 16 March 1999, before its term of office was completed. The Commission President Jacques Santer was replaced during the Berlin Summit of Heads of Government 24/25 March 1999 by Romano Prodi. The rest of the Commission remained in a 'caretaker' capacity until they were replaced following the European Parliamentary elections in June 1999.

THE ADMINISTRATIVE 'ARM' OF THE COMMISSION OF THE EUROPEAN COMMUNITY

The Commission of the European Community includes the largest part of the administrative organization of the EU's institutions. It has a staff of about 15 500 permanent and 3000 temporary officials and those based in research establishments. One fifth of the officials are employed in the translation and interpretation services. The European Commission is divided into specialized divisions or Directorates-General (DGs). The number of DGs has grown from 9 to 24. In addition to help from the DGs, the work of the Commission is also supported by 15 specialist service departments which include translation and legal services. DG XI, which has responsibility for the environment, was established in 1981 to replace a minor service department which had operated from 1971.

The number of personnel in each DG is much smaller than that in a national government department and varies considerably. D-G Xl (Environment) has 500 officials in contrast to DG VI (Agriculture), which has 800, or DG IX (Personnel), which has 2600. A senior official, a director-general, who reports to a commissioner, heads each of the DGs. Each commissioner is responsible for one area or portfolio (see Table 3.3) but that may be dealt with by more than one department or DG (see Table 3.4).

Table 3.4   Directorates-General and services of the Commission

DG	Area of responsibility
DG I	External relations
DG II	Economic and financial
DG III	Internal market and industrial affairs
DG IV	Competition
DG V	Employment, social
DG VI	Agriculture
DG VII	Transport
DG VIII	Development
DG IX	Personnel and administration
DG X	Information, communication, culture
DG XI	**Environment, nuclear safety and civil protection**
DG XII	Science, R&D
DG XIII	Telecommunications, information
DG XIV	Fisheries
DG XV	Internal market and financial services/company law

Table 3.4 continued

DG	Area of responsibility
DG XVI	Regional policy
DG XVII	Energy
DG XVIII	Credit and investments
DG XIX	Budget
DG XX	Financial control
DG XXI	Customs union, indirect taxes
DG XXII	Coordination of structural policies
DG XXIII	Enterprise, SMEs, tourism
DG XXIV	Consumer affairs

Services

Secretariat-General of the Commission
Forward Studies Unit
Inspectorate-General
Legal Service
Spokesman's Service
Statistical Office
Translation Service
Informatics Directorate
European Community Humanitarian Office (ECHO)
Task Force for the Accession Negotiations (TFAN)
Euratom Supply Agency
Office for Official Publications of the European Communities

DIRECTORATE-GENERAL XI RESPONSIBLE FOR THE ENVIRONMENT, NUCLEAR SAFETY AND CIVIL PROTECTION

The structure of the DGs which has evolved has led to much criticism because of overlap of areas of responsibility and the lack of congruence with responsibilities of the commissioners. As much of the work of policy formulation is done in committees and preliminary meetings rather than plenary sessions of the institutions, criticism has also been made of the lack of correlation between the structure within the European Commission and the EP's committee structure. The relevant EP committee is the Committee for the Environment, Public

Health and Consumer Protection – issues that are dealt with by DGs XI and XXIV and two different commissioners. This structure is the result of historical accident, political necessity and frequent minor reforms which have not been undertaken in a rational manner (Cini 1996: 102).

The hierarchical internal structure of the DGs has led to a failure of communication on issues which involve more than one policy area. The EU is committed to ensuring that environmental objectives are taken into account in all areas of sectoral policy. Failure of communication carries serious implications for environmental policy making. Since the adoption of the Fifth EAP in 1992 there has been a concerted effort within the European Commission to establish a structure which will overcome this problem. At the DG level a network has been established on the environment which meets regularly two or three times a year to review environmental issues. In each of the DGs an official at director or head of unit level is the designated environment integration correspondent with responsibility to ensure that information about proposed environmental measures is disseminated. Meetings of these officials are arranged on an *ad hoc* basis, depending on the nature of the proposal being made. Figure 3.2 shows the internal structure of DG XI, which is organized in such a way as to reflect the main areas of concern where environmental objectives must be taken into account.

Despite the introduction of these measures, establishing horizontal links between DG XI and the other DGs may remain problematic. However, as the policy is developing with increased emphasis on the integration of environmental objectives into other policy areas and the use of more framework directives, it is essential that mechanisms are found. The collaboration which led to the publication of a joint communication on employment and the environment by DG V and DG XI in 1997 provided an example of what is possible in terms of producing an apparent consensus (CEC 1997l) (see Chapter 4 for further discussion).

The European Commission's right of initiation of legislation means that without a proposal from the Commission no legislative act of the EU may be adopted. The formal right of initiation includes determining which treaty articles are to be used as the basis for the legislation. As a result, the European Commission sets the required majority for the proposals in the Council of Ministers. In turn this has an impact on the level of involvement which the European Parliament has in the formulation of policy. Sbragia (1996: 242) highlights the disagreements which have occurred between the Council of Ministers and the European Commission because there is lack of clarity in some cases between legislation which is linked to trade harmonization (article 95 TEC (100a TEC)) and protection of the environment (article 175 TEC (130s TEC)). The extension of the co-decision procedures made by the Treaty of Amsterdam will remove some of the ambiguity, but will also undermine some of the European Commission's impact on the decision-making process.

Director-General   **Deputy Director-General**

Units directly attached to the Director-General
Policy coordination, integration of the environment to other policies,
environment action programmes.
Human resources and administration
Budget, finances and contracts
Information technology

Directorate A Units	Directorate B Units	Directorate C Units	Directorate D Units	Directorate E Units
1. Inter-institutional relations	1. Economic analyses and environmental forward studies	1. Radiation protection	1. Water protection, soil conservation, agriculture	1. Industrial installations and emissions
2. Information and communications	2. Management and coordination of financial instruments in the environment field, environmental impact assessment	2. Safety of nuclear installations	2. Nature protection, coastal zones and tourism	2. Chemical substances and biotechnology
3. International affairs, trade and environment	3. Legal affairs, legislation and enforcement	3. Radioactive waste and management policy	3. Air quality, urban environment, noise and transport	3. Waste management
4. Technical cooperation with third countries	4. R&D, relations with EEA, education, health	4. Civil protection	4. Global environment, climate change, geosphere, biosphere, energy	4. Industry, internal market, products and voluntary approaches

Source: CEC (1993j).

Figure 3.2   Organization Chart, DG XI (Environment, Nuclear Safety and Civil Protection)

The right of initiation of the legislation is subject to constraints. The commissioners may have quite radical personal agendas but they tend to moderate their views and generally take care that any proposals do not damage their credibility. The credibility of the whole European Commission and the individual commissioners would be undermined if pieces of legislation were repeatedly proposed which were not accepted in the Council of Ministers. Whilst the European Commission is regarded as 'the motor of integration', the objective is to reach consensus on issues. This does not mean that all the European Commission's proposals will be accepted in the Council of Ministers. Proposals which are most likely to succeed are those for which the European Commission has first been able to mobilize support from some of the national governments. The European Commission will then seek to build up the level of support until the required level of national government support is reached.

Since the Maastricht Treaty the European Parliament has had the right to initiate some legislation. In practice this means that the EP has the opportunity to ask the European Commission to draft proposals for legislation. As this may be viewed as a poor substitute for Parliament being able to do this on its own behalf, it contributes to the accusations that the EU suffers from a democratic deficit. The directly elected representative of the citizens of the EU are not responsible for making the legislation. In the majority of cases the legislative power rests with the Council of Ministers and the European Commission. Concern about the lack of accountability of actions was instrumental in the changes made to the Maastricht Treaty which gave the EP the opportunity to question the appointment of the President of the European Commission and the commissioners. This did not alter the role of the European Commission in the decision-making process. It did, however, bring the European Commission under greater scrutiny by the EP.

In 1957 the Treaty gave the European Commission a responsibility to the citizens of the EU of developing proposals which are in their 'general interest'. Article 213 TEC (157 EEC) established the independence of the European Commission. Within the structure of the EU this independence from the national governments has enabled the Commission to be viewed as the key protector of the interests of small states (Laffan 1996: 82). The relationship between the Council and the European Commission in the formulation of policy is a close one but the Commission is not subject to supervision by the Council of Ministers. This independence of the Commission does not prevent the commissioners from developing special relationships with their national governments. As a check to this tendency, the Treaty provides for the compulsory retirement of any member of the European Commission who does not fulfil his/her duties or is guilty of misconduct (article 216 TEC (160 EEC)). Equally, as the commissioners are the nominees of the national governments, a commissioner suspected of 'going native' following appointment to Brussels may find that he/she is not nominated for a renewed term of office.

The European Commission is empowered to bring cases before the European Court of Justice (ECJ). Additional powers were given to the Commission in the Maastricht Treaty to recommend the level of fines which national governments would be subject to if they were found to be infringing legislation. Failure to implement environmental legislation provided the first cases to test this power in early 1997. In the majority of the test cases brought, the national governments took action within the time limits set, although both the German and Greek governments had a number of issues still to resolve in 1998 (see Table 4.3).

It is not institutions that make and influence decisions, but the individuals who are in them. The European commissioners are nominees of the national governments and tend to be politicians. Some of them have had very successful and high-profile national political careers. It is inevitable that as individuals they have specific agendas which they would like to fulfil. The individual priorities of the commissioner with responsibility for the environment and the president of the European Commission will therefore have an influence on the decision-making process. The influence of their personal agendas for environmental policy is tempered by the decision making within the College of Commissioners. Agreement has to be reached among the commissioners on their annual work programmes. Commissioners for other policy areas may have agendas which result in controversy within the Commission.

The European Commission as headed by Jacques Delors in the period from 1985 to 1989 was characterized by strong leadership. This may have been because the national government appointees for commissioners during this period were inconsequential national politicians (Grant 1994: 107). Whatever the reason, there were instances when the strong direction from the president of the Commission led to confrontation and limited opportunities for the individual commissioners to fulfil their own policy agendas. In 1989 Carlo Ripa di Meana was given the environment portfolio by Jacques Delors. Commissioner di Meana began a series of high-profile and vigorous actions against the national governments which had not implemented legislation. Among these measures was the action brought against the UK government in October 1991 because of failure to carry out the required environmental assessment of a number of large-scale construction projects. The letter sent by Commissioner di Meana to the UK government identifying the lack of compliance with the legislation was leaked to the press. The adverse publicity for the Conservative administration which followed caused a major political controversy between the UK government and European Commission.

During the negotiations in 1992 to ratify the Maastricht Treaty the priority which Jacques Delors adopted was to ensure that the principle of subsidiarity was applied to all policies, including environmental policy. Some of the more wide-ranging proposals made by Commissioner di Meana during this period were weakened by Delors as they were considered to be too regulatory and not in keeping with the application of subsidiarity. Among these proposals was one which would have established an EU environmental inspectorate.

The European Commission under the presidency of Jacques Santer was less directed by the president than that under Jacques Delors. At the beginning of his presidency of the European Commission in 1995 Jacques Santer identified a number of key priorities. They included the preparations for the 1997 Inter-governmental Conference, the achieving of economic and monetary union, the presentation of the Agenda 2000 framework for the EU's future, preparations for enlargement and proposals for the reform of the institutions of the EU. By 1995 the number of pieces of legislation to be introduced had slowed down as the legislation to implement the internal market was completed. The role of the European Commission as a policy formulator therefore changed in its emphasis. The introduction of some wide-ranging environmental legislation continued with an increased focus on framework directives for air and water quality and integrated pollution control. Proposals for other means of ensuring that envi-ronmental objectives were achieved gained in prominence, including strength-ening the mechanisms of policy implementation and advocating the use of economic instruments as a means of protecting the environment.

The change in style of the Commission under the presidency of Jacques Santer gave Ritt Bjerregaard, who was appointed Commissioner for the Environment in 1995, an opportunity to develop her own priorities, which included support for environmental taxation. However, there were constraints on the actions of Commissioner Bjerregaard. The independence of the other individual com-missioners undermined proposals forwarded from DG XI. Decisions about proposed legislation are taken within the College of the Commissioners on the basis of simple majority. If there is a lack of consensus within the European Commission, environmental proposals may be undermined by the interests of the commissioners with responsibility for trade, energy or industry. For example, among the proposals made by Ritt Bjerregaard in 1997 to suffer this fate was a proposal on domestic waste disposal and another on ambient air quality limit values. In the case of domestic waste disposal, Commissioner Bjerregaard proposed that an immediate ban be introduced on the total organic content in domestic waste to be buried in landfill sites. This was rejected by Trade Com-missioner Sir Leon Brittan. In its place a revised proposal was adopted that national governments should introduce measures to reduce the amount of food and paper waste to 75 per cent of 1993 levels by 2002 with further cuts to 50 per cent by 2005 and 25 per cent in 2010.

Proposals for targets for the emission of sulphur dioxide, nitrogen oxide, particulate matter and lead into the air which were made by Commissioner Bjerregaard were based on firm targets for each area. There had been a lengthy consultation process with industry and environmental groups because of the significance of the impact of any targets set. Industry lobbyists felt that the scientific evidence did not support the setting of firm targets and supported instead the setting of indicative targets for emissions of sulphur dioxide, nitrogen oxide, lead and poisonous dust. The argument advanced by industry was that Commissioner Bjerregaard was proposing introducing as firm targets standards based on guidelines for air quality in Europe adopted by the World Health Organization (WHO) in 1996. The proposal for firm targets led to controversy within the Commission, as support for the industrialists' view came from DG III (Internal Market and Industrial Affairs) and DG XVII (Energy).[5]

THE COUNCIL OF THE EUROPEAN UNION

The Council of the European Union is usually known as the Council of Ministers (CoM). Although it is a single body within the Treaty, in practice the Council is divided into meetings of the national politicians with responsibility for different policy areas. The foreign ministers of the EU states meet as the General Affairs Council and have a wide-ranging brief. Other groups of national politicians meet as the Technical Councils and are concerned with the sectoral policies of the EU. The meetings of the senior national politicians responsible for the environment and their advisers are in this category. Whilst the General Affairs Council or ECOFIN (the meetings of the ministers with responsibility for finance and economic affairs) may meet on a regular monthly basis, the meetings of the Environment Council may occur only two to four times a year.

Since 1990 a small number of Joint Councils have been organized which bring together ministers responsible for more than one policy, for example environment and energy or environment and transport. The advantage is that this enables the environmental objectives to be more carefully considered in other areas of policy. The disadvantage is that these councils are more likely to produce general policy statements than specific policy measures because of the range of conflicting national interests which are under consideration at these meetings.

THE COUNCIL OF MINISTERS

The Role of the Council of Ministers is to:

- provide the broad guidelines of policy;
- represent the interests of the member states;
- make decisions about the adoption of the legislation;

- provide a forum in which the differing national concerns may be reconciled;
- provide a forum in which differences between the institutions may be resolved;
- perform the pre-eminent role in the context of the intergovernmental 'pillars' of the European Union.

THE ROTATING COUNCIL PRESIDENCY

Each of the member states of the European Union holds the presidency of the Council of Ministers in turn (see Table 3.5). The civil service of the member. state holding the presidency takes on certain tasks during this period on behalf of the EU. The General Council Secretariat numbers only 2200 officials and therefore this assistance from the member states is vital. Providing this administrative support does, however, impose a financial burden on the smaller states of the EU during their presidencies.

Table 3.5   Rotating presidencies from 1 July 1995

	January	July
1995	–	Spain
1996	Italy	Ireland
1997	Netherlands	Luxembourg
1998	UK	Austria
1999	Germany	Finland
2000	Portugal	France
2001	Sweden	Belgium
2002	Spain	Denmark
2003	Greece	–

The advantage for a national government which holds the presidency is the greater control which they then have over the policy agenda. The legislation adopted during a particular presidency may reflect national interests. This advantage must not be overestimated. The role of the presidency is to ensure that deals are brokered among member states, and this may result in the national objectives remaining unfulfilled. Some criticism has been made that German presidencies of the Council have been characterized by attempts to take a lead role on environmental issues (Sbragia 1996: 247). These attempts have not always met with success. In a comparison of the presidencies of the UK government and Germany during the early and mid-1990s, little difference was found in the way in which the environmental issues had been managed. This was despite the differences in the national approaches to environmental issues (Wurzel 1996: 272).

The British government identified the protection of the environment as a priority during its presidency in the first half of 1998. Among the measures taken was one intended to enhance the importance of the Joint Councils. An informal Council of Environment and Transport Ministers was convened in Chester in April 1998. The outcome of this meeting was agreement between the UK governments and Austria, Germany and Finland[6] to introduce audits of the progress being made on environmental initiatives by each member state during its presidency. The objective of the proposal was to overcome any problems which might arise if the national governments tried to introduce short-term initiatives during their presidencies. Short-term measures might be designed to attract the attention of national electorates but would carry the potentially damaging effect of undermining the long-term strategy of the EU on the environment. The criteria for this auditing process were based on the first audit conducted by the UK government and presented at the Cardiff Summit in June 1998. A second proposal also came from the Chester meeting: that in reform of the European Commission a single commissioner should be appointed for both environment and transport.

VOTING PROCEDURES WITHIN THE COUNCIL

The White Paper of 1985 on the single market (CEC 1985) outlined nearly 300 measures to be introduced by 1992. It was acknowledged that this timetable could not be met as long as decisions continued to be taken by unanimous voting in the Council of Ministers. Amongst the initiatives which were introduced to speed the policy-making process was greater use of qualified majority voting (QMV) in the CoM for measures relating to integration within the market (article 205 TEC (148 SEA)). The differences in size of the populations of the member states were reflected in the number of votes which each national representative had on the adoption of legislation (see table in Chapter 2 note 11).

Decisions about agriculture, fisheries, the internal market, environment and transport are made using QMV. At least 62 votes are needed for a European Commission proposal to be adopted by the Council. As the objective of the Council's deliberations is to achieve consensus before voting, even by qualified majority, it is not often that a negative vote is registered. The Maastricht Treaty established the principle that decisions could be taken by either QMV or unanimity. This applies even if co-decision procedures are being used. Issues which involve environmental taxation, planning, the management of water resources or energy supply remained subject to unanimity voting. The German government raised objections to any extension of QMV to these issues during the negotiations for the Treaty of Amsterdam. The result was that areas which are particularly environmentally damaging or carry major financial implications such as energy choices or environmental taxation remain for unanimous action.

Following the accession of Finland, Sweden and Austria to the European Union in 1995, many environmentalists hoped that the three new states would work together on environmental issues within the Council of Ministers. Whilst there was evidence that the environmental commitment of the three states had not lessened as a result of their membership of the EU during the late 1990s, there was little evidence that the new member states were working together as a bloc in voting on environmental issues. The most significant impact which the Nordic states and Austria had on the development of the EU's environmental policy was achieved as a result of the Amsterdam Treaty negotiations. Pressure from the three states working together ensured that new language was introduced into the Treaty which confirmed the rights of the national governments to introduce stricter environmental legislation than that provided for in harmonization measures.

The Treaty of Rome established a support mechanism for the work of the Council of Ministers. This is the Committee of Permanent Representatives (COREPER) of the nation states. The members of this committee act as ambassadors for the individual states to the Community and are based in Brussels. The brief for this committee set out in the Treaty is that the members should be responsible for preparing the work of the Council of Ministers and carrying out any tasks requested by the Council. The COREPER is divided into two. COREPER 1 deals with environment, social affairs, transport and the internal market. The Deputy Permanent Representatives and their supporting staff make up the personnel of COREPER 1. COREPER 2 is the more senior of the two and works mainly for the foreign ministers and the European Council and ECOFIN. The whole structure of COREPER relies on the work done in various consultative committees and working groups which feed the views of interested groups and their advice to the two main committees. These views and accompanying recommendations are then forwarded to the Council of Ministers. This pyramidal structure with the working groups at the base, COREPER in the middle and the Council at the apex means that as a 'general rule of thumb ... decisions, including many which "set" policy, are taken as often as possible by the COREPER' (Peterson 1995b: 72).

THE EUROPEAN PARLIAMENT

The Members of the European Parliament (MEPs) have been elected by direct universal suffrage since 1979. Before that the Members were nominees from the member states.

The role of the European Parliament is to:

- reject or amend legislation;
- approve the appointment of the Commission;
- act with the Council of Ministers as the budgetary authority of the European Union;
- approve agreements with non-EU states;
- table questions to the Commission and the Council;
- receive petitions from the citizens of Europe;
- appoint an ombudsman.

The seats in the EP are allocated to the member states on the basis of population size. This results in some anomalies, the most obvious of which is the representation for Luxembourg (see Table 3.6).

Table 3.6   Number of seats in the EP allocated to the different member states

	1994[*]	1995[**]	1999
Belgium	25	25	25
Denmark	16	16	16
Germany	99	99	99
Greece	25	25	25
Spain	64	64	64
France	87	87	87
Ireland	15	15	15
Italy	87	87	87
Luxembourg	6	6	6
Netherlands	31	31	31
Portugal	25	25	25
UK	87	87	87
Sweden	–	21	21
Austria	–	20	20
Finland	–	16	16
Total EU MEPs	567	626	626

[*]   Number of MEPs at the time of the 1994 direct elections.
[**] Following accession of Austria, Sweden and Finland to the EU, the number of MEPs was increased to 626 after 1 January1995.

The elected MEPs do not sit in national groupings but are grouped according to political affiliations (see Table 3.7).

Table 3.7   Political groups in the European Parliament

Political grouping by number of MEPs	1995–99	1999*
Party of European Socialists	221	180
European People's Party	173	224
European Liberal, Democratic and Reformist Group	52	43
Confederal European United Left	31	35
Forza Europa	29	17
European Democratic Alliance	26	–
Green Group	25	38
European Radical Alliance	19	13
Europe of the Nations Group	19	21
Non-attached	31	55
Total	626	626

Source: European Voice 17–23 June 1999: 14

Notes
1. 1999* Membership of the political groups are based on the pre election composition of the EP. Final decisions about the formation of the political groups was made during the inaugural plenary session of the EP held in Strasbourg July 20 1999.
2. Forza Europa and European Democratic Alliance formed the Union for Europe Group in 1995.

The largest group returned in both the 1989 (197) and 1994 (200) elections were the Party of European Socialists (including the British Labour MEPs). The 1999 elections were characterised by a swing to the centre-right from a low turnout of an average of 49% of the total electorate of the EU (the highest turnout was in Belgium 90%, the lowest in the UK 23%). As a consequence 180 PSE MEPs were returned to the EP in 1999. The Green Group in the EP separated from the wider Rainbow Group following the June 1989 elections. The composition of the Green Group altered in 1994 as 12 of the 25 MEPs were from Germany. However the balance changed once more in 1999 as the French MEPs became the largest national group following a fall in the German national Green vote of 3.5%. In 1999 38 Green MEPs were returned from Austria (2), Belgium (5), Finland (2), France (9), Germany (7), Italy (2), Ireland (2), Luxemburg (1), the Netherlands (4), Sweden (2) and the UK (2). Although the number of Green MEPs is often a reflection of the level of interest in environmental issues within the national context the fall in the vote in 1999 in Germany was the result of national dissatisfaction with the 'red-green' coalition government headed by Gerhard Schroder. The disparate nature of the group in the past has not always led to the Green MEPs being able to act as an effective source of pressure to enhance environmental policy. Of much greater significance for the role of the EP in the formulation of environmental policy has been the way in which it has become a part of the mainstream of the EP's actions.

The importance of the European Parliament in the development of the European Union's environmental policy is the result of the way in which the MEPs have been able to utilize their powers. Because it is a policy area not defined in the Treaty of Rome, the EP has had a much greater opportunity to influence the development of the EU's environmental policy than other policies such as agriculture and competition. The EP played an important role in ensuring that the chapter on the environment was included in the Single European Act (Judge 1993: 189). The EP has used its budgetary powers to maintain pressure on the Council to boost expenditure to support a number of 'new' policy areas, including the environment (Corbett et al. 1995: 233). Particular support has been given by the EP for additional funding to be made available for the LIFE programme (see Chapter 4).

Environmental policy has also provided the EP with the scope to test and develop its powers, which have grown significantly since the Single European Act. The powers of the EP were limited in the original founding Treaty of Rome. The Parliament was known as the General Assembly and consisted of the nominees of the member states. They tended to be very committed to the ideal of European integration, but the Assembly was regarded as little more than a 'talking shop'. Following the introduction of direct universal suffrage in 1979, the powers of what then became the Parliament were increased to give the MEPs a greater share in the decision-making process. The Single European Act was influential in shifting more of the power towards the EP and the European Commission and away from the Council of Ministers. The Maastricht Treaty continued this trend of giving more powers to the European Parliament but placed some curbs on the activities of the European Commission. EP powers included more involvement in the enactment of legislation and the right of 'prior approval' of the appointment of the president of the European Commission and the commissioners.

Procedures for the adoption of legislation and the roles of the institutions of the EU had become increasingly complex with the passage of time. The Amsterdam Treaty brought some clarification to the procedures by reducing the number to three. This meant that the powers of the European Parliament to act as co-legislature with the Council of Ministers were increased. The cooperation procedure for decision making had been introduced in the Single European Act. Following the Treaty of Amsterdam, this procedure was largely abolished, apart from certain aspects of decision making which are required for economic and monetary union. The assent procedures were also introduced in the Single European Act and then strengthened in the Maastricht Treaty. This procedure required the agreement of the EP to legislative proposals with a single reading and no possibility of amendment of the legislation. This procedure is used for some international agreements which are negotiated or concluded by the European Commission and the Council of Ministers, for example reform of the Structural Funds and proposals by the EP for a uniform electoral system.

The co-decision procedures were introduced in the Maastricht Treaty and simplified and extended in the Amsterdam Treaty. The extension of these procedures to more environmental issues has increased the power of the EP in the formulation of environmental policy. If this procedure is used, the EP has the right to propose amendments to the legislation. Among the most important features introduced by the co-decision procedure were the setting up of a conciliation committee at the end of 1993 and the EP's right of negative assent.

The EP has the right to propose amendments to the legislative proposals. If these are rejected by the Council in its second reading, then the proposal is referred to the Conciliation Committee. The Committee is made up of members of the Council of Ministers and an equal number of representatives of the EP. The European Commission may also take part. The primary role of the Committee is to find a form of wording for proposed legislation which will lead to a settlement of any disputes. If the Conciliation Committee is able to find an acceptable form of words within six weeks, then the Council may still adopt the proposal unless it is rejected by a majority of the MEPs, in which case it may not be adopted.

The right of negative assent is still a power subject to constraint. The EP does not have a right to amend legislation following the final reading, and this means a great deal of the decision making power still rests with the Council of Ministers. It may be that MEPs will feel obliged to accept legislation with which they are not in full agreement, in order to have some legislation passed. In Maastricht the co-decision procedure was applied to article 95 TEC (100a TEC) (internal market harmonization), procedures which had an impact on the environment and article 175 TEC (130s (3) TEC) Environment (action programmes). In these cases the Council of Ministers used the QMV procedures.

The result of the changes made in the Amsterdam Treaty is that there is a transfer from cooperation to co-decision for legislation introduced using article 175 TEC (130s (1) TEC), action by the Community in order to achieve the objectives of article 174 TEC (130r TEC). This change has given the EP more say in the making of environmental policy. However, the impact of the EP on policy formulation remains limited by the failure of the national governments to agree to a general extension of the use of QMV in the Council of Ministers. The continued use of unanimity voting in some cases may frustrate the ambitions of the EP to have an increased impact on environmental policy making. Time limits have been placed on the procedures in an attempt to speed up what is often a lengthy process from the proposal of legislation to its adoption. Some of the complexity surrounding the procedure has, however, been removed.

PARLIAMENTARY COMMITTEES

The greater part of the work of scrutiny of legislation done by the EP is carried out in the specialist committees to which the members belong. The membership is organized so as broadly to reflect the differing strengths of the political groupings in the EP. The role of Chair of the Committees is allocated on the basis of the largest political grouping having the opportunity to nominate the largest number of chairpersons. The Environment Committee of the EP had been chaired from 1979 to 1984, and from 1989 until his retirement at the 1999 election by the longest-serving Committee Chair Ken Collins (UK Labour), of the Party of the European Socialists. The continuity of approach which this gave enabled the EP's Environment Committee to build a very proactive strategy in order to achieve environmental objectives.

The co-decision procedures have been used particularly effectively by the Environment Committee since they were introduced in 1993. By early 1995 more than 50 per cent of the co-decision legislation which had been adopted and published had involved the Environment Committee in the use of the new procedures. The result was a considerable increase in the Committee's workload. The development of preparatory 'trialogue meetings' between the Chair of the Environment Committee, a representative of the CoM and the desk officer with responsibility for specific proposals is one method of relieving some of the burden of work done during full sessions of the Conciliation Committee (see the discussion in Chapter 2 on the adoption of the European Commission report on the implementation of the Fifth EAP).

The high level of involvement of the Environment Committee in co-decision legislation has continued through the 1990s. In 1996, 30 pieces of legislation were introduced using co-decision, of which nine required referral to a Conciliation Committee. Seven were instances involving the Environment Committee (EP 1997b). None, however, were concerned with environmental legislation; rather with human health and consumer matters. The use of the procedures in connection with environmental legislation remained relatively untested in the late 1990s. Criticism has come from the EP that the Council of Ministers is undermining the importance of the co-decision process by adopting a minimalist stance and sending members of COREPER and not the relevant ministers to the Committee.

THE EUROPEAN COURT OF JUSTICE

The European Court of Justice (ECJ) is outside the decision-making process of the European Union. It is, however, the presence of the Court that makes the EU unique. It is the role of the ECJ in interpreting the European Union's agreed law which makes the decision-making process effective. The governments of the member states have agreed to be bound by the rulings of the Court based on the legislation adopted by the Council of Ministers.

The role of the European Court of Justice is to:

- apply directly the law of the Community;
- interpret the provisions of Community law;
- declare void any legal instrument adopted by the Commission, the Council of Ministers or the national governments which is incompatible with EU law;
- pass judgement on the validity or interpretation of points of EU law;
- deliver an opinion on agreements with non-EU states;
- ensure that the application of the law by the member states is consistent for the whole of the EU.

Throughout the history of the development of the environmental policy the ECJ has consistently upheld the view that the EU should have a broad-based legislative competence in this area (see the discussion in Chapter 2 on the legal basis for environmental policy). The Court's rulings have therefore helped to ensure that the EU is viewed as the single most important influence on the development of the national environmental policies of the member states of the EU. There is, however, some inconsistency in the strength of commitment that the Court has shown towards the development of the EU's environmental policy and in some judgements, doubts about the ECJ's own 'green credentials'.

The ECJ is subject to certain constraints. The powers given to the Court through the treaties mean that the Court may uphold the importance of environmental protection in a general sense. It is more difficult for it to rule on specific environmental issues, as these are not referred to in the Treaty. In addition the ECJ must be presented with reliable and objective scientific evidence to enable the judges to make informed decisions (see the discussion in Chapter 2 on changes to article 95 TEC (100a TEC) and Chapter 4 on the role of the European Environment Agency). The approach that the ECJ takes is to decide on a case-by-case basis. Individual judges may exert a considerable influence on rulings. As a consequence some of the judgements of the ECJ appear to be difficult to reconcile with an institution contributing to enhancing environmental protection.[7] Despite this, the ECJ has had an important influence on the way in which the EU's environmental policy has developed through its more than 100 rulings on cases in this area.

The Court rulings during the 1970s were based on the commitments made in the EAPs and article 94 TEC (100 EEC) which focused on the elimination of trade barriers. Through its rulings in this period the ECJ established the right of the EU to deal with trans frontier environmental problems. In the early part of the 1980s rulings made by the Court were based not only on article 94 TEC (100 EEC) but also on article 308 TEC (235 EEC) which gave the opportunity to introduce new areas of action into the EU. These rulings demonstrated more about the strength of the ECJ's commitment to furthering the process of integration within the EU than its desire to establish environmental policy. However, in case

240/83[8] in 1985 the ECJ ruled that environmental protection was one of the Community's essential objectives and, furthermore, that it is a mandatory requirement which may limit the application of article 28 TEC (30 EEC).[9]

The ECJ's ruling in the so-called 'Danish bottles case' upheld the national governments' right to introduce higher national environmental standards (case 302/86, Commission *v*. Denmark).[10] This established some green credentials for the ECJ as it was an important landmark ruling which appeared to be clearly pro the environment, and this has provided a precedent for future rulings. The ECJ accepted that Denmark's deposit and return system for empty drinks containers could be lawfully implemented, even though the result was to partition the market and prevent the free flow of drinks in containers to Denmark.

This does not mean that the economic issues were or have subsequently been ignored by the Court. Rulings which the ECJ makes on issues where there is a need to consider trade and environmental issues also include a requirement that a test of proportionality be applied. In any contested case it has to be established that the restrictions imposed on the movement of goods are necessary to achieve the environmental objectives set in the national rules. This is to ensure that the environmental benefit of a measure does indeed outweigh the potential for market distortion.

The inclusion of the chapter on the environment in the Single European Act in 1987 gave the ECJ more opportunity to show that it had environmental credentials as it gave a firm place to environmental protection policy in the Treaty. At the same time the Single European Act introduced some other uncertainties, as the principle of subsidiarity was introduced into the Treaty for the first time in the environment chapter. Concerns were expressed that, as a political principle, the ECJ would not be able to rule in some instances. The ECJ was not put to the test on the subsidiarity principle before it was incorporated into article 3b of the Maastricht Treaty and applied to a much longer list of policy areas. The Protocol on the principle of subsidiarity added to the Amsterdam Treaty provided additional guidance for the ECJ in its rulings in order to eliminate some of the uncertainties.

The other area of concern which emerged from the SEA was the requirement to integrate environmental objectives into other areas of policy. Again this was not tested by the ECJ before the strengthening of the article in the Amsterdam Treaty (article 6 TEC). Identification of a mechanism to evaluate the extent to which environmental objectives have been included in the legislation presented a similar problem to that of evaluation of the impact of environmental measures on trade.

During the 1990s the Court became more active on environmental issues as the number of reported cases of infringement of environmental legislation increased and interest in the enforcement of legislation grew among the general public. In 1997, ruling on a case brought by Greenpeace on behalf of a group of other environmental non-governmental organizations and local Canary Islands residents, the ECJ upheld the right of individuals to challenge the EU's decisions. The ruling did, however, undermine some of the advantage which the European Commission considered was an important aspect of the role of the non-governmental organizations in the monitoring and enforcement of policy (see the discussion in Chapter 4 of public participation in the implementation and enforcement of policy).

The powers of the ECJ to impose penalties on national governments were increased in the Maastricht Treaty changes with the introduction of article 228 TEC (171 TEC) giving the Court the right to fine member states which did not comply with earlier judgements. The first cases brought in 1997 using article 228 TEC (171 TEC) were concerned with infringement of environmental legislation. The threat of the penalty proved to be effective in speeding up the response of the German and Italian authorities (see Table 4.3).

THE ECONOMIC AND SOCIAL COMMITTEE AND THE COMMITTEE OF THE REGIONS

In addition to the main institutions of the EU involved in making decisions about policy, there are two committees which have the right to be consulted about and submit an opinion on proposed legislation. These committees have an important role to play: the Economic and Social Committe (ECOSOC) represents sectional interests and the Committee of the Regions (CoR) represents regional interests in the policy-making process. Whilst there are arguments to support their dissolution as the EP gains in power there are nevertheless advantages to be gained from their continued existence. Even in the event of future large-scale enlargement of the EU the size of the EP has been determined at 700 MEPs (article 189 TEC (137 TEC)). In order to ensure that all the interests are represented in the policy-making process, the work of the EP must be supported through these and other mechanisms.

The Economic and Social Committee was established by the Treaty of Rome in 1957. It is a consultative committee which brings together different economic and social interest groups. The membership comprises 222 appointees of the member states, who are based in Brussels and whose appointments are for four-year renewable terms. The membership structure for both bodies is shown in Table 3.8.

The primary role of the ECOSOC is to advise all the main institutions in the decision-making process. It is organized into nine specialist groups, one of which is concerned with environmental issues. It has the right to be consulted before certain decisions are made. The ECOSOC may also issue its own opinion on all aspects of European Union legislation and therefore may be considered to influence the making of policy. Criticism has been made in the past that proposals are not forwarded to the ECOSOC until a relatively late stage in the decision-making process. This may make it difficult for the Committee to contribute meaningfully to policy formulation, but nevertheless the Committee does provide a forum for the various interests to put forward their concerns. Among the more influential of the reports by the ECOSOC have been those on the operation of the single market, environmental labelling, and environmental management and auditing. Since the Amsterdam Treaty amendments to article 262 TEC (198 TEC) the EP also has the right to consult the ECOSOC on any matter.

Table 3.8   Membership structure for both the ECOSOC and the CoR

State		State	
Belgium	12	Luxembourg	6
Denmark	9	Netherlands	12
Greece	12	Austria	12
Spain	21	Portugal	12
France	24	Finland	9
Ireland	9	Sweden	12
Italy	24	UK	24
Germany	24	Total	222

Notes:
1. Three groups are represented on the ECOSOC Committee:

    - Employers – representatives of both the public and the private sector.
    - Workers – predominantly trade union representatives.
    - Various other interests – including small and medium enterprises, consumer groups and environmental organizations.

2. Representatives on the Committee of the Regions are drawn from regional and local authorities within the EU.
3. The number of members of these committees allocated to each member state is intended to reflect the size of the population of the individual countries of the EU. As with the other institutions of the EU there is a difficult decision to be made about how much representation should be given to countries so diverse in terms of population size.

Source: Art. 194 TEU and the Draft Accession Treaty.

When the Maastricht Treaty established the consultative Committee of the Regions (CoR), the powers which were given to the Committee were limited.

Its 222 members are recruited from the regional and local authorities within the European Union. Initially the CoR was not taken seriously in Germany. The ministers of the German *Länder* preferred to use the opportunities for more direct involvement in the policy process through the Council of Ministers. The calls by the Committee for the membership to consist exclusively of elected members of local and regional authorities which were made during the 1997 IGC were ignored by the Council of Ministers and no amendments were made to the recruitment of membership of the CoR in the Amsterdam Treaty.

The primary role of the CoR is to provide the Council of Ministers and the European Commission with information about the view of the local and regional authorities, particularly where the issues require cross-border cooperation. The Committee has emphasized the importance of the role which the local and regional authorities should play in the definition of policy and in the management and evaluation of the policy as it is operated. In the period between the TEU and the Amsterdam Treaty the CoR passed a number of own-initiative opinions on environmental protection measures, urban-related programmes and agricultural policy developments. Although the commissioner with responsibility for environmental policy between 1995 and 2000, Ritt Bjerregaard, courted the support of the CoR by speaking at several plenary sessions of the Committee, its powers and influence in the policy-making process remain limited.

CONCLUSIONS

The formulation of environmental policy is multi-layered and characterized by complexity because of the nature of the issues which are being dealt with as well as the many constraints on the policy process itself. The EU is searching for a policy-making strategy which will eliminate some of the constraints which these characteristics present. There are three issues which the policy makers have to resolve in this search: first, to establish that there is a need for the EU to take action on environmental protection; second, to ensure that there is commitment and willingness to act among the national governments; and third, to obtain enough resources to make the policy work.

The principle of subsidiarity has been proposed as the appropriate framework to provide the answer to the question of who makes the decisions within the EU (see Chapters 2 and 12). Decisions made as a result of the application of subsidiarity identify the most appropriate tier of government to tackle a particular problem. This establishes whether the need is for EU or national action and thus determines who the actors in the policy-making process should be. At the same time the transboundary nature of environmental problems makes the application of subsidiarity difficult and problematic. As environmental pollution is transboundary and environmental measures may act as barriers to trade in the internal market, this would seem to imply that all environmental action should be taken exclusively at the supranational level. The European Court of Justice has upheld the European Commission's view that the principle of proportionality of action should also apply as decisions are being made. Both principles are subject to a great variety of interpretation. As a result the national governments may try to use the subsidiarity principle to avoid the implications of supranational policy formulation. The application of the principle is not the panacea that some hoped it would be! In its application there are opportunities for increased fragmentation as the environmental policy-making process continues to be dominated by national self-interest and lack of transparency.

Decisions made during the forming of policy must be open to debate and scrutiny; otherwise the suspicion will remain that national governments are using the EU's environmental policy to support national self-interest and not to protect the environment. If fragmentation of the policy is not to result from decisions about the allocation of responsibility, then the issue of how to monitor and manage it must gain a higher profile in the early stages of policy design.

The primary purpose of the EU's environmental policy is to ensure that the process of economic integration within the EU is not frustrated. Changes are taking place in the type of policy measures introduced to meet this need, and the alternatives for the policy makers have increased. The Treaty of Amsterdam has brought a new focus for future policy making. The ambiguities left by the wording of some treaty articles in the Maastricht Treaty have been removed and the EU's commitment to a strategy of sustainable development has been strengthened. This commitment requires major changes to the formulation of policy so that the concerns of both environmental protection and economic development may be met. The commitment to sustainable development also gives a greater legitimacy to the participation of the public in the making of policy, as well as its implementation. Opportunities have been given, but there are new problems as the complexity of the policy formulation process appears to have increased rather than simplified as a result of the treaty revisions.

Policy making is often frustrated by the differing values and expectations of the actors involved. Whilst the institutional framework from which EU policy emerges was not designed to deal with the specific and complex issues which are included in environmental policy, that framework was designed to deal with often conflicting national interests. The sharing of responsibility for environmental policy has encouraged the emergence of coalitions of interests within the policy formulation process which may act as catalysts for action. The policy communities and issue networks approach to policy analysis allows some insights into the interactions which take place within these groups. What is clear is that on environmental issues the national governments of the member states have formed very stable policy communities, and environmental issues are often pursued because national policy initiatives force them on to the EU's agenda. Where differences do occur, the increased prominence of the integration of environmental objectives into all sectoral policies in the Treaty of Amsterdam will create pressure to ensure that mechanisms are adopted which will encourage the reconciliation of the differing values of the actors in the policy process.

Given that it has a policy-making process which is characterized by complexity, the EU appears to have become a major player in an international environmental context almost in spite of itself! The EU's achievements in the area of environmental policy since 1972 have been remarkable. There have been more than 200 directives adopted, plus 200 or so other measures. The EU is recognized as the major influence on environmental policy making at the national level. However, the policy-making process continues to display potential for major problems relating to fragmentation and lack of policy coordination. The effectiveness of the policy measures is undermined by the inadequacy of implementation and enforcement by the national governments, which is the subject of the following chapter. As enlargement of the EU to Central and Eastern Europe is achieved, this complex system will be placed under further strain, and reform of the institutional structure which was not addressed in the Treaty of Amsterdam has become more urgent!

NOTES

1. Although there is little evidence to suggest that they are effective across the board. If they were more effective, the environmental agenda might have made considerably more progress.
2. For example Manuel Marin (Spain) and Sir Leon Brittan (UK) served terms of office during the Delors and the Santer Presidencies of the Commission from 1989 to 1999.
3. It is nominally true that each commissioner is of equal importance, but this is not the experience in practice (see the following discussion of the role of the Commission President and the fate of proposals by Commissioner for the Environment Ritt Bjerregaard on the organic content of domestic waste to be buried in landfill sites).
4. Amongst specific examples which were brought against individuals were: Jacques Santer (failure to ensure adequate supervision of the Security Office (EP 1999: 9.2.8); and Edith Cresson (one case of favouritism (EP 1999: para. 9.2.10), failure to act in response to known irregularities which were identified in the funding of the EU's programme tor education and training – LEONARDO (EP 1999: para.9.2.7), Manuel Marin (failure to respond when cases of irregularities were identified (EP 1999: para. 9.2.5); failures in his responsibility to create the necessary management structure to deal with the irregularities (EP 1999: para. 9.2.6)).
5. Proposal for the directive setting new ambient air quality limit values for sulphur dioxide, nitrogen oxide, particulate matter and lead adopted by the Commission, 8 October 1997.
6. These three states held the presidencies following the British and the proposal therefore received support until the year 2000.
7. Case 252/85 in which the ECJ upheld the right of the French to apply national provisions on the manner in which certain species of birds were trapped on the basis that the numbers involved were low and the French government had applied to the European Commission for help (Sands 1996).
8. Case 240/83 Procureur de la Republique *v.* Association de défense des brûleurs d'Huiles Usagées (1985) ECR 531: para 13.
9. Article 28 TEC (30 EEC) on the prohibition of quantitative restrictions and measures with equivalent effect between member states.
10. Case 302/86, Commission *v.* Denmark. The judgement was based on article 95 TEC (100a (4) TEC).

4 Implementation and enforcement of policy

INTRODUCTION

At the centre of the development of the EU's environmental policy is a large number of pieces of legislation which have been adopted since 1972. The implementation process has therefore to focus in the first instance on the transposition of EU law into the legal systems of the member states, that is, legal compliance with the legislation. However, it also includes ensuring that the infrastructure is in place to enable the national authorities to introduce measures or procedures needed for practical compliance. Enforcement by the national governments includes monitoring, sanctions of various types, on-the-spot investigations and controls. Whilst it is possible to be cautiously optimistic about the amount of progress made on many aspects of EU environmental policy, there are still concerns about the lack of political commitment demonstrated in the implementation and enforcement of the policy by the national governments. If all the stages of implementation and enforcement are not carried through effectively, the EU's environmental policy will fail to achieve its goals.

The effectiveness of the EU's environmental policy may be undermined in a number of ways. If the national governments do not transpose the legislation into their national legislation according to the timetable set, the policy will be unable to operate. If they do transpose the legislation, but do not establish the relevant authorities or systems to carry out the terms of the legislation, the policy will be unsuccessful. Even if the legislation is transferred and the systems established, the objectives of the policy may still not be met without an opportunity for review, evaluation and monitoring of progress. These measures are essential, as they will identify problems such as unrealistic assumptions made in the legislation, the impact of changes in technology on the subject of the legislation, or a lack of funding frustrating the policy's operation.

The objective of this chapter is to discover the reasons for the lack of success in the implementation and enforcement of the EU's environmental legislation. The main argument put forward is that there is a wide gap between the formulation and the implementation of policy. This gap must be filled. Questions about how the legislation is to be implemented and enforced must be raised in the earliest phases of discussion and negotiation which lead to the drafting of the legislation. These issues should not be neglected until after the legislation is adopted.

Five key aspects of the implementation and enforcement of environmental policy are discussed in this chapter:

1. The drafting of legislation
2. The adoption and transposition into national legislation
3. Practical implementation
4. Enforcement through EU law and national law
5. Inspection and evaluation of enforcement.

The concluding section presents a critique of an approach to solving the problems of ineffective implementation and enforcement advocated by DG XI (Environment) in a comprehensive review of implementation undertaken in 1996 (CEC 1996h).

THE INCREASED PRIORITY OF IMPLEMENTATION AND ENFORCEMENT

Different methods to ensure effective implementation of legislation and enforcement were given a high priority in the Fifth Environmental Action Programme (CEC 1992a: 75). The proposals in the Fifth EAP reflected the disenchantment felt by the European Commission at the extent to which legislative commitments were being circumvented by the member states, many of which seemed to be attempting to gain a green credential at little or no cost by agreeing to the legislation but failing to act on it. This was not the result of lack of recognition of the need for action or lack of capacity to implement and enforce the legislation. It reflected a lack of political will to deal with the issues.

The Fifth EAP had been drafted at the same time as the 1991 Intergovernmental Conference was proceeding. Measures to ensure effective implementation and enforcement of legislation would not normally be dealt with in amendments to the Treaty, so it was hardly surprising that the Maastricht Treaty changes did not directly deal with these concerns. However, a number of changes were made to the Maastricht Treaty which provided support for the introduction of measures which would. Article 3 TEC (3b TEC) contained a reference to policy on the environment which confirmed the importance of the policy for the EU. Some aspects of the policy formulation process were dealt with, although these were not universally welcomed by environmentalists who felt that more radical changes could have been made. A declaration was added to the Treaty which committed the member states to transposing the Community directives into national law within the deadlines set out in the legislation. A financial penalty for national governments which continued to infringe legislation was introduced into Article 228 TEC (171 (2) TEC).

The Amsterdam Treaty introduced a number of amendments which will provide a stronger basis for the EU's environmental policy. Among these amendments changes to article 2 TEU (B TEU) and article 2 TEC (2 TEC) may have the most impact on the implementation process, as they include the commitment to sustainable development. Whilst there is a great deal of debate about the means by which sustainable development may be achieved, the public is recognized as having an important role to play in achieving any goals set in policy. The public, through environmental interest groups as well as through individual reports, already make a significant contribution to monitoring the EU's environmental policy at national level. The European Commission is actively searching for the means to increase public participation in the policy process and the treaty changes will give added weight to any proposals which may be made.

Table 4.1   Progress in transposition of environmental directives

Member state	Directives applicable on 31 December1997	Directives for which measures have been notified	%
Belgium	139	121	87
Denmark	139	139	100
Germany	141	133	94
Greece	144	140	97
Spain	143	142	99
France	139	133	96
Ireland	139	136	98
Italy	139	135	97
Luxembourg	139	136	98
Netherlands	139	137	99
Austria	135	131	97
Portugal	143	138	97
Finland	137	132	96
Sweden	137	133	97
UK	139	133	96

Source: CEC (1998c: 95–6).

Failures of implementation are recorded by the Commission in annual reports and tables on the application of European Community law. These tables do not necessarily reflect the state of the environment in the member states, but do give a good indication of the commitment of the national governments to implementing the EU's directives. They provide a 'league table of shame' which may be used as a form of political ammunition by the environmentalists to comment on the impact of environmental measures (see Table 4.1). At the end of 1997 Belgium and Germany were at the bottom of the table, with the worst record on the transposition of directives; Denmark was at the top, having transposed 100 per cent of the applicable legislation.

THE EUROPEAN UNION'S REGIME OF ENVIRONMENTAL REGULATION

The early history of the EU's policy on the environment was characterized by a regulatory command-and-control approach. This approach will not be abandoned in the future, although changes are being made to the nature of the legislation and the mix of policy instruments being used. The continued support for the command-and-control approach to environmental policy is because it has the following advantages:

- The EU is a relatively small geographical region and the problems are common, affecting all member states. This approach should guarantee coherence of policy.
- Allowing the free market to work without any government intervention is not a reliable way to deal with shared environmental problems. The approach allows a considerable degree of self-interest and 'free-riding' to dominate the policy area.
- It ensures that distortion of trade does not occur.

The disadvantages are that:

- Regulation may set a limit on the extent of environmental action – thus far and no further!
- The approach may ignore local conditions.
- It may foster a lack of commitment to the legislation unless there is cooperation between the numerous interested groups and the policy makers.

The source of the problem of ineffective implementation of policy in the EU is often seen as a lack of political will among the member states and the competent authorities. The Fifth Environmental Action Programme advocated a more varied use of legislation, economic instruments, increased funding and increased opportunities for the environmental interest groups to participate in the policy process to stimulate the national governments and competent authorities. The advantages of these recommendations were as follows:

- The environmental interests groups were able to become more actively involved. They are important as mobilizers of public opinion to ensure that issues are raised on policy agendas. They also have an important role to play in the monitoring of actions at the national and local level.
- Environmental degradation is the result of a failure to acknowledge that ownership of the environment rests with any group or individual. By establishing that everyone has shared responsibility to protect the environment, it is possible to achieve increased commitment to its protection.
- The use of economic instruments enables polluters to be more precisely targeted through a series of measures, for example effluent charges, tradable permits, taxation. In some cases subsidies may be used as an incentive to encourage polluters to find the most efficient and least costly way of limiting pollution.

Whilst it is generally accepted that there are many benefits to be gained from an effective environmental policy, it appears to be very difficult to overcome the lack of commitment to the implementation and enforcement of the EU's policy. The decentralization of the implementation process to the national governments and authorities introduces many more actors into the policy process than might be involved in the setting of environmental policy in an individual member state. There is much national debate about how to tackle specific issues or which should be given the most urgent priority. The authorities involved in the implementation of the policy will have their own set of agendas and priorities, and will be working within specific budgetary constraints. Each of these agendas and priorities may indeed be focused on improving environmental protection, but differences between them on methods or the importance of issues may be difficult to reconcile. Attempts to do so may compromise the environmental objectives of policy initiatives or delay crucial policy decisions.

Decentralization of the implementation process meets the commitment to shared responsibility for environmental protection. However, it can lead to the danger of fragmentation of the policy and may add to the opportunities for ineffective environmental policy to emerge. The problems of communication and the necessity of information availability and transfer within the multi-layered governance of the EU were highlighted in the Fifth Environmental Action Programme. Problems of communication were again highlighted in the 1996 progress report on the Fifth EAP (CEC 1996p). Communication has been the subject of a number of subsequent proposals by the European Commission (CEC

1996h). Initiatives such as the creation of the Consultative Forum on the Environment (Fifth EAP, 1992) and the Committee of the Regions (Maastricht Treaty, 1992) have a role to play in overcoming the problems of lack of communication (see Chapter 3). Through these initiatives there is an opportunity for regional and local authorities and other interested groups to become formally involved in the policy process.

'TOP–DOWN' APPROACH TO THE POLICY PROCESS

The process of implementation is further complicated by the complexity of the issues dealt with. Within the geographical area of the EU there is a wide variety of differing natural environments, each of which requires a different response to protect it from the problems of pollution. The national governments have ·responded to these challenges in different ways, establishing differing competent bodies to deal with the various national priorities. It is difficult to provide a framework for implementation and monitoring that will be the optimum structure for all these national authorities. This is why the EU has made such extensive use of the directive as the appropriate form of legislation for environmental issues.[1] Nevertheless the national and local authorities experience many difficulties in implementing EU legislation.

The underlying assumption is that once a directive is adopted, it will be the trigger for action, and implementation will follow. Implementation has been taken as given in the past, and the main reason for lack of effectiveness seen as inertia or ineptitude among the national authorities. In 1974 Pressman and Wildavsky's analysis of policy implementation in the US federal system warned of the consequences of such a view:

> The view from the top is exhilarating. Divorced from the problems of implementation, federal bureau heads, leaders of international agencies ... think great thoughts together. But they have trouble imaging the sequence of ideas that will bring their ideas to fruition ... People ... appear to think that implementation should be easy; they are, therefore, upset when expected events do not occur or turn out badly. (Pressman and Widlavsky 1974: 136)

Pressman and Wildavsky concluded that this implementation 'gap' could be overcome if there was an adequate flow of communication between the different tiers of government involved in the policy process.

As many EU directives have a 'reporting-back' requirement on the progress of implementation from the national governments, it would appear that measures have been put in place to prevent a similar problem occurring within the EU. The conclusions of the annual reports on the implementation of EU law show that this is not the case. National governments and authorities frequently do not meet the requirements for the submission of reports. The result is that the European Commission has to turn to other means of obtaining information, including individuals, non-governmental organizations and the European Parliament, which asks questions about implementation and enforcement.

Accepting the 'top–down' approach, with the implication of imposition of measures from the centre, provides a ready answer to the question of why there is a lack of commitment from the national governments and the national implementing authorities. The impression may be given that the national governments and the implementing authorities have had no involvement in the determination of the individual pieces of legislation. This view is represented in the popular media as the way in which the EU functions. As such it enables national governments which wish to do so to use the European Union as a 'scapegoat' to cover any lack of commitment to remedying environmental problems. Within the complex policy process of the European Union the answer to the question of lack of commitment requires a more exhaustive and rigorous explanation.

The EU's environmental policy is built upon the principles of shared responsibility for action, and subsidiarity. The mechanisms by which this may be achieved have been strengthened since the introduction of the Fifth EAP. A firm underpinning of the principle of shared action has been given by the inclusion of the principle of subsidiarity in the Treaty (see Chapters 2 and 12). The principle of subsidiarity imposes obligations on the actors in the policy process. They are not left with a decision about competence for action; that is outlined in article 5 TEC (3b TEC). Furthermore, whatever decision is made must be proportional to the effect achieved (protocol number 30 on Subsidiarity, Treaty of Amsterdam). Nevertheless, the sharing of responsibility requires commitment and involvement from all levels of government and all the actors in the policy process.

The Amsterdam Treaty raised the priority of environmental protection within the EU by adding the commitment to sustainable development. Through this the EU has acknowledged that it does have a system of shared values with regard to the environment. Protection of the environment, with a commitment to economic development and equity in society, is considered central to the concept of sustainable development and is now recognized as the core of the EU's environmental policy (see Chapters 2 and 12). The participation of the public and the sharing of the responsibility for environmental action are crucial if the objectives of sustainable development are to be achieved. However, there are still opportunities for the national governments to find ways to circumvent the implementation of legislation, especially if the measures have financial implications or threaten national political interests.

DRAFTING THE LEGISLATION

Despite 'the extraordinary information gathering which takes place before a proposal even reaches the Council' (Andersen and Eliassen 1993: 19), the EU's legislation is sometimes criticized because it is poorly drafted and does not take the differing national situations into account. The result is that the mechanisms which national governments use to implement and enforce the legislation become unwieldy, unnecessarily bureaucratic and cumbersome. These concerns were highlighted in the revisions of the regulation on the EU's eco-labelling scheme which were published in 1996. This regulation had included a lengthy consultation and discussion phase with industrialists and other interested groups between 1988 and 1992 before it was adopted, yet in its implementation it involved the introduction of cumbersome and bureaucratic procedures.

In December 1992 the Edinburgh Council had placed a high priority on finding a way to overcome some of the problems of poorly drafted legislation. Many of the environmental directives have been amended several times and have been published in different volumes of the *Official Journal* of the European Union over a number of years. In order to avoid confusion, work was begun by the European Commission to consolidate the texts of these directives. During the 1997 Intergovernmental Conference a declaration on the quality of the drafting of Community legislation was added to the Treaty. The declaration included the requirement that the EP, the European Commission and the Council of Ministers should lay down quality guidelines to be used in drafting legislation. The impact of this declaration was to raise the profile of this aspect of the policy process on the policy makers' agendas. It has also strengthened the role of the European Court of Justice in ensuring that the guidelines are adhered to.

Among other problems identified in the drafting of legislation is the lack of transparency about included requirements. A commitment was made in the 1994 Inter-Institutional Agreement to make legislation more accessible to the general public, and a number of measures have been introduced to make the discussion and drafting of legislation more open and transparent. These include the Code of Conduct concerning public access to Council and Commission documents (93/730/EEC), the Council Decision on public access to Council documents (93/731/EEC), and the Code of Conduct on Public Access to the Minutes and Statements in the Minutes of the Council (when it is acting as legislator – adopted October 1995). Conditions do nevertheless apply to the rights established by these measures. For example, requests for access to documents allowed under Directive 93/731/EEC have to be very precise requests, submitted in writing.

ADOPTION AND TRANSPOSITION INTO NATIONAL LEGISLATION

Although directives are a flexible form of legislation which do not need to be transferred word for word into national bodies of law, the member states must take the following steps to ensure that the directives are transposed. They must:

- introduce accompanying legal and administrative measures; and
- accurately transfer any definitions contained within the legislation. This is to ensure that the meaning of the actions taken within the legislation remains the same, even if the national measures are different.

The disadvantage of using directives is that there may be a wide range of national legislation, practices and procedures to be changed. Some member states may have to introduce several pieces of national legislation to transpose a single directive. This problem is most acute in member states which have federal structures. In Belgium the powers to regulate the environment are devolved to the regional governments within the federation. Each of the regions must therefore implement the EU legislation separately. Similar problems occur for Germany, where 16 pieces of legislation may be necessary to put one EU directive into place – one in each of the *Länder*. France, on the other hand, has a centralized system – the National Environment Code – which is an attempt to harmonize all environmental legislation into a single legislative framework. Directive 85/337[2] on the environmental impact assessments (EIAs) carried out of major public sector schemes required changes to more than 20 national measures in the UK to ensure its implementation and the necessary enforcement procedures. These differences result in time delays in the transfer to national legislation which may create distortion of the market or disadvantaged groups within the EU. Also, differences may be allowed in some directives to take into account the variety of environmental and economic conditions in each of the member states. For example, the large-scale combustion plants directive[3] contains different targets for the reduction of emissions and in some cases allows for increased emissions (see Table 4.2).

The introduction of the use of framework directives since 1992 may help to overcome some of the problems outlined above. In this legislative form general principles and requirements for the legislation in the different sectors are set out which give more flexibility to the national authorities. Only a limited number of framework directives had been adopted for water, air quality and waste management by the end of the 1990s. Among the benefits of the framework directive which established the future regulatory framework for EU water policy in February 1997[4] was the opportunity to repeal some outdated pieces of legislation. For example, the directives from 1975 on the quality of surface water[5] and from 1980[6] on the quality of groundwater were integrated and repealed. For the future the use of this legislative tool is likely to increase. Article 6 of the protocol on the application of the principle of subsidiarity included in the Treaty of Amsterdam contained a very clear statement that, 'other things being equal, directives should be preferred to regulations and framework directives to detailed measures'. However, framework legislation will only achieve its objectives if it is part of an overall holistic approach to the implementation and enforcement of environmental policy and if more emphasis is placed on the monitoring and management of the actions of national governments.

Table 4.2   Reduction of overall sulphur dioxide emissions from existing plants >50 MW capacity over 1980 levels (%)

	1993	1998	2003
Overall target	−25	−43	−60
Belgium			
France			
Germany	−40	−60	−70
Netherlands			
UK	−20	−40	−60
Portugal	–	–	+25

Source: Directive 88/609 EEC on the limitation of emissions of pollutants into the air from large scale combustion plants.

PRACTICAL IMPLEMENTATION

The practical implementation of legislation includes a wide range of national measures. Deadlines are included in directives and in some cases standards to be met and certain procedures to be adopted, but the national authorities have discretion about how to achieve the objectives of the legislation. In many cases more than one procedure is required at the national level. The complexity and diversity of the national measures needed will vary from directive to directive.

Practical implementation of Directive 80/778/EC[7] on the quality of water for human consumption gives just one example of this complexity. It required the following procedures and systems to be carried out within each member state:

- Monitoring, sampling and testing of drinking water, including tap water, either at the local, regional or national level.
- Identification of drinking water supplies which do not comply with the mandatory standards.
- Planning for compliance with measures relating to the removal of pollution of the water by treatment before distribution or removal of the source from use.
- Capital investment strategies in order to cope with the expenditures needed to construct or improve the necessary distribution or treatment systems.
- Assessment of the problems of nitrates and pesticides from agricultural sources as well as lead from lead distribution systems.
- Assessments of the costs to users.
- Assessments of the training necessary for staff.

As the number of legislative acts, including directives, regulations, decisions and recommendations, which the EU has adopted since 1972 exceeds 300, the result is a diverse pattern of measures which is very difficult to monitor. The European Commission places a high value on the public's involvement in the monitoring of practical implementation (CEC 1997g: 94). Reports by the public have identified cases of failure to transpose legislation correctly, and in others, the lack of requisite technical infrastructure. For example, complaints were made during 1996 about the smell and appearance of water being used for bathing in some member states. These complaints indicated either a failure to transpose Directive 76/160/EEC[8] on the quality of water used for bathing or a failure to construct sufficient urban waste treatment plants to deal with sewage disposal, which is the subject of Directive 91/271/EEC.[9]

A large number of complaints have been made by the public about infringements of the environmental impact assessment (EIA) directive in Spain, Greece, Italy, Portugal and Germany (CEC 1997g: 97). The complaints have centred on the lack of adequate national assessments, insufficient weight being given to enquiry findings in the final decisions about projects, or complaints that the work was begun before assessment was completed. The nature of these complaints does, however, highlight a problem of reliance on public involvement in the monitoring of legislation. The public shows a lack of understanding of the role of the European Commission and knowledge of the legislation. The EIA directive contains instructions about the content of EIAs, but the European Commission is not able to investigate national authorities' decisions about the choice of projects for which EIAs are carried out. The EIA directive was amended in 1997 in order to overcome some of the confusion. However, there is a clear and urgent need to inform the public of the role and responsibilities of the European Commission in many other cases.

IMPLEMENTATION AND ENFORCEMENT IN EU LAW

The primary responsibility for implementing and financing EU environmental legislation lies with the member states. Through various articles of the Treaty the European Commission is responsible for ensuring the proper functioning and development of the policies which relate to the integrated market. This includes environmental policy. The European Commission is able to perform its role because of a number of procedures and penalties which may be invoked, with the ultimate sanction of a case being referred to the European Court of Justice (ECJ). The objective of the penalties is, however, to settle any infringements of legislation before they need to be referred to the ECJ.

Article 226 TEC (169 TEC) of the Treaty identifies two actions which may be taken. One is the sending of a letter of complaint, and the second is the issuing of a reasoned opinion against a member state which fails to take note of the complaint in the original letter. In 1996 the number of article 226 TEC (169 TEC) letters issued rose by 9 per cent on the previous year from a total of 1044 in 1995 to 1142. The number of reasoned opinions issued rose from 194 in 1995 to 435 in 1996 (CEC 1997g: 11) The reason for this was an attempt by the European Commission to streamline the procedures and introduce a more structured timetable for action, so some measures were the completion of older actions alongside the new referrals. The majority of cases which were brought in 1996 were concerned with failure to notify the European Commission about the national transposition measures.

At the end of 1996 the European Commission undertook a major review of the practices which related to the speed and effectiveness of the internal rules of procedure based on articles 226 TEC (169 TEC) and Article 228 TEC (171 TEC) (CEC 1996h: 6). This review concluded that there are still a large number of unresolved problems associated with the use of the two articles: they do not provide an adequate guarantee that the national governments will both implement and enforce the legislation effectively. The procedures are lengthy and do not directly target the local and regional authorities responsible for implementation and enforcement.

The European Parliament criticized the European Commission in 1995 and 1996 on account of the time taken to introduce the provisions of article 228 (171 (2) TEC) of the Maastricht Treaty. The European Commission had not established the criteria to be used as the basis of the fines which the member states would be subject to if they infringed EU legislation. The European Commission proposed that the fines be levied daily until the necessary action be taken. The penalties are not applied retrospectively to the period before the Maastricht Treaty came into effect on 1 November 1993. Each case has to be treated individually. The European Commission finally published the criteria to be used in January 1997. The amount of the fine is calculated on the basis of a uniform flat rate of ECU 500 per day. This is then adjusted to take into account the seriousness of the case, the length of time over which the national government has failed to act and the ability of the national government to pay any fines. For example, fines levied against Germany range from ECU 13 200 to 792 000 per day; against the Netherlands from ECU 3800 to 228 000 per day; and against Ireland from ECU 1200 to 72 000 per day.

When the first fines were threatened in January 1997 against the German and Italian governments, almost immediate action was taken in most cases by the national authorities to ensure that the legislation was implemented. Table 4.3 shows the outcome of some of the requests for penalty payments under article 228 TEC (171 TEC).

Table 4.3   Examples of requests for penalty payments to the end of 1997

Member state	Subject	Penalty payment (ECU/day)	Rate of Commission decision	Settled
Italy	Radiological protection	159 300	29 January 1997	Yes
Italy	Waste management plan	123 900	29 January 1997	Yes
Germany	Surface water	158 400	29 January 1997	No
Germany	Wild birds	26 400	29 January 1997	Yes
Germany	Groundwater	264 000	29 January 1997	Yes
Belgium	Wild birds	7 750	10 December 1997	Yes
Greece	Waste water management in a village in Crete	24 600	26 June 1997	No

Source: CEC (1998c: annex III).

MONITORING THE IMPLEMENTATION OF LEGISLATION

Monitoring of environmental policy involves a number of other actors from groups as disparate as government departments to individuals, and carries with it several problems for effective policy. The basic assumption is that everyone involved in the implementation and enforcement of the legislation shares the same interests in ensuring that it is effective. However, the different actors have their own priorities and this may form the biggest single obstacle to their involvement in the monitoring process.

The responsibility for regulation of competition in the integrated market lies with the European Community as a necessity to avoid distortion of trade. As a result the European Commission has many more powers to investigate national actions in the area of competition policy than environmental policy. Commissioner for the Environment Carlo Ripa di Meana supported the idea of increasing the EU's powers through the creation of an EU environment inspectorate in 1989 (see Chapter 3). This proposal was rejected by Jacques Delors. The European Parliament proposed that the European Environment Agency (EEA) should function as an inspectorate when it was established. As this is unlikely to happen in the medium term, other ways have to be found to enable the European Commission more effectively to utilize the means of monitoring legislation which are at its disposal.

The officials of DG XI (Environment) rely on information supplied to them from a variety of sources. This information may be collected on an *ad hoc* basis and does not always provide a firm foundation for monitoring. The European Commission noted that there was a fall in the number of complaints made by the public about the implementation of environmental legislation in 1996, from 265 made in 1995 to 207 (CEC 1997g: 94). This fall did not necessarily reflect an improvement in environmental performance. There were a number of other possible explanations, including lack of enthusiasm on the part of the public, lack of appropriate legislation, lack of sufficient information and the adoption of legislation which seemed to have no bearing on public concerns!

Many, but not all, directives contain the requirement that reports should be made to DG XI on the progress of implementation. Some confusion exists as the 'reporting-back' requirement differs from directive to directive. In some cases reports are required periodically, in others regularly. Often the reports are concerned with the transposition process and not practical implementation questions. The failure to provide these reports makes it very difficult for the European Commission to fulfil its role of monitoring the implementation of legislation. Directive 91/692/EEC[10] on standardizing and rationalizing reports on the implementation of certain environmental directives was introduced as a measure to harmonize reports from the member states. The European Commission is required to draw up basic questionnaires for each of the main sectors of policy – water, air and waste. These are then passed to the member states for the appropriate national authorities to complete and return. From the returns the European Commission then prepares reports for each sector every three years. An exception has been made in the case of the directive on bathing water

(76/160/EEC), which requires annual reports. Whilst the directive does deal with some of the problems, it is difficult to evaluate its impact yet. The directive was adopted in 1991 but the first reports were not completed until July 1997 for the water sector and not until 1998 and 1999 for the others.

THE ROLE OF THE EUROPEAN ENVIRONMENT AGENCY

The European Commission is heavily dependent on the quality and availability of the environmental information that comes from the national governments. There is a problem of lack of comparability of some information. The monitoring and collection of data is governed by the nationally set priorities in the individual member states. Different national approaches to environmental protection policy require different information to be collated. National variations are also affected by the degree of centralization of the monitoring process. Comparison may be difficult where the member states have national definitions of the region or locality for the collection of environmental data.

In order to overcome some of these problems, the European Commission launched the Coordination of Information on the Environment initiative in 1985 (CORINE). CORINE was an experimental project to determine the need for accurate and consistent data on the state of the environment within the EU. The primary purpose of the initiative was to provide an accurate view of environmental degradation to assist the legislative process. The CORINE programme was limited and it was apparent that more detail was required to establish specific targets for different environmental issues. To fulfil this need the European Environment Agency (EEA) was established in 1990 (Council Regulation EEC 1210/90).[11] The results of the CORINE programme became part of the basis of the functions which the EEA carries out. Whilst the EEA provides information to the European Commission, it is an autonomous agency with its own management structure and organization, and is not part of DG XI.

Theoretically the EEA has no role in the policy-making process itself. The work of the EEA is 'to record, collate and assess data', 'to draw up reports on the environment', 'the production of timely, objective information on the quality of the environment, the pressures to which it is subject and its sensitivity' (Council Regulation EEC 1210/90:1, article iii). Despite the recognition that accurate information is a crucial element of the policy process, the early years of the operation of the EEA were delayed as the national governments left decisions about the location of a number of EU agencies unresolved. Once agreement was reached, the EEA became operational in October 1993 in Copenhagen.

The primary objective of the European Environment Agency is to evaluate all the alternatives open to policy makers through the production of State of the Environment Reports. The scope of these reports was extended in 1998 to include the identification of future trends and prospects (CEC 1998b: 2). It is not part of the role of the Agency to make decisions about the alternative strategies. As such the EEA may be described as 'a watching dog with no teeth' (Señor Beltran, Director General, EEA 1994 (House of Lords 1995: 3)). However, to continue the metaphor, 'if the Agency ... does not have teeth it has a very strong jaw!' (Lord Geddes (House of Lords 1995: 3)) because of the importance of the role it can play in providing accurate information and scientific assessment. It is hoped that in this role the EEA will contribute to the ability of the policy makers to manage the environment successfully.

The debate which led to the establishment of the EEA included support from the European Parliament for the Agency to have the necessary powers and resources to function as an environment inspectorate. The UK government had also supported this view initially, recommending in 1988 that an inspectorate of inspectorates along the lines of the Fisheries Inspectorate should be established (House of Lords 1989). The argument was that this would help to overcome the problem of enforcement of policy at the national level. This was not accepted by the other national governments as an appropriate role for the EEA when it was founded. The UK government has also come to share this view.

> If a Community level inspectorate of inspectorates were to be established the logical home for it would be the EEA. But we agree with the Commission that the question of formal machinery for auditing national inspectorates need not be pursued for the time being. (House of Lords 1997a: 38)

The number of staff involved in the EEA is not sufficient to engage in a direct inspectorate role. Its initial complement was 40–50 technical and administrative staff, to build up to 100–150 once it became fully operational.[12] The EEA is an administrative organization, not a policing one, but in its role as presenter of alternatives to the policy makers it is more than merely a scientific institute. For the EEA to take on a direct inspectorate role would be to undermine the EU's commitment to shared responsibility for environmental protection between the national level environmental inspection authorities and the European Commission in its monitoring role. It would also undermine the neutrality of the role the EEA is required to perform in the identification of policy alternatives. In the 1998 review of the regulation founding the EEA, even peer review undertaken by the EEA on its own initiative was identified as potentially an inspectorate role, which would exceed the terms of reference given to the Agency (CEC 1998b: 2).

The desirability of an independent and EU-wide inspectorate to ensure the effective implementation and enforcement of environmental legislation remains. The EU relies on the national authorities for effective inspections and monitoring, with some supporting measures. One such initiative was the formation of the 'Chester' network of the national environmental authorities during the UK presidency of the Council of Ministers in 1992 to exchange examples of 'best practice' in inspection and monitoring procedures. The Chester network has been adapted and the informal EU network for the Implementation and Enforcement of Community Law (IMPEL) established in its place. It is jointly chaired by the European Commission and the state which holds the presidency of the Council of Ministers. DG XI acts as host for the IMPEL secretariat and distributes its reports.

The objective of IMPEL is to consider questions of implementation which will ensure better enforcement by national, regional and local authorities. Projects which have been completed include:

- exchange of information and comparison of the national permits given to industrial installations;
- exchange programmes for national environmental inspectors; and
- publication of a report on monitoring and enforcement mechanisms for the transfrontier movement of hazardous waste.

IMPEL has a valuable role to play in increasing the flow of information from and between the local and regional authorities which have responsibility for implementation and enforcement of EU policy. However, it has only limited powers and is based on voluntary action. The current structure does not provide the basis for IMPEL to develop into an inspectorate. The national competent authorities which form the network have very different powers given to them. In some states the role of the inspection authorities is limited to inspecting for compliance (the Netherlands); in others the competent authorities also make decisions on permits or court actions for enforcement (Denmark, the UK). Nevertheless, within its narrow constraints the IMPEL network could be very useful in identifying minimum criteria for environmental inspections.

PUBLIC PARTICIPATION IN THE MONITORING OF IMPLEMENTATION AND ENFORCEMENT

Sustainable development relies on a high level of public participation in the development and monitoring of policies. The Fifth EAP identified the following groups as important partners and sharers of the responsibility for environmental protection with the EU and national governments:

- Public authorities
- Private and public enterprises

- Non-governmental organizations (NGOs)
- The general public.

It is through the NGOs that the general public as well as the environmental interest groups have the greatest opportunities to influence the whole policy process. The NGOs are non-profit-making organizations. The charitable funding of the NGOs guarantees them an element of independence and autonomy. The environmental NGOs have made much progress in finding ways to participate at all stages of the policy process. Some groups are able to feed in opinions and views at the beginning of the process. Others are involved in the implementation directly, and yet others play an important role in monitoring the actions at the national level. However, the most effective participation of the NGOs in the policy process comes at the beginning, during the policy drafting and discussions. Once the legislative proposal has been passed to the Council of Ministers, it is difficult for the NGOs to make any alterations (see Table 3.1). The role of the NGOs in the policy process becomes important again after the legislation has been handed on to be transposed into national legislation. The NGOs are able to play a very active role in monitoring its implementation and enforcement.

The NGOs receive a high level of support from the European Commission for a number of reasons. Primarily this support stems from a recognition that the NGOs represent a large number of the citizens of the EU. The NGOs facilitate the participation of the general public in the monitoring and implementation of policy because they provide information. As information gatherers, the NGOs assist the European Commission where it has limited resources to deal with particular problems and they are a cost-effective way for the European Commission to obtain access to scientific expertise.

The impact of the environmental NGOs may be undermined by the way in which they are structured. Often the reason why many have come into existence is because the members have been involved in campaigns to ensure implementation and enforcement of specific measures in a local or regional context. For example, the implementation of the bathing water directive in the UK was of interest to a number of organizations. The Coastal Anti-Pollution League, which monitored the directive in the late 1970s and early 1980s, was concerned with the problem of sewage pollution at all UK beaches. The Marine Conservation Society, which took over the monitoring of bathing water quality at all UK beaches in the late 1980s and 1990s, was interested in a broader range of issues affecting the aquatic environment in the UK. At the resort of Scarborough, the quixotically named and somewhat eccentric membership of the 'Sons of Neptune' were concerned with monitoring the two beaches at this resort only. These groups were involved with monitoring the same directive but each had very different priorities in relation to the legislation.

If the NGOs collaborate, they can bring court actions which would otherwise prove too costly for groups on their own and can also withstand the consequences when actions fail. In 1997 Greenpeace headed a group of other environmental non-governmental organizations and local Canary Islands residents in bringing a test case which it was hoped would open up the rights of individuals directly to challenge EU decisions in the European Court of Justice. The case involved a decision by the Court of First Instance not to deny the right of challenge to a European Commission decision made in 1993. An award of ECU 40 million was authorized by the European Commission towards the building of two fossil-fuel power stations in the Canary Islands. The basis of the complaint made by Greenpeace and the other plaintiffs was that the projects had received approval before an adequate environmental impact assessment had been completed, and that it was contradictory for the European Commission to ratify the UN Convention on Climate Change on behalf of the EU while spending taxpayers' money on new sources of carbon dioxide emission. The complaint was not successful. The court ruling was based on the precedent set in the 1962 Plaumann case that individuals could only challenge an EU decision if it affected them directly (Plaumann and Co. *v.* the European Commission, Case 25/62).

Collaborative action among some of the environmental NGOs led to the establishment of the European Environmental Bureau (EEB) in 1974. This was following the adoption of the First EAP when the European Commission (particularly DG XI) realized the importance of an NGO movement as a counterweight to the industry lobby. At the end of the 1990s the EEB was a federation of 130 NGOs from 24 countries. As the EEB has a base in Brussels, it has more direct access to the European Commission and the European Parliament than nationally based groups which might be involved in the formulation and monitoring of environmental policy. It has a small permanent staff and the primary objective of the federation is to monitor the performance of the institutions of the EU on environmental issues and to ensure that environmental protection is integrated into other aspects of EU policy. Specific measures which have been the subject of special reports by the EEB include the environmental management and audit regulation and the EU's eco-labelling scheme.

The EEB has an annual budget of ECU 1 250 000 (1996 budget of the EU), which is provided by the European Commission and contributions from its member organizations. The amount of funding made available by the Commission for all NGOs has increased steadily throughout the 1990s. In 1995 and 1996 ECU 2.5 million were given in subsidies each year to the NGOs. In May 1997 an action programme was adopted for the environmental NGOs with a budget of ECU 10.6 million for the period to 2001. Greenpeace, Friends of the Earth and the World Wide Fund for Nature maintain offices in Brussels and, whilst they have links with the EEB, they function separately. These organizations have a very high profile at the national level. They concentrate on exerting pressure on the national policy makers rather than at EU level. Greenpeace deliberately avoids EU funding in order to preserve its independence. The World Wide Fund for Nature has a limit of between 10 and 15 per cent of its funding coming from public sources for the same reason.

The NGOs have their own information-gathering capacities but this requires legal support to ensure that there is freedom of access to the information. Directive 90/313/EEC[13] is intended to ensure that the public is able to play a full and active role in the partnership to protect the environment. The directive establishes the right to have questions answered within specific time scales, and national governments are requested to make periodic reports on the state of the environment. The implementation of this directive has raised a number of important issues for some national governments. The presumption in the directive is that of unrestricted access to information. However, this has raised questions about confidentiality of information which have been difficult to resolve within some member states. The directive requires the national governments to put in place clear procedures such as public registers of information. In order to fulfil the requirement of publication of periodic reports on the state of the environment, the national governments have also had to introduce appropriate systems of information collection and analysis. This has been a particular difficulty in those cases where monitoring of compliance is carried out by different authorities.

There are also specialist environmental agencies which have developed strong specialism or expertise in issue-specific areas. The Institute for European Environmental Policy (IEEP), which was established in 1976 and has offices in Arnhem, Bonn, London, Paris and Brussels, is the most important of these. It is responsible for disseminating information about environmental protection measures to a wide range of groups, the mass media and informing national governments. Its personnel have direct links with DG XI and the European Parliament.

FUNDING FOR ENVIRONMENTAL POLICY

A major criticism of the EU's environmental policy in the 1970s and the 1980s was the lack of financial support for its development from the supranational level. Despite this criticism, the primary responsibility for funding environmental policy continued to rest with the national governments throughout the 1990s. Before 1992 it was possible to obtain some limited funding for environmental projects from the Structural Funds,[14] but the mechanisms to do so were cumbersome and bureaucratic. The main objective of the Structural Funds was to help to overcome regional disparities within the member states. The 1988 reform of the Structural Funds introduced a more interventionist approach by the EU to these problems.

It also increased the opportunities introduced for funding programmes which contained environmental measures. These opportunities were not, however, based on meeting an environmental need, but were part of the overall regional development plans which were submitted to the EU for support.

The 1993 and 1999 reforms to the Structural Funds regulation and proposals for the future contained in the European Commission communication 'Agenda 2000' published in July 1997 (CEC 1997o) did not alter this position. The assistance given under the Structural Funds is based on the co-financing of operational programmes and national aid schemes which may include environmental aspects. However, there are two requirements in the Structural Funds regulation which are of significance for environmental protection:

1. The inclusion of an environmental appraisal in national and regional funding plans.
2. The requirement that funded projects comply with EU environmental policy.

Since 1992 two new initiatives have made EU sources of funding available for a limited number of aspects of environmental policy. The regulation establishing a Financial Instrument for the Environment (LIFE) was adopted in 1992 with funding allocated until 1995 (Council Regulation EEC 1973/92).[15] Funding under this regulation was exclusively to contribute to the development and implementation of environmental policy. It was an attempt to bring some coherence to the limited funding available from the differing sources in the EU and enable it to have a greater impact. This is not a substantially funded programme, and the main projects covered are demonstration projects or preliminary actions supported on the basis of co-financing from the national governments. A second allocation of funding for projects was made in 1996–99 under the LIFE II Programme. The total budget for LIFE II was ECU 450 million for four sectors of activity:

- Environment
- Nature
- Third countries
- Improving the implementation of the policy.

The Cohesion Fund was established as a result of extensive lobbying by the governments of Spain, Ireland, Portugal and Greece during the 1991 Intergovernmental Conference. It is not an environmental fund, but projects which are financed from the Fund have to be primarily concerned with improving transport or environmental infrastructure. When the funds were first allocated in 1993 there was criticism of the division made between the categories, as 38 per cent was committed to environmental projects and 61 per cent to transport, but by the end of the 1990s this imbalance had been removed (see Table 4.4). The environmental criteria used for funding from the Cohesion Fund are not as rigorous as those included in the Structural Funds regulations. There is no requirement to carry out environmental appraisal of projects to be funded. This has resulted in criticisms being made by the Court of Auditors, as sewage plants which have been financed from the Cohesion Fund to implement the urban waste water treatment directive have been built in an environmentally damaging way.

Table 4.4 Cohesion Fund – balance of commitments to the transport and environment sectors, 1993–97

	1993	1994	1995	1996	1997	1993–97 (ave.)
Environment	38.7	49.8	48.4	49.8	54.4	49.1
Transport	61.2	50.1	51.5	50.1	45.5	50.8

Source: Rapid Report IP/97/1169, 19 December 1997.

The financing of environmental policy carries with it many problems for the applicant states of Central and Eastern Europe. In September 1997 the Commissioner for the Environment Ritt Bjerregaard warned the environment ministers of the Eastern European applicants that they faced a bill of ECU 120 billion to reach EU standards (*European Voice* 1997: 9) (see Chapter 12). There are some funds available through PHARE[16] for Central and Eastern European states which may be used for environmental projects. The levels of funding have been increased since the programme began in 1989 but remain limited.

CONCLUSIONS

In the 1996 review carried out by the European Commission of the implementation of environmental law (CEC 1996h) the conclusion was reached that a more holistic approach had to be adopted to ensure that the problems associated with implementation and enforcement of legislation would be overcome. The European Commission proposed that this process should be viewed as part of a 'regulatory chain' which included the transposition of legislation into the national legislation, the design of the legislation, the institutional structure which was involved in its implementation, and education and information dissemination. If the recommendations of this report are taken into account, the future of the EU's environmental policy will be more soundly based. The European

Commission views the European Environment Agency as being able to provide the link in the chain between evaluation and design of legislation (see Figure 4.1).

This approach is a crucial development within the EU for the following reasons:

- The EU is drafting more environmental legislation in the form of framework directives. The early consideration of the problems of national implementation and enforcement will ensure that this form of legislation achieves the stated objectives.
- The policy will become effective as the evaluation process becomes more wide-ranging and reports and analysis are fed back into the review of legislation once it has been adopted.
- The commitment to integrate environmental considerations into the sectoral polices of the EU will be easier to fulfil.

There are, however, constraints on the ability of the European Commission to ensure that this method is adopted. The political willingness of the national governments to support the more holistic approach outlined above has to be

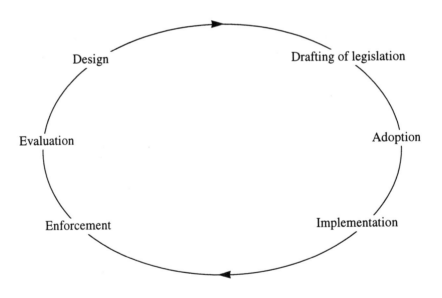

Source: Based on definition given in CEC (1996h, Annex 1)

Figure 4.1   The regulatory 'chain'

ensured. There will be an increase in the involvement of the European Commission, especially DG XI, in the preparatory work of the legislative process. Questions must therefore be asked about the capacity of the European Commission to deal with the extra workload.

Other recommendations outlined in the 1996 review were that:

- in the absence of an EU environmental inspectorate, EU-wide criteria for the completion of inspection tasks by the national authorities should be provided;
- an environmental complaints and investigations procedure within the member states which would receive and examine complaints from the public about the implementation of EU environmental law should be introduced;
- there should be increased opportunities for environmental cases to be dealt with by national courts through broader access to justice on EU environmental law issues.

Among recommendations made to overcome some of the problems of enforcement of policy is increasing the opportunities for the national courts to deal with cases of infringement of environmental legislation. This has several advantages. It is in accordance with the application of the principles of subsidiarity and shared responsibility. It has the practical advantage of enabling quick and low-cost settlements of issues to be made in a way that is more accessible to the citizens of the EU. The European Court of Justice could be consulted as a last resort. At the same time, if these opportunities for the national courts to deal with cases are made available, there will be more requirements for the introduction of mechanisms to monitor enforcement of policy at the supranational level. Otherwise the danger of increased fragmentation and undermining of the attempts to achieve a concerted and harmonized environmental policy within the EU will grow.

The review's recommendations are an acknowledgement of the fact that the 'top–down' approach to policy making is not providing effective environmental protection. The structure outlined would create a more holistic approach to the implementation of environmental policy which would ensure that the problems of enforcement and monitoring receive a much higher profile in any future developments. A more holistic approach is essential if the commitment to the application of the principles of subsidiarity and sharing of responsibility is to be met. It will provide a firm basis on which to build to meet the growing pressures on the environmental policy as the EU enlarges to include Central and Eastern Europe. However, it represents a 'virtuous circle' of desirable action and will be difficult to achieve in the short or medium term as the EU faces the twin challenges of the single currency and enlargement. Many of the difficulties of enforcement and implementation lie in the legal and technical complexity of the issues under discussion. Numerous questions of interpretation and technical application are associated with the EU's environmental legislation, and there are many problems of ensuring proper coordination of differing national authorities. If these problems are not addressed, the EU's environmental policy will fall short of the ambitions which it expresses for environmental protection and economic development.

NOTES

1. Forms of legislation available to the EU:

   Decision – the least important form of legislation for environmental policy. For example, a decision may be used to amend legislation, e.g. additions to the lists of waste carried under the directive on the transfrontier movement of hazardous waste.
   Regulations – about 10 per cent of the EU's environmental legislation take this form. Regulations are directly applicable in all the member states and supersede any existing conflicting national legislation. As such they do not need to be transposed into national legislation.
   Directives – the most frequently used form of legislation for environmental measures. It is the most flexible form as it enables the national government to use the most appropriate national means available to implement the EU's legislation.

2. Council Directive 85/337 on the environmental impact assessments (EIAs) carried out of major public sector schemes, OJL 175, 5 July 1985.
3. Council Directive 88/609 on the limitation of emission of pollutants into the air from large-scale combustion plants, OJL 336, 7 December 1988.
4. Adopted by the European Commission.
5. Council Directive 75/440/EEC on the quality of water intended for the abstraction of drinking water in the Member States, OJL 194, 25 July 1975.
6. Council Directive 80/68/EEC on the protection of groundwater against pollution caused by certain dangerous substances, OJL 20, 26 January 1980.
7. Council Directive 80/78/EC on the quality of water intended for human consumption, OJL 229, 30 August 1980.
8. Council Directive 76/160/EEC on the quality of bathing water, OJL 31, 5 February 1976.
9. Council Directive 91/271/EEC concerning urban waste water treatment, OJL 135, 30 May 1991.
10. Council Directive 91/692/EC on standardising and rationalising reports on the implementation of certain directives relating to the environment, OJL 377, 31 December 1992.
11. Council Regulation EEC 1210/90 on the establishment of the European Environment Agency (EEA) and the European Information and Observation Network (EIONET), OJL 120, 11 May 1990.
12. Staffing levels had reached 66 persons by late 1998.
13. Council Directive 90/313/EEC on the freedom of access to information which is normally held by publicly accountable bodies, OJL 158, 7 July 1990.
14. The EU's Structural Funds are the European Regional Development Fund (ERDF), the European Social Fund (ESF) and the European Agricultural Guarantee and Guidance Fund (EAGGF).

15. Council Regulation EEC 1973/92 establishing a unified financial instrument for the environment (LIFE), OJL 206, 22 July 1992.
16. PHARE began in 1989 to help with the process of transition to liberal democratic systems of government and market economies in the states of Central and Eastern Europe. Since 1994 a new phase of support has begun with more emphasis on longer-term objectives and preparations for the accession of some of these states to the EU.

5 Market forces and the environment

INTRODUCTION

Man's economic activity is based upon the use of resources. Many of these are finite, and because some economic activities may damage the environment, choices have to be made. These choices concern not only the quantity of the earth's scarce resources that should be depleted at any particular time, but also how they should be managed and exploited. Can we leave these choices to individuals, without taking heed of society's needs? Whilst environmental protection is a moral and cultural issue, it is also tied to the economic process. Economic activity and economic mechanisms are therefore at the forefront of the process of controlling environmental degradation.

This chapter considers three key issues:

1. The failure of the unregulated market to deliver an acceptable level of environmental protection.
2. The use of economic instruments as a mechanism for the protection of the environment.
3. The EU's role of encouraging and monitoring the use of economic instruments at the member state level.

Environmental protection cannot be left to unfettered market forces alone. However, this does not mean that the power of the market mechanism can be ignored. There is a need for the member states and the EU to take an active role in supplementing and regulating market forces. Environmental taxes and charges are used in all the member states, and they are playing an increasing role in the applicant states from Central and Eastern Europe. As a consequence, the EU has a significant role in managing the implications of economic instruments with respect to the single market. This involves the monitoring of economic instruments to ensure that they do not become barriers to trade. Whilst these trade issues are important, they may have distracted policy makers from achieving the full potential of using economic instruments to control society's behaviour with respect to the environment.

Environmental degradation happens for a number of complex reasons. Pollution may occur through society's ignorance, in which case the problem can be solved by better education. If environmental problems arise because people simply do not care, it is very difficult to reawaken moral standards to the extent that citizens are prepared to take action. Casting the problem in moral terms may not therefore be helpful in generating solutions. This leaves us with a third avenue to explore; that is, environmental degradation comes about because of failure of the economic system. Whilst not all decisions are driven by the profit motive, it is a powerful factor in the way that many people think. If the environment is regarded as being free and if it can be exploited for profit, then the likelihood is that it will be abused. This leads to the phenomenon of market failure. That is, the market does not fully take into account the cost of environmental degradation and the benefits that arise from a clean environment. Central to the EU's strategy to deal with this failure of the market mechanism is the attempt to make polluters acknowledge the cost of their activities by implementing the polluter pays principle (PPP). This requires that all instruments of environmental policy should result in the polluter bearing the full cost of pollution control. The hope is that all pollution-related costs will be internalized within the firm, so that managers realize that they must pay a price for using the environment. Thus the adoption of PPP should be an incentive to move towards significantly reducing the effects of pollution. This is an idea that appears deceptively simple; however, in practice it has been difficult to implement on an EU-wide basis.

Throughout this chapter we implicitly support the paradigm of ecological modernization. That is the belief that economic development and environmental protection can be integrated and make a positive impact. The positive impact comes about because measures to improve environmental protection can be a spur to innovation and greater efficiency. However, there is a problem of gaining the acceptance of the member states to the EU taking a lead on any strategy that challenges their right to articulate economic policy.

MARKET FAILURE AND THE ENVIRONMENT

The market has failed to take account of environmental degradation because of the existence of externalities (spillover effects) and public goods. There is an aspect of environmental benefits which economists describe as public goods, which leads to failure of the market mechanism. The basic feature of public goods is that it is difficult to prevent users from exploiting them.[1] Unless society is prepared to take action to protect the environment, some citizens will soon realize that the environment can be abused, without their making any contribution towards its upkeep. This abuse of the environment has been called 'free-riding'. Whilst the activities of one person 'free-riding' are harmful, additional problems occur because there is a temptation for others to follow, even though this will be even more harmful in the long run. An example of free-riding is the dumping of waste into the sea.

Externalities occur when economic decisions are made which impose costs on or give benefits to people other than the economic decision maker. These are described as social costs or social benefits: a clean environment is a social benefit; a polluted environment is a social cost. It is evident in many cases that environmental benefits such as clean air and unpolluted water are not available in the quantities that society would wish (but it is difficult to say precisely what value should be placed on them). In deciding their levels of production, investment and consumption, it is assumed by economists that individuals and firms normally consider costs and benefits to themselves, and not the impact of their decisions on society as a whole.

Whilst individuals can act independently, they rarely have the economic power to counteract the activities of polluters, particularly if they are large corporations. Indeed, they may also be unwilling to challenge the unsociable behaviour of specific companies. Polluters can indulge in 'free-riding' because the enforcement costs are often too high to bring about a remedy. This is particularly true where there is no ownership of the environment.

Failure of the market gives a rationale for collective action. The state (or international organization) is needed because collective action is required in order to ensure that all citizens participate in maintaining and improving the environment. What is needed is either regulation to control the market, or the introduction of economic incentives that will help to make the market work more effectively. Collective action is likely to be more effective if there is an agreement to stick by any rules of conduct that are laid down. This is not to suggest that state intervention in environmental issues will guarantee that society's aspirations for improvement will be met. It should be remembered, for example, that in many Eastern European states before the collapse of communism, the environment was not protected. Instead of initiating collective action to improve the environment, the state led the process of environmental degradation by concentrating on industrial production to the exclusion of all else.

The international nature of many environmental problems has particular implications for the use of economic instruments. Environmental protection is essentially a regional, national and global problem: it is not easy to see where costs and benefits end because costs may be imposed on societies in other parts of the globe. It may be possible for the state to control externalities within its own borders, but what about global externalities? If a country like Germany decided to stop burning fossil fuels, this would be at an enormous cost to the country, and there is no guarantee that others would follow suit. 'Free-riders' who would simply take advantage of the gesture, and the impact on the global environment would therefore be limited. It would be far more advantageous for an effective international agreement to be in place which reduced all countries' use of fossil fuels.

Where economic instruments are used, they have to be agreed by all parties on an international basis; however, the wider the international element, the less certain it is that action will be taken and will be effective. The difficulty of trying to control by using international organizations is that they normally have little real leverage to persuade signatories to a treaty to honour their agreements. Trade sanctions might be an answer in some cases, but history suggests that they are largely ineffective. However, the EU is better placed than most international bodies, because it has significant powers to enforce legislation once this has been agreed by the member states.

The EU has very limited financial resources to deal with the problem of environmental degradation on its own account. Member states may also feel that they lack the financial resources to be able to cope with problems of pollution control. The more affluent the society, the higher the level of environmental protection that can be afforded. If we compare the levels of public and private expenditure on provision of control in member states, we find that the UK and Germany each spend 1.5 per cent of GDP compared to Greece and Portugal, which each spend only 0.5 per cent of GDP on this task. When these figures are adjusted for the differing industrial structures and levels of pollution, the highest-spending member states are devoting more than nine times that amount per capita to solving their pollution problems compared to the lowest-spending states (Bjerregaard 1996b). This may mean that if the EU expands to the east, there will be a need to ensure that those new member states can meet their environmental obligations.

ECONOMISTS AND THE ENVIRONMENT

Economists showed little interest in environmental problems until the 1970s. Before then the economics of the environment was not the subject of significant debate. Classical and neo-classical economics assumed that, apart from certain key roles, state intervention was undesirable; it was the market that gave the best results. The most dominant economic philosophy was that of Adam Smith, who in his *Wealth of Nations*, published in 1776, said that it was the actions of individuals following their own self-interest that gave the best results for society overall. That is, he believed that an *invisible hand* would lead society to maximize its welfare. Classical and neo-classical economists believed that there was a limit to production of goods in society. The law of diminishing returns determined that society would finally arrive at what has been described as the stationary state, where resources were economically fully utilized, and economic growth would cease.

Neo-classical economists such as John Stuart Mill, in his *Principles of Political Economy* (1857), recognized that there was a problem where the market failed to demonstrate consumers' preferences. A.C. Pigou, in his

Economics of Welfare (Pigou 1920), took further the criticisms of unrestricted market forces by suggesting that consumers' choices in the marketplace do not necessarily indicate the social importance of the goods and services that are being provided. So, for example, using his logic, if a tax were placed on a product that caused pollution, this would have the dual benefit of allowing individual choice and at the same time improving society's welfare by reducing pollution. Whilst Pigou's ideas were of importance, it should be noted that they were not particularly influential at the time. Indeed, the major problem in the 1920s and 1930s was mass unemployment, and in the period after the Second World War the major concern was how to maximize the rate of economic growth.

Throughout the period from the Industrial Revolution to the 1970s environmental concerns were largely associated with public health issues rather than general and environmental degradation. In the postwar period there was a strong belief that just as economic growth could be maintained on a permanent basis, so it was possible to find technological solutions to the difficulties associated with depleted resources. It was not until it was clear that society was heading for an environmental crisis that economists started to address the problems associated with the rational exploitation of the environment.

PROPERTY RIGHTS

One feature of the environment that makes it difficult to manage is that there is often a lack of clear ownership of it, and as a consequence it is frequently abused. This leads to what has been described as 'the tragedy of the commons' (Hardin 1968). 'The tragedy of the commons' describes a situation where there is unregulated access to an asset such as common land, which existed before agricultural enclosure in England. In such circumstances, individuals tend to maximize their individual benefit by grazing as many animals as possible on the common land. This leads to excessive use. The result is that the quality of animals deteriorates, they become disease-ridden and there is a lack of food to maintain their overall health. Whilst it makes sense for the individual to exploit the land, the result is a disaster for society. Indeed, individuals may realize this, but everyone is locked into the cycle of overexploitation because the land is not owned. In this situation, any individual reducing the number of his grazing animals will find that others, with rights to use the common land, will increase the size of their herds. The tragedy of the commons was resolved by enclosure of land, and by private ownership superseding the collective holding of land. Once the land was privately owned, overexploitation was reduced. In modern times, the tragedy of the commons is particularly acute where assets are internationally available. An example of this is fishing in the world's oceans, where the lack of ownership rules has led to overfishing and a significant threat to stocks. Voluntary agreements to restrict fishing have only worked to a limited extent, because of the failure to enforce regulations on the size of catches. The EU's attempts to regulate the industry by means of the common fisheries policy have had only limited success. It has been argued that the only way to improve the protection of stocks would be by national ownership of fish stocks. This is a policy that has worked well for Norway, but has not been a success in the case of Iceland (Barnes 1996: 222).

It has been suggested that an alternative approach to solving the problem of environmental degradation can be found in the adoption of a system of property rights (Coase 1960). This approach assumes that if the environment is owned, as any other property, the costs could be internalized. Because the environment is an asset, care will be taken to protect its value. If pollution takes place, there will be a demand for compensation to be paid to the owner of the environment who finds that their property has been damaged. This approach assumes that it is the courts that enforce environmental policy.

The property rights approach does not take into account the costs of environmental degradation for future generations. Negative externalities fall on future generations as well as on today's. If we take, for example, the storage of nuclear waste, this not only poses a burden on society now, but could prove a health hazard for many years to come. The same problems also arise from global warming, as it may be that actions taken now are creating problems for the future. Typically, economists value benefits that will come in the future at a discounted rate; that is, they assume that consumers place a higher value on what they have now. It could be argued that the discount on future benefits should be zero, and the environment should be in as good a state in the future as it is now, or even better. This may not, however, be practical. The problems of the future are real, and inevitably they are a price we have to pay. Unfortunately they are not normally something which is included in the calculation of individual rationality. At a collective level, there are also few votes to be won from offering to protect the environment for the future.

The above approach to environmental economics runs contrary to the EU strategy, which is based upon the polluter pays principle (PPP). The ownership of property rights assumes that PPP is invalid, because if society found that it did not own the environment, it would have to pay polluters to regulate their behaviour and reduce the level of pollution. Another problem with respect to property rights to the environment is that it is difficult to define them, especially in the international context, where ownership rules are unsatisfactory.

THE USE OF ECONOMIC INSTRUMENTS

Environmental policies traditionally relied upon command and control policies in the form of regulations to achieve standards of environmental protection. An example of this is building regulations in which minimum energy efficiency standards are set. Each regulation carries with it a cost that is either met by the company or by the individual, unless the state decides to offer a subsidy to offset this. The principal advantage of regulations is that if they are enforced, environmental targets are met. They also offer a degree of standardization where, ideally, the rules are clear. Costs are therefore predictable for business, thus offering a degree of certainty.

The use of a regulatory approach has been criticized because of its static nature. This approach disguises the true cost of meeting environmental standards demanded by the consumer, and often fails to give an incentive to improve environmental performance beyond the standards set. Also, it may not allow for the exploitation of cost differences.

The use of economic instruments is widely advocated with respect to the operation of effective environmental policy. Support for their adoption reflects a move in society away from the view that resorting to regulation can solve all problems. A financial burden is placed upon the polluter, which can either be used to pay for the cost of abatement, or provide a financial incentive to reduce pollution. A number of economic instruments are appropriate for controlling environmental degradation. These are as follows.

Charging

A policy of charging was well understood in areas such as water pollution. Traditionally funds gained from this source have been earmarked for clean-up operations and to improve the general infrastructure for treatment of pollution. Whilst this strategy will continue, charges might also be used rather more as a means of discouraging the production of pollution at source through market signals.

Taxation

Different levels of taxes are applied to products depending on whether they are regarded as being environmentally friendly or not. This is seen as an extremely economical way of affecting behaviour and reducing environmental degradation. Such taxes do not necessarily have to be applied so that they increase the overall burden of taxation.

State Aids

Financial assistance is offered to producers to encourage a change in their behaviour. Subsidies can include direct payments to businesses, tax allowances, loans at preferential rates of interest, services provided at below-market costs and tax allowances to encourage investment in more environmentally friendly production methods.

The Creation of Artificial Markets

Artificial markets might include emissions trading, that is, buying and selling the right to pollute. Under this system, firms are set emissions targets and, if they fall below their limit, they may have the right to trade their allowances with other firms.

Financial Penalties Related to Enforcement

Financial penalties are imposed on firms which do not comply with environmental targets. The aim is to charge a fee that is equal to or greater than the excess benefit a firm gains from damaging the environment.

Deposit Schemes

A refundable deposit is charged on the sale of a good that is potentially polluting, for example, packaging. This is refunded on the return of the product.

The case for the use of economic instruments is that they:

- exert a flexible and continuous pressure for the improvement of environmental performance;
- give an incentive to improve the production process and innovate so that environmental standards can be raised;
- allow a choice to be made between the cost of intervention and environmental benefits to be gained from that intervention;
- avoid excessive state interference. Whilst many firms and environmentalists prefer state regulation because of its consistent approach, economic instruments allow a balance between treatment and prevention;
- help to avoid the burden of environmental regulation on the public purse.

In addition to the above, economic instruments may have a fund-raising aspect. This is of particular importance given that many environmental measures are expensive. But the purpose of these measures can be misleading. Many economic instruments are regarded with some cynicism by the general public, and are seen as no more than attempts to raise revenues. An example of this might be the raising of excise duty on petroleum without providing an alternative of improved public transport. The element of this policy associated with reducing environmental degradation is frequently secondary and often minimal.

Economists do not normally recommend that pollution be totally eliminated. If zero pollution were required, the price for abusing the environment would have to be set at a very high level. Normally they have in mind an optimal level, which balances the cost of reducing pollution with the benefits that this brings, in a way that is acceptable to society. This approach makes sense partly because the environment itself has some capacity to assimilate pollution, and partly because it is possible to abate the effects of pollution by resources generated in the production process.

There are a number of problems associated with the practical aspects of using economic instruments. Their use should involve financial stimulus to encourage firms to take action, but there should also be a degree of voluntary action, to permit firms to take what they believe is the most effective form of action. There is awareness that whilst the use of economic instruments has traditionally been a matter for the member states, there is a need to ensure that the charges do not affect competition. Wide differences in the application of economic instruments can encourage firms to relocate in order to reduce their costs.

Enthusiasm for economic instruments is not universal. Business organizations complain that they are being charged for the use of the environment, whereas in the past they believed that its use was free. This gives rise to active and well-funded opposition. Polluters are very adept at reducing the cost of economic instruments. In the real world, political lobbying can ensure that the harshness of many measures is mitigated, by gaining exemptions from and reductions to taxes and charges.

The most important criticism of economic instruments is that, despite the theoretical precision of many of them, the actual impact of measures is frequently unclear. Accurate information on which to base decisions is frequently not available, and in general there is no clear understanding of what environmental costs and benefits are. Only a few attempts have been made to evaluate the effect of economic instruments, despite their wide advocacy by policy makers. Social costs and benefits are in any case highly subjective, and as a consequence they are open to differing interpretations. Economic instruments tend to be targeted at particular environmental indicators and are narrowly focused. They very rarely consider the wider picture, despite the global effects of policy initiatives, which means that costs and benefits are likely to be apparent in different locations. Even if the problems are serious, it could be that leaving environmental problems to be sorted out in the future might be beneficial if better and cheaper technology might then be available (Wolf 1997).

However, if we search for certainty with respect to environmental information, we put off solving the problems to some future date. This is a prescription for inaction and a worsening of environmental damage. It is for this reason that the EU's response is to adopt a 'no regrets' philosophy, that is, that action should be taken to tackle environmental problems now, rather than later. Economic instruments make sense if some improvement takes place, even if the precise extent of the benefits is unclear.

The Polluter Pays Principle

The polluter pays principle (PPP) has been at the heart of the EU's strategy to employ economic instruments to limit environmental damage. PPP is based on the principle that polluters should not be subsidized. That is, all instruments of environmental policy should result in the polluter bearing the full cost of pollution control. In the long term the idea behind PPP is that pollution-related costs should be internalized within the firm. Thus the operation of PPP should act as an incentive to sectors of the economy to move towards reducing significantly the effects of pollution.

PPP involves firms meeting the cost of environmental standards once they are set; it does not mean that firms have to meet costs of environmental damage below that minimum standard. Once polluters realize that they must pay the cost of meeting environmental standards, the costs should be fully internalized and the total cost of production be understood. Either prices will rise to take account of the full cost of production, which includes the costs of reducing the environmental damage, or firms will take action to deal with environmental degradation on a cost-effective basis. This internalization may in turn help prevent market failure and force the firm to move away from the market optimum level of production to a socially optimum level.

PPP poses a number of problems in practice. These include:

- A lack of clarity as to who is to blame for pollution, if that pollution comes about as a result of implementing government policies or responding to government incentives. This is a particular problem with respect to pollution resulting from agricultural activities. It could be said, for example, that the common agricultural policy (CAP), with its incentives to increase agricultural production, was a major indirect cause of agricultural contamination of water sources.
- Dealing with pollution when it comes from a number of sources, and where it is impossible to identify the polluter. Greenhouse gases cause particular problems because they are generated in varying amounts by all countries of the world. However, no world government exists to make all the polluters pay.
- Increasing costs as a result of adopting PPP, where the ability to meet these by charging the customer is limited. The costs may therefore fall on an industry on an inequitable basis, which has advantages for some producers

while penalizing others. This is particularly important with respect to international trade.

- The need to apply PPP internationally rather than just nationally. If one state is insisting that manufacturers pay the full environmental cost, while another does not, this gives a competitive advantage to those firms operating in countries with low costs, and may lead to the inappropriate location of industry.

The main policy instrument used to support PPP is taxation. However, the EU has only limited powers in this respect, and none of these powers applies directly to environmental policy. The main attempt to introduce PPP at the EU level was the carbon/energy tax, which was ultimately not adopted. The common fisheries policy in particular runs counter to PPP, with its side payments such as decommissioning grants being used to control the overexploitation of the seas. Owners of fishing vessels are paid to take their vessels out of the industry in order to reduce the incidence of overexploitation.

THE EU'S ADVOCACY OF ECONOMIC INSTRUMENTS

The origins of the EU's adoption of a policy of recommending economic instruments to protect the environment can be dated to the memorandum of the Commission in March 1971 which advocated charging for the use of transport infrastructure. The First Environmental Action Programme was adopted on 22 November 1973 and covered the years 1973 to 1976 (CoM 1973). This called for the use of economic instruments and a common method of accounting that allowed for the costs of pollution. It was recommended that the polluter pays principle should be adopted and that 'this should be taken as the guiding principle for applying economic instruments to carry out the environmental programme without hampering the progressive elimination of regional imbalances in the community' (CoM 1973: 33). This implied judging the effectiveness of economic instruments and harmonizing the methods of applying them. It also called for the rules on state aids to be respected. However, it did envisage certain exceptions and special arrangements, in particular where transitional periods were involved, and made the proviso that this would cause no significant distortion to international trade or investment.

The EU's environmental strategy for the 1990s was the Fifth Environmental Action Programme, published in March 1992 (CEC 1992a). The section dealing with economic instruments was entitled 'The Economic Approach: Getting the Prices Right'. This indicated the continued interest in economic instruments to protect the environment. The Commission stated that 'in order to get the prices right and to create market based incentives for environmentally friendly economic behaviour the use of economic and fiscal instruments would have to constitute an increasingly important part of the overall approach'. The Commission's long-term goal was increasingly to internalize environmental costs incurred during the whole life cycle of products, that is from the production stage through to their final disposal. The intention was that environmentally friendly products should not be disadvantaged in the marketplace. Two approaches were discussed in the document, the first being the pricing approach to economic incentives. The second approach, regarded as a possible option, was the use of tradable permits to control and .educe the quantity of pollution.

In line with the economic concern of the time, the Fifth EAP stressed that instruments would have to be applied in a cost-effective way in order to avoid unnecessary adjustment costs to the economy. Also, there was a need to take note of the distributional effects of any measures and their impact on regional economies. Economic instruments that were examined in the Fifth EAP included charging taxes to reduce consumption, and state aids.

In addition to the above measures, the Fifth EAP recommended two instruments which would not be seen as directly market-based, but would have an economic impact. These were:

1. *Environmental auditing*   This is to encourage firms to become more aware of their environmental performance. This would, it was hoped, feed through into the way that firms viewed their production processes. (For a discussion of this topic see Chapter 7.)
2. *Viewing the protection of the environment as a shared responsibility*   If firms failed to take note of their environmental responsibility, in the last resort the use of legal means to punish firms which damage the environment was seen as a legitimate way forward (see the section on Civil Liability and the PPP below, page 139).

In many respects it appears as though there is little difference between the statements with respect to the EAPs of 1973 and 1992 advocacy of economic instruments. The aspirations of 1973 were not fulfilled and in 1992 the message was still largely about advocacy of economic ·instruments rather than their successful application. The problem here is the lack of authority of the EU with respect to fiscal matters. This is made more noticeable when the EU's attempts to construct policy come into play. The establishment of an environmental tax involves a number of different parts of the Commission: DG III (Internal Market and Industrial Affairs), DG XXI (Taxation), DG XI (Environment), DG XV (Internal Market and Financial Services/Company Law) and DG XVII (Energy). Each of these needs to be consulted in order to launch a new initiative and to gain support from the member states.

ECONOMIC INSTRUMENTS AND THE SINGLE MARKET

The most active aspect of the EU's role with respect to economic instruments is the supervision of the activities of the member states. In particular it has been seen as an important part of the policy implementation process within the Commission to manage the tensions between member states which have aspirations to high environmental standards and those which are more concerned about competitiveness. This is particularly important with respect to state aids.

National taxes to control pollution have been very much the order of things, as the EU lacks powers to impose taxes without unanimous support. Typical of such a tax would be the kerosene tax proposed by the Dutch government. The rationale behind imposing a kerosene tax on aircraft is that flying can generate three times as much carbon dioxide and five times the amount of nitrogen oxide as the equivalent train on the same journey. The problem with such taxes is that, if they are applied by just one member state, airlines would be tempted to divert to other airports for refuelling, which in turn would do little to preserve the Dutch environment (Shan 1996).

The EU's role is now one of monitoring and controlling the use of economic instruments at the member state level. That is, it has tried to ensure that state aids and taxation do not distort the single market. The EU has increasingly tried to promote the view that economic instruments applied at the member state level can be compatible with EU legislation and that there is considerable room for action to use fiscal instruments which respect the obligations of the treaties (CEC 1997a).

For environmental measures to be acceptable they should be justifiable on the basis of resolving a specific environmental problem. Thus:

- Particular attention should be paid to articles 174–176 TEC which set out the objectives of environmental policy (130r, s, t. TEC) and the Fifth Environmental Action Programme.
- Charges should not discriminate against foreign products articles 23 and 25 TEC (9 and 12 TEC).
- Domestic taxes cannot be levied at a higher rate on products from other member states than on domestic products article 95 TEC (100a TEC).
- Any charges that are applied with respect to the environment must comply with the secondary legislation on indirect taxes. This is especially with regard to article 93 TEC (99 TEC) on indirect duties and taxes. Member states may increase taxes on certain products for environmental reasons, for example, incentives to use more environmentally friendly fuel.
- Quantitative restrictions on trade or equivalent measures can be applied even if they are normally banned under articles 28–30 TEC (30, 34, 36 TEC) if they achieve environmental objectives.

- State aids must comply with articles 87 and 88 TEC (92.-93 TEC)

State aids are policy instruments designed to affect the outcome of the market process. In the case of environmental policy, they can be used either to encourage investment in more environmentally friendly production processes or to give an advantage in the marketplace to environmentally friendly products. State aids are targeted at particular sectors of the economy or industries or products. They are paid by the state sector to the non-state sector, although there is no clear definition of what they are, apart from government intervention in the market economy. They can include payments directly from the budget, lower taxes, lower prices given by state industries, credits and equity participation in commercial investment. Generally the EU seeks to ensure that state aids are transparent and that they do not give an unfair advantage to goods traded in the single market.

Article 87:1 TEC (92 TEC) makes the following point with respect to state aids:

> Save as otherwise provided in this Treaty, any aid granted by a Member State or through State resources in any form whatsoever which distorts or threatens to distort competition by favouring certain undertakings or the production of certain goods shall, insofar as it affects trade between Member States, be incompatible with the common market.

The above clearly indicates that state aids should not be granted unless they have the approval of the European Union. The member states are required to notify the Commission of any state aids they give. Directive 83/189 requires prior notification of technical standards and regulations; environmental regulations are no exception to this. The EU's task with respect to state aids given by member states is to regulate them so that they do not interfere with the operation of the single market. (The EU tends to be less concerned about state aids with respect to the environment and the global market.) The Treaty sets out the kind of aids that are compatible with the single market and those that *may* be considered compatible. Included in this are 'Such other categories of aid as may be specified by decision of the Council acting by a qualified majority on a proposal from the Commission' article 87 (e) TEC (92:3.e TEC).

An example of a permitted state aid is Sweden's increase in its taxes on CO_2 in fuel, which was then matched by a tax reduction for companies using large amounts of fuel. These reductions represented a state aid, but the Commission viewed them as being justified because they were in line with the EU's environmental objectives (*Europe* 1996b). That is, firms in Sweden were being encouraged to improve their efficiency because fuel was to be more expensive, but at the same time they would not be at an overall disadvantage in the international market.

New rules with regard to state aids and the environment were adopted on 8 December 1993 (revising the 1974 framework). These were designed to take account of EC competition policy, the needs of the Fifth Environmental Action Programme and the wish to move towards the polluter pays principle. The rules said that state aids could be given for investments that help to improve the quality of the environment, but only in respect of the extra costs needed to meet environmental objectives. A ceiling of 15 per cent gross was allowed in the case of existing plant more than two years old to help them to reach new mandatory standards. Up to 30 per cent was to be allowed where investment improved on mandatory standards. Smaller and medium enterprises were allowed an extra 10 per cent in the form of state aids to take account of their limited resource base. In 1994, the first year of the application of the new guidelines, a number of projects were approved, including measures to assist energy conservation, waste management and development of new technologies.

Whilst state aids to assist investment were allowed, in principle operating aid was to be prohibited and would only be authorized on an exceptional case-by-case basis on the condition that the aid would be temporary and wound down over time. Operating aid would only be provided to launch new and more costly environmental protection policies or to maintain international competitiveness (CEC 1993i: 44–5).

The EU's general rules on state aids for environmental protection did not apply to the steel industry, which was still subject to the regime laid down by the ECSC.

TRADABLE PERMITS

Emissions trading is an attempt to create a market where none exists. In the US, power companies can trade their right to emit sulphur dioxide. Each plant is allowed to emit to a certain level against a target set by government. Those plants that can reduce their emission levels cheaply can sell their rights to emit to those companies facing higher costs. For example a power company running a dated coal-fired station might conclude that it is easier to buy the right to keep emitting its current level of sulphur dioxide than to switch fuels. Where costs of reducing sulphur dioxide are low, standards can easily be met and improved on, with the prospect of profiting from the sale of rights to emit which are not required.

Emissions trading is believed to be successful in the United States. It was the US that promoted the idea of an international system at the UN Framework Convention on Climate Change (UNFCCC) in Kyoto, Japan in December 1997. A power plant in Russia might easily be able to switch to natural gas, and therefore might wish to trade its emissions rights with an Italian company that finds it costly to reduce its emissions. Under this arrangement, those people directly affected by the Italian plant would not experience any significant improvement, but globally there would be an improvement. Similar arrangements could be made between differing sectors and types of environmental problem. So, for example, emissions reduction could be traded against deforestation, which might allow trading between developed and underdeveloped countries. (It is normally assumed that it will be the rich countries paying the poor for the right to pollute.)

Whilst trading arrangements may work within the nation state, there are doubts about their desirability and feasibility. A sense of justice demands that the rich countries of the world should compensate developing countries for their cooperation. Should rich countries simply be able to buy the right to pollute the planet? Surely all the world's population has an equal right to exploit the world's environmental resources. How can agreements be enforced, given the inevitably complex nature of these arrangements?

CIVIL LIABILITY AND THE PPP

The United States was a pioneer in the use of civil liability to ensure that the polluter pays for the damage done to the environment. The US Superfund legislation came into existence in 1980 with the Comprehensive Environmental Response Compensation and Liability Act (amended in 1986). This introduced the concept of strict liability, which meant that the plaintiff did not have to prove either negligence or causation on the part of the defendant. The idea behind this is that the polluter must pay to rectify environmental damage and that companies will be subject to very considerable legal costs associated with the damage that they cause. Effective civil liabilities legislation means that firms must behave with the utmost caution, because of the threat of significant legal costs being imposed upon them if they are found to have been the source of pollution. As a consequence most impose self-control over their activities and internalize environmental costs. This legislation should have a preventive and a precautionary effect, which implements the PPP and improves the enforcement of environmental rules. In the US, however, the scale of litigation following the introduction of this legislation has led to the view that it is the lawyers who have cleaned up rather than the environment.

The Seveso[2] and Sandoz[3] incidents led to calls for the EU to consider introducing measures to promote civil liability. Environmental liability legislation has been introduced in a number of member states within the EU, and although the nature of the legislation varies, it has a common feature: polluters are responsible for remedying damage. The case for the European Union's involvement in civil liability is that many environmental problems are transnational. Consequently, there is a danger that a patchwork of initiatives at the member states level will lead to a less than comprehensive regime. There is a need for legislation that covers all aspects of environmental degradation, including that of flora and fauna. In addition, the rules with respect to the legal processes involved should be harmonized and the process needs to be effective, but at a reasonable cost.

The variety of different national systems may lead to distortions in the competition process across the EU that might be exploited. For this reason there is business support for the idea of an EU-wide policy. A survey conducted for Green Alliance suggests that, in the UK, 73 per cent of businesses favour the strict EU code on environmental liability (Parkinson 1997). The prospect of wide-ranging legislation with respect to environmental civil liability raises the expectation of a considerable business opportunity for the insurance industry, should it ever be adopted. Any liability will be difficult to insure against, however, if it is made retrospective, or indeed if the extent of any liability is unclear. The banking sector is also likely to feel considerable unease about lending money to areas, where there is a fear of environmental blight.

The picture is confusing with respect to opposition to an EU-wide approach to civil liability. Some member states are opposed to the detailed aspects of many of the proposals, while others believe that national laws are already adequate to cover most situations. Finally, there are those who believe that EU involvement will contravene the principle of subsidiarity.

In 1989 the draft directive on 'Civil liability for damage caused by waste' (CEC 1989) was published, and this was modified substantially in 1991. The EU's draft directive of 1989 declared in article 3 that 'the producer of waste shall be responsible under civil law for the damage and injury to the environment caused by the waste, irrespective of fault on his part'. The draft directive called for damages to be paid and for restoration of the environment that was in a previously undamaged state. The issue remained the subject of debate and was an element of the Green Paper 'Remedying environmental damage' (CEC 1993a). By 1997, the Commission was still proposing no-fault liability in line with national regimes, and that the regimes should cover only future damage. The prospect of trying to unravel the problems of the past, especially in Eastern Germany and within an enlarged EU involving states from Central and Eastern Europe, meant that any other option would be impractical.

In 1993, a European-wide initiative was launched to harmonize approaches to civil liability by the Council of Europe with the Lugarno Convention on Civil Liability for Damage Resulting from Activities Dangerous to the Environment. However, by 1997 only five member states had signed the Convention. These were Finland, Greece, Luxembourg, Italy and the Netherlands, with the UK and Germany opposing it, as the Convention differed from their own established regimes.

Attempts to introduce an EU-wide perspective on civil liability foundered on the basis that no one scheme appeared to be acceptable to all members. In particular, the larger member states feel that their national schemes are superior and they are reluctant to be constrained by EU-wide initiatives. This has left three basic options that might be adopted at some time in the future:

- A directive covering traditional and environmental damage. This would include damage to persons and property, as well as the problem of cleaning up of sites and ecological damage. The drawback to the proposal was the opposition of France, Germany and the United Kingdom.
- Accession of the EU to the Lugarno Convention of 1993. Membership of the Convention would not require specific EU legislation and would be easy to extend to Central and Eastern Europe.
- An EU directive on liability for environmental damage alone. This would tie up the loopholes of national legislation, most notably the sharing of liability for ecological damage. This kind of directive would be a guide to national authorities, which would introduce their own legislation. Once again there was opposition from France, Germany and the United Kingdom (European Report 1997a).

TAXES AND SUBSIDIES

Consumers generally consider only the monetary cost of their purchases, and generally they pay as low a price as possible. They find it difficult to understand that many environmental resources are underpriced, and as a consequence are overused. In the case of water and energy, for example, the price of the goods fails to capture their environmental cost. Indeed, governments often see their provision as a social service, which leads them to give environmentally perverse subsidies and tax allowances, because they worry about the impact of their prices on the distribution of income. Pigou believed that it was possible to devise a system of taxes and subsidies to correct the social costs that were not incorporated into private decision making. This was an essentially pragmatic approach, where state officials or agencies evaluated the level of taxation that was required to reduce pollution to a socially acceptable level. Taxes would be applied to reduce output and to make firms understand the true cost of production. Pigou also advocated the use of subsidies as a compensation to be paid to citizens harmed by pollution. This does not, of course, help to reduce the level of pollution (Pigou, 1920).

The problem with this approach is that it is oversimplified. It does not take into account that in the real world many problems are interrelated. It is also not very often clear what the actual cost of environmental degradation is either to the firm or to society. Although the use of taxes might move society towards a more efficient solution, some groups will still inevitably suffer as a result of the pollution that takes place.

In the private marketplace equilibrium is reached when demand for the product is equal to the marginal private cost of the product (supply price). If motor cars and petrol were left untaxed, the number of vehicles on the roads would increase very substantially. We are aware, however, that the motor car causes environmental damage and severe congestion, and we would like to reduce its use in society. That is, the marginal social cost of motoring is far higher than the marginal private cost.[4] This is illustrated in Figure 5.1.

In Figure 5.1, the demand for vehicle miles is *D*. This is also the marginal benefit curve (*MB*). Marginal private cost is shown by *MPC*, but this is lower than society would prefer, because it does not take account of the problems associated with pollution and congestion. Vehicle miles are too high at *OQ*. The

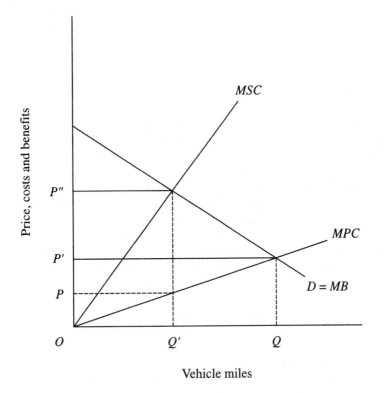

Figure 5.1   Social versus market equilibrium

true cost to society is shown by the marginal social cost (*MSC*) curve. If the market is to be in social equilibrium, taxes should be set at such a rate as to reduce the number of vehicle miles from Q to Q'. This means that a tax of P, P'' should be imposed.

There are benefits to be gained from imposing taxes on goods that cause pollution; they include charging the user for something which is unpriced, and making it possible to estimate the optimum rate of pollution. This is of course dependent on knowing what the damage costs and abatement costs are.

There are also disadvantages, however, which include the objections put forward by industry that taxes may well be set too high. That is, taxes might be set at a level beyond the optimum level of pollution. Because it is difficult to judge the damage caused by pollution, it is difficult to set the optimum rate of taxation. Also, taxes that are set on a national basis may reduce a country's international competitiveness. Ideally, environmental taxes should be imposed on all the players in the market, which means that they should be set on a global basis in some cases. This is difficult in practice.

THE APPLICATION OF ENVIRONMENTAL TAXES

Despite the fact that the Fifth Environmental Action Programme recommended a greater use of environmental taxes, little progress has been made in implementing them at the EU level. However, the European Environmental Agency (EEA) pointed out that the use of taxes at the member state level increased substantially in the period from 1990 to 1996. As a proportion of overall taxes, ecotaxes only amounted to 1.5 per cent of the total, but if energy taxes are taken into account, this percentage rose to 5.2 per cent. In some countries it was higher: for example in the Netherlands and Denmark it rose by 1.5 per cent and 4 per cent respectively. Energy taxes have, however, proved to be more important, accounting for 5.2 per cent of all EU taxes. In Portugal and Greece they represented 10 per cent of all taxes, while in Italy and the UK they were between 6 and 7 per cent (Chemical Business News Base 1996). The reason for member states' reluctance to introduce environmental taxes is their perceived impact upon competitiveness, employment and the distribution of income.

The EEA, however, suggested that a well-designed tax could stimulate competitiveness, and in a study of 16 environmental taxes, they found that these were environmentally effective at a reasonable cost (European Environmental Agency 1996: 52–61). The EEA found that certain taxes at the national level are particularly important in reducing environmental problems. For example, a Danish scheme to place a charge on the disposal (via dumping and incineration) of non-hazardous waste was found to have made a significant contribution towards encouraging the recycling of waste. However, a Swedish levy on lead batteries had only a limited impact, because a viable alternative product was not available. A Dutch levy on aircraft noise also had a very limited effect on noise levels, although it was successful in raising revenue. The EEA believes that the use of eco-taxes can provide a multiple dividend, and that their use should be extended by adopting them in more European countries, increasing their harmonization and compatibility at the EU level, and developing a new tax base for applications of such taxes to the transport sector, tourism, land management, and water and mineral resources.

The adoption of eco-taxes at the EU level is, however, likely to be resisted by the member states, as the setting and collection of taxes is close to the heart of national sovereignty. As a consequence, the EU uses unanimous voting for taxation issues as stated in article 93 TEC (99 TEC). This means that any member state can prevent EU policy which it believes to be against its national interest from being adopted. Any EU-wide initiative is likely to conflict with national taxes, subsidies and regulations, because taxes have to be set at a relatively high rate to have an impact. If taxes just add to industrial costs, this could significantly reduce European competitiveness. Where member states apply taxes, these might interfere with the operation of the single market and as such might be challenged by the Commission. Finally, there is a fear that eco-taxes applied within Europe might interfere with world trade rules.

Advocates of eco-taxes within the EU believe that these objections can be removed by the careful design of taxes, and the use of environmental taxes as part of an overall policy package. Extensive consultation and a gradual approach could ease their implementation (European Environment Agency 1996: 7). None of these tactics is likely to work at the EU level, but at the national level there have been some successes, the most important one being the use of fiscal incentives to encourage a switch to unleaded petrol.

In most member states, unleaded petrol is taxed at a lower rate of excise duty than leaded petrol. In 1986 unleaded petrol only took 1.7 per cent of the market, but this had risen to 40.7 per cent in 1991, 56 per cent in 1993, 62.4 per cent in 1994 and 76 per cent in 1998 (CEC 1996p). The switch to unleaded petrol can therefore be attributed to its immediate price advantage, combined with the changed technical specifications for cars, which came about because of the rising popularity of unleaded petrol (see also Chapter 10).

THE CARBON/ENERGY TAX: A CASE STUDY IN THE USE OF ECONOMIC INSTRUMENTS

The proposal to introduce a carbon/energy tax was the source of active debate within the EU. Although it was the subject of intensive study by the Commission and others (CEC 1992e: 65), no progress was made towards its introduction on an EU-wide basis, making it an ideal case study in the failure of such initiatives. Because it was designed to have a significant impact upon business behaviour, it cut across national policies to a significant extent, and was consequently regarded as unacceptable.

In 1990, the Council of Ministers agreed to take action to stabilize the level of carbon dioxide emissions at 1990 levels by the year 2000, that is, to stop the inexorable increase in carbon dioxide emissions which arise mainly through the burning of fossil fuels. The reason for attempting to stabilize this level was that carbon dioxide was seen as a major source of global warming. A carbon tax was believed to be a viable means of control because there were no practical methods of absorbing CO_2 at source. It was proposed to introduce a tax which would be equivalent to $3 per barrel of oil in 1993 and additionally $1 per barrel would be imposed until the year 2000, giving a total tax of $10 per barrel. The commissioner proposed that the tax should be levied on the basis of 50 per cent according to the carbon content of fuel and 50 per cent according to its energy content. This was, therefore, not a straight carbon tax. The reason for not imposing a pure carbon tax was that it would be a major incentive to switch fuels, for example from coal to nuclear power. There was, moreover, a wish to ensure that nuclear power was not treated too favourably and that the security of the coal industry would be guaranteed.

The principles behind the proposed tax were that it should be efficient, by achieving the target for CO_2 emissions at least cost, and it should be equitable, in the sense that it did not have significant distributional consequences. The adoption of the tax would have been in line with the concept of 'no regrets'. That is, even if the greenhouse effect should pose no problems, reducing CO_2 and energy consumption would make sense. This is because the energy savings would promote greater efficiency, and therefore there would be long-term gains to be made.

The impact of the tax would have varied according to which particular member state it was applied to, because of the different structures of indirect taxation. In the UK it was estimated that it would increase real energy prices by about 25 – 30 per cent on average, with the heaviest burden falling on oil products and coal. The burden would be significantly less in terms of the final price on fuels which were already heavily taxed, such as petrol and diesel (House of Lords 1992a). It was thought that the tax would raise £2.5 billion at $3 per barrel, rising to £8 billion at $10 per barrel. This was assuming that there would be no switching away from carbon products. Clearly if the tax were successful in reducing consumption of carbon fuels, then the tax take would be significantly less. The degree of support for the tax depended on the particular standpoint of the interest groups involved. For example, the nuclear power industry and the environmental group Friends of the Earth were generally in favour of the tax; industrialists, the coal industry and other heavy users of carbon fuels were generally sceptical about its effectiveness. The reasons for the scepticism varied, ranging from a fear that the tax would make industry uncompetitive to a belief that imposing the tax would simply encourage end users to switch to other sources.

The purpose of the tax was simple. It was designed to increase the supply price of carbon fuels and thus reduce consumption. In practice there are a number of problems with this view. First, the demand for energy tended to be uncertain over time, partly because it depended upon the pace of economic growth. If economies are growing rapidly, energy demands tend to increase sharply. Second, the rate of technological process is uncertain. Only if industry and the consumer believe that there is an adequate incentive will they invest in energy conservation and, even if they do, it takes time for new technology to come on stream. Third, world energy prices are uncertain. They depend on a complex interaction between demand and supply on a worldwide basis. So, for example, new discoveries of energy sources can bring prices down quite rapidly, whilst political unrest can raise them quite quickly. Finally, the elasticity of demand for carbon energy sources is uncertain. However, there is a general consensus that it does tend to be fairly low, meaning that, if energy prices rise, this would still not choke off a significant level of demand. The reason why the level of elasticity demand for energy is relatively low is that the market tends to be imperfect.

Many firms regarded the carbon/energy tax as just another cost, and there is certainly no guarantee that it would quickly have led to reduced consumption. Sectors like coal would have suffered very badly because it was anticipated that prices would have risen by as much as 58 per cent, compared to the transport sector, where gasoline and diesel prices would only have risen by 6 to 11 per cent respectively (House of Lords 1992a: evidence 29).

If an energy tax were compensated for by a reduction in other taxes, the impact on overall tax revenue would be neutral. Alternatively, the tax could be earmarked for spending on additional government programmes, which would increase the overall tax burden and expand the share of government spending as a percentage of GDP. The purpose of this tax was, however, to change relative prices rather than permit the expansion of government spending. Unless all member states adopted the same level of carbon/energy tax, this may have had an impact on trade; hence the suggestion of a common rate and tax base. However, where global competition was involved, there was a fear that some industries would lose out to global competitors who are able to take advantage of cheap energy supplies.

The tax would have sectoral effects, but these would depend upon the energy mix used within the firm, and the overall energy intensity. It would also have an impact upon individual income distribution, with a relatively high burden being placed on poor households in terms of domestic heating. Better-off households would pay more in terms of fuel cost for motor cars. It would also affect other products that people buy.

Any tax of this type would have an effect on world energy markets, if it were a success. It would reduce the demand for energy, or at least move some way towards stabilizing it. This in turn could reduce the price of international energy supplies, in particular oil.

The carbon/energy tax was not adopted on an EU-wide basis, but it did become an element of national environmental strategies. Denmark introduced a carbon tax in 1992 and simultaneously reduced excise duty so that prices were not raised. The tax was not applied to alternative energy sources. In 1992 the Netherlands also introduced a tax on fuel based upon energy and carbon levels, but lowering excise duties did not compensate this tax.

At the Florence European Council in June 1996, the Council of Finance Ministers suggested developing a tax system 'taking into account the need to create a tax environment that stimulates enterprise and job creation and promotes a more effective environmental policy' (*European Report* 1996). The October 1996 Commission responded to this by proposing a widening of the tax base on energy sources. The only tax that applies to energy across the whole of the EU and that is likely to have an effect on consumption is the excise duty, which applies to mineral oils. However, natural gas and coal are responsible for 30 per cent of CO_2 emissions, which seems to point to a justification for broadening the tax base. The first step in the process would be to bring about a closer convergence of excise duties, so that market distortions are not created by firms moving to take advantage of lower energy prices. In addition to this, there is an element of cross-border shopping associated with the movement of vehicles. Restrictions are still in place with respect to the amount of fuel that can be carried across borders in the tanks of trucks.

It was suggested by the Commission that a movement towards taxing energy in a more harmonized way would offer the possibility of reducing energy consumption, while at the same time maintaining the overall level of taxation in an economy. The additional revenue from the energy tax would have given scope for reducing taxes on labour, which would assist industrial competitiveness. Generally, industry was somewhat sceptical of these claims. In Germany, for example, industry lobbied against the proposals because it was felt that the overall level of taxation was too high, and it did not trust the government to reduce payroll taxes (Boulton 1996b).

CONCLUSION

Economic instruments are generally underutilized by the EU and the member states with respect to environmental policy. Whilst there are many problems associated with the use of such instruments, they do widen the range of policy tools available. In particular, they can provide an important incentive to improve environmental standards beyond the minimum levels laid down by the regulatory approach.

There will doubtless be many proposals for an EU-wide use of economic instruments, but these are unlikely to be adopted. The member states are unwilling to cede their powers of taxation to the EU, and the EU's budget is too small in its own right to have an impact. The EU's role is therefore more likely to be that of monitoring the schemes which have been implemented by the member states. Consequently, the complaint that the EU's role with respect to economic instruments will inevitably be tied to monitoring the single market appears to be justified.

The member-state focus of economic instruments may mean that they will become widely adopted. The budgetary pressures facing the member states mean that they will be tempted to use any viable excuse to widen their taxation base. With this in mind, the preservation of the environment will be the cause that will be cited, in many cases where the taxation burden increases. What would be more helpful to the case for adopting eco-taxes is if the burden to taxation were shifted so as to offset the increased costs to firms in one area by a reduction of costs in another.

NOTES

1. Also, if we take a narrow technical definition of public goods, additional users should not add to the cost of provision. Clearly this is a condition that does not apply to the exploitation of the environment. Additional users do imply additional environmental costs. For example, the more internal combustion engines that discharge into the environment, the greater the risk of environmental damage.
2. In 1976 a disaster at Seveso near Milan in Italy led to the surrounding area being polluted by toxic dioxin dust. No one was killed immediately, but animals had to be slaughtered and land became sterilized.
3. In 1986 an accident at the Sandoz plant at Basle in Switzerland led to extensive pollution along the whole length of the Rhine.
4. It is estimated that the external costs of road transport may be as high as 4.2 per cent of the EU's GDP (European Environment Agency 1996: 15).

6 Trade and the environment

INTRODUCTION

The purpose of this chapter is to examine the interrelationship between trade and environmental policy. This brings together two basic and related themes. The first is the impact that trade liberalization has on environmental policy. The second is the role of the EU in combating environmental nationalism (protectionism). The view that trade and environment policies can be designed in a way that supports sustainable development has been central to the EU's policy. This orthodoxy is based on the belief that an open multilateral trading system leads to the most efficient use of resources, and consequently reduces the demands on the environment. Not only does an open trading system allow countries to exploit their comparative advantage and specialize in what they do best; it also facilitates the transfer of environmentally sound technologies. Finally, because trade assists the growth of income, it can generate resources that can be devoted to environmental improvements. Indeed, no one would consider restricting trade if it were not for the existence of nation states and their national political agendas.

The reality is that national political agendas do exist and they are driven by social, cultural and economic factors. International trade is becoming ever more important. The European Union must therefore manage the process of reconciling a growth in trade, which is part of its *raison d'être*, and the need to deal with any environmental issues created by a more open European and global economy. Negative effects can arise as a result of trade, for example the economic growth process can lead to pressure on environmental resources. Also, the trade process may undermine national environmental policies, as countries with lower standards seek to gain a trade advantage.

The internationalization of environmental concerns can be attributed to a number of factors, including:

- improved international scientific understanding of problems, which has not only helped to define the problems, but has also provided a range of possible solutions;
- increased pressure from domestic and international environmental groups;
- the progress that many countries have made with domestic environmental problems, which has led those countries to consider a broader agenda;

- the increased extent of regional and international economic integration (Blackhurst and Subramanian 1992: 249).

The 1992 UN Conference on Environment and Development (UNCED), held in Rio de Janeiro, led to the adoption of the action programme Agenda 21. Chapter 2 of this sets the objective of making international trade and environmental policies mutually supportive. The EU's Fifth Environmental Action Programme also considered the integration of trade and environmental policies as one of its main priorities (CEC 1996b). In this respect there is a degree of harmony between what the EU is trying to achieve within its own competence and what it wishes to support on a global basis through organizations such as the World Trade Organization (WTO). However, the EU has made little progress with its international agenda, compared to what has happened domestically.

Regulation with respect to the environment is a legitimate policy tool, and reflects consumers' wishes via the political process. Despite this, industrial lobbying can be well organized in particular sectors of the economy, and industries frequently complain that excessive regulation is a threat to their competitive position because of the risk of eco-dumping. Demands are made to protect jobs either by restricting trade or by deregulation.

Related to this issue is the fear that 'eco-duties' might be imposed on imported goods in order to compensate for the unfair advantages that lower environmental standards can offer. There is also the threat that higher environmental standards can, in some cases, lead to trade restrictions being imposed by states wishing to lead the world in this area.

THE ENVIRONMENTAL IMPACT OF TRADE

The links between trade and environmental policy issues have become increasingly complex as national policy makers have recognized the extent to which the effectiveness of domestic policy is constrained by regional and global influences. In economic terms, there is a need to reach agreements between countries because of a lack of enforceable property rights. Trade has an impact on the environment because it affects where goods are produced and sold in the global economy. Even where environmental policies are set within nation states they can have an impact on other countries; for example, environmental taxes, subsidies and standards can alter market conditions. These can not only change the competitiveness of domestic producers, but also reduce the access of foreign producers to markets. Trade policy can have a beneficial effect in promoting cooperation between countries that have specific environmental objectives. Table 6.1 sets out the potential that trade has to generate both positive and negative environmental effects.

Table 6.1   The positive and negative environmental impacts of trade

Effects	Positive	Negative
Products	Increased trade in goods that are environmentally beneficial, e.g. biodegradable containers	Increased trade in environmentally damaging products, e.g. hazardous wastes
Technology	Reduced pollution per unit of output	Spreading dirty technologies, e.g. toxic pesticides
Scale effects	Better environmental protection if trade gives the resources for environmental protection because of economic growth	Increased production without improved environmental protection
Structural effects – changes in patterns of economic activity	Improved method of production, e.g. more extensive methods of agriculture	The need to increase agricultural production for overseas markets leads to the drainage of wetlands
Policy	Improved policies because of international agreements	Reduced standards because of the need to become internationally competitive

Source: OECD (1994a).

There are some aspects of environmental degradation that can be contained if the movement of goods is restricted and the transport system is kept as a means of serving discrete regions. Environmental degradation may be caused by pollutants being transported across borders as part of normal trading activity, or because the act of engaging in trade encourages processes which are harmful. It is therefore possible to construct a case that suggests that trade should be restricted in order to protect the environment. Added to this, there is the prospect that a very competitive international economy will lead to a situation where traded goods are forced down in price to the point where they are below their 'true cost' of production. That is, the trading system disregards negative externalities (see Chapter 5). A middle ground should be found between the supporters of free trade who believe that the cost of protectionism is generally underestimated, and the view of many environmentalists who believe that the cost of environmental degradation is generally misunderstood.

Circumstances have therefore dictated that the EU accommodate these developments in its international relations. Not unnaturally, the EU takes the view that trade is not automatically a bad thing for the environment. Indeed, it might lead to more efficient use of natural resources and the development of new technology to encourage sustainable development (*Europe* 1996a). The environment industry has created an important world market valued at somewhere in the region of $250 billion per year – and one that is growing at an annual rate of 8 per cent. In a macroeconomic sense it may well be that environmentally friendly production processes are not a drag on economic growth. The EU has argued that whilst environmental measures can increase the cost of industry, overall these costs are not decisive, representing only 1–2 per cent of production costs in the EU (*Europe* 1996a). That does not, however, mean that environmental costs are not a considerable burden on some industries. They are costs that many would do without, if they were offered a clear choice. The process of trade might provide this opportunity.

There is a need to consider how standards and rules are set with respect to the environment, whether at a global or regional level. Rules must take account of the comparative environmental advantage that some areas enjoy and the particular sensitivity of ecosystems to pollution. There must also be an acknowledgement of the difficulties that certain states will have in reaching environmental standards and their unwillingness to obey any rules that are set. A pattern is emerging of certain countries taking the lead with respect to environmental issues, but this leadership is not always a welcome phenomenon. Indeed, excessive zeal might be seen as a form of environmental imperialism, imposing values and cultures upon people in other states. The key issue of who sets environmental standards and how they are enforced must be dealt with sensitively. In the EU, enforcement is dealt with by its institutional structures, and ultimately by the European Court of Justice. At the global level, sanctions tend to be brought against countries breaking environmental rules, but not on a consistent basis. The larger states and larger groupings of states can resist international sanctions unless there is concerted action. The international community, once it has exhausted its political processes, normally resorts to the use of trade sanctions in order to make its environmental case, but this is far from ideal.

THE NEED FOR INTERNATIONAL RULES

The long-term trend is for international trade to grow faster than national economies. In 1998 the volume of world merchandise exports grew by 3.5 per cent while world output declined by 2 per cent (WTO, 1999). This trend is likely to continue as the influence of the WTO grows. The expansion of global trade and the prospect of market failure with respect to the protection of the environment have created a powerful case for establishing an international set of rules to address the problem. Unfortunately, progress in this area has been slow, in part because of an inability of the world's major trading blocs to come to a clear consensus on the action that should be taken. Resolving this problem must be a priority for the future.

The driving force behind the growth in the world system has been the liberalization of trade. The collapse of the communist states of Central and Eastern Europe removed the last major obstacle to the acceptance of free trade ideas. It made membership of the WTO an important aspect of most countries' international strategy. In July 1999 the WTO had 135 members and covered 90 per cent of world trade. Membership of the WTO places significant obligations on its members to avoid trade restrictions that are discriminatory. This provides much of the context of the EU's international trading relations. Trade and environment issues were not central to the Uruguay Round negotiations, but it was inevitable that environmental issues would be addressed. Indeed the preamble to the WTO Agreement included a direct reference to the objective of sustainable development and to the need to protect and preserve the environment. For example, the Agreement on Technical Barriers to Trade took account of governments' use of measures to protect human, animal and plant life and health and the environment. The Agreement on Agriculture exempted direct payments under environmental programmes from WTO members' commitments to reduce domestic support for agricultural production, subject to certain conditions. Both of these are examples of where EU policies match WTO requirements.

In 1991, discussions about trade and environment were initiated in the General Agreement on Tariffs and Trade (GATT) in the working group on Environmental Measures and International Trade (EMIT). When the Uruguay Round was approved in April 1994, the trade ministers picked up the issue more formally by starting work on a trade and environment programme. A WTO Committee on Trade and Environment (CTE) was established to bring sustainable development issues on to the agenda of the multilateral trading system. Their first annual report was presented to the Council of Ministers at the 1996 ministerial conference in Singapore. The CTE has a remit for all areas of trade, but it is not intended to be an environmental agency. Its task is not to review national environmental policies or to set global standards, but to safeguard the principles of the multilateral trading system. Whilst the CTE was initially welcomed when it was launched, it was later criticized for being slow and losing direction and focus. Renato Rugiero, the Director-General of the WTO, commented that the 'committee clearly needs fresh political impetus' (*Europe* 1998d).

The rules of the WTO with respect to the environment are restricted to ensuring that the flows of world trade are not disrupted. Articles I and III of the GATT oblige partners to treat imports from any other member of the GATT in a non-discriminatory way. Also, they should ensure that imports are not discriminated against with respect to domestically produced items. However article XX of the GATT permits trade restrictions that are 'necessary to protect human, animal or plant life or health' or which 'relate to the conservation of exhaustible natural resources', but they should not infringe the rules on transparency and non-discrimination.

It is in the nature of many environmental problems that they are transboundary or global. In response to this, governments generally prefer cooperative solutions, and one way of achieving this is via multilateral environmental agreements (MEAs).[1] MEAs do not have all-embracing memberships and may have only limited environmental objectives. The benefit of this approach is that it helps to link together participants who share common objectives. It was an approach endorsed by the 1992 Earth Summit at Rio de Janeiro.

Although some MEAs contain trade restrictions, they are not accommodated within the rules of the WTO. Compliance with WTO requirements may create problems because each body may have a different membership. Trade problems can arise where MEA rules conflict with the requirement of market access, but there is little evidence of this. In expressing the EU's endorsement of MEAs, Leon Brittan suggested that they should not be frustrated if they enjoyed widespread support. However, he believed that trade restrictions should be used with care against non-members (Brittan 1998). For the future, article XX of the GATT should be amended to include methods of dealing with MEAs. It may even be that special arrangements could be put into place to deal with trade and environment issues at the WTO level. These would have to be incorporated into the WTO's dispute mechanisms, however, because of the danger that jurisdictional disputes might arise.

The size of the WTO and its very disparate membership mean that it will always take time to make important decisions. The 15 members of the EU, with its regional focus, have a greater chance of reaching a clear consensus about policy. This has led to a situation where the various institutions of the EU have criticized the performance of the WTO. In addition to the Commission, whose observations we noted above, the European Parliament has also been critical.

THE SINGLE MARKET

The creation of a single market (internal market) is a fundamental provision of the Treaty of Rome and is the driving force behind the process of economic integration. Until recently progress towards implementing the 'four freedoms' (free movement of people, goods, capital and services) was disappointing, Whilst tariff barriers within the EU were quickly removed, non-tariff barriers (NTBs) still remained more than 40 years after its creation. These barriers to trade ensured that traded products that had an environmental impact would have only a limited circulation throughout the EU. In particular:

- goods were stopped and subjects checked at frontiers;
- most products had to comply with different national laws of the member states;
- transport systems were mostly nationally based and not subject to international competition.

The launch of the single market programme in 1985 signalled a realization that NTBs were one factor contributing towards slow growth in the European economy. It was recognized that removing barriers to trade would reduce the transaction costs of doing business across the whole of the EU, and as a consequence expand trade. Following this, competition would become more intense, with industry becoming increasingly specialized within regions. The White Paper on 'Completing the Internal Market' (CEC 1985) did not deal directly with environmental policy, although it was concerned with the free movement of goods that have an environmental impact. It categorized NTBs under three main headings: physical barriers such as customs posts; technical barriers that related to differing national standards; and fiscal barriers, including differing taxation and subsidy regimes. Many of these NTBs protected the environment of individual member states either by design, or as a by-product of their existence. The Single European Act (SEA), which came into force in 1987, speeded up the single market legislative process. It dealt with the problem of harmonization of standards as well as the need to include environmental protection considerations in other policy areas (see Chapter 2 for a more detailed analysis of the SEA).

The White Paper initially identified nearly 300 measures that would complete the single market. Of these, 221 required directives that necessitated legislation to be passed in each of the member states. In addition to this, a number of other measures were passed, leading to nearly 1400 pieces of legislation being brought into force to bring the venture to its conclusion. Despite some legislative success, a late start to the programme and a degree of national intransigence meant that the deadline had to be extended from 1 January 1993 to 1 January 1999. In reality it may take many decades to rid the EU of all its NTBs.

There were delays in transposing legislation at the national level, which resulted in a very uneven implementation. By June 1999, 87.2 per cent of the White Paper's measures had been transposed in their entirety into the 15 member states. Portugal's transposition deficit was the highest at 5.5 per cent (CEC 1999a). This suggests that the EU had made considerable progress in achieving completion by the revised 1999 deadline. The pattern was not uniform across all sectors. The detailed statistics show that 14.3 per cent of the 89 directives concerning the environment and the single market were not transposed in all member states (CEC 1999e). Also, much of the legislation had been transposed poorly, adding to the uncertainty facing business. It could be argued that many of the delays in the transposition could be justified on the basis of an improved quality of national legislation. However, there is some evidence to suggest that the opposite might be true. There is a correlation between those countries that have the greatest number of infringement cases and those that are the slowest in transposing legislation (CEC 1998l: 8–9).

Uneven enforcement of EU legislation has been seen as a further complication leading to concerns about market distortion. A Commission survey found that 46 per cent of small and medium-sized enterprises (SMEs) were unaware of the procedure for registering complaints about the single market, and nearly 80 per cent of all firms found the effort of complaining outweighed the advantages (CEC 1997dd). The survey found that 59 per cent of large enterprises and 55 per cent of SMEs had encountered at least one obstacle to engaging in business across borders. Of these, 14.8 per cent of SMEs and 19.4 per cent of large firms cited environmental regulations as a barrier (CEC 1997dd). The EU monitors progress in its annual reports on the single market, and these are complemented by the member states. A successful example of this is the UK's Single Market Compliance Unit, which is part of the Department of Industry. Here firms can make complaints about trade restrictions and request assistance in their removal.

There were early fears that the completion of the single market would have a negative effect on the environment, because it deprived the member states of their national control over traded goods. It was felt that economic growth might accelerate the depletion of resources and that open borders would encourage trade and the expansion of road haulage and air transport as well increasing the movement of nuclear and hazardous waste (CEC 1992f). In fact, as we have seen above, the completion of the single market is a process that is taking place over a number of years. This has allowed the creation of a greater body of common environmental rules governing the conduct of industry and markets.

The single market programme has not contributed towards a significant growth in consumerism. Indeed, its impact on EU living standards has been somewhat disappointing, as it contributed to a rise of between 1.1 and 1.5 per cent over the period 1987–93. The sweeping aside of many NTBs has led to growing competition between companies and an accelerated pace of industrial restructuring. The volume of inter-industry trade (IIT) has increased significantly. It has been estimated that the volume of manufactured goods traded increased by between 20 and 30 per cent in the period to the mid-1990s (CEC 1996s: 4). The completion of the single energy market has led to environmental improvements because of an increased use of gas. Gas is cleaner than many other fuels and its greater use should reduce CO_2 emissions by an estimated 105 million tonnes per year. The removal of border controls, liberalization and improved documentation have led to a faster and cheaper transport system. Between 1990 and 1995, there was a 300 per cent increase in the volume of road transport services delivered by road hauliers from different member states (CEC 1996s: 14). In part, this represents an improvement in the efficiency, but the growth in cross-border road traffic is an environmentally sensitive issue. The volume of cross-border road traffic is expected to increase further when the 1997 liberalization of EU road haulage has had its full effect. The areas where the additional volume will have its greatest environmental impact will be the transit regions (for example the Alps).

COMPETITION AMONG RULES

In the past, organizations had to accept the regulatory regime that the political process presented to them. Without mobility it was not possible to choose to apply the rules that existed in other countries, even if these were more advantageous. Once trade liberalization took a grip it was possible to choose different regulatory regimes, either as a consumer or producer. Producers in Europe can now choose where to locate, supported by the free movement of goods and services and by capital liberalization. Competition among rules is a global problem, but the creation of the single market within the European Union has increased the potential for this phenomenon to occur. In particular, with the movement towards mutual recognition of technical standards as a result of the 1979 Cassis de Dijon case,[2] products can now circulate freely throughout the European Union as long as they are safe and pose no threat to the health of the consumer.

A variety of cultural influences and legal traditions, along with differences in capacities of environments to absorb pollution, have all helped to shape the contrasting environmental regimes across Europe. These offer a potential for business exploitation, especially if public attitudes to environmental degradation or a lack of resources reduce willingness to reform in line with the rest of the EU. Also, a government might manipulate environmental rules in order to encourage industry to locate in its territory or offer an advantage to domestic industry already located there. These differences in approach to environmental protection can be seen when we compare the UK with other member states. The UK approach stresses the capacity of the environment to absorb pollution, in contrast to that of the Netherlands and Germany, which stress the flow of resources around the economy and not the production line approach. Before the completion of the single market these approaches could coexist; the removal of barriers has exposed the incompatability of the two systems (Weale 1994).

The advantage of competition among rules is that of choice and diversity. Standards can be made appropriate to the circumstances of the state concerned. If fewer restrictions result from the process, there should be less risk of regulatory failure and the system can be simplified. A variety of different regulatory systems may allow greater national sovereignty, although this may be eroded by the need to respond to the competitive process. Finally, differing rules can lead to experimentation and innovation, whilst a monolithic approach to environmental regulation may be somewhat static.

A problem may arise if competition among rules leads to the bidding down of standards. Initially, differences in environmental standards can generate competition, during which a degree of arbitrage takes place, with the commercial and industrial sector taking advantage of opportunities offered by the different rules. Finally, in order to protect their industrial base, countries may feel obliged to remove any environmental protection that is eroding national competitiveness. Alternatively, there could be a drift towards reimposing restrictions on trade in order to keep the system of environmental protection in place at the expense of the trading system. There is therefore a risk of market failure caused by 'free-riding' on different environmental standards, with the result that either the trading system does not work as it should, or the standard of environmental protection is reduced. (see Table 6.2)

Table 6.2   The consequences of completion of the single market for competition among rules

Positive if:	Negative if:
• There is a common commitment to higher environmental standards	• There is a weak commitment to higher environmental standards relative to other social/political/economic priorities
• Industry is not compelled to pursue the lowest-cost option and firms can take a long-term view	• Business is driven by a short-term profit motive
• High environmental standards are seen as a source of competitive advantage	• There is a strong emphasis on industrial competitiveness
Result	Result
• There is a bidding up of environmental standards	• Environmental 'free-riding' takes place. Either there is a general bidding downwards of environmental standards, or free trade is restricted

The gap between these positions can be bridged if there are no costs associated with higher environmental standards. Society might also learn from its past experience and develop an environmental consensus. This is, however, at best a long-term consequence of the competitive process.

TAX COMPETITION

A similar concept to competition among rules is tax competition. This arises where the process of trade liberalization exposes the incompatibility of different tax regimes. The movement of goods and enterprises erodes the ability of countries to maintain different tax bases and levels of taxation. This weakens their ability to impose environmental taxes, because it might result in loss of industry rather than acting as an incentive to produce more efficiently and in a more environmentally friendly way. Attempts to gain agreement about imposition of carbon/energy taxes have failed because of a lack of willingness of the big players in the world economy to agree on a common implementation. Japan, the United States and the European Union refused to agree to impose such taxes unless everyone agreed to implement them. Without such general agreement there is a fear that some countries will 'free-ride' by taking advantage of the lower costs of being outside these agreements. Suggestions that the European Union might go it alone with respect to carbon/energy taxes have come to nothing.

Within the European Union, there has only been limited progress towards harmonization of taxes because this area is at the heart of the sovereignty of the member states. Article 93 TEC (99 TEC) maintains the right of member states to insist on unanimous agreement with respect to tax harmonization. Within the EU there is no suggestion that tax competition in relation to environmental taxes is taking place, although it could happen. In 1997, the Commission decided that it needed more information on the 'harmful' effects of 'unfair competition'. It was also felt that a 'code of good conduct' should be developed to stop harmful tax competition (*Economist* 1997a). It is, however, reasonable to assume that member states take care to ensure that their environmental taxes do not damage their own national competitiveness.

COMBATING ENVIRONMENTAL NATIONALISM

One consequence of the completion of the single market is the fear that national environmental standards will become a barrier to trade. In 1994 the Economic and Social Committee warned of a general and increasing trend towards protectionism through the use of national environmental measures (ECOSOC 1994: 14). An increasing number of product-related national environmental laws, decrees or voluntary agreements were emerging as new non-tariff barriers to trade to protect national industry. The consequence of this was that the EU's collective investment in the creation of the single market was threatened.

The justification for the continued maintenance of national standards is based either on the desire of the member states to achieve environmental improvement for their national citizens, or the wish to retain an environmental comparative advantage which will benefit economic development. The result of the flight to the 'moral high ground' is to foster 'environmental nationalism'. The Commission believes that an EU-wide framework could be the best guarantee of striking the right balance between single market and environmental objectives. They assert that 'Environmental policy is an essential component of the creation of the internal market ... Moreover, effective environmental protection, which goes beyond national borders, can only be achieved in the framework of a functioning internal market and common environmental rules' (CEC 1996a: 62). To make this a reality demands an adequate regulatory framework. Without this, the member states may adopt diverging legislation in the environmental field that could fragment the single market.

Trade restrictions have frequently been used to assist declining national industries or to promote the growth of new ones. Generally economic protectionism tends to be universally condemned as destructive to the trading system. Environmental nationalism is different because, instead of being justified on the basis of narrow self-interest, it presents itself as synonymous with health and safety regulations. That is, it is portrayed as essential to protect citizens from a significant nuisance. More stringent national environmental measures are said to offer an example for other states to emulate. The measures are justified as being the way forward that all 'right-thinking' environmentally concerned states should follow. Environmental protectionist states frequently wish to be seen as pioneers who are making sacrifices in order to demonstrate to the world a better way to manage the protection of the environment. They are often admired rather than condemned. For these states trade distortion is seen merely as an unfortunate price to pay for environmental protection.

It may be perceived to be in the interests of the poorer states of the EU to maintain lower environmental standards as a means of attracting industry, which is looking to locate where there are reduced financial implications from national environmental standards. Advocates of the removal of regulation portray this as the freeing of the economy from the constraints of bureaucracy. It is seen as a way to release the dynamics of the market, which in turn will help to create jobs and stimulate economic growth. Deregulation is believed by many to be the cure for the slow growth of the European economy and part of the solution to persistently high levels of unemployment.

There are a number of developments within the EU which have led to concerns about the emergence of environmental nationalism. These include:

- article 95 TEC (100a: 4 TEC) which allows member states to 'opt out' of harmonization measures on environmental grounds;
- continued uncertainty about the application of the principle of subsidiarity;
- the inadequate transposition of EU legislation into national law and poor implementation.

The impact of the maintenance of national environmental provisions acting as a barrier to trade is difficult to measure, especially if environmental protection is the declared justification. Relatively high trade costs, coupled with a small environmental benefit, would indicate that the true role of the measure is to restrict trade. If this is so, then there is a case for claiming that environmental nationalism exists. However, proving this is difficult, as definition of what is environmental protection remains very subjective. The imposition of differing product-related environmental measures is the most obvious and easily recognized example of this form of economic protectionism. However, within the single European market environmental nationalism may manifest itself in the existence of differences in environmental protection regulations for producing plants.

Lower national environmental standards for producing plants have the same effect as if the member states had given a subsidy to the industry. Differing technical standards can lead to a situation where there is potential for 'eco-dumping' and the creation of 'pollution havens', where industry will settle in order to avoid having to improve their own environmental standards. Profit-maximizing rationality dictates that firms should produce in the lowest-cost locations. Governments will seek to justify lower environmental standards on the grounds that domestic industries cannot afford to update their industrial practices. They may also argue that the national economic situation needs the investment and employment possibilities that accompany industrial relocation. Lower environmental standards are therefore an important tool for attracting inward investment. Finally, governments may assert that a comparative environmental advantage exists, and there is no need to introduce stringent standards. This is a defence that the British government has used, claiming that the North Sea is less susceptible to environmental damage than other areas of water within the EU.

Companies located in states with lower environmental standards can avoid the cost implications of the introduction of measures that will increase environmental protection. As a result trade is distorted because such companies gain an unfair advantage. Within the single market they can undercut their competitors and produce more cheaply. Not all companies can take advantage of the gains offered by lower environmental production standards. Those that can do so tend to be concentrated in the heavy manufacturing or extraction sectors which are linked to a particularly hazardous product and have major environmental impacts, for example pesticide production. Companies that can take advantage of lower production costs, because of lower environmental standards, are doing so at the expense of the environment. They may not only be imposing costs upon the citizens of the state where they are located, but also throughout the whole of the EU because of the close geographical proximity of the member states to one another.

WHO WILL HAVE THIS DIRTY INDUSTRY?

Unfair trade practices are a blunt instrument with which to deal with the problems of unemployment and structural changes in industry (Brack 1995: 509). Whilst eco-dumping amounts to an implicit subsidy for industry with low environmental standards, there is not much evidence that it is a tactic employed widely (OECD 1997b: 79). It is difficult to be certain of the cost to industry of differing environmental standards, and their potential for distorting competition. Even if environmental standards are different, it does not mean that industry will migrate because:

- environmental costs are only part of the costs facing a firm;
- customers may be prepared to pay more for products subject to higher environmental standards;
- schemes can be used to mitigate the cost of higher environmental standards, for example the use of subsidies, rebates and exceptions.

Even if industries would like to migrate to take advantage of lower environmental standards, they will not always be welcomed elsewhere. Low national environmental standards may be a sign that a country is unable to meet the cost of higher environmental standards for its existing industrial base, but it does not mean that it wants to attract more dirty industry. These migrating industries may generate higher levels of pollution and impose significant social costs due to health problems created by environmental degradation. In addition to this, they may be producing goods that have problems in finding markets in countries with higher environmental standards, because they are produced by dirty industry. Finally, dirty industries are often the ones that are stagnant or decaying, and have little long-term future.

THE IMPACT OF TREATY CHANGES

Treaty changes have increased the chance for environmental nationalism to develop. The Single European Act (SEA), the Maastricht Treaty and the Amsterdam Treaty all contained opportunities for the national governments to exploit loopholes in order to protect national industrial interests. Article 95 TEC (100a SEA and TEC) is concerned with harmonization measures necessary to enable the market to operate. It allowed for a national 'opt-out' for member states wishing to protect their environment, providing they were not introducing a disguised restriction on trade.

The precedent for use of the 'opt out' was set in the decision of the European Court of Justice[3] that allowed Germany a derogation from Directive 91/173/EC on the marketing and use of pentachlorophenol (PCP). Germany had imposed a national ban on the production, marketing and use of this chemical. In 1991 the European Union adopted a directive restricting the supply and use of PCP via qualified majority voting. The German government opposed this legislation and notified the Commission of its intention to continue to use the national regulations. In its ruling the ECJ decided that the health and environmental considerations given by Germany should have higher priority than economic or trade considerations and the derogation was allowed.

The ruling of the ECJ depends on establishing a basis for a concept of proportionality. If trade restrictions impose costs, then it is important that these costs are proportional to the environmental benefits being sought. If high trade costs and a low environmental benefit were the result, then clearly the underlying role of the measure is to restrict trade and not to improve the environment. What the ECJ ruling demonstrates is the vital need for relevant and independent information to be available before a judgement is made.

In the consolidated version of the Treaty, taking account of the changes introduced in Amsterdam, chapter 3 deals with the approximation of laws, regulations and administrative provisions of the member states that directly affect the establishment and functioning of the common market (single market). This is one area where the Treaty has been changed to promote higher environmental standards. Instead of merely making harmonization proposals, article 95 (100a TEC) requires the Commission, in making proposals in the areas of health, safety, environmental protection and consumer protection, to take as a base a high level of protection. They must also take particular account of any new development based on scientific facts. There are provisions for the member states to retain higher environmental standards and even to improve on those that currently exist.

- Member states can retain national environmental provisions on the grounds of the need to protect their environment. However, they must inform the Commission of these provisions and the reasons for retaining them (article 95:4 (100a:4 TEC)).
- Member states can introduce national provisions based on new scientific evidence relating to the protection of the environment. This applies to problems specific to that member state. This can happen after the adoption of the harmonization measure (article 95.5 TEC). The member state is required to notify the Commission of the envisaged provisions as well as the grounds for introducing them. This increases further the ability of member states to follow divergent national strategies.

It is then up to the Commission to decide if this provision is genuine or if it is really a form of arbitrary discrimination or disguised restriction on trade. The Commission then has six months to approve or reject the national provisions. If it does not respond, the national measures will be approved by default. (The Commission can request a further six months to deliver its response.) If the Commission believes that the member state is abusing its powers, the case can be referred to the Court of Justice. The Commission is expected to consult with member states if it believes that a national measure is distorting trade, and make recommendations on how this can be avoided. If a member state does not comply with the Commission's recommendation, other member states will not be required to amend their own provisions in order to eliminate such distortion. Finally, if the member state that has ignored the recommendation of the Commission causes distortion detrimental only to itself, sanctions will not apply.

The original provisions of the SEA were the result of pressure brought to bear by the Danish government during the negotiations to revise the Treaty. In protecting their own national standards the Danish government has supported opportunities for fragmentation of environmental policy. The potential use of the Treaty to protect national environmental standards was highlighted in the Pimenta Report to the European Parliament on the accession of Sweden, Finland and Austria (EP 1994b). It is not possible for Sweden, Finland and Austria to attempt to apply the provisions of the Treaty to existing EU legislation in retrospect. In ratifying first the European Economic Area Agreement and then the Accession Treaty, the governments of the three states have accepted all the EU legislation already adopted. However, the potential remains for the three new states of the EU to invoke the provisions of articles 95.4 and 95.5 in the future (see above).

In its 1996 overview of the single market, the Commission commented that fears that environmental legislation might lead to new market fragmentation by indiscriminate use of the Treaty 'opt-out' clause by member states had not been justified (CEC 1996s: 100). They believed this was because environmental objectives had been taken into account, and therefore there was less reason to resort to the 'opt-out'. In addition, because the 'opt-out' had only been used in a very limited number of cases, effects on the single market were minimal and the few cases concerned have had little impact on its trade and functioning. The Commission noted that 70 per cent of the chemical companies surveyed had found that EU environmental legislation has had a positive or neutral effect on overcoming barriers and obstacles to trade. However, 28 per cent of companies still considered that the introduction or the maintenance of national environmental measures that were stricter than those adopted by the EU had led to a loss of relative competitiveness.

SUBSIDIARITY

There is a great deal of debate about what the principle of subsidiarity means and much controversy surrounding its application. Concern continues that the national governments will attempt to use the subsidiarity principle as an excuse for maintaining national environmental standards. In the Sutherland Report on the operation of the single market (1992), it was suggested that the fragmentation of the single market might result from the application of the subsidiarity principle. Consequently, consistency in environmental measures had to be seen as a key element in achieving the single market (Sutherland 1992: 18).

The debate surrounding the inclusion of the principle of subsidiarity in the TEU showed the lack of consensus about its definition. The opportunity to use the application of the principle so as to protect national interests continues, as there has been no significant progress in reconciling these differences. (For a fuller discussion see Chapter 12.) A significant threat to the single market is the fact that governments are permitted to close their domestic markets by adopting higher environmental, health, safety or consumer standards (due to national exemptions permitted by the treaties). However, these concerns should not be overestimated and up to 1997 there have only been eight instances where these higher standards were invoked.

ECO-LABELLING

The EU adopted legislation on eco-labelling in 1992.[4] The rules are based on voluntary action, but they carry the potential to act as technical barriers to trade because they discriminate between products on the basis of environmental characteristics. (For a fuller discussion see Chapter 7.) The benefits to the environment accrue if the rules alter the pattern of consumers' behaviour and encourage the purchase of environmentally friendly products. The EU's scheme is based on national bodies establishing the relevant criteria for the different product groups. Involving the national governments and national testing agencies is in keeping with the commitment to apply the principle of subsidiarity to policy. The national governments are required to designate the competent bodies to propose the product groups and award the eco-labels. Once the system is established, the Commission has the responsibility for the adoption of the criteria and the management of the consultation between the national bodies.

The 'cradle to grave' approach has been utilized by the EU in its eco-labelling legislation. This approach relies on mechanisms being in place that enable some monitoring of the extraction and production processes to be undertaken, in most cases before the product is exported. These mechanisms remain the responsibility of the national governments and can therefore be used by national governments to protect domestic producers. Despite the extensive consultation procedure, and piloting of the eco-label scheme before it was adopted, trade distortion may result from:

- a lack of transparency in the national decisions about the environmental criteria on which the eco-label will be awarded;
- differences in the methodologies adopted by member states to identify the environmental criteria;
- the voluntary nature of the scheme;
- the continued widespread use of national labelling schemes for other products.

Other complications occur when EU regulation is partial (as in the case of emissions of titanium dioxide) and national legislation is comprehensive (as in the case of emissions of solvents). Also national eco-labelling schemes are in some cases mandatory, for example in life cycle analysis, but if consumers become accustomed to a national eco-label they may not purchase unlabelled imported goods.

DISPOSING OF WASTE PACKAGING

The packaging of goods is an essential element of the consumer society, but its disposal has become a pressing global issue. This has arisen because the cheaper and easier methods of disposal, such as the use of landfill sites, have become less viable, and because of growing consumer awareness. Most of the member states have national schemes to dispose of waste packaging. The basis of the schemes is varied, including in some states voluntary measures, in others a form of taxation. A large number of companies have been established within the EU to deal with the recovery, recycling and disposal of waste. Waste has become a tradable commodity as well as an externality generated by the production process. This does not mean that governments generally welcome the import of waste from abroad, largely because of negative public opinion.

The trade-distorting impact of the national eco-packaging schemes may be more damaging than the impact of eco-labelling within the EU. As member states' regulations covering packaging are based on positive discrimination, some impact on trade is both desirable and inevitable, if the cost of disposing of the waste is to be internalized into production costs. However, this becomes a problem in the single market if the packaging legislation is used as a form of positive discrimination against imported products. For companies that have to comply with differences in national packaging legislation, there are cost implications and the possibility of loss of competitiveness. Companies frequently find it difficult to penetrate a market due to a lack of information or misunderstanding about the national measures. The emergence of national regulations on waste and its disposal, particularly those introduced by the Danish and German governments, have become very contentious within the EU. The EU framework directive on packaging and packaging waste was adopted in December 1994 in an attempt to harmonize national legislation to avoid these problems.[5]

The conflict between the member states and the EU's packaging rules became apparent in 1977 and 1982, when the Danish government introduced strict requirements to cover containers used for drinks of various types. Beer and soft drinks could only be sold in refillable containers that also carried a refundable deposit. (This requirement precluded plastic bottles.) Metal cans were banned for all beers and all beverage containers in use had to have the prior approval of the Danish national authorities. These requirements led to accusations of protectionism from the other member states. The EU introduced legislation to harmonize the national approaches in 1985, but this did not achieve its aim. As a result of its terms the Danish government was able to continue with its mandatory scheme. Following numerous complaints about the difficulties of entering the Danish market, the Commission brought a case against the Danish government in 1988.

In the 'Danish Bottle Case', the European Court of Justice supported the environmental objectives of the national legislation. However, it found that the requirement for prior approval was disproportionate to the environmental benefits, and was therefore a barrier to trade. In making its ruling the ECJ highlighted the need for common rules within the EU to avoid environmental measures forming barriers to trade.

The German government's 1991 Ordinance on the Avoidance of Packaging Waste had a much wider economic impact. The ordinance required the producers and distributors of packaging to take it back after use. Recycling or reuse was then required under the terms of a further piece of German legislation. The ordinance covered both German companies and those of other member states which wished to export to Germany. Targets were set in the legislation for the reuse or recycling of secondary packaging (that is, the packaging used by the distributor of the goods to the final customer) and transport packaging.

As the ordinance required a deposit on one-way packaging, except where more than 72 per cent of the material was reusable, this was a barrier to trade. It discriminated against large volumes of imported one-way packaging, especially recyclable aluminium and tinplate. The organization that had the responsibility to administer the ordinance (the Duales System Deutschland) was subsidized by the state, and not required to charge German recycling firms for the packaging waste they collected. Not unnaturally the German ordinance created a huge increase in the volume of waste that required recycling. This flooded the reprocessing plants throughout Germany and the rest of the EU. Growing quantities of recyclate were also exported to the Far East and Eastern Europe. The value of waste was undermined, so that in the UK, for example, commercial collection of waste became less viable. In 1996 the German Environment Ministry revised the ordinance by lowering the recycling quotas – from 72 per cent for glass and tin packaging to 70 per cent, and from 50 per cent in 1996–97 for aluminium, cardboard and paper to 60 per cent from 1997.

Directive 94/62/EC was an attempt to implement the EU's strategy on packaging waste and to overcome some of the problems mentioned above. It aimed to harmonize national packaging waste management measures, to minimize environmental impacts of packaging waste and at the same time avoid the erection of trade barriers. The directive covers packaging and packaging waste, industrial, commercial or domestic, regardless of the materials used. The member states were expected to adopt the legislation fully by 1 July 1996, and were required to reach established recovery and recycling targets within five years (ten years for Greece, Ireland and Portugal). It was required that, by 30 June 2001, between 50 and 65 per cent of packaging waste should be recovered, and between 25 and 45 per cent of all packaging waste should be recycled, with at least 15 per cent of each packaging material being recycled. Reuse, recycling and other forms of recovery (including incineration with energy recovery) were accepted and seen as equally valid methods. Recycling included reprocessing and organic recycling (composting). Incineration without any energy recovery was unacceptable.

On the date when the directive was to take effect, only Austria, Belgium, Luxembourg and Sweden had proposed national legislation to implement it. Germany and Denmark had notified their intention to continue with national measures according to the terms of article 100a (article 95 Treaty of Amsterdam). By the middle of 1998 (two years after the deadline had passed), it was clear that the directive had not been transposed satisfactorily into national legislation. As a consequence of this the Commission decided to serve Reasoned Opinions to several member states for their failure to comply with the directive.

GENETICALLY MODIFIED ORGANISMS – A NEW THREAT?

Genetically modified organisms (GMOs) should be the basis of the next agricultural revolution if the scientific speculation about their impact is to be believed. In some cases they promise better crop yields; in others they are said to offer a greater resistance to disease. It all depends upon the genetic feature that is being sought and designed into the organism. The difference between

GMOs and other experiments in plant breeding is the greater degree of scientific intervention, with genes being transferred between species. Some feel that the processes are unnatural and that they offer a 'Frankenstein' approach to farming. Environmental groups such as Friends of the Earth argue that there are too many questions unanswered with respect to genetically engineered foods and crops, and that they may pose a major environmental risk for the future. Their increased use may reduce biodiversity by squeezing out other plant varieties or damage other varieties by contamination. Many of the benefits are in any case somewhat marginal. Productivity may not be much better than in existing high-yielding varieties. Organic farmers who do not use herbicides have countered claims that they are essential for successful farming, and therefore there is no need to breed herbicide-resistant strains. Other farmers believe that better control of applications of herbicides may work just as well.

In 1997 the EU introduced a directive designed to ensure that all genetically modified foods were labelled.[6] This development came about in part because of the disquiet caused by the decision in May 1996 to permit ge:ietically modified soya beans to be marketed in the EU. A similar decision followed with respect to the market release of genetically modified maize which was roundly condemned by the European Parliament on the grounds that it displayed a lack of caution with respect to consumer health, environmental protection and producers' concerns. The Commission's view was that labelling was desirable because the public would then be able to make up its own mind with respect to any, as yet to be revealed risks (CEC 1997b). The wording of labels for goods containing GMOs has been criticized. Labels that distinguish between those products that *actually* contain GMOs and those that *may* contain GMOs may be confusing to many purchasers who have only a limited understanding of the distinction. However, it is open to all manufacturers of products not containing GMOs to assert that they are GMO-free.

The EU's trade policy with respect to GMOs has been subject to criticism both within the EU and internationally. The problem arises because of ethical fears of a potential threat to public health and biodiversity. Here the EU is torn between a wish to be seen to be transparent in its policy process, and being sensitive to concerns about food safety. This runs contrary to WTO rules, which require that a product must be shown to be harmful before it is excluded. Environmental concerns that are based on the precautionary principle appear to outsiders to amount to a disguised form of trade protectionism. Critics see them as playing upon the public's neurosis with respect to food safety.

Generally the US government tends to place a greater reliance on scientific opinion, whilst many of the EU member states have felt let down in the past. Experience has taught them to be cautious about the safety of food products. The US government's 1998 report on 'European trade barriers' denounced the EU's 'restrictive distribution practices, certain customs duties and unpredictable demands relating to the approval, labelling and licensing of products' (*Europe* 1998a). One of the main concerns was that the EU lacks common standards, uniform evaluation methods, fair labelling rules and certainty regarding the licensing and certification of products. This was particularly the case with respect to GMOs. The US bemoaned the 'laborious and highly unpredictable approval procedures which are affected by concerns of a political nature linked to consumer opposition in several Member States' (*Europe* 1998a).

CONCLUSIONS

In an ideal world, trade policy with environmental objectives should be integrated in a way that prevents trade barriers emerging, but at the same time does not weaken environmental protection. This is perhaps easier to achieve within the EU than in the international arena, although enlargement will complicate this process. However, it is still the case that the two areas tend to be considered in parallel rather than together. The single market taken as a whole is probably working as well as might be expected given the programme's late start, but removing barriers to trade has had negative consequences where environmental policy has been developed on a national basis. If comprehensive regimes can be developed within the EU and internationally, the negative effects of unco-ordinated national action might be avoided.

The EU needs to ensure that a degree of harmonization takes place so that the regimes covering national environmental standards are broadly equivalent. The effectiveness of environmental and trade policies will be undermined as long as the member states continue to pay lip service to the implementation of environmental policy. If the EU can establish its ability to ensure that its environmental policy is consistently effective, trade barriers within the single market will be removed, as will the additional costs for those involved in trade.

Some national variations in environmental measures can exist within an international context, but they need to be designed so as not to spill across borders, as in the case of German packaging waste (see above). It is not necessary for the EU to take on the role of setting all environmental regulations, as standards set in this way may be inappropriate for the different national conditions of the member states: it is not necessary to achieve complete harmonization of all the national regimes. Some differences in the national environmental standards may remain without distorting trade. Information about national regimes must, however, be readily available for consumers to make appropriate choices and for industrialists who wish to export within the integrated market.

NOTES

1. Examples include the European Convention for the Protection of Animals During International Transport (1968) and the Convention on International Trade in Endangered Species (1973).
2. Court of Justice, 20 February 1979; case 120/78, OJC 256, 3 October 1980, pp 2–3.
3. Decision 94/783/EC, OJL 316, 9 December 1994, Commission Decision of 14 September 1994 authorizing Germany to continue to prohibit imports of PCP and products treated with PCP.
4. Regulation on a Community eco-label award scheme, OJL 99, 11 April 1992, p. 1.
5. Directive on packaging and packaging waste, OJL 365, 31 December 1994 p. 10.
6. Commission Directive 97/35/EC, 18 June 1997, adapting to technical progress for the second time Council Directive 90/220/EEC on the deliberate release into the environment of genetically modified organisms, OJL 169, 27 June 1997, pp. 72–3.

7 Environmental protection and the maintenance of industrial competitiveness

INTRODUCTION

During the last 30 years a massive restructuring has taken place in the manufacturing sector in Europe. Despite this process of deindustrialization, manufacturing remains an important aspect of the European economy. The sector still provides 25 per cent of the national income and 25 per cent of the employment in the member states of the EU. The manufacturing sector is often regarded as one of the major sources of environmental degradation in Europe. Modern European manufacturing is, however, characterized by two underlying features that have contributed to lowering the levels of environmental damage caused by its industries. First, as the number of producing plants has fallen in the EU due to closures and changes in production processes, so too has the level of pollution. Second, many companies have begun to view improving their environmental performance as both cost-saving and good for their public image. The chemical and oil industries in particular have introduced a large number of environmental protection procedures.

This does not mean, however, that the EU can be complacent about the prospects for environmental improvement in the future. The late 1980s and early 1990s was a period of strong economic performance. The mid- to late 1990s was marked by a downturn in the European economy, accompanied by rising and persistent levels of unemployment (CEC 1997j). Included within the manufacturing sector are industries that have a particularly serious impact on the environment – paper and board manufacture, the processing of non-metallic minerals, chemicals, iron and steel production, cement and glass manufacture. Many of these industries have had a higher than average growth rate in comparison with other sectors of economic activity during the mid- and late 1990s. They are heavy users of energy and raw materials, and responsible for the generation of large amounts of hazardous waste. The possibility of environmental degradation has not gone away; nor has the necessity to counterbalance it with an effective and targeted environmental policy.

The enlargement of the EU to the states of Central and Eastern Europe (CEE) will increase the problems of environmental degradation from manufacturing industry. Initial investment costs for the ten associated countries[1] to meet the requirements of the environmental acquis were estimated to be up to ECU 120 to 150 billion (CEC 1997o: 5). Of this, equal levels of investment of 40 per cent for air pollution abatement technology and water and waste management, 20 per cent for solid and hazardous waste management were needed. This is of course not just manufacturing industries' requirements; the sector will absorb a considerable proportion of any investment made in a 'clean-up' process. As the restructuring of industry continues within the CEE states, and former producing plants are closed, the levels of pollution may also fall. However, enormous problems will remain because of the residue from the manufacturing processes and the dismantling of the redundant producing plants. In addition the dismantling of redundant nuclear power generation plants within the CEE states will provide both opportunities and tremendous challenges for the EU.

The necessity remains for measures to be continued and new means adopted to ensure that the more polluting sectors of the manufacturing industries become committed to improving their environmental performance. The objective of this chapter is to analyse current policy measures and proposals targeting the manufacturing sector, including the debate about the extent to which measures should be based on voluntary action or stringent legislation. There is support from some sectors of industry for the introduction of measures based on voluntary action. There are many advantages from continuing with stringent legislation for both environmental protection and the operation of the integrated market. The catalyst for the changes made in the chemical and oil sectors was the introduction of stringent legislation on the industries at both national and supranational level during the 1970s and 1980s.

The chapter will also include an evaluation of the extent to which environmental protection measures will assist in the EU's current preoccupation with employment creation. The rising and persistent unemployment levels within the EU during the mid- and late 1990s have highlighted problems of lack of competitiveness within the European economy as a whole. Support from the EU for schemes to advance the developments in the eco-technologies because of their job creation potential has therefore grown. Developments in the eco-industries may make a positive contribution to lowering the levels of unemployment by creating new jobs. However, the problems of unemployment in the EU are the result of a combination of factors which have characterized the labour market during the greater part of the 1990s and no single solution will be adequate.

Among the measures advocated since the Fifth EAP to ensure that industry change its practices is the use of economic instruments. These include taxes, effluent charges, and subsidies for technological changes to introduce more efficient filters to factories. Just how problematic this approach may be within the EU has been demonstrated by the heated controversies and debates surrounding the proposed introduction of an EU carbon/energy tax (see Chapter 5). Developments are taking place within individual member states to introduce various forms of national eco-taxation which will affect industry. The enlargement of the EU in 1995 encouraged this progress, as the Nordic states already had eco-taxes in place. Whether the support of the Nordic nations for eco-taxes will help to bring the Commission's proposals on an EU carbon/energy tax to fruition is, however, very uncertain. Whichever approach or combination of approaches is adopted, questions and concerns about implementation, enforcement and monitoring of policy are apparent.

Improving environmental protection raises a number of issues for manufacturing industry which may be viewed as amounting to diminished competitiveness[2] and a loss of profitability. Short-term compliance with environmental protection measures often carries a financial penalty. This is particularly the case where legislation is the driving force and companies are working to deadlines or standards which they have not introduced themselves. In order to fulfil the environmental requirements, industry in many cases has focused on implementing end-of-pipe solutions such as fitting dust filters to outlet pipes. This represents a 'pure cost' to the companies (CEC 1997l: 7). The introduction of clean technology which is designed to minimize waste production and material use has the potential to improve efficiency and bring cost savings, but the initial investments may be high. There is no guarantee that there will be a return on any long-term investments made by companies in this way to improve their environmental performance.

PARTNERSHIP BETWEEN THE POLICY MAKERS AND INDUSTRY

The European Commission took the view in the Fifth Environmental Action Programme that it was the responsibility of the companies in the manufacturing sector themselves to change current patterns of activity to protect the environment (CEC 1992a). Following the adoption of the Fifth EAP in 1992 the Commission published a consultative Green Paper on 'Industrial competitiveness and the protection of the environment' (CEC 1992d). This Green Paper opened the debate about how industrial competitiveness could be reconciled with environmental protection. Subsequent initiatives have outlined the policy to be adopted in more detail (CEC 1993g, 1994d, 1995c, 1997l). The role of the EU is to provide a supportive framework in which the necessary changes can take place. In addition to encouraging industry to become mobilized on environmental protection, any policy measures introduced must ensure that there is no distortion of the integrated market or loss of competitiveness. Much of the discussion about the response of industry to the EU's environmental policy has therefore to focus on the question of the extent to which it is possible to have partnership between the EU policy makers and industry. The dangers of not being able to produce a working partnership will undermine the process of economic integration in the market as well as progress on industry's environmental performance.

Proposals made by the European Commission in 1992 (CEC 1992d) started from the assumption that improving the quality of the environment and enhancing industrial competitiveness were not incompatible. Some companies believe that taking environmental protection seriously can improve competitiveness. This is not a view shared by all. There is no clear and conclusive evidence that the introduction of measures intended to improve environmental performance will not undermine competitiveness and lead to increased costs. Certainly for the majority of companies there are significant short-term cost implications which could undermine competitiveness. However, for high energy users, introducing environmental protection measures carries the potential for significant cost savings. If all manufacturing companies are to take action, a stimulus must be provided, either through economic incentives or a tighter regulatory structure.

The chemical sector is one of the EU's most important and prosperous industrial sectors. Within the sector major investments have been made in new technologies in order to ensure competitiveness in global markets. The sector has more than 9000 European companies but 40 per cent of production is in the hands of just five companies within the EU. As a result of the stimulus of legislation and regulation since the 1970s, a great deal of innovative new technology has been introduced into the sector which has brought long-term cost and time savings. The sector has therefore become more committed to environmental protection than some other areas of industrial development. It has been recognized that industrial competitiveness has been enhanced and not necessarily eroded by environmental legislation. The result has been that since the 1970s the chemical industry has been able on average to double its production but at the same time halve its pollution impact.

The evidence from the chemical sector suggests that the regulation of the industry through environmental legislation has met with success without hindering competitiveness. This has been achieved because of the wide-ranging nature of the legislation at national and supranational level, which has affected all companies in the sector to the same extent. For the future, pressures are growing from the chemical companies as well as other industrialists to introduce more flexibility into the environmental measures with which they are asked to comply. Policy makers are now under pressure to find alternatives ways of achieving environmental objectives apart from legislation. Among the most important of these within the EU is the commitment to developing policy based on the principles of subsidiarity and shared responsibility (see Chapters 2 and 12). Other proposals which have emerged during the process of consultation on policy measures have concentrated on ways in which the regulatory centralized control may be combined with voluntary instruments to increase the levels of EU funding for environmental projects. This is an important switch in emphasis on how policy is formulated. It allows for greater flexibility in the measures adopted without removing the tool of legislation which has been successful in the chemical sector.

In order to achieve the twin objectives of environmental protection and enhanced industry competitiveness, the Commission has advocated a two-pronged approach. First, environmental objectives must be more closely integrated in any policy measure adopted. The Treaty of Amsterdam has provided a firm legal basis for this requirement, with the amendments made to article 6 TEC (3 EEC). Legislation affecting manufacturing industry has to contain some assessment of how the environmental objectives are being incorporated into the development of competitive industrial policy. This gives the European Court of Justice a 'benchmark' to use in ruling on the treaty obligations. It nevertheless remains difficult to ensure that the integration of environmental requirements is accomplished, moreover, integration must be achieved at several different levels. It is not sufficient to include it in the Treaty as a requirement without mechanisms to ensure that it can be carried out.

The complexity of the policy-making process within the EU was discussed in Chapter 3. The priorities of policy makers concerned with protecting the environment and those whose objectives are to stimulate industrial growth may not necessarily coincide. There are many actors involved in the policy process. Within the institutional structure of the EU integration of policy objectives has required the creation of procedures and political and administrative mechanisms to bring together the policy makers with responsibility for very differing areas. The Directorates-General of the European Commission that are most closely involved in the development of effective environmental policy and support for industry include DG XI (Environment), DG IV (Competition), DG XXIII (Enterprise, including small businesses), DG XII (Science, Research and Development) and DG V (Employment and Industrial Relations). Each of these DGs has its own priorities and agendas which continue to cause controversy and undermine effective policy developments. Within DG XI a number of changes have been made to the administrative structure to respond to the concerns that policy may be undermined by the differing policy agendas of the DGs (see Chapter 4). In November 1997 DG XI and DG V (Social Affairs) cooperated on a joint communication on environment and employment (CEC

1997l). This was an example of the possibilities which exist within the European Commission to bring the officials of differing DGs to work on joint proposals.

A prerequisite for integration of environmental requirements into policy is the creation of a partnership between policy makers and the manufacturing sector. During the mid- and late 1990s a number of initiatives in the form of consultation (such as the establishment of the 'Green Forum'; see Chapter 2) and changes to the nature of policy instruments were adopted to facilitate this partnership. Bringing these groups together in order to enable discussion and collaboration about policy measures is difficult, as the manufacturing sector is disparate, covering a very wide range of companies from family-run businesses which employ fewer than ten workers to semi-autonomous units of large multinationals. Each one of these will have its own priorities and concerns. Each sector of manufacturing will require different conditions to support the development of its individual products. The relationship between the different sectors of the manufacturing industry and the national governments will vary, as will the strength and influence of the lobbyists attached to the sector.

COST-EFFECTIVE POLICY

The OECD (1997d) has estimated that the economic value of the services provided by ecological systems is in the range of US$16–54 trillion per year, with an average of US$33 trillion per year. The global gross national product is US$18 trillion per year. The conclusion reached in the OECD report on these figures was that most of this ecosystem value was outside the market, and that the environment provides economic goods and services which are at least as valuable if not more valuable than those provided by the markets. This OECD report is an attempt to cost the benefit to the global economy from the environment and to cost failure to protect it. If there is a lack of coordination between economic activities such as manufacturing which are heavy polluters and environmental protection there will be inefficiencies in the utilization of resources. In turn this will cause increased pollution and higher pollution control costs.

The main preoccupation of the EU in the environmental area is the development of a policy that will deliver the objectives of sustainable development. To do this requires objective data on the interaction between the operation of the economy and the protection of the environment. The national governments of the member states have varying systems and approaches to deal with the collection and collation of these data. In 1994 the European Commission (CEC 1994c) outlined an EU-wide framework for the integration of economic and environmental information systems. This framework was seen as instrumental in the attempt to integrate economic aspects into environmental policies and environmental concerns into economic policy. It is difficult to decide which environmental indicators to use as economic accounting tends to be of short-term and market-oriented flows, but costings dealing with environmental issues, for example climate change, are very long-term. As a result the costs of environmental damage may be severely underestimated.

Following from the 1994 framework proposal, the European Commission produced in 1997 a more detailed prototype for use by national statistical offices in the collation of environmental statistics. The prototype was piloted in a study of volunteer member states before its adoption in 1999. The areas of statistics included in the pilot were:

- Natural resources (forests, subsoil assets, and water)
- Emissions (into air and water)
- Other data which had environmental significance (environmental protection expenditure, eco-taxes and eco-industries).

For companies the cost of damage to the environment is a less visible and urgent priority than the costs which they incur in complying with EU legislation. The costs causing most concern include:

- The introduction of appropriate pollution control and abatement technologies
- Information and data collection costs
- Administrative and testing costs
- Levels of financial penalties for non-compliance
- Lack of certainty about regulations and standards are to be introduced
- Lack of knowledge about the costs of implementation may discourage investment.

The costs of implementation of environmental protection measures may be why industrial activity is transferring outside the EC, and evaluation is therefore an important element of the introduction of environmental policy. The 1992 Green Paper on industry and the environment (CEC 1992d) advocated the use of cost–benefit analysis (CBA) in evaluating environmental measures. These proposals raised concerns from the manufacturing sector about their appropriateness. CBA measures social as well as private costs and benefits. These social costs and benefits are not easy to quantify in terms of hard cash. The existence of social benefits does not offer a business anything in a direct way. Indeed, inadequately carried out, CBA may lead to loss of competitiveness if decisions are taken on the basis of incorrect information.

Common standards are needed for measuring environmental performance and impact on the environment, for example the EU's framework on national green accounting and environmental indicators. In addition, changes are required to accounting practices used by companies to reflect the environmental costs of trade and industry, and common criteria to devise life cycle analyses which measure the product's environmental impact over its whole lifetime. The problems of obtaining the level and type of information required to introduce these procedures are evident. The European Environment Agency (see Chapter 4) has an important role to play in this area.

VOLUNTARY VERSUS REGULATORY APPROACH TO ENVIRONMENTAL PROTECTION

Since the Fifth EAP there has been growing support from the policy makers within the EU for the introduction of different approaches to environmental protection, including greater reliance on voluntary action. If a more voluntary approach is to be used, then incentives must be developed which will ensure that action is taken; otherwise a fragmented and ineffective environmental policy will result. Increased consultation between companies and policy makers is one way to avoid this, as is a requirement for general participation by companies in any one sector.

In some sectors of industry, for example the chemical industry, there is a considerable level of support for the development of more initiatives based on the use of a voluntary rather than a regulatory approach to protection of the environment. A somewhat sceptical view may persist that the support from industry for voluntary action results from their belief that voluntary action need not be implemented! It must be recognized that the chemical sector has been subject to stringent regulation since the early 1970s at both national and supranational level. The improvements in environmental performance made by this industry have been in direct response to that legislation. Since 1972 the EU has introduced 47 directives which target the chemical industry and its practices and, together with measures by national governments, this legislation has been the catalyst for change. The presence of the body of EU regulation has also ensured that the industry is operating within a level playing field in the market.

Following the Fifth EAP the EU has introduced a 'new generation' of measures which combine the legislative approach with voluntary action and also use market-based instruments to persuade industry to alter its more environmentally damaging practices (see Chapter 5). Two measures which were given a high profile in the Fifth EAP were the introduction of the regulations to establish the eco-labelling scheme[3] and the Environmental Management and Audit Scheme (EMAS).[4] The Commission has also made considerable progress on the development of voluntary agreements with sectors of industry to achieve specific environmental objectives. This type of voluntary environmental agreement began at the national level, and not only has the EU adopted the approach but the Commission has also developed guidelines in order to harmonize what is being done within the member states.

ENVIRONMENTAL AGREEMENTS

Support for voluntary agreements between industry and public authorities to achieve environmental objectives grew at national level during the 1990s. Agreements of this type took many different forms and were applied in differing ways. In some cases legally binding obligations were set in the agreements. In others unilateral commitments were made by industry which were then recognized by public authorities. However, there were a number of features common to the national agreements, the most important of which were that they should:

- contain a requirement for prior consultation with the interested parties;
- be in a binding form;
- establish quantified and staged objectives;
- include mechanisms for monitoring results;
- include publication of the agreement and results.

Environmental agreements have a number of advantages. They may supplement legislation or be an important alternative to it. They provide an opportunity to promote a proactive attitude from industrialists because of the requirement for consultation and involvement from a much earlier phase of their development than may occur in the development of legislation. Environmental agreements may enable the introduction of more cost-effective measures as the agreements contain more 'tailor-made' solutions to environmental problems. Quicker and smoother introduction of environmental objectives may result because of the early commitment they can encourage among industrialists.

However, there are also disadvantages associated with the use of voluntary agreements, particularly with regard to any requirements for clearly defined objectives and enforcement procedures. Probably the biggest single criticism which may be made is that as they are voluntary they are only binding on those already committed! The risk therefore emerges of 'free-riders': companies that do not participate in the agreement may benefit by avoiding any costs shared by those that do. This may be overcome either through the threat of introducing legislation or by the identification of the 'free-riding' companies in the negotiation phases of the agreements by their competitors. This view was endorsed by the Union of Industrial and Employers' Confederations in Europe (UNICE) in March 1997: 'environmental agreements will neither replace all legislation and regulation, nor be a panacea for solving present and future environmental problems. Appropriate legislation will remain necessary to set the democratically chosen targets for achieving sustainable industrial development' (UNICE 1997: 4).

In December 1996 the European Commission attempted to provide general guidelines to the national governments which would ensure transparency of these agreements (CEC 1996l). The European Commission checklist highlighted the elements of best practice from the national level which would guarantee that the most effective structure was implemented in the agreements. In addition to providing a framework for use in agreements between national policy makers and industry, the Commission had also entered into agreements with sectors of industry.

The Auto-Oil Programme was instigated in 1992 by the European Commission as an attempt at consultation and partnership between the policy makers and industry in a voluntary agreement (see Chapter 10). The primary objective of the collaboration was to set environmental goals through consultation with industry. The intention was to use the results of scientific research to find the most cost-effective means to reach those targets. The European Commission encouraged a high level of involvement by the vehicle and fuel industries from the beginning of the programme in an attempt to overcome the rivalries between these groups. As road transport is one of the biggest producers of pollutants such as carbon monoxide, nitrogen oxides, benzene and ozone, establishing emission targets for these industries is also a crucial part of the development of an EU policy on air pollution.

Table 7.1   Targets for air-polluting emission from motor vehicles

Pollutant	Emissions in 1990, % of 1990 level	Emissions in 2010 without the Auto-Oil measures, % of 1990 level	Emissions in 2010 with Auto-Oil measures, % of 1990 level
Urban particulates	100	56	34
Urban carbon monoxide	100	47	23.7
Urban benzene	100	49	25.4
Total nitrogen oxides	100	52	33.8

Source: M. Smith and L. Boulton *Financial Times*, 17 February 1998, p. 2.

Whilst industry groups supported the overall approach, the cost implications for them made the Auto-Oil Programme extremely controversial. The legislative proposals which were needed to make the agreed strategy work were adopted in 1996 for passenger cars. Quality standards for petrol and diesel cars, with further legislation containing the emission standards for light commercial vehicles and heavy duty vehicles, appeared in 1997. The agreements on cutting back on air pollution emissions included stricter standards than those which the US was setting at the same time.

The costs of implementing the cuts in emissions were estimated at more than ECU 80 billion over 15 years. The main source of the controversy about the programme was the fact that the bulk of this cost fell on the vehicle manufacturers (ECU 4.1 billion annually), with a much lower cost on the fuel industry (ECU 766 million). Estimates were also made that the proposed fuel standards would cost the consumer about ECU 12 per annum. In February 1998 the European Parliament supported more stringent standards for petrol and diesel fuels to be introduced by 2005, despite the concerns of industry about the cost implications. As a consequence of the EP's recommendations, conciliation procedures were invoked to reach an acceptable compromise. The EP proposed more than 100 amendments of the legislation and the discussions within the Conciliation Committee were, as a result, very detailed.

By July 1998 agreement was reached on all three dossiers contained within the programme. These included measures to be taken against:

- air pollution by emissions from passenger cars (amending Directive 70/220);[5]
- emissions from light commercial vehicles including pick-up trucks and light vans (amending Directive 70/220);
- quality of petrol and diesel fuels (amending Directive 93/12).[6]

The issues which were dealt with were difficult to resolve but the model of consultation which was established by the Auto-Oil initiative was considered to be successful and laid the basis for future developments. In October 1998 the European Commission proposed that the approach should be used in the negotiations to revise the 1994 waste packaging directive.[7] This proposal to set up a structured dialogue was supported by the European Organization for Packaging and the Environment (EUROPEN), the interest group representing the packaging industry. One of the main problems which had emerged following the 1994 directive was the length of time that action was taking against the Danish and German governments, which had adopted stringent national recycling rules. As a consequence the free movement of packaged goods was being restricted. In October 1998 the European Commission initiated the second stage in infringement proceedings against the Danish government for failing to implement the directive (see Chapter 4).

THE EU'S ECO-LABELLING SCHEME AND ITS IMPACT

Eco-labels are the logos displayed on products that inform consumers of the products' environmental performance. They are certification marks confirming that the environmental impact of the product has been independently evaluated. The evaluation is made against a specific set of criteria which are used for all products in a particular product group. As the number of national eco-labelling schemes increased, and with them the danger of distortion of trade, the European Union adopted a regulation which established an EU eco-label scheme in 1992. The EU's scheme joins the more than 20 others established worldwide since the late 1980s. All the schemes are based on voluntary registration by the manufacturers for the licence to use the logo. Some schemes, for example, the Nordic White Swan and the German Blue Angel, are government sponsored. Others such as the Swedish Good Environmental Choice and the United States Green Seal are privately sponsored. In addition to these schemes, some manufacturers have devised their own logos based on eco-criteria set by the company involved (see Table 7.2).

Table 7.2   National eco-labelling schemes in operation within the EU[1]

National scheme	Date begun	Geographical area covered	Product groups	Licences awarded	Products labelled
Nordic Swan[2]	1989	Sweden, Finland (Norway and Iceland)	40	287	>1000
Blue Angel	1977	Germany	71	>1000	4350
NF Environn -ement	1992	France	N/A		
Stichting Milieukeur	1992	Netherlands	Mainly paper products	26	32

Notes:
[1] Also in development within the EU:
   Sweden   Good Environmental Choice
   Spain   Medio Ambiente
   Catalan   Medi Ambient
   Austria   Umwelt Zeichen, which operates in Germany, Sweden, Finland, the Netherlands, France, Spain and Austria
[2] The Nordic Swan label is used in Norway and Iceland, countries that are not members of the EU.

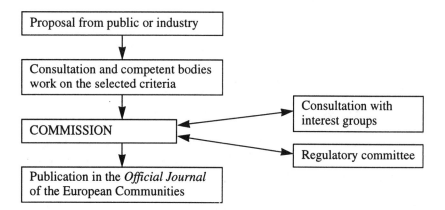

Figure 7.1a   The eco-label system

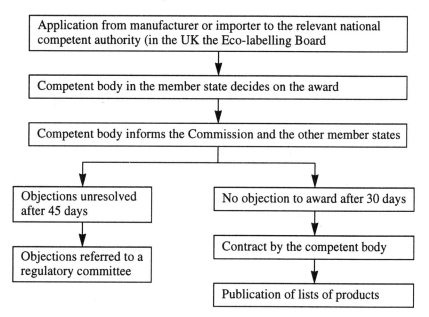

Figure 7.1b   The eco-label award process

The EU's eco-labelling scheme has two objectives. It attempts to persuade consumers to change their environmental behaviour and, through them, to target the behaviour of the producers. At the same time it is part of the EU's approach to supporting the competitiveness of European industry and persuading companies of the benefits of compliance with environmental measures. Late in 1998 eco-label criteria had been published for 12 product groups, with 42 licences for their use granted to 31 manufacturers and 2 importers for a total of 216 products. As a result of the number of licences granted, the European Commission considered the scheme a success (for example CEC 1997x). However, the number of licences granted represents a tiny proportion of the products being sold within the single market. The meaning of 'success' must be considered carefully with regard to this scheme, as numbers of awards may not be the most appropriate measure, for a variety of reasons! It may be that the number of products bearing the blue flower logo of the scheme will never be large. What will provide a more accurate judgement will be the number of companies applying to join the scheme and an evaluation of the effort made to meet the criteria.

Among the advantages of the EU's eco-labelling scheme for both the consumers and the manufacturers is the uniform approach to labelling the selected product groups. There are clearly defined eco-criteria to be used by all the products in a selected group which help consumers to identify those companies whose products have a reduced impact on the environment. The scheme raises awareness of which products are better in environmental terms and covers a number of environmental impacts during the life cycle of a product.

However, the disadvantages must not be ignored. There may be some biased weightings of the criteria, especially those which relate to non-renewable resources. The scheme does not allow for national differences in industry and may not work in very diverse industrial sectors. Eco-labels are not a reward for improved environmental performance but are marketing tools. There is evidence that more support may be forthcoming from manufacturers for the EU's Environmental Management and Audit Scheme (EMAS), which takes a more holistic approach to changing environmental performance. Eco-labels are based on rewarding the least environmentally damaging and not the most environmentally friendly. On its own, therefore, an eco-label does not give enough information to the consumer about the environmental credentials of the product. The eco-label system and award process are shown in Figures 7.1a and 7.1b.

Given the disadvantages which are attached to the scheme, evaluation of its success must be made by a consideration of consumer and manufacturer perceptions of what the award means and its impact. The objectives of the scheme will be tested by the extent to which the behaviour of both consumers and manufacturers is permanently altered, taking a more environmentally concerned path. Increased interest in registration for the scheme does not indicate that this has been achieved. Among the reasons for this is the considerable confusion over what eco-labels show and the existence of rival and more familiar national eco-labelling schemes. This is particularly true of the German Blue Angel scheme which was introduced in 1977 and was the model for the others.

The rationale behind the introduction of the EU's scheme is to avoid the possibility of barriers to trade emerging because of unfair discrimination between products. The scheme presents a somewhat paradoxical situation as in itself it is discriminatory in identifying and singling out certain products within broad product groups for 'recommendation' to the consumer! Despite supporting the eco-labelling scheme, officials of DG XI acknowledged that 'the key difficulty of the European industrial associations vis-à-vis the Community eco-label is related to its selective nature' (CEC 1996o: para. 15).

There are a number of other contradictions inherent in the use of eco-labelling as a tool of environmental policy and increasing industrial competitiveness which are difficult to remove. Only those least environmentally damaging manufactured products in a product group will be eligible for the award if the manufacturers apply for a licence. Competition for the label should encourage manufacturers to change their behaviour, but in some sectors, for example detergents, there are only a few major manufacturers. As the national authorities are involved in consultation with the manufacturers over the setting of the eco-criteria, some industrialists may have an unfair advantage because of their influence on the national authorities.

In establishing the aims and objectives of the scheme the primary objective is clearly to ensure that trade is not distorted. Concerns have been expressed in a number of quarters that this will in fact be the case. The view of DG XI and the European Environment Bureau (EEB) is that as long as the scheme remains voluntary, it will not distort trade as producers may decide whether to adopt the scheme or not.[8] On the other hand concerns have emerged amongst officials of DG II (Economic and Financial Affairs) and DG III (Internal Market and Industrial Affairs) about the potential trade impact.[9] In 1996 the Greek government attempted to introduce a requirement that all imported products in the identified product groups should carry the EU's eco-label. This blatant attempt to protect its own infant companies was, however, ruled to be discriminatory by the Commission's legal services. The conclusion would appear to be that the eco-label scheme will not distort trade as long as it remains a voluntary and fairly low-key initiative.

In requiring the national authorities to work on the selection of the eco-criteria, this regulation may have provided an example of where applying the principle of subsidiarity undermines the objective of the scheme. The responsibility was devolved to the individual national authorities to set the criteria for use on products traded in the European single market. This led to much criticism and complaints that national interests were influencing the selection of the eco-criteria. The national authorities were, however, required to establish eco-criteria which were more rigorous than merely a limited identification of a few consumption-related criteria.

The orthodox view is that increased competition will lower prices and therefore consumers will support intensity of competition. Some consumers perceive that environmentally friendly products are more expensive, and this will lower support for 'green' purchases. Eco-labelling requirements may be perceived by the consumer as a way of removing unlabelled products from the marketplace and providing a 'justification' for increasing prices. Evidence is also emerging that consumers *say* that they are environmentally concerned and aware but their purchasing behaviour is not consistent with this.

Mobilizing support from consumers for the EU's scheme is difficult. Within the EU there are wide disparities in income (the 10 richest regions having a per capita GDP of 160 per cent of the EU average, and the 10 poorest 50 per cent of the EU average (CEC 1999d). There are differences in culture and consumer tastes in the marketplace. The history of product labelling is littered with examples of manufacturers making extravagant claims for their products. Environmental labelling is no exception to this. This behaviour is costly for a number of reasons. First, marketing costs for a company may be increased by excessive labelling. Second, ineffective warnings to consumers may result in lack of confidence and lead to deliberate purchasing decisions away from the labelled products. Third, it is not always clear if the consumer requires all the information provided on the label.

Consumers may claim that environmental factors influence their purchasing decisions but there is some evidence to suggest that what is claimed and what is done are not the same (National Consumer Council 1996: 4). The report of the UK National Consumer Council (NCC) was funded by the Department of the Environment and involved the UK Eco-labelling Board. It found that consumer decisions were more likely to be influenced by brand name, price and product performance than environmental considerations. However, that does not mean that environmental considerations will not become part of the purchase decision in the future. Respondents to the NCC's survey were placed in five categories (see Table 7.3). These findings suggest that whilst there is a large element of sceptical people who doubt that they can do anything to protect the environment, some 36 per cent believe they can (affluent Greens and young Greens). Common to both groups of Greens, however, was confusion about what was causing the environmental problems and the most effective way of overcoming them. Current eco-labelling was considered by these shoppers to be inadequate to overcome this information gap.

Consumers appear to be looking for more information; however, there is confusion in the public's mind about what is meant by an eco-label. If a comparison is made with the impact of the government-sponsored national scheme which has existed longer than the German Blue Angel, it is possible to show the importance of eco-labelling. It must, however, be seen as just one part of a strategy to raise environmental awareness. In the case of the German scheme, other elements included increasing the importance of environmental issues in education and the reinforcing action of other types of mandatory environmental actions.

Table 7.3   Do consumers care?

Category	% of respondents
Affluent Greens	19
Recyclers	19
Careful spenders	19
Young Greens	17
Sceptics	26

Source: Adapted from NCC (1996: 15).

The European Commission outlined a number of revisions to be made to the scheme in December 1996 (CEC 1996o). Among the changes was the introduction of a graduated label designed to give more information, an independent European eco-label organization to develop the eco-label criteria and a ceiling on the cost of fees, with special rates for small and medium-sized enterprises. For many companies this new fee structure was a positive step forward. However, the main area of confusion was left untouched, as there was a continued commitment to complementarity of national and EU schemes:

> The present stage of development of the Community scheme does not make it possible to assert that the Community scheme might automatically supersede national schemes in the long run. The developments in the last few years seem to support the contrary view. In the absence of positive action to stop it the proliferation of schemes and the corresponding eco-label criteria is likely to continue. (CEC 1996o: 26)

The reforms have therefore done little to overcome the continued lack of commitment from producers and continued scepticism from the consumers.

THE ENVIRONMENTAL MANAGEMENT AND AUDIT SCHEME

There is evidence to suggest that the regulation establishing the EU's Environmental Management and Audit Scheme (EMAS) has more industrial support and will have greater long-term impact in encouraging changed behaviour amongst producers.[10] The scheme emerged from a lengthy process of consultation which brought together policy makers, policy implementers and targeted groups of industrialists. It was generally accepted by the policy makers and industrialists that a scheme was necessary to encourage better environmental management practices. A number of broad-based concerns emerged at the beginning of the consultation process. These included:

- whether the scheme was to be based on voluntary or mandatory registration for the use of the logo;
- what industries should be covered;
- whether the scheme should be centrally organized in Brussels or in the individual member states.

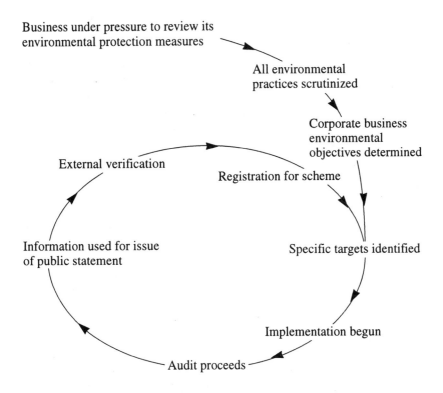

Source: Adapted from Council Regulation 1836/93, allowing voluntary participation by companies in the industrial sector in a community eco-management and audit scheme, Annex I.

Figure 7.2   The environmental management and audit cycle

The first proposals were made in January 1991, followed by successive drafts of the legislation, each of which was discussed with the national experts and industry representatives. The initial proposals had identified the need for three directives. The final decision was to adopt a single regulation,[11] with the target group of industries being in the manufacturing sector. The terms of the regulation left the opportunity for other sectors to be included, and the UK government took advantage of this to include public authorities providing a range of services.

The use of the legislative form of a regulation made it obligatory for the national governments to adopt the legislation in all its elements and provide the infrastructure for the scheme. This was designed to avoid any distortion of competition which might result if the national governments were given the flexibility of choice contained in the legislative form of a directive (see Chapter 4). EMAS is not a measure that covers products, but rather the environmental procedures of producing plants. It encourages improved performance from a base identified by the manufacturers themselves. It is not a point-in-time measure but allows a manufacturer the opportunity to adapt and change practices that have an environmental impact. The scheme also allows a longer-term strategy to be adopted by a manufacturer with concerns about major outlays of capital investment, as it 'rewards' the evolution of environmental change.

Eco-audits were first carried out in many large-scale multinationals in the late 1970s, and by the early 1990s this form of auditing was a well-established management tool in some sectors of manufacturing. The trend was for any eco-audit carried out to be regarded as a 'one-off' and not part of a continuous and regular pattern. Eco-audits were essentially seen as internal management tools which brought savings for companies in a number of areas. Knowledge of existing practices was beneficial when new legislation was proposed. As a result of conducting an eco-audit, companies had a clearer idea of what procedures would be required to implement new measures. Eco-audits were able to identify procedures which might have resulted in prosecutions and fines. It was possible to make savings by changing the methods of waste disposal used. Following increasing claims for damage from environmental incidents, insurance companies began to add eco-audits to their list of requirements. The results of eco-audits or the fact that they are conducted may also be used in company advertising.

As national and company schemes had proliferated during the 1980s, the introduction of the EU's regulation was intended to provide a common framework for the various approaches. In order to register to use the EMAS logo in its publicity a company must:

- establish an environmental policy;

- set objectives for environmental performance and put the management systems into place to achieve these objectives;
- introduce a pattern of eco-auditing to assess environmental performance and to provide the information needed to develop the environmental management systems. The timing of these eco-audits must not be less than every three years;
- provide an independently verified public statement once the initial audit is completed.

Once the initial eco-audits have been carried out, the procedure must become part of a regular cycle and the updated material published in an environmental statement (see Figure 7.2). The verifiers of the public statements must consult with the companies on the details to be made public. The member states had to establish independent and neutral bodies for the accreditation of the independent environmental verifiers and the supervision of their activities by April 1995. Early in 1998 not all the national governments had complied with this requirement. The European Commission began to target national governments which were failing to put in place the necessary procedures to implement the regulation by initiating action against the Portuguese government.

The contents of the public statement are set out in a very structured way in article 5 of the regulation. The provision of this independently verified public statement is probably the single most controversial issue associated with the scheme. It requires more than a mere acknowledgement that an eco-audit has been carried out. Companies have to demonstrate that over a period of time they have used the information to alter their approach to environmental protection. It may be that this will have implications for a company's purchasing, production, marketing or sales policy. It may even result in the closure of a particular facility. Company concerns remain that the public statement may give information to their competitors.

Certain safeguards were built into the regulation to deal with these concerns. The procedures in the EMAS presuppose that both the auditors and the verifiers have a high level of technical expertise. A company considering registration for the scheme will not do so if there are any doubts at all about the expertise of the auditors and the verifiers of the audit. The release of incorrect information would be too damaging to the company concerned. This is less of a problem in the UK than in other member states, as the UK already has a well-developed structure of accreditation arrangements for the two quality management standards BS 5750 and BS 7750 through the National Accreditation Council for Certification Bodies (NACCB). The NACCB was designated as the competent authority to monitor the EMAS in the UK. A company applying for certification to act as the independent verifier for the BS 7750 is also able to apply for additional certification to act for the EMAS.

A total of 700 sites of manufacturing companies within the EU had been registered for the scheme by the beginning of 1998. This represents a small number of potential locations. In introducing the scheme to the UK in 1992, the UK authorities had identified more than 100 000. If this voluntary legislation is to be more widely adopted, then certain reservations which companies share must be considered in any reviews of the legislation undertaken. Otherwise the number of companies which register for the scheme will remain limited, and its effectiveness will be undermined.

INTEGRATED POLLUTION PREVENTION AND CONTROL AND ITS IMPACT ON INDUSTRY

In its recognition that a more holistic approach to pollution prevention and control produces more effective environmental policy, the European Commission proposed a directive on integrated pollution prevention and control (IPC) in 1993 (CEC 1993d) which was adopted in 1996.[12] The primary objective of the legislation was to encourage an approach at the European level which was already used in various forms in many of the EU's member states. The directive started from a recognition that no part of the environment is separate from any other. If legislation is adopted which targets one medium, the consequence may be that there is a release or transfer of pollutants to another medium. This legislation was a significant change to the approach adopted by the EU which in the past had concentrated to a great extent on protection of individual environmental media.

The target of the 1996 directive was the manufacturing sector, but it also included energy production and waste management. The directive provided a framework for the licensing of polluting emissions from industrial installations. It was based on the use of the 'best available technique' (BAT) approach. BAT is defined in the directive as the 'most effective and advanced stage in the development of activities and their methods of operation which indicates the practical suitability of particular techniques for providing ... the basis for emission limit values designed to prevent or reduce emissions and their impact on the environment as a whole' (article 2 (12), Directive 96/61/EC).

The national governments are required to impose emission limit values for the targeted sectors. Applications for permits for emissions must include:

- Details of the installation, its raw and auxiliary materials and energy use or energy generated
- Sources of emissions, with their effects on the environment

- Techniques being used or to be used to prevent or minimize emissions
- Recovery or recycling operations to be carried out
- Measures to prevent major accidents
- Measures for monitoring emissions
- Measures for minimizing pollution
- Measures to protect the environment when the process finally ceases.

The cost implications of compliance with the legislation were taken into account. For small companies the thresholds were established so as to exclude them from the terms of the directive. For medium-sized companies the directive was only to be applied if their polluting potential was considered significant.

The IPC directive was established as a very flexible piece of legislation in order to accommodate a range of existing national practices and at the same time give national governments which did not have IPC legislation in place an opportunity to incorporate it into national law. Denmark, France, Greece, Luxembourg, Belgium, the Netherlands, Ireland and Portugal already had IPC in place when the EU legislation was proposed in 1993. In the UK the regulators were left with a great deal more discretion over implementation of the IPC legislation than was favoured in Germany.

Within the German federal structure of government the individual states' (*Länder*) governments have a great deal of autonomy over the implementation of environmental legislation. The degree of flexibility allowed in the implementation of the IPC directive was of concern to many industrialists in Germany. Their view was that there was a danger of a large number of differing systems developing in the different *Länder*. They had therefore favoured a stricter 'top–down' approach to prevent this from happening.

The directive was intended to enable the European Commission and the member states to compare standards established at the national level. This was to pave the way for the future introduction of regulation in areas where there was a great deal of diversity. The exchange of information envisaged within the IPC directive was seen as an important part of the establishment of EU environmental quality standards and a way to overcome the problem of imbalance in techniques used to protect the environment within the EU. In late 1998 it was clear that the far-reaching ambitions of the legislation had not been met, as some of the national governments had still to ensure that the procedures were in place.

EMPLOYMENT CREATION

The debate about how to reconcile the two objectives of industrial competitiveness and protection of the environment has become of greater importance with growing concern about the high levels of unemployment within the EU

(Eurozone[13] seasonally adjusted rate in February 1999 was 10.5 per cent; Eurostat rate for the EU 15 was 9.6 per cent). There is much debate about the employment effect of environmental policy, but an OECD report in 1997 reached the conclusion that the result was a small, positive net employment impact (OECD 1997b: 10). Whilst it is not the primary objective of environmental policy to create employment, there are direct linkages between environmental policy and job creation potential.

A broad definition of competitiveness encompasses three elements: productivity, efficiency and profitability. At the macro-level, economic indicators of competitiveness include growth, productivity and employment. At the micro-level of an individual company, competitiveness also includes market share and profitability (CEC 1996r: 3). Much of the problem with industry's attitude is that the introduction of environmental protection measures carries costs that are very visible in the short term. The potential for benefits only becomes visible in the long term. It is necessary to look at the issue of competitiveness from two points of view with regard to the potential for job creation created by the linkage with environmental protection. One question is the extent to which the introduction of environmental protection measures will affect the competitiveness of a company by constraining its share of a particular market or by increasing costs and lowering levels of profitability. This will in turn affect their ability to increase the levels of employment offered. The second question is how new developments may enhance the growth of employment in those companies that are involved in the production of the new eco-technologies.

To what extent is the view of industry that competitiveness is undermined by environmental protection measures an accurate one? There is evidence that jobs are lost by the introduction of such measures, for example in the US, which has many more dedicated anti-environmental groups than can be found in Europe. These groups are prepared to fund research into the costs of environmental measures as a way of offering support to lobbyists. Their activities are seen as adding to the environmental debate rather than running contrary to the consensus, as might be the case in the EU. This has been seen in the debate concerning the US's commitment to the Kyoto Agreement. Under this the US was required to reduce its greenhouse gas emissions to 7 per cent below 1990 levels by 2012 – 16 per cent below emissions in 1998. On the one hand the US government's assessment of the cost of implementing the agreement was put at between $70 and $110 per household in any one year. They suggested that costs would be largely offset by the benefits to consumers stemming from the planned deregulation of the electricity industry. An alternative assessment was sponsored by the Global Climate Coalition, an industry-led group opposed to the Kyoto Agreement which suggested that it would cost 2.4 million US jobs and reduce gross domestic product by as much as $300 billion annually. The survey found that it would cause energy prices to double, with severe implications for the rest of the economy. The need to replace capital equipment and the lowering of disposable incomes would result in a real GDP loss of $2728 per household by 2010 (Suzman 1998).

A similar sceptical view was supported by findings in the UK. In the third of its annual reports, ENTEC-UK and the Green Alliance, a UK-based green lobby group, identified a rise in the number of large companies citing costs as a limiting factor when implementing environmental programmes. Their report of 1997 identified 58 per cent of companies surveyed expressing this view; by mid-1998 this had risen to 73 per cent (ENDS 3/6/1998). It is extremely difficult to estimate the extent to which company competitiveness will be lost in the long term. What does emerge from much of the evidence presented is that there is a cost disadvantage for many companies from meeting the requirements of environmental protection, and this might undermine their ability to provide employment. On the other hand companies can make cost savings as a result of less wastage in production processes and lowering of energy usage. However there is no guarantee that new employment will result from the increased profits of a company.

In 1994 the market for eco-industry was valued at $280 billion globally, with the EU market reaching ECU 90 billion – Germany accounting for one third of that total. In addition, it was expected that globally the eco-industry would grow to US$640 billion in 2010, a growth rate of about 8 per cent per annum (CEC 1997l: 8, note 12). Within the EU the market for eco-technology appeared to suggest that there was a significant possibility of job creation in the developments which were taking place (see Table 7.4).

Table 7.4   Market in the EU for eco-technology by % of EU output and industrial turnover as % of EU GDP

Market for Eco-technology	% of EU output	Turnover of eco-technology industry	% of GDP
Germany	35	Austria	2.3
France	20	Netherlands	2.3
UK	12	Germany	2.0
Italy	10	France	1.5
Netherlands	8	Sweden	1.5
Austria	4		

Source: CEC (1997l: 21).

Evaluating the potential of the eco-industries to provide new jobs is difficult because of problems of identifying and then targeting the industries in need of support. The definition that has been adopted by the European Union is that of the OECD. The core activities of environmental protection are 'the production of goods and services to measure, prevent, limit or correct environmental damage to water, air, and soil or activities that deal with problems related to waste, noise, and eco-systems'. This includes companies in the following sectors:

- Air pollution control, for example production of catalytic converters
- Waste water treatment, for example products and services associated with the removal of pollutants from sewage
- Waste management, for example products and systems for the collection of municipal, commercial and industrial wastes
- Systems for the reclamation of contaminated land
- Products and services associated with noise abatement
- Environmental R&D
- Environmental monitoring products
- Environmental consultancy services.

Other forms of employment may be created in areas that are not concentrated in one sector of activity but occur in other parts of the economy, for example the adoption of production methods that minimize environmental damage.

At the national level it is possible to discern a growth in the numbers of people directly employed in these areas (see Tables 7.5 and 7.6).

Within the EU this positive employment effect was first highlighted in the White Paper on growth, competitiveness and employment (CEC 1993g: ch. 10). It also formed part of the debate about employment creation that resulted in the unique joint communication from Ritt Bjerregaard (Environment Commissioner) and Padraig Flynn (Social Affairs Commissioner) in November 1997 (CEC 1997l). The direct employment impact of the eco-industries within the EU is estimated to be about 1 million jobs, that is, about 0.7 per cent of total EU employment, providing ECU 90 billion of goods and services per annum. Although it is more difficult to estimate employment where the environmental impact is less direct, it is possible to conclude that 3.5 million jobs exist within the EU in environment-related employment. It is estimated that a further 500 000 could be created by 2010 in renewable energy technology, with investments in renovation of housing and public transport adding another 500 000 (see Table 7.7)

Table 7.5 Positive employment effects of environmental policies in Germany (000s)

Sectors	1980	1984	1990	1994	2000[*]	forecast
West Germany	434	433	597	642	786	
Directly involved in environmental protection	158	172	255	284	290	
Supply of goods and services for environmental protection	–	–	341	358	496	
East Germany	–	–	–	314	336	
Directly involved in environmental protection	–	–	–	224	66	
Supply of goods and services for environmental protection	–	–	–	90	280	
Total	434	433	680	956	1122	

[*] Forecast of employment post 2000.

Source: OECD (1997b: 36).

Table 7.6 Positive employment effects of environmental policies in France (000s)

Sectors	1985	1986	1987	1988	1989	1992
Market activities	–	–	–	176.1	179.0	–
Direct employment effects	–	–	–	96.2	98.7	–
Indirect employment effects	–	–	–	75.9	80.3	–
Administration	–	–	–	123.4	124.0	–
In-house production	–	–	–	53.5	56.0	–
Total	343.5	349.2	349.4	353.0	359.0	418.0
% labour force	1.6	1.6	1.6	1.6	1.7	1.9

Source: OECD (1997b: 37).

There are many different types of jobs associated with environmental protection. Some employment is to be found in the introduction of the new technology that is needed to implement environmental legislation. The response of industry to much environmental regulation in the past has been to adopt end-of-pipe technology, which is often the cheapest solution for companies in the short term. The introduction of these technologies may impose a financial burden on companies, depress competitiveness and result in job losses. Employment may be lost in some companies required to introduce the technology, but there are arguments to support the view that losses will be compensated by creation of jobs related to the introduction of waste management or treatment technology. There is no conclusive evidence to support this view. For example, the introduction of flue-gas desulphurization equipment (FGD) to power stations proved to be costly (taking around 10–20 per cent of the total capital costs of a power plant) and also caused a reduction in operating efficiency. In a 1995 study of a Japanese company that had been among the first to begin commercial production of the technology, investment had been required for a period of 15 years before there was a net return (CEC 1997u). Of the producing company's labour force of 3000, 200 were directly employed in the production of the technology.

Table 7.7   EU initiatives for job creation

Target area	Potential for job creation
Environmental protection	Up to 1 million
• Maintenance of natural and public areas (local waste recycling)	
• Water purification and clean-up of polluted areas	
• Monitoring of quality standards	
• Energy-saving equipment, particularly in housing	
Improvements in the quality of life	Up to 1 million
• Renovation of run-down areas	
• Development of local public transport services	
Local services	
Leisure and cultural facilities	Up to 1 million
Audio-visual	

Source: OECD (1997b: 62); based on CEC (1993g: ch. 10).

The clean, lean technologies, on the other hand, have long-term environmental benefits. These technologies are designed to minimize the use of materials and to reduce the production of waste. Much R&D effort surrounds the introduction of this type of technology, which tends to reduce energy use as well as costs for raw materials. The primary objective of these measures is to improve process efficiency. Consequently the environment is protected and at the same time there are clear long-term cost advantages for companies. This will only translate into job creation under specific conditions. The job creation potential of clean technologies is dependent upon a number of factors, including the competitiveness of the companies involved.

For a company involved in the production of the eco-technology there may be a 'first-mover' advantage to be gained from being the first to supply it. The overall competitiveness of the company will be strengthened if any increase of price which might have to be passed on to the consumer is small. It may not increase competitiveness if the price is perceived to be unacceptably high. Maintaining competitiveness is also crucially dependent upon other countries or companies being obliged to use the new technology. If that does not happen, companies may be left bearing higher costs for long periods of time and experiencing diminished competitiveness.

The EU is attempting to provide a framework to support the development of eco-technology. This can be done through funding for R&D programmes or by the reduction of controls on state aid to some sectors of industry. Following a joint conference held in May 1997 by the European Commission and the European Parliament on Employment and the Environment, a database was established which recorded details of 2100 companies involved in the production of more than 60 different environmental technologies and products and services within the EU. The purpose of the database was to collate information about companies and use it in the preparation and evaluation of policy. The companies included in the initial database operated in what were considered to be the seven core areas of environmental protection. The database was by no means definitive, as there are between 20 000 and 30 000 large and small companies involved in these eco-industries within the EU! The value of the database may be proved in the future from the information which it is able to provide to help with future developments.

More than 70 million people within the EU are in employment provided by small and medium-sized enterprises (SMEs) (see Table 7.8).

Table 7.8   Number of small and medium-sized businesses in the EU, 1996

	Very small	Small	Medium	Total
No. of enterprises (000s)	17 285	1 105	165	18 555
Employment (000s)	37 000	21 000	15 070	73 180
Average size of enterprise	2	20	90	4
Turnover per enterprise (ECU mn)	0.2	3.0	16.0	0.5

Source: *European Voice* (26 February 1998, p. 27).

Many companies involved in the eco-industries are in this sector. The European Commission's (CEC 1997l: 9) view is that reorganization of work and enterprises in the late 1990s will release more employment in the form of sub-contracting to the SMEs. The employment effect of the linkage with environmental protection will therefore be seen mainly in SMEs. However, they are subject to the same concerns about costs and loss of competitiveness as larger enterprises.

The consumer drives the developments in the SMEs. A great part of the advantage which small businesses have lies in their ability to innovate and to be flexible in their production systems so as to react to the changing patterns of consumer demand. Lack of a coherent and clearly defined EU consumer policy based on accurate information may be seen as a limit to their competitiveness. The public has to be encouraged to ask for environmentally friendly products and the results of increased production will in turn lead to job creation. Whilst there is a growth of environmental awareness and interest in the purchasing of so-called 'green' products, it must also be acknowledged that there is some evidence to suggest that consumers say one thing and do another (National Consumer Council 1996: 4).

The categorization of small and medium-sized enterprises together may often cause problems in the development of policy as on the one hand the category includes very many small concerns which employ fewer than ten workers and may be family-run businesses. In the UK, for example, more than 95 per cent of companies employ fewer than 50 people. On the other hand an SME may employ several hundred people in branches of multinational companies. For the smaller company, compliance with environmental legislation will have a disproportionately greater impact than it will on the subsidiary of a multinational. Ensuring that SMEs remain competitive also involves them in disproportionately higher R&D costs. The SMEs are thus put in the position of trying to reconcile the needs of a competitive market, low-cost production requirements and high costs of environmental improvements. The main question for SMEs is who should shoulder these costs. If higher unit costs are or are perceived to be a result of the introduction of environmental procedures, the SMEs will try to find ways to avoid compliance with that legislation.

The concern that the SMEs have about the financial implications of compliance with environmental legislation have been recognized by the EU. The overall conclusion of the European Commission about where support for SMEs should come from is that it is an issue for national governments to deal with. Furthermore, in the context of increased economic growth within the EU the Commission believes that there will be an opportunity for the SMEs to benefit without specific measures being introduced. This does not mean that the concerns of SMEs are being ignored by the EU.

A number of measures have been put in place to assist the SMEs, and new initiatives are being included in legislation which has been adopted since the mid-1990s. In 1994 the Commission initiated the 'Integrated Programme for SMEs and the Craft Sector' which highlighted the job creation potential of the eco-technologies. The 'Environment and Growth Initiative for SMEs', which was allocated ECU 9 million from the budget for the purpose of supporting small firms that were carrying out investments which would either contribute to energy savings or environmental improvements, was launched in 1995. Within the Structural Funds ECU 1 billion (1993–99) was set aside for support to national programmes intended to assist with developments within SMEs. The commitment to support the SMEs was continued in the proposals of Agenda 2000 (CEC 1997p, vol. 1: 20) for reform of the Structural Funds. 'There will be special emphasis on improving competitiveness, which is vital if jobs are to be created and maintained. This will require support for measures to assist infrastructure, innovation, SMEs and human resources.'

Informing companies of the implications of legislation and involving them in consultation is considered by the European Commission to be the role of national authorities. Uncertainty about the meaning of legislation is a concern for the SMEs as it is for the larger companies. The benefits of face-to-face consultation between the policy makers and the representatives of industry about the costs of compliance with legislation are clear. The SMEs are, however, less likely to be large enough to maintain their own environmental division or staff to identify the implications; they rely on other agencies for this information. A complaint made by some SMEs is that in some instances the national officials to whom they turn are themselves unsure of the full implications of legislation. In its progress report on the implementation of the Fifth EAP in 1996, a survey undertaken on behalf of the Commission concluded that the national governments weren't addressing the needs of the SMEs (CEC 1996p: 10).

In order to try to alleviate this problem, legislation has begun to be drafted and prepared by the Commission to include an assessment of how the proposals would affect SMEs. When the Directive on integrated pollution control (96/61/EC) was adopted in 1996 it introduced specific measures that affected the SME sector. The smaller companies were exempted from the legislation and medium sized companies were only affected if they had a significant pollution potential. The proposals made at the end of 1997 in the directive for the disposal of end of life vehicles (CEC 1997i: 31) included a section which identified measures which could be taken to minimize any adverse impacts of the legislation on the SMEs.[14]

The directive attempted to deal in a very direct way with the concerns of the SMEs. Problems of consultation were overcome to some extent because trade organizations representing small companies were targeted. Information was made readily and clearly available to explain what the SMEs had to do to implement the legislation. Producers of cars, apart from a few specialist companies, are very large-scale enterprises located in a small number of member states, but those involved in the disposal of vehicles may include many small companies scattered throughout all the states. Two proposals were made in the 'end-of-life' directive following extensive discussion between a large number of organizations representing these companies and the European Commission to assist them in the introduction of this legislation. First it was proposed that more time should be given to enable companies to introduce the required disposal procedures; and second, two- and three-wheeled vehicles and special-purpose vehicles were also exempted from two of the articles of the legislation.

Employment creation may be helped by investments made by the EU. A number of studies have been carried out which attempt to quantify the cost of jobs created which have received funding either wholly or partially from the EU's funds. For example:

- Analysis of the LIFE nature programme for 1996 projects – 63 projects with a value of ECU 45 million created 500 full-time job equivalent. The projects had an average life of 3.3 years. Each job therefore cost around ECU 30 000 (CEC 1997aa).
- In an analysis of projects carried out in Objective 1[15] regions in the context of the EU funding programme for environmental projects in the less developed regions (ENVIREG) in 1993 – the total investment of ECU 627 had created around 5400 jobs. They were in sectors such as urban waste water treatment, municipal solid waste management and public water supply – an investment of ECU 116 000 for each job (CEC 1997u).
- Within the context of the Energy Technology Support Programme (THERMIE) a proposal for upgrading of all single-glazed windows in the EU housing stock to high-performance double glazing is considered to bring a double benefit as it would enable energy to be conserved and would create employment. Investment required: ECU 84 million creating 127 000 for ten years (CEC 1997aa).

In their joint communication in 1997 (CEC 1997l) officials of DG V and DG XI identified a number of areas where the linkage of employment and environment will have a positive impact on job creation. These areas include renewable forms of energy, changes to agricultural practices, changes in consumer demand, developments in urban areas, and the construction industry. Each of these must be treated circumspectly as employment creation potential in each sector depends on the competitiveness of the companies involved. There is no guarantee that employment creation will follow from the developments taking place. Restructuring in a sector or a company does not necessarily result in new employment creation. The main questions to be asked are where investment is to come from and what type of employment is to be created.

In the case of employment in the renewable energy sector, DG XVII (Energy) is engaged in modelling based on employment created by the use of renewable energy. The Commission's view is that by the year 2002 the EU should meet 12 per cent of energy needs from renewable sources. Estimates suggest that this would create 1 million jobs. The current level of energy production in the renewable sector is about 6 per cent of the EU's domestic requirements. The downside is that such a change requires massive investment.

Within DGV (Social Affairs) of the European Commission there is a great deal of desire to establish a sustainable strategy which would have an impact on the environment and on employment. Its officials support a move away from end-of-pipe solutions to environmental problems as the way to guarantee job creation. The question asked within DG V is 'Is it possible to renew capital stock and move to clean and integrated technologies?' It is difficult to persuade industry to engage in process innovation, which is based on a long-term strategy requiring a longer time scale than end-of-pipe technology. It is also difficult to quantify such a strategy in terms of human resources and training: it requires flexible competence from the labour force. 'Flexibility' here should not be viewed as flexibility of workers and their hours: it should be much more associated with workers' skills and competencies and their ability to transfer these skills to another sector.

The introduction of environmental technology is most likely to affect those who are in employment. It is they who will be likely to receive retraining in order to move into a different type of work in the same company. Those groups that are excluded from the labour market as a result of structural changes in the manufacturing sector will continue to find it difficult to enter for the first time or re-enter once they have become unemployed. There is an acceptance in the late 1990s of the idea that retraining will be essential throughout most individuals' working life. Support for reskilling of employees is most likely to come from local level or national government. The EU helps with set-up costs for companies or with support for schemes for those entering the job market,[16] but not with what might be considered as ongoing working costs. If a company receives funding, as soon as it comes to the end of its contract with the EU it must demonstrate that it is viable for the future without additional support.

Greener jobs are assumed to be more labour-intensive and also to absorb some of the less skilled of the unemployed groups (this is not necessarily the case). In reuse sectors there is clearly an opportunity for lower-skilled work. Recycling technology, on the other hand, is likely to require more skilled people as technicians and operators. The construction industry has been emphasized in the proposals made by the European Commission in late 1997. At present it provides 10 per cent of the labour force. The industry offers opportunities for recycling and reuse. Urban renewal schemes are being encouraged by all the national governments, with funding opportunities being sought in public and private sector investment. The construction industry would therefore appear to be an important sector where environmental employment may be created. However, this does not take into account the fact that the construction industry responds very rapidly to changes in economic development. Growth in the construction industry will only come if there is growth in the European economy.

Through its programmes for research and technology development (RTD) the EU has an opportunity to influence the development of the eco-technologies. The Fourth RTD Programme covered the period between 1994 and 1998 and had a maximum overall total budget of ECU 13.1 billion. One of the specific areas which the EU was prepared to support through this programme was the development of research into innovative environmental protection technology. The three predecessors of the Fourth RTD Programme had been criticized for low levels of funding and the way in which the funding was allocated. Competition for the funds was intense and many projects, especially those involving SMEs, failed to attract funding. There were a number of strings attached to the way in which funding was allocated. All projects had to be cooperative ventures, which undercut the competitive incentives of the market. Those companies involved in transnational collaborations complained of a cumbersome bureaucratic system associated with contracts with the European Commission. Funding went to strategic industry and therefore to high-profile projects. This did not help the SMEs. Low-cost solutions to the implementation of environmental legislation were allowed for, but the EU provided little support for projects to find them.

The objective of the Fifth RTD Framework Programme (1998–2002) was to concentrate on technology developments which were of most concern to the people of Europe (employment, quality of life and competitiveness). The structure of this programme included support for actions in the following sectors:

- Environment and sustainable development
- Energy
- Land transport and marine technologies
- Sustainable marine ecosystems
- Socioeconomic research.

The concentration on energy and environment was a result of the input and commitment which the EU had made during the UN Conference on Climate Change held in Kyoto in 1997 (see Table 7.9).

Much of the criticism of earlier programmes still applied to the Fifth RTD Programme. No proposals were made to change the way in which funding was allocated. The programme had an overall budget of ECU 14 billion. This budget was substantially lower than the original proposals of the Commission and the European Parliament (ECU16.3 billion and ECU16.7 billion respectively). It was even below the level of funding for the Fourth programme in real terms since merely maintaining its value at 1998 prices would have required ECU 14.5 billion. The budget meant a reduction of support for the research effort despite the job-creation opportunities in the eco-technologies.

Table 7.9   Budget for the Fifth RTD Framework Programme, 1998–2002

EC framework programme	Budget (millions of euros)
Thematic programmes	
Quality of life and living resources	2 413
Creating a user-friendly information society	3 600
Promoting competitive and sustainable growth	2 705
Energy, environment and sustainable development	2 125
Energy, environment and sustainable development – Euratom	979
Horizontal programmes	
International role of Community research	475
Promoting innovation and participation of SMEs	363
Improving human research potential and the socio-economic knowledge base	1 280
Joint Research Centre	1 020
Total	14 960

Source: Council common position adopted 12 February 1998.

CONCLUSIONS

Within the EU, companies have been particularly concerned not to lose their competitiveness through the application of environmental policy. There is no firm evidence to support the view that companies will suffer loss of competitiveness if they introduce measures to improve their environmental performance. The introduction of end-of-pipe solutions (such as waste water treatment, dust filters, solid waste treatment) in reaction to specific problems may result in short-term additional costs. The introduction of clean technologies into the workplace, on the other hand, may produce significant savings in energy and raw material consumption in the long term. Those companies that have adopted innovative technology have had to bear an initial investment cost but, as has been shown in the chemical sector, the overall impact has been a positive one.

The new generation of measures which the EU has turned to since 1992 relies on the successful conclusion of the search for a model of cooperation between policy makers and industrialists. To achieve this, dialogue is necessary between companies and the policy makers so that cost-effective measures are introduced. As with many issues which relate to the EU's environmental policy, information collection and dissemination is of fundamental importance for checking implementation of policy and evaluating the impact on competitiveness of environmental protection policy. Companies are reticent about the levels and nature of information which they make available as it may be used by their competitors to undermine their share of the market. Many of the means by which this information may be obtained require further development.

The EU has introduced two major pieces of legislation since 1992 establishing information-based voluntary instruments which are designed to change the behaviour of industry. The regulation (Regulation EEC 1863/93) to establish an Environmental Management and Audit Scheme (EMAS) with voluntary registration by companies is designed to target company behaviour directly. The other regulation (Regulation EEC 880/92), establishing a voluntary registration eco-labelling scheme, targets consumers and, through them, industry. Encouraging companies to register for the EMAS has an important part to play as a mechanism to evaluate environmental performance and publish the results to 'consumers' of the products. The consumers in the case of this piece of legislation include suppliers, other companies supplied and company shareholders. The publication of results provides important feedback to a company and ensures their commitment, particularly if their suppliers are looking for the eco-audit logo. The eco-labelling scheme, on the other hand, is a marketing tool to be used by a company in direct relationship with the end user of the product. As a tool to change the behaviour of a manufacturer it is less successful because of the indirect way in which it is envisaged to work. As the case studies in this chapter show, these regulations have met with variable success in different sectors and in different member states.

Individual companies may feel that the introduction of eco-technology will undermine their competitiveness because of the additional costs of introduction of the technology. Investment in eco-technology is important for the competitiveness of the whole European economy. The evidence of the OECD and EU companies already involved in the development of eco-technologies shows the contribution which they may make to job creation. This contribution must, however, be recognized as part of a strategy to improve the competitiveness of European companies and evaluated in terms of what it may contribute to a more general approach to stimulate growth in the European economy.

The EU has set in place the basic regulatory framework for the protection of the environment. The element which now requires strengthening is the means by which effective implementation is ensured, and broadening of the policy instruments is an important way of guaranteeing this. The necessity of improved implementation, increased monitoring and raised levels of the penalties imposed on the individual companies in cases of infringement of the legislation is apparent. The overall picture emerging from the 1990s is that environmental protection and industrial competitiveness are compatible and beneficial to both individual company performance and that of the European economy as a whole. However, the benefits are slow to appear, and constant review of the policy measures and increased dialogue with companies in the manufacturing sector should be developed, as should the adoption of measures which bring together a number of differing approaches to tackling the problems of environmental degradation from the manufacturing industry within the EU.

NOTES

1. See Chapter 12, note 4.
2. A broad definition of competitiveness encompasses three elements – productivity, efficiency and profitability. At the level of an economy, economic indicators of competitiveness include growth, productivity and employment. At the level of a sector of the economy such as manufacturing, competitiveness also includes market share and profitability (CEC 1996r: 3).
3. Council Regulation 880/92 on the Community award scheme for an eco-label, OJL 99, 11 April 1992.
4. Council Regulation 1863/93 allowing voluntary participation by companies in the industrial sector in a Community eco-management and audit scheme, OJL 168, 10 July 1993.
5. Council Directive 70/220/EEC on the approximation of the laws of member states relating to measures to be taken against air pollution by gas from positive ignition engines of motor vehicles, OJL 76, 6 April 1970.
6. Council Directive 93/12/EEC on the creation of a single limit value for sulphur content of gas oil, OJL 74, 27 March 1993.
7. Council Directive 92/62/EEC on packaging and packaging waste, OJL 365, 31 December 1994.
8. Interviews held with Dr Karola Taschner, EEB and officials of DG XI, May 1997.
9. Interviews held with officials of DG II and DG III, May 1997.
10. ECOSOC (1994), The EU Ecolabel Award Scheme. Interviews with Silvia Calamandrei and Robert Wright, authors of this report, in May 1995; second interview with Robert Wright, May 1997. Interviews with Dr Karola Taschner EEB and officials of DG XI, May 1997.
11. See note 4.
12. Council Directive 96/61/EC on integrated pollution control and prevention.
13. The Eurozone comprises the 11 countries that introduced the single currency on 1 January 1999.
14. In October 1998 this proposal continued to cause a great deal of controversy. The European Automobile Manufacturers' Association (ACEA) found that even though the proposed directive contained many positive elements, the overall impact represented a significant threat to the European economy, as it would interfere with the operation of the free market.
15. Objective 1 regions are those regions of the EU that are experiencing the highest levels of economic difficulty. They are therefore considered to be regions most in need of funding from the EU in addition to the support being provided by the national governments to improve their economic development. A number of criteria are used to identify these regions. The criteria

include: the level of unemployment, the level of wealth measured by the per capita GDP, the size of the population, the rate of economic activity (rural or industrial). Funding is provided through the EU's Structural Funds (ERDF, ESF, EAGGF and FIFG) and the Cohesion Fund for these areas.
16. Assistance for job creation schemes may come from the European Social Fund.

8   Agriculture and the environment

INTRODUCTION

Agricultural land occupies over 50.5 per cent of the European Union (27.9 per cent is woodland) (CEC 1997r: 7). The proportion devoted to agricultural land in each state varies, as it occupies less than 10 per cent of the territory of Sweden and Finland (Stanners and Bourdeau 1995: 452). The purpose of the sector is primarily to meet human demand for food, an objective that has been satisfied within the EU. The relative economic importance of the agricultural domain has declined since the creation of the EU, both in terms of its contribution to GDP and its employment potential. At the same time the industrial and service sectors of the economy have assumed an ever-greater importance. In 1997 agriculture contributed only 0.8 per cent to the GDP of the German economy compared to 7.4 per cent to the less developed Greek economy. Despite this declining role, agriculture is heavily subsidized for producers throughout the EU. In 1997 the sector received a subsidy equivalent to 42 per cent of the value of its production compared to 16 per cent for the US (OECD, 1998c).

There is a general assumption that the relationship between agriculture and the environment is a harmonious one, so that farmers are frequently described as the guardians of the countryside. This is an image that is politically convenient, in that it does not confront politically powerful farming pressure groups. It is invoked because it offers a reassurance of compromise rather than confrontation when the issue of reform is mentioned. Yet the reality is far from that. The farmer does not necessarily preserve all that is best in rural life. Farming in Europe is largely profit-driven, and has radically altered the shape of the countryside. A large part of the countryside has been altered by man's activities since the earliest times. For example, farmers have been responsible for removing large tracts of Europe's forests, often leaving just poor-quality scrubland in its place in many upland areas. At best, therefore, farming can be described as a sector generally seen as having a role in preserving the environment that it has created. Indeed, from an environmental perspective, farming and the countryside have the potential to be in almost permanent conflict.

The common agricultural policy (CAP) was designed as a method of integrating the agricultural policies of the original six member states. In 1958 the main concern was to establish a system which guaranteed as far as possible security of the food supply and farmers' incomes. The policy was based upon a price support system designed to maintain the viability of even the least efficient farmers. This meant that the consumer paid higher than world market prices. Initially the system was based upon cereals, but by the late 1990s there were 23 commodity regimes plus schemes to promote the agri-environment.

It is important both that the EU's agricultural sector is economically efficient and that its harmful environmental effects are reduced. At the same time it should be possible for the sector to make a positive contribution to the goal of sustainable development. The CAP has shown that it is possible to influence the behaviour of farmers by the use of incentives, which in the past have been devoted to improving efficiency and increasing output. However, it should be possible to use economic incentives, such as payments, as well as taxes and charges, for environmental purposes. It is also possible to use cross-compliance measures, such as linking income supports to environmental practices. Any economic incentives introduced take time to work, especially in a sector such as agriculture. This means that some degree of regulation is important to deal with particular agricultural practices that damage the environment, such as the careless discharge of animal waste or overuse of pesticides.

Whilst the CAP's price support system remained largely intact until the 1990s, after that the policy went through a number of modifications Most of these were designed to eliminate the inconsistencies within the sector, and to refocus policy to meet changing market conditions. In particular there was a need to address problems associated with overproduction of commodities, which not only added to the high budgetary cost of the policy, but also damaged world trade. The Fifth EAP pointed to problems of overexploitation and degradation associated with water, oil and air, the resources which are essential to the sector. The increasingly intensive nature of the industry was also thought to have contributed to rural depopulation (CEC, 1992a: 7). For this reason, EU policy is moving slowly away from maximizing production to protecting natural resources and enhancing the countryside. Agricultural policy has been moving forward to the situation where farming is regarded as part of a wider rural canvas. The quality of the environment is important in terms of creating attractive living and working conditions, as well as providing recreational space.

By the late 1990s a wide range of measures was associated with the CAP. These included:

- *Support for agricultural markets* This is achieved by a combination of intervention in the market by purchasing surplus supplies, the use of export subsidies, and tariffs. The tariffs favour domestic producers by making imports more expensive.

- *Controls on supply* This includes a range of mechanisms such as quotas which limit the supply of milk.
- *Direct payments to farmers* These were an important aspect of the 1992 MacSharry reforms, because they led to a partial decoupling of the link between production and payments paid to farmers.[1] By 1997 direct payments accounted for almost two thirds of the budgetary cost of the CAP. They cover both the livestock and arable sectors. These payments are not tied to the level of production, and are subject to national and regional limits.
- *Accompanying measures* These were introduced as part of the 1992 reforms, and are designed to encourage environmentally friendly farming.

ENVIRONMENTAL DAMAGE CAUSED BY AGRICULTURE

With or without the CAP, there would have been problems with respect to the management of the agricultural sector in a way that promotes environmentally acceptable outcomes. Farmers tend to make their own decisions about what takes place on their farms. Other effects will, however, occur outside the farm, but the farmer will not necessarily take account of these costs. All agricultural practices will have an impact on the environment as man attempts to modify nature in order to produce food. The concern is that this activity may not be sustainable, and indeed may be destructive in the long term. Agriculture has done a great deal to modify the rural landscape, and some of these changes have been subject to criticism. This is particularly the case with respect to the changes which the European Union has stimulated via the support for the sector with the CAP. This has created a dichotomy between the goal of maximizing the production of food from the land and the goal of sustainability. Where there has been extensive use of fertilizers, these have affected the water supply. The overuse of pesticides has reduced the extent of biodiversity. The degradation of the environment can therefore be seen in some cases as a negative consequence generated by EU policy. This in turn requires the EU to respond by adapting its policy so as to improve the position for the future.

Many of the problems related to agriculture and the environment are of very long standing. As soon as man started to cultivate the soil and rear animals, there was some abuse of the resource. In the context of modern times there is no question about our ability to manage the agricultural environment in a more beneficial way should we choose to do so. Chemical-based fertilizers date back to the nineteenth century, and pesticides have been in use for more than 50 years. Indeed, many modern agricultural practices show a significant improvement on what has happened in the past. It is where we have abused modern technology to damage our agricultural potential that the EU must address its policy. This issue has become of great concern to the EU because of its central role in the CAP. Although the CAP is among the most developed of the EU's policies, farming is still a very individualistic activity, and the implementation of many policy initiatives is still very dependent on the member states. The way that the CAP has encouraged production has created problems in the following areas:

- *Increased crop production* The trend towards monoculture creates the ideal conditions for pests to multiply. This has led to the greater use of weed-killers and pesticides to protect crops and thus retain higher yields. These chemicals have an impact on soil and water pollution and are associated with reduced biodiversity.

    It is difficult for farmers to apply exactly the right amount of fertilizer to the soil. If too much is applied, this can lead to surpluses leaching into the water supply. Excessive use of nitrogenous and phosphate fertilizers can cause eutrophication, in which the fertilizers simulate the development of toxic algae and cause the removal of oxygen from the water. This can kill fish and make the water unusable.
- *Inappropriate management of the land* Mismanagement of the land can lead to a reduction in the quality of soil, and increase the danger of soil erosion. It can also lead to a destruction of wild habitats.
- *Intensification of livestock farming* Intensive livestock rearing can mean that animal diseases become more difficult to deal with. The disposal of animal waste can test the drainage system. If water supplies are polluted, this can attack fish stocks. At the same time human water supplies may also be affected.

    Overgrazing may occur, unless there is an intensive application of fertilizers, which causes problems in its own right.
- *Land drainage* Improving the quality of drainage may improve crop yields, but it can lead to a reduction of biodiversity and depletion of wetlands.

RESEARCH AND TECHNOLOGY DEVELOPMENT PROGRAMMES

One way of improving the environmental performance of agriculture is to investigate alternative strategies to perform essential tasks. The EU's research efforts are managed in the context of framework programmes. The Fourth

Framework Programme, which ran from 1994 to 1998, had only limited funds available to it compared to commercial organizations and national governments. Certainly these funds are not comparable to those available to develop commercially oriented products designed to increase production. Nevertheless, an agricultural research programme was developed which had the objective of establishing the scientific basis for sustainable agriculture. The total budget of this programme was ECU 607 million.

The Commission estimates that up to one third of EU-financed agricultural research projects contribute to sustainable development, and criteria have been established to ensure that projects are not funded which are incompatible with the EU's aspirations for sustainability (CEC, 1996q: 37). The programme supports research into the techniques of animal and vegetal production, socio-economic research on rural development, and economic research on the links between environment and agriculture.

The Fifth Framework Programme (1998–2002) had an initial budget allocated to it of ECU 14 billion. (CEC, 1998j). The programme area dealing with 'Quality of Life and Living Resources' took about 16 per cent of resources. It contained within it a sub-heading dealing with sustainable agriculture, fishing and sylviculture, including the integrated development of rural regions.

PRESERVING BIODIVERSITY

One of the impacts of modern farming, and the excessive use of fertilizers and differing chemicals to control the growth of weeds, is that biodiversity is significantly reduced. Animal types are also prone to disappear over time, as they become less fashionable because of lower yields. It would be difficult to envisage the EU having the funding or the motivation to try to promote the preservation of biodiversity from the centre. This is a case where the arguments for subsidiarity are particularly strong, even though there is a degree of interdependence with respect to these resources. The work of the member states needs to be coordinated, however, so that data are compatible, and there is a general reassurance that all the member states are playing their part. In 1994, the EU fully recognized the need to preserve biological and genetic diversity in agriculture, and at the same time to respect its commitments to the Convention on Biological Diversity ratified by the EU in 1993. The regulation on the conservation, characterization, collection and utilization of genetic resources in agriculture[2] provided the programme with a budget of ECU 20 million over a period of five years. The purpose was to supplement the work of the member states, not to initiate work on behalf of the EU, so that best use was made of existing efforts. The regulation took account of the fact that both plants and animals are genetic resources.

The regulation called for the member states to provide the Commission, at least once a year, with technical, economic and financial information on measures they had carried out or were planning for the conservation, characterization, collection and utilization of genetic resources in agriculture. The Commission was then to keep an inventory of these measures, and to facilitate their exchange. The Commission would then be in a position to comment on trends as they developed across the EU. It produced an interim report on the action taken by the member states in the third year of the programme. However, given that this is only a modestly funded programme with very limited initial aims, it will simply generate information on which to base further action.

NITRATES

The problem of winning compliance with EU legislation is illustrated once again with attempts to reduce the harm caused by nitrates. The benefits of a lower use of fertilizers and pesticides are that farmers will produce fewer crops on environmentally fragile land and grazing will be less intense. There will also be less risk of the nutrients and pesticides leaching into the soil or running off into land drainage. Although some fertilizers move quickly into the water supply in periods of heavy rain, for example, it can take many years for some to reach underground supplies.

The pollution of drinking water by nitrates is a problem throughout the EU. In many of the member states the drinking water exceeds the EU maximum level set at 50 mg/l which was set on public health grounds. The drinking water directive set a guide level (25 mg/l) for nitrate concentration. This may be exceeded in groundwater beneath more than 85 per cent of agricultural land in Europe, with the maximum concentration limit (50 mg/l) being exceeded in waters beneath approximately 20 per cent of agricultural land (Oppenheimer, Wolff & Donnelly 1997: 2–3). The nitrates leach into watercourses and into seas, leading to the growth of algae, which in turn damages the ecosystem. The intensification of agriculture means an increased use of chemical fertilizers, and the rearing of livestock by factory farming methods. Unless efforts are made to dispose of the manure in a satisfactory way, it can be highly polluting.

Farming is the largest contributor to the pollution of fresh waters and marine waters by nitrates, and consequently the nitrates directive was agreed in 1991.[3] The objective of the directive was to reduce or prevent water pollution caused or induced by nitrates from agricultural sources. The directive called upon the member states to identify surface waters and groundwater which was either affected or which could be affected by nitrate pollution. These areas were to be designated 'Nitrate Vulnerable Zones'. The member states were then expected to establish and implement action programmes that limited the spreading of any fertilizer containing nitrogen. Limits were also to be set on the spreading of livestock effluent. The deadline for implementation of the legislation in the member states was 19 December 1993 and the mandatory restrictions should have been in place by the end of 1995.

In 1997 a Commission report on the implementation of nitrates directive (CEC, 1997k) reviewed progress. It expressed concern about the lack of progress on implementing the directive and the serious threat that this posed to the environment and public health. Only Austria, Denmark, Germany, Luxembourg and Sweden had established action programmes, none of which, however, were considered to comply with the directive. In response the Commission opened infringement proceedings against 13 of the 15 member states.

It could be argued that the threat of the legislation plus market forces was a greater influence. Total nitrogen fertilizer consumption declined in the 1980s, but the 1992 MacSharry reforms had a further impact. The fertilizer industry went through a considerable restructuring, pushed on by lower agricultural support prices. This led to the closure of 66 plants within the EU and the halving of the workforce. European fertilizer manufacturers predict a 5 per cent fall in nitrogen consumption and a 9 per cent fall in demand for phosphates and potash in the ten-year period 1997–2007. Full implementation of the nitrates directive by the end of 1999 is expected to lower further the application of nitrates. In the Netherlands, where there is the most intensive usage of nitrates, the fall is expected to be as much as 27 per cent. In Spain and Portugal the use of nitrates might rise, with greater intensification of fruit and olive oil production (Maitland 1997).

A fall in the use of pesticides was also evident. In the period 1986–88 to 1993–95, of the EU member states surveyed, only Belgium, Greece and Ireland increased the use of pesticides, whilst the quantities used fell in the others. A similar situation was evident with respect to nitrogen surpluses in the period 1986–88 to 1994–96, where only Ireland and Belgium showed an increase (OECD, 1998a: 14–15). However, the volume of pesticides was not the only concern. There were increasing concerns about the toxic side-effects of those being used, as we learned more about the compounds that we have been using.

THE COMMON AGRICULTURAL POLICY

The CAP was devised when the memories of food shortages during and after the Second World War were still uppermost in policy makers' minds. Protecting the interests of the substantial number of farmers was also important. Because agricultural markets were either in balance or in deficit, the objectives of the CAP could be heavily oriented towards increasing production. There was no adequate mechanism to control production, because the sanction of falling prices was removed. Article 39 of the Treaty declared these objectives to be:

- to increase agricultural productivity by promoting technical progress and by ensuring the rational development of agricultural production and the optimum utilization of factors of production, in particular labour; and thereby
- to ensure a fair standard of living for the agricultural community, in particular by increasing the individual earnings of persons engaged in agriculture;
- to stabilize markets;
- to ensure the availability of supplies;
- to ensure that supplies reach consumers at reasonable prices.

Within the above there are no environmental objectives set for agriculture: no reference is made to rural development, or to farm animal welfare. Indeed the impact that agricultural practices can have on the air and water quality, or on the soil quality, was not an issue of active debate at the EU level at the time of drafting the Treaty. The first time environmental policy and agriculture are linked is in the First EAP in 1972 (CoM 1973: 38–40). This document noted with concern the trend towards an intensification of agricultural production and, for example, recognized problems such as the overuse of pesticides. In particular it called for the adoption of the directive on less favoured areas (LFA). This was achieved in 1975.[4] Calls were also made for measures to promote forestry.

The basic shape of the CAP remained the same from the 1960s to the early 1990s, despite growing criticism. At its heart was a support mechanism which speeded up a process of change in the sector. Farmers were given a guaranteed price for their production, pitched at a level that offered a living to the least efficient farmer. The rewards were such that more efficient producers could gain a very good living. The support was set far above that paid on the world market. At the same time, the market was protected from imported competition. As a consequence farmers maximized production. Any surpluses were purchased on behalf of the EU and either stored or exported at a cut-down price. What could not be sold was simply destroyed. The need to control the surplus production led to the creation of an ever more elaborate bureaucracy surrounding production quotas, high costs and dissatisfied farmers and consumers.

Many traditional agricultural practices declined in importance and farming became more intensive. Production techniques were improved, with a greater degree of mechanization and the use of more effective chemical treatments of soils and plants. The sector was able to achieve higher yields and greater labour productivity, so that farms grew in size and became more specialized. This trend is particularly apparent in the north of Europe, principally in the UK, the Netherlands, Belgium, Northern France and Germany.

The dramatic increase in agricultural production in the EU was a policy success in terms of moving towards self-sufficiency. Until the 1990s, agricultural production increased, on average, at about 2.5 per cent per year, despite 10 million workers leaving the land in the period from the start of the CAP. Surpluses started to appear as early as the late 1960s, as consumption was growing by only 0.5 per cent per year. Eventually the sector faced a major crisis of overproduction and demands for reform. The emphasis of policy needed to be towards extensification, so that the structure of the industry was not damaged (that is, a lower input–output model). This then gave an opportunity for the EU to consider introducing policies that were less environmentally damaging.

Despite the declining role of agriculture in European economies, the CAP absorbs around 0.6 per cent of the EU's GDP. The justification for this level of spending could reasonably be challenged, bearing in mind the declining share of agriculture in the economy and the constant pressure on public expenditure in the member states. Spending on the CAP is distinct in the sense that it falls under that part of the EU's budget that is compulsory, and as a consequence is far more secure. It has always enjoyed high levels of funding. At its peak the CAP was taking over 60 per cent of the total budget, but by 1997 the percentage had fallen to 54 per cent. The size of the budget should give policy makers scope to influence the development of the sector. To date this is an opportunity that has not been taken advantage of.

Table 8.1   EU budgetary spending on agriculture (ECU million)

	1994	1995	1996	1997[1]	1998[2]
EU budget	59 909.1	65 498.1	80 456.5	80 880.0	81 433.6
Net cost of the CAP	33 378.0	36 057.2	41 128.3	43 964.1	43 645.3
Accompanying measures	490.1	832.1	1 852.3	1 889.0	2 297.0
Accompanying measures as % of the CAP budget	1.47	2.3	4.5	4.3	5.26

[1]   Payment appropriations entered in the 1997 budget.
[2]   Appropriations entered in the letter of amendment to the 1998 preliminary draft budget.

Source: Adapted from European Commission Directorate-General for Agriculture document of 24 November 1997.

Whilst Table 8.1 represents a huge commitment by the EU, insufficient benefit from it reaches the smaller farmers it is supposed to help, in that 80 per cent of the subsidies go to the richest 20 per cent of farmers. The consumer also feels threatened. A wide range of food safety issues have started to emerge and there was also concern about animal welfare related to production methods, and the pollution caused by intensive farming.

The MacSharry Reforms

The Council of Ministers agreed to a major reform of the CAP at the Council of Ministers meeting on 21 May 1992. The MacSharry reforms[5] were important for a number of reasons. First of all they incorporated into the CAP environmental reforms. Indeed the Commission had stated that environmental issues were central to the reform process (CEC 1991c). The measures to reduce market support contained only a limited and indirect environmental incentive, but the regulations governing the so-called accompanying measures were designed to have a direct impact.[6] These referred to environmental measures and forestry respectively. The funding for the accompanying measures came from the guarantee part of the agricultural budget (European Agricultural Guarantee and Guidance Fund – FEOGA). This was an important development, in that it came from the part of the budget that was used to support prices and to assist with the export of surplus production. There was a legal obligation on the member states to introduce these measures, unlike previous attempts to support environmentally sensitive farming.

The CAP reforms covered about 75 per cent of the EU's agricultural production, and are outlined below.

- The link between agricultural support and production was diminished when prices for the arable and beef sector were reduced. Cereal prices were reduced by 29 per cent and beef prices by 15 per cent over a three-year period. CAP prices became much closer to world prices. This may have had indirect environmental benefits, although this would be difficult to verify fully.
- In order to compensate for the loss of income and to maintain their viability, farmers received compensatory payments on a historical basis for the reductions in EU support prices.
- The payments to larger producers of arable crops were dependent on the withdrawal of a proportion of their land from production (set-aside). All but the smallest farms (those producing not more than 92 tonnes of cereals) were expected to participate by leaving at least 15 per cent of their land fallow. This was later reduced to 12 per cent in the crop year 1995–96, 10 per cent in 1995–96 and then 5 per cent in 1996–1998. The rate was set at 10 per cent for the crop year 1999–2000.

- Compensation payments for the beef sector were subject to individual or regional ceilings on the number of cattle per hectare.
- The budgetary costs of the CAP rose with the advent of direct payments to farmers, but this was simply making the cost of assistance to farming more transparent.
- There were accompanying measures that covered agri-environment,[7] afforestation[8] and early retirement measures. These created new opportunities for farmers, while at the same time providing the first step towards a solution to some of the environmental and structural problems of the CAP. These structural measures were seen as an important aspect of the reform.

The objective of the accompanying measures as set out in Regulation 2078/92 was to combine the reduction in food production with improvements in the environment, and at the same time to encourage income divergence and rural development. The member states were required to draft schemes that had a positive environmental effect on the countryside. These might provide aid to farmers, for example schemes to reduce the use of fertilizers and promote organic farming. More extensive production methods were encouraged, as well as the use of farming practices that protected the natural environment and promoted the maintenance of the countryside.

Set-aside

A major feature of the 1992 reforms was the introduction of a set-aside regime to reduce food production. There are other reasons to introduce it, for example as a mechanism for soil conservation, and as a way of preserving natural habitats. The EU version of set-aside was effectively a voluntary production quota. Compensatory payments were only available to larger farmers (whose production of cereals, oilseeds and protein crops exceeded 92 tonnes per year) if they participated in the scheme. Two regimes were offered to farmers, rotational set-aside and free set-aside, but in 1996 it was decided that there would be just a single set-aside rate.

The length of time that land is set aside from crop production may be an indicator of its capacity to help the environment. Short-term set-aside is largely concerned with the control of crop production. Rotational set-aside refers to land taken out of food production for a year, and then returned to production. This can improve soil quality, but it is essentially designed to reduce the cost of management of land that is not required for crop production. This fallow land has to be managed and plant cover is required. In order to improve the economics of the process, farmers could still receive the set-aside premium and use the land for growing non-food crops, including ingredients of pharmaceutical products and biodegradable plastics, and biomass and biofuel, which can be used as renewable energy sources. Non-food set-aside amounted to 1 020 000 hectares in 1995/96.

There are several reasons why set-aside can distort the market and only give a limited environmental benefit. Rotational set-aside is usually managed by farmers to ensure that the least productive land is taken out of production first. The hope is that the regime will have run its course by the time prime land is being considered. Certainly the EU's decision to reduce the set-aside requirement from 15 to only 5 per cent rewarded those farmers who delayed taking high quality land out of production. Farmers may also devote a greater intensity of resources to the land that remains in production. If prices rise as a result of limiting production, that in turn will result in production being stimulated (Bowers 1987: 8). Certainly the period of high prices in the mid-1990s encouraged increased production, so helping to bring back the surpluses that set-aside was designed to reduce. The Commission's preferred option was to abandon the use of rotational set-aside, but the need to reduce surpluses meant that it was retained as a means of controlling production as part of the 1999 Fischler Reforms.[9]

The accompanying measures also brought with them a separate scheme which enabled farmers to commit themselves to environmental set-aside of between five and 20 years. This voluntary set-aside amounted to 50 per cent of the total 4 million hectares set aside in the period 1997–98 (CEC 1998m). This kind of set-aside initiative has a much greater chance of having an environmental benefit, especially if it is accompanied by measures to reduce the intensity of agricultural production elsewhere. The member states were required to draw up schemes to be co-financed with the EU. This posed design problems for the member states but gave them considerable freedom to create schemes appropriate to local conditions. The level of funding to farmers depended upon their income foregone and the costs associated with the scheme. The measures applied to any farmland, not just that dedicated to arable production. Long-term set-aside can create small natural parks or biotopes and valuable habitats for a variety of animal and bird life. Typically the scheme works best with marginal land, which is environmentally fragile.

The results of the MacSharry reforms

The new instruments of the CAP agreed in 1992 did take better account of the environment, but did not systematically integrate environmental concerns. Indeed, by the late 1990s there was little evidence that they had had a measurable effect. However, there may have been secondary effects that were positive, which arose from the reduction of price supports. The decision to weaken the link between agricultural production and support for farmers was important. If high prices were a stimulus for more intensive agriculture, as farmers sought to maximize the use of their assets, then it was reasonable to argue that price reductions would work in the other direction. It could be a stimulus for extensification of production (moving from a high-input high-output method of production to a low-input low-output method of production). So, for example, the demand for fertilizers should fall, as indeed it did. Lower agricultural prices could mean that there is less pressure to convert natural wetlands, forests and grasslands to agriculture. Indeed, afforestation and forage production can be an important device to reduce soil erosion.

If price support falls too far, farmers may abandon the land, especially in marginal areas. After a time such land may return to its natural state, but there is no guarantee that this will happen. The process needs to be monitored, because in a number of cases man's activities protect the countryside by helping to prevent flooding and the damage caused by landslides. Without this protection, there would be a loss of biodiversity and damage to the landscape (CEC 1996q: 34). There are also cases where we place a high value on the aesthetic value of the cultivated landscape, or where it supports a rich variety of plant and wild life.

As a result of the reforms and poor harvests, 1994 and 1995 stocks diminished, and the EU looked as if it had achieved a balance between production and consumption in the cereals market. Beef stocks fell from 1.1 million tonnes to zero, until the 'mad cow' disease crisis reduced consumption and caused stocks to rise suddenly. By 1997 the stocks of beef had risen to 450 000 tonnes (Southey 1997). Cereal stocks fell from 33 million tonnes in 1993 to less than 3 million tonnes at the end of the marketing year 1995/96.

Indeed, there was a feeling that production had been cut by too much, because the cuts coincided with a poor harvest globally and a period of high prices. During the period 1992–96 farm incomes rose by 4.5 per cent a year and in many countries they were above the national average. Cereal farmers were fortunate on two accounts. The rise in world cereal prices meant that they did not actually suffer from a fall in prices, but they still received compensatory payments. The Commission believed that this situation amounted to an 'overpayment' which gave the farmers ECU 8.5 billion more than had been intended (*Economist* 1997b).

The problem of overproduction started to return. In September 1997 intervention stocks of cereals were 5.3 million tonnes and by December 1998 they had risen to around 16 million tonnes. Without increasing the extent of set-aside, it was estimated that stocks could stand at 30 million tonnes by June 2000 (CEC 1998m). Longer-term predictions were for a rise to 58 million tonnes in the period to 2007, unless action were taken. Surpluses were expected to grow in other areas. This would not only create problems for the EU in terms of its external relations; it would create pressure on the EU's budget at a time when there were new priorities with respect to enlargement (*Economist* 1997a). In its evaluation of the reforms, the Commission (CEC 1998g) believed that the effects of reform on the environment had been mixed. There had been a more rational use of fertilizers and pesticides resulting from the reduction in support prices. However, the regionalization of direct payments to cereals, oilseeds and protein crops had encouraged the irrigation of crops. The Commission also believed that there had been environmental benefits as a result of well-managed set-aside. The incentives for lower intensity of livestock rearing had been a positive feature. But this had been offset to some extent by lower feed prices, and subsidizing silage encouraged greater intensity of rearing.

The EU missed a substantial opportunity to use fiscal incentives to steer environmental policy. Referring to Regulation 2078/92, which saw the payment to farmers who protected the environment and maintained the countryside, Commissioner Bjerregaard commented that 'we already suspect that agri-environmental premiums ... of the agricultural budget are not attractive enough compared with subsidies for intensive production, covering 90 per cent of the budget. They cannot compete' (Bjerregaard 1996a). Indeed, these were precisely the sentiments that were put forward at the time the regulation was introduced (House of Lords 1992d: 7). As participation in agri-environmental measures is voluntary, payments to farmers to participate should be at least as high as the income they forego, as an incentive to participate.

The Environmental Future of the CAP

The nature of the agricultural methods employed has a specific impact on the extent of environmental damage. After the MacSharry reforms had been in place for some time, there was a concern to move forward to complete the task. At the Madrid European Council in December 1995, the Commission presented its agricultural strategy paper (CEC 1995d). This concentrated on improving the competitiveness of European agriculture, but also outlined the need for an integrated rural policy to accompany the reform process. In the first cohesion report, published in November 1996, the Commission argued for a parallel effort to enhance the economic potential and the environmental value of rural areas and their capacity to provide sustainable jobs (CEC 1996f).

In its policy document Agenda 2000 (CEC 1997p), the Commission set out its objectives for the future of agriculture as follows:

- Farmers should be given the opportunity to enjoy a fair standard of living.
- Agriculture should be competitive within world markets without being oversubsidized.·
- Production methods should be environmentally friendly and the products should be of the quality that consumers want.
- The sector should retain its diversity and not just be output-orientated.
- Rural communities should be maintained.

- Agriculture should have a policy that is more understandable, with the sector being able to justify its role in society.

The document was optimistic about the commercial aspects of the policy: demand would be assisted by the increase in world population and rising income per head, which would stimulate world agricultural production, but this would be constrained by the process of urbanization taking land out of production and environmental considerations. Although a slowdown in the growth of yield was predicted, it was felt that this might be offset by developments in genetic engineering, providing these methods proved to be acceptable to consumers.

The Commission's view may have been overoptimistic. Apart from the fall in demand for beef because of the BSE crisis, competition within world markets became more intense. By 1997 there were signs that surpluses were starting to appear in cereals, sugar, wine, olive oil, skimmed milk powder and some other dairy products. Bumper harvests in 1988 and the effects of the economic crisis in South East Asia made this problem worse.

The new multilateral trade negotiations scheduled to start in 2000 would, it was felt, follow the trends established by the Uruguay Round, with pressure to reduce export subsidies. This will have implications for internal support prices. The link between support from the EU budget and production is likely to be reduced further. At the same time there will be greater emphasis on environmental and social standards at the international level, and the Central and Eastern European enlargement will pose problems with respect to the sector's ability to absorb labour. Similarly the cost of support prices and direct payments may prove prohibitive.

The CAP's role at the centre of the EU's sectoral policies would seem to make it an ideal focus for implementing article 3c of the Amsterdam Treaty. This requires that environmental protection be integrated into the definition and implementation of common polices, with a view to promoting sustainable development. In its Agenda 2000 strategy, the Commission recognized the importance of agri-environmental policy. It saw the task as the creation of instruments to support a sustainable development of rural areas and a response to society's increasing demand for environmental services. The policy was not intended to be just a price-driven phenomenon, as issues such as food safety were to be considered. Linked with this, it was noted that many consumers were also concerned with issues of animal welfare and the environmental impact of agriculture. These ethical concerns have the potential to place the farmer in the role of manager of the landscape in EU policy terms. If this is to be a reality, however, the nature of support arrangements needed to be changed yet again, and the review of EU policies carried out under the Agenda 2000 provided an opportunity to do this.

The Agricultural Council of 11 March 1999 came to a political agreement about the substance of CAP reform for the period leading to the accession of new states (CEC 1999a). The 1999 Fischler Reforms were expected to stay within the guidelines for agricultural spending, which allowed it to rise by no more than 74 per cent of GNP growth. However, there was some doubt whether this had actually been achieved. The main substance of the Fischler Reforms, as amended by the Berlin European Council of 24–25 March 1999, was that:

- intervention prices for cereals were to be cut by 15 per cent;
- direct payments to farmers were to be increased;
- compulsory set-aside was to be retained, with the basic rate set at 10 per cent for the marketing years 2000–2006;
- voluntary set-aside was to be retained, but the scheme was to be improved, in particular to take account of environmental considerations;
- the support price of beef was to be cut by 20 per cent;
- the milk quota regime was extended until 2006 and the future of the regime after 2006 would be reviewed in 2003;
- the intervention price for butter and skimmed milk was reduced by 15 per cent (CoM 1999).

The cut in support prices was somewhat lower than had been expected, and reflected the ability of the agricultural lobby in the member states to defend the sector against radical change. The retention of compulsory set-aside was surprising, given the general lack of enthusiasm for the mechanism by the Commission and by the farming community. Its retention indicates a belief that the support prices were still not low enough to deter production and keep surpluses under control. Indeed it is difficult to see the reforms fully satisfying any of the EU's policy objectives for the sector. EU markets will still largely favour domestically produced agricultural products, which will bring them into conflict with the WTO. The cost of the settlement may in any case be too high to be fully affordable once the EU has expanded to take in the Central and Eastern European states. What the budget settlement did bring was increased resources for rural policy and environmental measures. This is shown in Table 8.2.

In order to demonstrate a greater commitment to environmental objectives, other measures were introduced, although these were not fleshed out in detail. Member states were expected to define appropriate environmental measures to be applied by farmers. Penalties were to be introduced for environmental infringements involving, where appropriate, the reduction of direct payments. It was suggested that funds made available from aid reduction could be used as an additional support for: agri-environment measures, less favoured areas, and afforestation. The member states will administer these measures, which will be tailored to specific regional circumstances. The measures offer financial incentives to farmers who, on a voluntary and contractual basis, provide environmental services or improve the environmental soundness of farming practices. It will be a test of these measures if, rather than offering funding for good agricultural practices, they make payments for additional environmental gains.

Table 8.2   Agriculture and rural policy budgets, 2000–2006 (millions of euros at 1999 prices)

	2000	2001	2002	2003	2004	2005	2006
Agricultural expenditure	40 920	42 800	43 900	43 770	42 760	41 930	41 660
CAP expenditure (excluding rural development)	36 620	38 480	39 570	39 430	38 410	37 570	37 290
Rural development and accompanying measures	4 300	4 320	4 330	4 340	4 350	4 360	4 370

Source: CoM (1999).

The Commission had proposed that the member states should be able to make compensation payments and market support conditional on environmental requirements (CEC 1997p). However, these proposals were watered down in the Fischler Reforms, in an attempt to reach an overall agreement. The payments system can be utilized to improve the environmental performance of agriculture, but it needs to be operated in a transparent way. Also the measures need to be evaluated to ensure that their environmental effects are achieved at the lowest cost. Finally, payments have to be monitored to ensure that there is compliance (Legg and Portugal 1997).

The less favoured areas (LFA) scheme is also to be improved by reorientating it towards more environmental schemes with strong links to sustainable farming and nature protection. The LFA scheme currently makes payments to farmers who face permanent natural handicaps in using their land, for example those in mountainous areas, on arid plains with difficult climatic conditions, on steep hills and in Arctic zones. The Fischler Reforms extended the concept of the LFA by giving member states the opportunity to include areas where farmers faced specific environmental constraints. The additional allowances under the LFA scheme are intended to ensure continued sustainable land use, which should help to maintain rural communities and traditional landscapes. It is likely that much of the support will go to extensive farmers (low input–low output) since the Commission seeks to promote sustainable farming as a condition for receiving payments.

Whilst it is important that incentives are made available to farmers within the EU budget to improve their environmental performance, the application of the polluter pays principle (PPP) is generally absent. This applies to both current payments and future plans. It would appear reasonable to pay farmers to adopt more environmentally friendly practices, but they should not be paid to desist from environmentally damaging practices. To do so would be contrary to the idea of the PPP.

RURAL DEVELOPMENT POLICY

Agriculture can help to maintain certain rural environments that are especially valued, and have become part of our cultural inheritance. The value that society attaches to these areas runs contrary to economic forces. As agriculture has become more intensive throughout the whole of the EU, the extent of economic divergence within the sector has grown. This has led to areas where agriculture has become only a very marginal activity, and where there is a danger that farmers will abandon land, or where insufficient effort will be made to maintain environmental standards. This applies to many areas at the margins of the system, such as uplands or wetlands. Maintaining an approach that sustains or even improves on the existing balance between agriculture and the environment is particularly important, and yet these areas are often the least profitable.

The idea of integrating agricultural structural policy into the wider economic and social context of rural areas has been on the EU's agenda for almost two decades. The pattern of life is changing, with a significant fall in the numbers of people employed in agriculture and the total number of farms. Agriculture (and forestry) are no longer the basis of the rural economy. Farming accounts for only 5.5 per cent of total EU employment, and the number of farmers is declining at a rate of 2–3 per cent per year.[10] Only in a few regions does the sector account for more than 20 per cent of employment. The strength of rural policy is its ability to integrate across sectors other than farming, which means that it is not just concerned with a dwindling band of farmers, but incorporates all those who live in the countryside.

Expanding the scope of a rural development policy offers a way of gaining wider political support for the agricultural sector, while at the same time removing the emphasis of policy away from supporting production. Rural development has generally been regarded as the poor relation of the main business of the CAP in terms of offering support to the countryside. The EU's rural development policy assists farmers with the task of diversifying into other activities so as to supplement their income. It also provides aid to change the structure of agriculture and encourages environmental improvements. Included within this are schemes to encourage the development of forestry. Some activities that might have been economically marginal are supported, for example rural tourism, growing and selling of high-quality produce, investment projects linked to environmental improvement or regional culture. Non-farmers who live in the countryside also benefit from projects to regenerate villages and schemes to encourage tourism.

The 1999 Fischler Reforms promised the introduction of the new rural development policy, with a more generous level of funding. The weakness of the rural development policy in the past was that it lacked adequate funding. Politicians believe there are votes to be gained from supporting farmers, despite the declining numbers. There is only limited support for the general rural lobby, despite the Commission promoting what appears to be a rational policy. For this reason the EU is likely to continue with its greater emphasis on direct support for farmers.

CONCLUSION

The CAP was not designed as an environmentally friendly policy, and it was not until 1992 that it started to be integrated into the mainstream of policy. At the very best, environmental improvements are seen as only one of many competing priorities. By far the greatest concern is for farm incomes and security of food supplies. This has added to the financial strain that the sector imposes on the EU. Despite the progress that has been made in the 1990s, the EU's CAP has so many problems that the main priorities for reform are likely to be maintaining farm incomes, reducing surplus production and the incorporation of Central and Eastern Europe into the EU.

The conflict between agriculture and the environment may be resolved in the future if environmentally friendly production can be seen to offer a lower-cost option. This is not to suggest that there will be a general movement towards organic farming. This is still carried out on a relatively small scale, and consumers appear to be generally resistant to paying a significant price premium for its perceived environmental benefits. It is more likely that the use of high technology, such as satellite monitoring and tracking of applications of fertilizers and pesticides, will be the way forward for large-scale farmers. The use of satellite mapping combined with satellite dishes on machinery now means that the application of fertilizers and pesticides can be very precise.

The concern with high levels of unemployment and rural depopulation suggests that broadening the basis of policy to include rural development has great potential. Whilst there is a capacity to incorporate environmental objectives into such a policy, there is evidence of a lack of political support for the policy overall. The alternative is to link CAP financial support to environmental objectives. In the past, agriculture was the buttress of the rural economy, now it is not. It can, however, generate environmental benefits, which sets it apart from a great deal of industry. This may be an argument for making payments to farmers for environmental services. Indeed, given the problems caused by overproduction, this represents the strongest political case for continued EU support to the sector. Such payments may contradict the PPP, but they offer a pragmatic solution to the problem of changing farmers' attitudes, and could be achieved without any additional costs. The problem for the EU is not a lack of financial support for the sector, but a lack of policy direction. This radical strategy, which has been proposed by the Commission, offers a way of ensuring that the industry remains economically viable, while at the same time improving its environmental performance. It remains to be seen if the 1999 Fischler Reforms will deliver this.

NOTES

1. Small farms received the payments without being expected to set aside land. Also, the intervention arrangements still remained in place.
2. Council Regulation 1467/94 of 20 June 1994 on the conservation, characterisation, collection and utilisation of genetic resources in agriculture, OJL 159, 26 June 1994.
3. Council Directive 91/676 concerning the protection of waters against pollution caused by nitrates from agricultural sources, OJL 375, 31 December 1991.
4. Council Directive 75/268/EEC on less favoured areas, OJL 128, 19 December 1976.
5. Named after Ray MacSharry, the agricultural commissioner who championed the reforms.
6. Council Regulation 2078/92 of 30 June 1992 on agricultural production methods compatible with the requirements of the protection of the environment and the maintenance of the countryside, OJL 215, 30 July 1992 and Council Regulation 2080/92 of 30 June 1992 instituting a Community scheme for forestry measures in agriculture, OJL 215, 30 July 1992.
7. These schemes aimed to encourage farmers to introduce or maintain production techniques which encouraged the protection of the environment, the landscape and natural resources.
8. These were intended to encourage farm forestry, as an alternative to producing surpluses. Promoting afforestation does not necessarily lead to environmental benefits.
9. The Fischler Reforms were named after Franz Fischler, the commissioner responsible for agriculture. These proposals came under the Agenda 2000 package of reforms.
10. This figure ignores the significant numbers of rural service providers who sell to farmers, such as vets, seed firms and technicians. All these services have a considerable multiplier effect.

9 Energy and environmental policy

INTRODUCTION

The development of the EU's common energy policy (CEP) has taken place in the context of a growing global concern about a whole range of political and economic issues related to the sector. It is notable that two of the first three treaties were concerned with the integration of energy policy across Europe. These were the European Coal and Steel Community (ECSC) Treaty in 1951 and the European Atomic Energy Community (Euratom) Treaty in 1958. Despite the existence of the treaties, there have been continuous conflicts between the role of the member states and that of the EU. The reality has been that the dominant hand has been held by the member states, largely because of their ownership of parts of the energy sector and their control over fiscal policy. The security of energy supplies has been central to national industrial policy, and has been seen as a strategic issue. This is especially the case where there has been an external threat, such as an oil crisis. However, as the EU's single market has become more important, so has the development of the internal energy market (IEM).

The EU's energy consumption is relatively high compared to that of the developing world, but has tended to grow by only 1 per cent per year compared to a global consumption increase of 2 per cent per year. Although this appears to be a relatively good performance, it reflects the slow growth of the EU's economy, which has dampened energy demand. However, energy is a sector that is subject to change, and a number of important events have had an impact on it, including:

- The energy market has become more globalized due to improved transport systems.
- The liberalization of Central and Eastern Europe and the newly independent states (NIS) from the former Soviet Union.
- The signing of the European Energy Charter.
- The strengthening of environmental concerns, with an increasing desire to ensure that sustainable development is integrated into energy policy goals.
- Technological developments which have had an impact on the competitiveness of all sectors of the economy, improving access to energy

resources, increasing energy efficiency, contributing to the diversity of fuels and helping energy saving.

This chapter suggests that there are no instant solutions to problems relating to energy and the environment. Energy is essential for man's existence and is the basis of European industrial society. The chapter is therefore concerned with how to manage the process of exploiting energy sources so as to minimize damage to the environment. Energy and environment policies need to address the problem of global warming and sustainable growth and to formulate a cost-effective approach to integrating energy into environmental policy. This involves improving upon energy efficiency and at the same time introducing new energy sources with little or no environmental impact. Energy use not only affects the atmosphere, at the same time there are significant problems related to waste disposal as a result of energy production, particularly with respect to nuclear energy. There are also by-products of the energy industry's activities which need to be taken into account, such as coastal pollution due to oil spillage.

The rapid rise in oil prices in 1973/74 and 1979/80 were caused by Middle Eastern conflicts and had a very detrimental effect on the growth of the European economies. This meant that security of the sources of energy supply became crucial issues for Europe, as well as competitiveness and protection of the environment. The political process is therefore complicated by a need to reassure member states that any EU-wide initiative will not expose domestic supplies to additional threats. However, the oil price rise did provide an incentive to improve energy efficiency, and encouraged innovation with respect to renewable energy sources (RES).

ENERGY PRODUCTION AND RESOURCES

A wide range of energy sources is available, including solid fuels, such as coal, gas, oil and nuclear. In addition to this there are renewable energy sources such as wind and water power and derived energy sources such as electricity. The mixture of fuels consumed depends on many factors, for example environmental regulation, prices, technological developments and decisions taken to maintain the security of supply.

Energy activities can be divided into three stages. The first is the production of primary energy; the second is its conversion into derived energy; and finally consumption. Primary energy in Europe rose to 689.8 million tonnes of oil equivalent (toe) in 1995. Figure 9.1 shows the breakdown of production by product.

There is an uneven distribution of primary energy sources throughout Europe, which affects the production of primary energy. The UK, because of its supplies

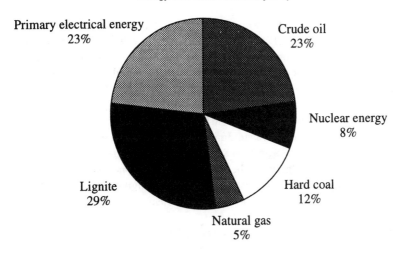

Source: Eurostat (1996a).

Figure 9.1   Primary energy production broken down by product, 1995 (EU 15)

of North Sea oil, is the most important producer of primary energy within the European Union, with other countries being much more meagrely endowed (see Table 9.1).

Table 9.1   Primary energy production (m toe)

	1994	1995	1995/94 (%)
EU 15	677.5	689.8	1.7
Belgium	10.6	11.0	4.4
Denmark	13.7	14.0	2.2
Germany	137.4	137.1	−0.2
Greece	7.8	7.9	0.4
Spain	28.0	26.9	−3.8
France	110.3	114.1	3.4
Ireland	3.4	3.3	−4.1
Italy	27.8	27.2	−2.0
Luxembourg	0.0	0.0	−24.1
Netherlands	64.6	65.0	0.6
Austria	5.7	5.8	1.2
Portugal	1.1	0.8	−24.4
Finland	7.9	7.9	−0.4
Sweden	23.4	23.2	−0.9
UK	235.9	245.7	4.2

Source: Eurostat (1996a).

The main factors that determine the quantity of energy consumed within a country include the size of its population, income levels, the structure of the economy, the rate of technological progress and the price of energy. Total EU gross inland energy consumption reached 1360.4 million tonnes of oil equivalent (toe) in 1996. As Table 9.2 demonstrates, Germany, which has the largest economy in the EU, is a major consumer of energy, which reflects its population size and overall industrial development. However, energy consumption per person averaged 3650.6 kilograms of oil equivalent (kgoe), ranging from 1778.0 in Portugal to 8157.6 in Luxembourg. These differences largely reflect living standards, heating needs and economic structure, with Luxembourg being a special case because of the high energy consumption related to its industrial sectors and to foreign consumption (mainly transport).

Table 9.2   The EU's energy balance sheet, 1996

	Gross inland consumption (million toe)	Rise on 1995 (%)	Energy dependence ratio (%)	Consumption per person (kgoe)
Belgium	55.5	6.0	80.7	5 468.7
Denmark	22.8	13.8	29.1	4 335.0
Germany	343.8	3.6	59.5	4 201.6
Greece	23.7	5.0	69.1	2 267.2
Spain	95.7	−3.8	74.2	2 437.7
France	230.3	4.4	49.1	3 953.6
Ireland	10.7	4.3	70.8	2 950.1
Italy	158.4	−0.7	82.6	2 763.0
Luxembourg	3.4	3.1	99.4	8 157.6
Netherlands	75.0	4.5	17.2	4 840.5
Austria	23.2	3.4	75.5	2 878.9
Portugal	17.6	−3.6	91.9	1 778.0
Finland	21.5	10.3	62.7	4 204.9
Sweden	47.6	12.6	52.1	5 390.1
UK	231.3	5.7	−11.6	3 940.2
EU 15	1,360.4	3.6	48.2	3 650.6

Source: Eurostat (1996b).

The EU's energy dependence ratio – net imports as a proportion of gross consumption – was 48.2 per cent in 1996. Twelve member states had dependence ratios higher than this, but the UK as a net exporting country (−11.6

per cent), and low dependence by the Netherlands (17.2 per cent) and Denmark (29.1 per cent) kept the average down. Not only do individual member states show disparities in terms of their energy balances; they rely on different sources of fuel. So, for example, the UK has the largest oil reserves in the EU, Germany is far more dependent on its coal industry for reasons of both energy security and employment. Technological development should limit the growth in EU energy consumption to about 1 per cent per year. However, the EU is becoming increasingly dependent upon imported energy sources, which could rise to 70 per cent of total consumption by 2020. This is because of the declining use of coal and a switch to the use of gas, which is far more environmentally friendly (CEC 1997a). As Europe becomes ever more dependent on energy sources from outside, foreign policy will be an important consideration.

Energy efficiency has improved since the early 1970s, so that unlike in the past, there is only a weakened link between the growth in population, national income and energy consumption. This demonstrates that it is possible to obtain the same level of energy output with less input, and shows that there is not an automatic link between economic growth and increased energy consumption. Improvements in energy efficiency also have implications for the environment, because they may result in a reduction in the level of emissions of greenhouse gases, particularly carbon dioxide. This means that improving energy efficiency can be economically profitable as well as environmentally desirable. It also indicates that there are opportunities for further efficiencies, particularly as consumers can improve to the most efficient level in all sectors and across all member states.

THE DEVELOPMENT OF EU ENERGY POLICY

The central role of energy in the European economy is illustrated by the fact that two out of the three treaties that established the EU had energy at their heart. The ECSC Treaty that came into force in 1951 aimed to create a common market for coal and steel. These provisions were designed to bring about equality of access to sources of production, improved productivity and growth in trade. The ECSC Treaty reflected the priorities of the time and in particular the relative importance of coal. It led to the removal of import and export duties throughout the EU and abolition of certain restrictive trade practices. So, for example, state aids were to be authorized through article 67 of the ECSC Treaty and would only be granted if they existed to promote economic viability, solve social and regional problems created by industry closures or to help the coal industry to adjust to environmental protection standards. The Euratom Treaty that came into force in 1958 concentrated on the nuclear industry and had a strong focus on research and dissemination of knowledge, as well as safety. This reflected the optimism that nuclear energy would provide a safe and cheap high-technology energy source for the future.

It was not until the 1973/74 oil crisis that the need for an energy strategy arose within the EU. Since that time, energy policy has largely focused on reducing the consequences of an oil crisis and on security of supply. In 1983 the Council of Ministers defined the common energy objectives and stressed the need for EU coordination to strengthen national energy operations and launch specific Community initiatives. The EU has a shared responsibility for energy policy, but the instruments with regard to energy policy are not integrated within the treaties. However, the adoption of the Single European Act and its contribution to the creation of the single market had a profound effect on the energy sector. This sector is a prime target for liberalization and deregulation, and it was anticipated that improvements here would lead to improvements in overall competitiveness within the European economy.

In 1988 the Commission started the process of trying to develop a more meaningful internal energy market (IEM) (Matláry 1998). Their proposals had the following features:

- Harmonization of indirect taxation
- Transparency of price and investment decisions
- Competitive public procurement
- Third-party access to oil and gas
- State-aid restructuring for coal
- Integration of electricity and gas grids.

Whilst the above proposals were not designed to have a direct impact on environmental aspects of the CEP, the competitive process which drove them did. In particular, coal, which is one of the most polluting of energy sources, is also vulnerable to price competition from oil and gas. Few deep coalmines can survive without subsidy. Similarly, nuclear power has a problem competing in the open market.

The Maastricht Treaty did not include an energy chapter; neither did the Amsterdam Treaty. However, there is a role for the EU with respect to the creation of trans-European networks (TENS), which are designed to link the national energy distribution networks. The Maastricht Treaty also had an impact on the energy sector by stressing the operation of the internal market, promotion of economic and social cohesion, common commercial policy and environmental policy as well as research. Article 2 of the TEC called for 'sustainable and non-inflationary growth respecting the environment' (article 2 TEC), which was significant for energy policy in the sense that it required that there be a balance between price stability, economic growth and environmental protection. This requirement was maintained in the Amsterdam Treaty.

THE PRIORITIES FOR EU ENERGY POLICY

The EU can only achieve its energy and environment strategy by working in partnership with member states. The rational use of energy sources means developing partnerships with industry and gaining the support of the consumer. The provision of information and incentives is essential, for example the use of tax allowances to promote better use of energy sources. Each energy source has a different impact on the environment, which means that it is important to internalize the external costs so that comparisons can be made. Increasing energy efficiency is partly driven by market forces, so that the liberalization of energy markets will remove some of the least efficient practices by a competitive process. In addition to this, standards should also be set to promote energy efficiency. The EU has assisted with research and technology development by promoting cross-border collaboration and supporting parts of the schemes. The funding of these types of initiatives is, however, limited because of EU budgetary constraints. More promising is the broadening of the mix of instruments that can be used by the member states. This includes withdrawal of some subsidies that give the wrong market signals and the promotion of voluntary agreements with industry. Finally, changing attitudes among the member states is a very important aspect of policy – perhaps the most important – in that it helps to generate the political will for action to be taken.

The EU's energy policy aims to balance three priorities (CEC 1995f):

- *Overall competitiveness* Competitiveness with respect to energy policy helps the development of economies and also ensures international success for EU companies. The EU's competitiveness derives from the functioning of the single market, minimization of regulation and an appreciation of the economic value of energy efficiency. This market-based approach means that the EU member states still use processes that are not necessarily the most environmentally friendly.
- *Security of supplies* This is an important consideration, because it creates an environment that is favourable to economic activity. It drives forward the need to encourage energy saving, the development of energy networks and the strengthening of international cooperation. It also means maintaining the coal industry at a level that can meet an emergency created by an international energy crisis.
- *The environment* In an ideal world, there should be synergy between the competitiveness and energy security aspects of policy. Where conflicts arise between these objectives, measures need to be taken to adjust them. Part of the key to this is internalization of external costs of energy so that the full cost of externalities is realized. This implies a need to integrate environmental considerations fully into energy policy, so that emission

levels and energy production processes can be regulated by fiscal incentives, voluntary agreements or legal means.

There are aspects of energy policy that cannot be fully reconciled. The failure to win agreement with respect to a global carbon/energy tax can be blamed on the threat of free-riding by major industrial powers, that is, any pricing policy must take account of global competition. If there is a significant loss of competitiveness due to high energy prices, then there is likely to be only limited political support for the internalizing of external costs. Security of supply is also a problem, because it is based on assessment of political threats, which are impossible to price. The search for policy coherence is also complicated by the fact that aspects of it fall under different EU policy areas, such as External Relations, Environmental or Agricultural Policies, Research and Technological Development or Structural Funds.

In the Fifth Environmental Action Programme, the Commission declared that energy policy was a key factor in the achievement of sustainable development (CEC 1992a: 6). The challenge was to guarantee economic growth along with security of energy supplies and a clean environment. To achieve this by the year 2000, the Commission called for an improvement in energy efficiency. The development of strategic technological programmes would be towards a less carbon-intensive energy structure and, in particular, renewable energy sources. The reasoning behind this was the projected doubling of the world population from an estimated 5 billion in 1990 to 10 billion in 2050. It was thought that this might bring about an increase in energy demand from 9 billion tonnes of oil equivalent (toe) in 1990 to 20 billion toe in 2050. Even with a significant improvement in energy efficiency, this figure was set to rise to 13 billion toe. The consequences of this development for Europe were that there would be a significant increase in the emission of greenhouse gases as well as a considerable problem with respect to security of energy supplies. Because at that time it was believed that there would be a heavy reliance on coal supplies, even the lower level of 13 billion toe implied an increase of 60 per cent in CO_2 emissions on a global level. This growth in energy demand would naturally create problems with respect to security of energy supply, and it was therefore felt that there should be greater emphasis on renewable energy sources as well as higher energy efficiencies. The strategy that the EU proposed took into account the need to reverse previous trends towards increasing CO_2 emissions. In October 1990, the European Council had concluded that aggregate CO_2 emissions should be stabilized at 1990 levels by the year 2000.

In the period from 1990 to the end of 1994, the EU appeared to make good progress with respect to reduction in emission levels of CO_2, achieving a fall of 2.2 per cent. The main reason for that success was the decline in emissions from households and industry, as can be seen from Table 9.3.

Table 9.3   EU 15 CO_2 emissions by sector (in millions of tonnes)

	1990	1992	1994	Share, 1994 (%)	Change, 1994/90 (%)
Total CO_2 emissions	3174	3153	3103	100	–2.2
Thermal power stations	966.2	981.2	955.7	30.8	–2.7
Other emissions by energy sector	135.7	137.5	143.3	4.6	+5.6
Transport	757.9	793.0	815.2	26.2	+7.5
Households etc	683.0	661.5	625.5	20.1	–8.4
Industry	631.6	569.6	563.1	18.1	–11

Source: Derived from UNICE (1996).

It is interesting to note that this position has been achieved without the imposition of a carbon/energy tax and perhaps reflects the fact that the EU's targets were rather unambitious. However, the slowdown in the economies of Europe in this period (1990–94) would certainly go some way towards explaining the reason for the decline in industrial CO_2 emissions. As the economies started to speed up, so the doubts as to the attainability of the targets returned. At the December 1997 Kyoto Summit, the EU's aspirations were revised with a promise to reduce emissions of greenhouse gases by 8 per cent below the 1990 levels between 2008 and 2012. However, this challenge will be difficult to meet given that CO_2 emissions from energy alone are predicted to increase by 8 per cent between 1990 and 2010, unless there is a radical change in policy (Bjerregaard 1998).

ENERGY EFFICIENCY

Energy efficiency can be achieved in one of two ways: an increased level of investment, or a change in consumer behaviour. It is important because it helps to reduce the use of natural resources, and comes about as a result of producers and consumers of energy products reducing energy use per unit of output without affecting the level of service they provide. Efficiency improvements can therefore be brought about at various stages of the fuel cycle, through improvements in technology, software, energy management and operational practices. Energy efficiency improvements tend to be most rapid at times of energy crisis, where very strong price signals such as the quadrupling of oil prices in 1973/74 are received. These lead either to greater efficiencies or changes in the fuel mixes adopted to produce energy. Generally energy efficiency will improve over time due to the replacement of old equipment with new equipment and the adoption of new technology. In periods of rapid growth, efficiency will improve because new equipment will be installed more quickly. The instruments to improve energy efficiency include provision of information, regulation, pricing, taxation and government action.

It is important to distinguish between energy efficiency and total energy consumption. For example, total energy consumption has risen in the transport sector, even though vehicles are generally more energy-efficient. The need, therefore, is to concentrate on those areas where the problem is greatest. The link between energy efficiency and environmental protection is not an automatic one. Indeed, there have been particular problems with respect to diesel fuels in the past, but the movement towards the improved fuels that combine energy efficiency and low emissions has been an important point of progress, as has been the encouragement of cleaner-running cars. As early as 1985/86, car taxes were instituted in Germany, the Netherlands and Sweden to encourage the purchase of cleaner-running cars. Other states have since followed this initiative (International Energy Agency, 1991).

Energy efficiency makes most progress when prices are high, but interest tends to fade once this price signal diminishes. If global warming became a reality, this would be a stimulus for companies to offer energy-efficient goods and services: it has been estimated by the International Institute for Energy Conservation that the market could be worth US$1800 billion over the next 40 years (Boulton 1996a). The energy companies themselves are, of course, not particularly concerned that energy conservation takes place (although they may appear to because of the public relations value) because they make their living selling energy products. Apart from the environmental benefits, promoting greater energy efficiency offers cost savings, so that even if global warming does not, there will be other benefits. Countries that are highly dependent on imported energy tend to put more effort into promoting energy efficiency and in this respect the use of carbon taxes would be a particular help in combating global warming. However, examples of this are relatively limited. More progress has been made with respect to phasing out energy subsidies in some countries and this will continue as long as there are pressures on national budgets.

In 1986, the Council set a target of improving European Union energy efficiency by 20 per cent in the period to 1995. By the end of 1995 it was clear that this objective would not be met (CEC 1995f: 7). It could be argued that this target was perhaps too ambitious, given that many improvements in efficiency had been implemented in the period between 1973 and 1986 and that many of the new opportunities to save energy related to the introduction of new technology. In 1998, the Commission suggested that it would be possible to save

18 per cent of the EU's total energy consumption between 1995 and 2010 by being more efficient. It suggested that this could be achieved by greater energy efficiency in buildings, better equipment and improved energy management (*Europe* 1998b).

The main EU vehicle for developing technology to improve energy efficiency is the SAVE (Specific Actions for Vigorous Energy Efficiency) Programme. SAVE I ran from 29 October 1991 to 31 December 1995 and had only a limited budget of ECU 35 million, with which it established 200 pilot projects, with a special emphasis on developing regions. The SAVE II Programme covering the period 1996 to the year 2000 had a budget of ECU 45 million.

The SAVE Programme was designed to assist the EU in meeting its targets for stabilizing CO_2 emissions by the year 2000 at the 1990 level. The threat was that energy consumption was still set to rise despite these targets, between 5 and 8 per cent in the period 1995 – 2000 (CEC 1996q). The SAVE Programme aimed to improve energy efficiency by 1 per cent per annum over and above what would have been obtained by taking no action at all.

In its evaluation of the SAVE I Programme, the Commission recognized that the EU's capacity to act with respect to promoting energy efficiency was limited. This was partly because of the introduction of a subsidiarity principle and also because of the absence of an energy-related article in the Maastricht Treaty (CEC 1995f: 10). Nevertheless, it was felt that there had been considerable value-added in SAVE I, particularly with respect to pilot projects and the information programme, although the cost of a large-scale promotional exercise was beyond the scope of the programme.

The experience of the SAVE I Programme was sufficiently positive for a SAVE II Programme to be proposed. The aims of the programme were to stimulate energy efficiency and increase investment in energy conservation. The programme had a number of instruments at its disposal, including:

- Studies and other actions leading to the implementation and completion of Community energy efficiency measures
- Pilot schemes aimed at accelerating energy efficiency and/or improving energy use patterns
- Measures to assist the exchange of information
- Means to monitor energy efficiency
- Specific actions in favour of energy management at a regional and urban level.

RENEWABLE ENERGY SOURCES

Renewable energy sources (RES) are at the heart of the move towards sustainable development. Greater use of hydroelectricity, wave power, sunlight and wind power all seem to offer significant savings in terms of non-renewable energy sources such as oil and at the same time have fewer pollution effects. The EU has developed a clear commitment to developing and promoting these sources (CEC 1995g, 1996m, 1997m). EU Commissioner Christos Papoutsis declared that 'renewable sources of energy constitute an economically valuable and environmentally friendly indigenous energy source. Despite the fact that we have developed the technologies to harness renewable energies, they are far from being fully exploited' (Papoutsis 1996).

A number of member states have specific targets with respect to RES. For example, Denmark is calling for the achievement of 12 per cent utilization of RES by 2005 and, in the longer term, 35 per cent by 2030 (CEC 1996m: 9). The achievement of national targets is supported by a number of national incentives such as capital subsidies, fixed buy-back rate, for example the German *Stromeinspeisungsgesetz*, surcharges on fossil fuels and fiscal incentives.

Renewable energies are non-depletable forms of energy. They include hydropower, wind and solar energy (both thermal and photovoltaic), biomass and geothermal energy. Although it is depletable, organic waste is normally also classified as a renewable source of energy. Added to this list are wave, tidal and hot dry rock energy, but either the technologies are still at an experimental stage or they have still to prove their economic viability. The established forms of RES are as follows:

- *Hydroelectric energy* has been exploited some time. Most large-scale sources within Europe are fully exploited (these are generally the most efficient). There is, however, potential for small-scale sources to be exploited, particularly in Germany.
- *Wind energy* is harnessed by using wind turbines to generate electricity. These turbines have become increasingly economically viable, and are now frequently established in clusters to create wind farms. Wind power to generate electricity was popularized in California in the 1980s, but budget cuts and technical problems have tended to slow down its US development. Europe is now the biggest market for wind power, and in 1995 there was 2420 megawatts (MW)of installed capacity, as against 1700 MW in the United States, according to the European Wind Energy Association (Nairn 1996). Technology has improved significantly in this area, with the largest turbines growing from 75 kilowatts (KW) in the mid-1980s to 600 KW in the mid-1990s, with reliability close to 100 per cent. This makes it one of the most viable of the RES, and therefore any new plan to generate 2 per cent of electricity by wind power by the year 2005 is viable. Indeed, Denmark hopes to generate 10 per cent of its electricity from wind power by the year 2000. Wind power varies across the EU, with the UK having one of the best positions. However, there are diffi-

culties associated with it, including the fact that its fluctuations are difficult to manage and many other sources of supply are well away from centres where the power can be used. This means that it has to be transmitted across long distances, which can be inefficient.

- *Solar energy* is derived from the sun's light and heat. It is converted into electricity by using solar collectors, photovoltaic cells.
- *Biomass* is either cultivated as an energy crop, or is a by-product of agriculture and forestry activities used to produce fuels.
- *Geothermal energy* is generated by tapping the heat below the earth's surface through boreholes driven into a hot aquifer, or by injecting cold water through hot dry rock. The hot water produced is brought to the surface and is either used directly for heating, or to drive turbines (CEC 1996m). The use of hot aquifers is an established technology, but injecting cold water into hot dry rocks has yet to become financially viable.
- *Organic waste* from the agricultural or municipal sector can be treated thermally or biologically to produce energy.

As early as September 1986, the EU was calling for the promotion of renewable energy sources. In September 1993, the Council of Energy Ministers adopted a Programme for the Promotion of Renewable Energy Sources (ALTENER). This was designed to reduce CO_2 emissions by 180 million tonnes by the year 2005, by increasing the proportion of energy production by renewable sources from 4 per cent to 8 per cent for the EU 12 over the 1991–2005 period. The Commission later revised this target. The new proposed target for RES is 12 per cent of overall energy demand by 2010 for the EU 15 (CEC 1997m). In adopting the target, the Council of Energy Ministers downgraded the target to a 'useful guideline'. This wording suggests that the majority of member states had refused to set quantitative objectives on the development of renewable energy (*Europe* 1998c).

ALTENER 1 had a budget of ECU 40 million. Whilst it was generally regarded as somewhat underfunded, it supported four different types of actions to assist RES:

- Technical studies and appraisals to define technical standards and specifications
- Support for national measures to create an infrastructure for renewable energies
- Help in coordinating national activities, particularly those setting up an information network
- Studies on the industrial use of biomass and its advantages for the economy and the environment.

The ALTENER 1 programme was not a major research programme; it was more concerned with the promotion of RES. In March 1997, the Commission launched its proposals for ALTENER 2, which covered the period 1998–2002. This was finally adopted at the Energy Council in May 1998 for the period 1998–99, with a budget of ECU 22 million. One priority must be to reduce the cost of renewable energy sources to make them competitive with other sources. The resolution stated that some of the tasks should be financed entirely by the EU, whilst others would qualify for 50 per cent funding support. ALTENER 2 promised support for:

- Studies on implementation
- Development of standards for products and equipment in the RES market
- The setting up of new financial arrangements and instruments for RES
- Pilot actions to help with infrastructure
- Improved information dissemination and coordination
- Actions to encourage investment in RES
- Actions to monitor the implementation of RES throughout the EU.

The substitution of RES for other energy sources is not a universal panacea. There are some key issues that require investigation including:

- How much RES is available?
- How competitive is it in price, relative to other sources of energy?

Table 9.4 illustrates the extent to which exploitation of RES varies across the EU. It shows that RES is becoming increasingly important in all economies, although there is a huge gap between the performance of Austria and Sweden compared to the UK.

The use of renewable energy sources depends upon specific national regional constraints; not all locations are ideal for the kind of infrastructure that RES requires. Technological development is also a problem, given that RES tends to provide low-density energy and the costs associated with concentrating that energy to make it viable are considerable. Even simple designs require high levels of investment to make them workable. There are also costs associated with the storage of such energy, as it is not available as a continuous stream. Typically, therefore, costs tend to be higher for RES in terms of investment, and payback periods tend to be longer. These factors mean that it has limited credibility in some cases, with many projects often being small-scale and experimental. RES also competes with the high levels of investment already put into delivering fossil-fuel-based energy and the technology associated with it. Investment in RES is not without its environmental impacts, and the local impact of RES schemes, which can be quite visible, have to be balanced against the effects of global warming. In some states, the public does not understand the benefits to be gained from RES, and this tends to lead to a reluctance to invest in the public authorities.

Table 9.4   Share of renewable energy sources in gross domestic consumption, 1990 and 1995

	1990	1995
Austria	22.1	24.1
Belgium	1.0	1.0
Denmark	6.3	7.0
Finland	18.9	19.3
France	6.4	7.2
Germany	1.7	1.9
Greece	7.1	7.2
Ireland	1.6	2.2
Italy	5.3	6.4
Luxembourg	1.3	1.3
Netherlands	1.3	1.4
Portugal	17.6	17.5
Spain	6.7	6.2
Sweden	24.7	24.0
United Kingdom	0.5	0.6
European Union	5.0	5.4

Source: Eurostat, taken from CEC (1997m: 33).

The EU's attempts to promote RES have been subject to some criticism, for example by Eurelectric (the European grouping of the electricity supply industry) (*Europe* 1997d). Whilst acknowledging that RES has an increasing role to play, Eurelectric sees the doubling of RES by 2010 from 6 per cent to 12 per cent as having implications for the electricity industry. In 1997, electricity production by RES was 15 per cent and this would have to be doubled to 30 per cent, leading to a significant burden on the electricity industry. Eurelectric argued that:

- RES projects have an environmental impact because of their construction, their visual impact and their noise;
- RES makes only a limited contribution towards security of supply;

- some renewable sources of energy are already mature, such as hydro-electricity, whilst others are not yet fully commercially viable, such as wind power and biomass;
- RES is not competitive in a financial sense;
- the adoption of RES would put an unfair burden on consumers, because of its cost relative to other energy sources.

The EU has attempted to promote the development and use of clean and safe energy via the JOULE-THERMIE Programme. This was research that covered the non-nuclear area and was aimed to be very market-related. The programme was sub-titled 'Technology for Clean and Efficient Energy and Non-Nuclear Energies'. The objective of the THERMIE Programme 1990–94 was to demonstrate and promote new clean and efficient energy technologies, renewable energies and solid fuels and hydrocarbons. THERMIE supported technological demonstration projects and encouraged uptake of the successful projects through information and promotion measures.

In 1995, it became the JOULE-THERMIE Programme and had a budget of ECU 967 million to cover the period 1995–99. It was then part of the EU's Fourth Framework Programme and once again focused on the need for technological solutions associated with the production and use of energy sources. The JOULE-THERMIE Programme contained five sectors which covered strategies in the energy field, development of technologies which would help to cut energy consumption in building this industry and transport, renewable energy sources, promoting the cleaner use of fossil fuels and the dissemination and promotion of technology.

THE ENERGY PRODUCT TAX

The use of fiscal instruments is an important part of the EU strategy for promoting energy conservation and a reduction in greenhouse gases. Raising the price of energy means that consumers can make choices about the most appropriate way to accommodate the cost increases. As we discussed in Chapter 5, the Commission launched two attempts to introduce a carbon/energy tax in the period 1990–95, but these failed because of lack of unanimity in the Council of Ministers for agreeing to proposals dealing with taxation. In October 1996 the Commission decided to try to promote the idea of widening the tax base on energy sources.

Excise duty on mineral oils is the only tax that applies to energy across the whole of the EU that is likely to have an effect on consumption. The first step in the process is therefore a convergence of excise duties, so that firms moving to take advantage of lower energy prices do not create market distortions. In addition to this, there is an element of cross-border shopping associated with the movement of vehicles. This development means that some restrictions are still in place with respect to the amount of fuel that can be carried across one border to another in the tanks of trucks.

In 1997 the Commission proposed a draft directive for an energy product tax (CEC 1997c), but this still fell under the requirements of article 99 (now article 93 TEC) which requires unanimous agreement. The directive suggested that, for the first time, there was scope for a tax on all energy products for the first time, apart from mineral oils already covered by excise duty. Its main purpose was to eliminate the distortions in the way taxes applied to fuels and to strengthen the single market. This was not a proposal for an environmental tax as such, but it was thought that if the measures were implemented, they would have a positive impact, especially as natural gas and coal are responsible for 30 per cent of CO_2 emissions. It was envisaged that the taxes could be above the minimum level, in order to achieve environmental objectives appropriate to national circumstances.

The proposed energy product tax covered mainly coal, natural gas and electricity, with taxes being applied by the member states and not by the EU itself. The member states could also refund tax paid by consumers who wished to encourage the use of renewable energy sources. The draft directive covered energy for motor fuels and heating, as well as for industrial purposes. Exempt from the tax would be aviation fuel, which was subject to international agreement. Fuel used by shipping in Community waters could be exempt. Also there could be exemptions or reduced rates for renewable energy sources for bio-fuels, and for railway transport and inland waterway transport. The Commission was also sensitive to the need to maintain competitiveness, so there could be reduced rates for firms whose products were high in energy use, particularly where it accounted for 20 per cent or more of production costs. In terms of consumer prices it was anticipated that the proposed measures would lead to a limited rise in the cost of unleaded petrol and diesel. Not surprisingly, the Union of Industrial and Employers' Confederations of Europe (UNICE) disagree with the whole concept of energy taxes as a way of promoting environmental goals. They argue that it is investments in modern industrial techniques that have the most important impact on energy saving, as well as a shift in industrial investment towards activities which are less energy-intensive. The imposition of taxes to achieve environmental goals, they argue, simply reduces companies' profitability and therefore their ability to invest in modern equipment (UNICE 1996).

At the heart of the proposal was the concept of fiscal neutrality. Article 1 of the draft directive proposed that member states 'shall endeavour to avoid any increase in their overall tax burden' as a result of taxation of energy products. The proposal was therefore for a broadening of the taxation base, rather than for an increase in the overall level of taxation, with member states being able to apply different rates to the same product, provided they were higher than the minimum proposed rates laid down in the draft Directive. The aim is to move towards a more environmentally friendly energy production. The hope was that any increase in tax revenue from the energy product tax could be diverted towards reducing taxes on incomes or reducing employers' social security payments. If employers' costs are reduced, this may encourage them to take on more workers. The first article called for 'Member States to promote the objective of tax neutrality' (*Europe* 1997b). The proposed tax would favour freight transported by rail and inland waterways rather than road haulage, but the impact on road freight in some countries would be largely limited, because their minimum rates were in excess of the EU excise duties, for example in the UK (Rogers 1997). The European Parliament Greens Group (Europe 1997a) immediately criticized the proposals. They pointed out the following:

- The proposed minimum tax rates were too low to have any real impact on the level of CO_2 emissions.
- The exemption of kerosene for the air transport industry was a mistake. Despite the Chicago Agreement, air transport is a major source of pollution, and should not be sheltered by international agreements.
- There were too many exemptions for heavy industry. There was no reason why this group should be specially privileged.

The EP Greens Group wanted to extend the range of taxation further to include high-energy products from third countries. They believed this would be acceptable as long as the taxes within the EU were at the same rate.

Denmark and Sweden are the two countries that have led the way by imposing their own national carbon taxes. The UK has removed the subsidies for energy and introduced the policy of an annual 5 per cent real increase in energy duties. In 1994, the German government increased taxes on oil products to reduce the debt of the national railway company and to finance extensions to its transport network. This is a good example of the uses of taxes on energy that are fiscally neutral. In 1996, the German government also removed the coal levy on electricity. The levy had been used to force German utilities to buy domestically produced coal at above market prices, although there were still concerns about subsidies made to the German coal industry in 1998.

EXTERNAL RELATIONS

The EU has had to address the dual issues of security of supply and the environment in its external relations with other states, particularly those in

Central and Eastern Europe. Whilst the case for energy security is particularly strong in periods when supply is under threat, the problem of pollution is ever present. Many of these problems are related to the energy industries, either because of the damage to the atmosphere and watercourses as a result of industrial activity, or because of the problems associated with the disposal of waste materials. In the case of the nuclear industry, though, the real threat is of significant environmental damage caused by accidents. This problem was highlighted by the Chernobyl disaster, which even ten years after the event was having an effect on its immediate environment.

The SAVE and ALTENER Programmes are open to members of the European and economic area, and SAVE II is associated with the Central and Eastern European states. The THERMIE Programme and later the JOULE-THERMIE Programme set up the Organization for the Promotion of Energy Technology (OPET), which established energy centres in Central and Eastern European countries. The Technical Assistance to the Commonwealth of Independent States and Georgia (TACIS) programme then extended the energy centres to the newly independent states of the former Soviet Union.

The European Energy Charter is an attempt to construct a European-wide energy strategy. The European Council meeting in Dublin on 25 June 1990 debated the idea of creating a European Energy Community. This led to a proposal to establish a European Energy Charter at the Conference on Security and Cooperation within Europe (CSCE) in Paris, 19–21 November. The purpose was to make available technology, know-how and capital to explore the oil and gas resources of Central and Eastern Europe and particularly the newly independent republics that made up the former Soviet Union. It was hoped that this would bring economic benefits for those countries, while giving greater security of supply to Western Europe. One of the most important aims was to ensure that investment was legally protected while at the same time giving assistance to the economic development of Central and Eastern Europe. The Energy Charter has a chapter dealing with the environment and two sectoral protocols dealing with energy efficiency and nuclear safety. Article 22 of the Charter requires the contracting parties to minimize harmful environmental impacts in a safe and economically efficient manner. The Charter also adopted the PPP within its rhetoric, although it is difficult to say whether this will have practical implications. The protocol dealing with energy efficiency set out measures to improve energy efficiency and promote energy saving, so that environmental damage would be limited.

In Lisbon on 17 December 1994, 45 countries, including the European Union member states and the European Union acting in its own right, signed the Charter Treaty (51 countries took part in the actual negotiations). The Charter came legally into effect in April 1998.

The EU has made available, via its budget, subsidies to assist developing countries' cooperation in energy matters since 1980. In that year, ECU 650 000 was spent on energy cooperatives, but this increased over time, rising to ECU 9 million. With the collapse of the former Soviet Union, the SYNERGY Programme to promote international cooperation in the energy sector became more important. In 1995 the Commission proposed that the programme covering the period 1996–2000 be launched, with the aim of helping the fight against pollution and improving security of supply as well as fostering energy efficiency. This time period was reduced to cover the period January to December 1997, because of the need to develop the energy framework programme, but was finally extended for a further year to December 1998. The programme was also supported by complementary policies within PHARE and TACIS.

CONCLUSIONS

The EU has not developed a sustainable energy strategy but, in conjunction with the member states, has taken action to reduce the environmental impact of energy consumption. At the member state level there are a large number of initiatives that complement EU activity. Indeed, many of the measures that have been introduced reflect national priorities rather than those of the EU. However, the various national schemes, such as standards of building regulations and insulation and fiscal incentives, are expected to be transparent and not to damage the integrity of the single market.

Many of the EU programmes can be criticized for being underfunded and, as such, their impact is limited. However, their value in promoting cooperation and assisting the search for common solutions should not be undervalued. Three areas where the EU has a strong role are those of RES, energy efficiency and promoting collaboration with respect to new technology. These all offer a long-term dividend that is worth striving for, but it is likely that many of the benefits will simply offset the growth in energy demand.

10 Transport and the environment

INTRODUCTION

The European Union is striving to achieve the goal of sustainable development, which for the transport sector can be translated as the objective of sustainable mobility. The EU has attempted to reach this by a mix of regulatory measures and of economic instruments at the member state level. However, this is something of a lost cause. The growth of the economy, and citizens' increasing desire for mobility, have placed a growing demand for transport services, which inevitably imposes an environmental cost.

The importance of the transport sector can be judged by the fact that the common transport policy and the common agricultural policy were the only sectoral policies to be part of the Treaty of Rome. The transport industry is essential for both the production and distribution of goods and services across the EU, and it is a key element in the process of economic development and integration. Travel by EU citizens continues to grow as incomes rise and populations move out of the cities. Between 1970 and 1992 the average distance travelled by members of the public increased from 16.5 kilometres per day to 31.5 kilometres per day, of which 75 per cent were by car (EP 1997a). The transport sector has seen considerable technical improvements, which have helped to reduce the level of emissions per vehicle.

The introduction of legislation to enforce emission standards will reduce levels further. The agreement to move ahead with the Auto-Oil measures concluded in 1998 should ensure that new cars, when they come into service, comply with higher emission standards.[1] From the year 2000, new models of cars will be expected to comply with the standards after five years or 80 000 kilometres (50 000 miles) on the road. This figure will rise to 100 000 kilometres (65 500 miles) in 2005. As part of the series of measures associated with this development, it was proposed that on board diagnostic systems (OBDS) be made mandatory for petrol cars from 2000 and diesels from 2003 (EP 1998). However, the industry is growing faster than the rate of technical and regulative achievements, which means that the goal of sustainable mobility is becoming more distant. Despite a number of policy initiatives over recent years, the level of emissions is not consistent with the capacity of the environment to absorb them.

It is clear that the energy needs of the transport sector are not sustainable. Transport was responsible for 20 per cent of final energy consumption in the 1970s, but by 1995 this figure had risen to over 30.7 per cent (CEC 1998h). Little use is made of renewable energy sources. The introduction of three-way catalytic converters has been slow in many member states, and the development of electrical cars has not been as rapid as was hoped. At the same time the industry is placing excessive demand on the available land resources. The transport sector affects the environment via the transportation infrastructure, the type of transport mode (air, sea, inland waterway, rail, road and pipeline), the intensity of the mode of transport used, and the technology being employed. Despite this, it is possible for the transport sector to improve its environmental performance by switching to relatively benign transport modes (Whitelegg 1992: 5).

The EU's policies have, in a number of cases, added to the environmental problems created by the transport sector. An example is the growth in traffic that has arisen as a natural consequence of economic development and the single market. This has stimulated cross-border trade and increased the demand for transport services. In addition to this, the EU has pushed forward the liberalization of the transport sector, which has enhanced the efficiency key sectors such as road and air. The improved cost advantage of these two sectors has added to environmental problems as they have won business particularly at the expense of the more environmentally friendly rail system. The creation of the Trans-European Transport Network (TEN-T) is having the practical effect of removing bottlenecks, but once again it has had the greatest impact upon improving the competitiveness of road transport. The TEN-T does offer opportunities for the rail system to improve its relative position, but only if there is a greater use of intermodal transport. Without this, the investment in transport infrastructure in response to demand is likely to strengthen further the position of road and air transport.

THE NATURE OF THE TASK

The task for the EU transport and environmental programmes is to restrict the overall impact of transport on the environment. This involves reducing total pollution and limiting the impact of the development of infrastructure on land use. There is also a need to reduce traffic congestion, especially in urban areas, and there are linked issues such as the transport of dangerous goods and waste products that need to be taken into account. This suggests that action is needed in a number of areas, including:

- A strategic environmental assessment (SEA) of transport networks, and the integration of environmental and transport concerns into land-use planning at the local, regional, national and EU level. The assessment should incorporate the real costs to the environment in its appraisal.
- The development of initiatives to promote alternatives to long-distance road freight.
- The internalization of the external costs of transport by the use of fiscal measures to control usage. That is, the price of transport services should reflect the full environmental costs.
- The improvements of the competitive position of more environmentally friendly transport modes such as railways and water-borne transport.
- The development of better public transport in urban areas.
- The continued technical improvement of vehicles and fuels to ensure that the private car is used in a more environmentally friendly way.

Many of the above policy areas are the responsibility of the member states, which need to work together to overcome the problems created by the Europe-wide transport system. The Commission has estimated that if all the available strategies are implemented, it would be possible to reduce CO_2 emissions by the transport sector by as much as 180 million tonnes over the period to 2010 (CEC 1997v: 8). The greatest saving would be reduced emissions from car transport, which could make a saving of 100 million tonnes of CO_2, whilst intermodal shifts (mainly from road to rail) would reduce CO_2 emissions by 50 million tonnes.

THE GROWTH AND STRUCTURE OF THE TRANSPORT SECTOR

The transport sector accounts for 7 per cent of the EU's GNP (CEC 1998h). From 1970 to 1996 the annual growth of passenger transport was 3.1 per cent and 2.2 per cent for goods. Passenger travel by air grew more rapidly, achieving a rate of 7.7 per cent per annum over the period. However, the number of railway passengers only grew by 0.9 per cent, and indeed declined slightly over the period 1990–95 (–0.3 per cent) (CEC 1998i). The growth in road freight was 3.8 per cent annum over the period 1970–96, faster than the economic growth rate.

The relative importance of the transport modes has changed as a result of their differing growth rates, with an increased emphasis on road transport in particular, as is shown in Tables 10.1 and 10.2.

Table 10.1   Distribution of EU freight transport by mode, 1970–97 (EU 15)

	1970 %	1980 %	1990 %	1995 %	1997 %
Road	48.9	57.7	68.2	73.1	73.2
Rail	31.8	24.9	18.4	14.1	14.4
Inland water	11.9	9.4	7.9	7.3	7.2
Pipeline	7.5	8.1	5.5	5.5	5.2

Source: CEC (1999c).

Table 10.2   Distribution of EU passenger transport by mode, 1970–97 (EU 15)

	1970 %	1980 %	1990 %	1995 %	1997 %
Passenger car	73.8	76.4	79.0	79.5	78.7
Bus and coach	12.3	11.0	8.5	7.9	7.9
Railway	10.1	8.2	6.5	5.8	5.8
Urban rail	1.8	1.3	1.1	0.9	0.9
Air	2.0	3.1	4.9	5.9	6.7

Source: CEC (1999c).

There are various explanations for the above trends, relating to rising income levels and the failure of public provision for passengers and freight. If no action is taken to change current trends, road freight traffic will continue to predominate, because of its lower relative price and greater flexibility. The trend towards 'just in time' production, with low levels of stock held by manufacturers, means that deliveries need to be more frequent, and individual consignments may be smaller. Similarly, car traffic is expected to dominate as a consequence of rising income levels and the failure of public transport to meet the needs of society. There has been a marked increase in transport of goods between the north and south of the EU, leading to specific problems for the Alpine Regions of the transit states – Austria within the EU and Switzerland outside it. Air transport is expected to grow by 182 per cent in the period 1990–2010 (CEC 1996p: 26).

THE COST TO SOCIETY

The total growth of the transport sector, along with an increasing emphasis on less environmentally friendly transport, is one of the most serious problems facing the EU's environment policy. This growth has led to a rise in CO_2 emissions, total fuel consumption, the number of motor vehicles and the miles of motorway. It has led to severe congestion and increased environmental degradation, which have reduced economic well-being. The annual economic cost of traffic pollution and congestion could be as high as ECU 260 billion, or ECU 700 per person throughout the EU (CEC 1997q: 11). The EU's estimates of the cost are set out in Table 10.3.

Table 10.3   External costs of transport (estimate, in % of GDP – no year specified) ·

External cost	% of GDP
Health problems associated with localized air pollution	0.4
Accidents	1.5
Noise	0.2
Congestion	2.0
Total	4.0

Source: CEC (1997a: 11).

The OECD suggests that the costs might be higher than those shown in the table, which do not include non-local pollution costs (for example acid rain) of between −1 and −10 per cent of GDP (OECD 1995a: 16). All of this is in addition to the cost to individuals of the failure of public transport systems and the sense of isolation that this creates.

Emissions

All the main transport modes impose some environmental cost on society. Air transport creates particular problems with respect to nitrogen oxide (NO_x) emissions from subsonic civil aircraft, and only slow progress has been made with respect to reductions (CEC 1996p: 26). Most concern is, however, directed at road transport. In urban areas, traffic causes almost 100 per cent of CO_2 emissions. In addition to CO_2 problems there are difficulties with other pollutants such as lead. There was a slight overall reduction of 1.3 per cent in the level of CO_2 emissions within the EU 15 over the period 1990–95, but transport still remains a worry. In 1995, the transport sector was responsible for 26.4 per cent of CO_2 emissions. Over the period 1990–94 CO_2 emissions by transport grew by 7.4 per cent, and by a further 1.4 per cent between 1994 and 1995 (Eurostat 1997b). The Commission's prediction was that without action being taken, CO_2 emissions from the transport sector would grow by 39 per cent over the period 1990–2010 (CEC 1997v: 4). The share of the different modes of surface transport is shown in Table 10.4.

Table 10.4   *EU 15 CO_2 emissions by the transport sector, 1990–95 (millions of tonnes of CO_2)*

	1990	1992	1994	1995	Share, 1995 (%)
Rail transport	9.22	8.82	8.4	8.5	1.0
Road transport	644.58	675.16	690.7	677.9	84.4
Air transport	83.30	86.80	94.4	96.5	12.0
Inland navigation	20.81	22.28	21.8	20.6	2.6
Totals	757.92	793.08	815.2	803.5	100

Source: CEC (1999c).

The increase shown in the table reflects the problem of growth of the transport sector, and the absence of a satisfactory technology to remove CO_2 from exhaust gases. Other substances are produced where there is incomplete combustion, for example carbon monoxide and unburned hydrocarbons.

Whilst there is an urgent need to develop alternatives such as electrically driven vehicles, the EU's approach to reducing these emissions is to encourage the adoption of ever-more stringent standards in terms of fuel and engine performance. This strategy, along with voluntary action by industry, has led to some success, most notably in the fuel economy of motor cars.

Fuel economy and CO_2 emissions are directly related, and in this respect European car manufacturers have done well. In 1998 it was estimated that a new car produced in the EU consumed an average 7.1 litres of fuel per 100 km, compared with 10.8l per 100 km in the US and 7.2l per 100 km in Japan. Technical progress has meant that cars are now less polluting. For example, Ian McAllister, the Chairman of Ford UK claims that 'Fifty new Ford Kas produce the same level of emissions as one original 1976 Fiesta' (Haig 1998). However, fuel consumption is compromised by many of the advances in car design, for example the inclusion of air conditioning. Also, improved safety features can add to a car's weight, and hence increase fuel consumption.

In July 1998 the European Automobile Manufacturers' Association (ACEA) accepted a voluntary timetable to cut CO_2 emissions on new cars by 25 per cent by 2008 compared with 1995. This should reduce the CO_2 emissions from new cars to an average of 140g/km by 2008, compared with 186g/km in 1995.

Progress will be reviewed in 2003 with a view to lowering emissions towards 120 g/km by 2012 – the EU's target.

Paying the Full Price

Public opinion on transport issues often appears to be contradictory. In a survey of attitudes to a range of energy issues, the Commission found that 32.8 per cent of those questioned supported clear preference being given to public transport to the detriment of private cars, whilst 44.8 per cent favoured preferential treatment for public transport with only certain disadvantages for private cars. Better traffic management was thought to be important by 86.9 per cent, and 75.5 per cent favoured cutting pollution by tougher traffic controls during peak times (CEC 1997aa). However, the reality is that the public still prefers private forms of transport, as is demonstrated by the continuing upward trend in car ownership.

As private forms of transport grow, so public transport services deteriorate and become more expensive. In 1995 road transport consumed 83 per cent of the energy used in the sector, compared to 2.8 per cent consumed by rail. The reasons for the growth in demand for private cars are purchases related to changed social expectations and a movement of employment and retailing activities away from the city centres. Car ownership in the EU has increased from 23 per cent of the population to 43 per cent in a period of 20 years. This has been made possible by rising incomes and a financial system that has increased the capacity of households to buy cars and maintain them.

The real cost of motoring has fallen in many countries. It took a typical UK household 40 hours and 52 minutes of work to purchase a car licence in 1971, and 8 minutes to purchase a litre of petrol. By 1992 these times had fallen to 16 hours 43 minutes and 5 minutes respectively (OECD 1995a: 34). The trend in the 1990s was for low fuel prices, with oil markets being awash with surplus production. This tended to remove some of the incentive for technological developments to improve fuel efficiency (OECD 1997a: 15).

The environmental damage caused by the transport sector can be reduced by better use of technology, but this comes at a price. It is estimated that the Auto-Oil Programme, which comes into full effect by 2005, will cost EU car makers and fuel producers $60 billion each to implement (a price that will have to be met by the consumer in the end). The car manufacturers argue that they will need to make a considerable investment in developing lean-burn engines and better catalytic converters. Fuel producers will face the cost of adapting refining capacity (Haig 1998).

More efficient use could be made of the existing transport capacity and the overall volume of transport reduced. However, one of the best strategies lies in shifting the mode of transport. The Commission maintains that the prices paid by individuals for transport services should reflect the real costs of journeys (CEC 1995h: 4). The subsidies that are still being given to car users could be reduced, for example by removing free parking places, subsidies for company cars and the tax deductions which are still available in some countries. Withdrawing the duty-free shopping concession at airports and on ferries for journeys within the EU on 30 June 1999, removed a subsidy on mobility.

As Table 10.5 shows, there are significant differences in the environmental costs associated with the various transport modes, with the cost of rail transport being very much lower than the road alternative. These external costs are not reflected in prices paid by the user. Adopting an appropriate pricing system is therefore integral to the process of achieving the shifts required to achieve the desired environmental and transport goals.

Table 10.5 External cost of transport by mode, 1991 (EU 15)

Effect	Cars[1]	Buses[1]	Road freight[2]	Rail passengers[1]	Rail freight[2]	Air passengers[1]	Air freight[2]	Ship freight[2]
Accidents	32.3	9.4	22.2	1.9	0.9	–	–	–
Noise	4.5	4.2	12.7	3.1	4.7	3.0	16.5	–
Air pollution and climate	13.2	6.8	23.6	5.0	1.8	14.8	76.8	6.1
Total[3]	50.1	20.4	58.4	10.0	7.3	17.8	93.2	6.1

[1] In ECU per 1000 person kilometre
[2] In ECU per tonne kilometre
[3] Figures do not add up due to rounding.

Source: CEC (1995a), Annex 10).

If the prices charged for transport internalized the full social and economic costs, including the infrastructure costs, this would mean a significant increase in taxation and charges. The degree of success of this strategy will depend upon the availability of alternative transport modes, and the extent to which each is price-sensitive. This internalizing of costs would probably not affect the volume of long-distance freight that moves around the EU, but it would assist the rail industry in relation to road. It would make rail more competitive against air journeys over medium distances. The rise in costs of road usage would also spur greater efficiency and encourage the use of public transport in urban areas (Kågeson 1996). If a more realistic pricing system were in place this might reduce mobility, thus encouraging greater use of telecommunications.

The required price increases may be unacceptable. An EU survey found that only 43.4 per cent of those questioned thought that it was important to cut pollution by higher taxation on private vehicles and fuel (CEC 1997aa). This is a clear signal to politicians that price increases are unpopular and may cost them votes. As in many other areas of EU environmental policy, most action is required at the member state level, because of their desire for fiscal autonomy and the application of the principle of subsidiarity. Whilst the EU can encourage action, its direct role tends to be confined to ensuring that charges do not discriminate against other member states and harm the single market. As national charges are introduced for using roads, the EU will also need to consider the level at which excise duties are harmonized.

The taxes that are most often applied to the use of motor vehicles are those levied on their purchase and use. These tend to be small (between 1 and 6 per cent of government revenue) relative to energy taxes. Significantly higher rates of value added tax (VAT) have now been largely phased out, in an attempt to harmonize across the EU. Excise duties provide two thirds of the tax revenue for the road sector. In 1992, the minimum level of duty within the EU was harmonized at the relatively high level of ECU 245 per 1000 litres. The tax on goods vehicles is fixed in relation to their gross permissible laden weight and the number and types of axle. In 1995 the minimum tax rate on a conventional 2+3 axle vehicle weighing up to 40 tonnes was fixed at ECU 700 per annum (Van Vreckem 1996). Member states are allowed to impose tolls and other charges, but there must be no direct or indirect discrimination based upon the haulier's nationality. Tolls must not lead to the introduction of controls at the frontier. Member states themselves need to consider the determinants of transport demand and issues such as business location. There is a need to reduce mobility in urban areas by offering alternatives such as car-free city centres and traffic management schemes, and by encouraging teleworking. This latter idea appears to be attractive, but has a number of problems associated with it, including the feeling of social isolation that it creates.

As early as 5 December 1973 the Commission sent a proposal to the Council that suggested that the member states should harmonize their laws with respect to the composition of petrol. At that time, motor vehicles were responsible for a high proportion of lead released into the urban environment, which was a particular threat to public health. Also, different legal and administrative standards with respect to the lead content of petrol was creating an obstacle to the free movement of fuel for motor vehicles across the EU. The directive was finally adopted in 1978 and stipulated that, from 1981 onwards, the maximum lead content of petrol should not exceed 0.40 grams per litre. The directive also specified that a reduction in lead should not significantly increase the quantity of other pollutants in the environment.

In 1993, new standards were laid down with respect to emissions from new light commercial vehicles and this provision was extended to all new commercial vehicles from 1994. From 1996 onwards, new standards were laid down for petrol- and diesel-driven cars. The hope is that these new standards will reduce the overall levels of emissions, although this will depend partly on the total number of vehicles that appear on the roads. Proposals have also been made to set targets with respect to air quality.

Lead-free Petrol – A Policy Success

Governments can give signals to change consumer behaviour by the use of the taxation system. The most successful aspect of this has been the lower rates of excise duty applied to unleaded fuel. In 1985, the Council adopted a new directive on the lead content of petrol and the introduction of lead-free petrol.[2] Whilst still making leaded petrol available across the Community, the directive required that member states should reduce the lead content of petrol to 0.15 grams per litre as soon as possible. The main innovation, however, was the introduction of lead-free petrol after 1 October 1989 (Johnson and Courcelle 1995: 142). From 1993, new cars were expected to be capable of running on unleaded fuel. As an incentive to switch to unleaded fuel, the excise duty has been lower than on leaded fuel. This fiscal incentive meant that in 1998 unleaded petrol was on average 7 per cent cheaper in those countries where the two fuels were available. The result of the various pressures has been that unleaded fuel commanded a 76 per cent share of the EU market in 1998. In Austria, Denmark, Holland, Finland and Sweden leaded fuel had almost disappeared. However, it had only 54 per cent of the market in Italy, 51 per cent in Portugal, and 46 per cent in Greece and Spain. Over the period 1990–98 lead emissions declined by 75 per cent (Eurostat 1998).

The success of the campaign to phase out leaded petrol led to an agreement in 1998 to prohibit its sale from 1 January 2000. However, a member state can request a derogation until 2005 if it is able to demonstrate that the ban will result in severe socioeconomic problems or would not lead to overall environmental or health benefits. Given the relatively low adoption rate in Southern European member states, it seems likely that they will be forced to seek this derogation, although the vast majority of cars will be converted to unleaded fuel.

Where leaded petrol remains on sale, the lead content should not exceed 0.15 g/l. Small quantities of leaded petrol will still be available for use in vintage cars, but this will be distributed through special interest groups which will be exempted from the ban (sales should not exceed 0.5 per cent of total petrol sales) (EP 1998).

Despite their higher purchase price, the greater fuel efficiency of diesel engines has caused consumers to move increasingly towards their use throughout most of the EU. The exception to this was Sweden, where a diesel driving tax, based upon the number of kilometres driven, existed between 1973 and 1993. This has now been replaced by higher excise duties. Excise duties on diesel fuel have tended to be lower throughout the EU, so encouraging its use;

however, this can be criticized because the gains in terms of fuel efficiency have to be offset against the higher risks caused by diesel particles and oxides of sulphur.

Following the success of tax reductions on unleaded petrol, it has now been advocated that similar tax incentives be offered to users of city diesel. In 1991, Sweden introduced tax incentives for switching to ultra-low sulphur diesel and, in 1996, this took 75 per cent of the market. City diesel reduces emissions by up to 85 per cent, black smoke by 50 per cent and sulphurous oxides by 98 per cent compared with the standard product. City diesel is now widely available. Progress has been made to improve the quality of fuel. The 1998 agreement with respect to the Auto Oil Programme should ensure that after 1 January 2000 standards are in place to reduce the sulphur and benzene content of fuel (EP 1998). The EU's new directive obliges oil companies to introduce 'reformulated fuels', such as low-sulphur diesel. By 2005 fuels should have a sulphur content of just 50 parts per million – a three-fold reduction on 2000 in the case of petrol and a seven-fold cut for diesel.

A more radical approach would be to use the price system to allocate scarce road space. The use of toll roads is a crude example of this, and can be a useful method of paying for infrastructure. However, there are only a few cases where pricing operates in a detailed sense, and, given the available technology, it is in cities that it is likely to be most effective. The best example of this is Singapore, where the number of cars is limited by quota, and access to the city centre at peak times carries a premium charge. The system operating in Oslo is a successful example within the EU, but the coverage of the scheme is not as comprehensive or as technically advanced as in Singapore. The Netherlands proposes to introduce a smart-card system of charging for the use of roads within the four main cities within the Randstad conurbation (Amsterdam, The Hague, Rotterdam and Utrecht) in 2001.

One possible innovation would be for the EU to move towards a standardized model of road pricing. This might involve a standard measurement system and a system of charges that would reflect the cost of providing and maintaining the infrastructure and could include environmental costs. The price would need to be adjusted depending on the time of day and the day of the week, in order to assist the flow of traffic. Technical advances mean that trucks and cars could be fitted with electronic devices that could charge the users. This kind of charging might be attractive, given that the road user already pays a high price for the congestion faced on a daily basis.

The Commission adopted a White Paper in 1998 that proposed a new harmonized approach to paying for infrastructure use across all commercial modes of transport. It was hoped that this would replace the existing charging arrangements over a period of time, and would generate savings of at least ECU 50 billion a year that could be passed on to consumers. The White Paper,

'Fair payment for infrastructure use: A phased approach to transport infra-structure charging in the European Union', sets out how a new 'user pays' charging system could be developed by the Commission working with a specially created committee of transport experts appointed by the member states (CEC 1998f). Such a system would take some time to introduce because there are various systems of charging within the EU, and the extent to which the rail sector has been liberalized varies considerably. The aim of the charging process would be to develop a method of taking account of marginal social costs that would include pollution, accidents and congestion. However, because of the differences in national and regional circumstances, it was not thought desirable to introduce a common set of charges. It was proposed that between 1998 and 2000 the Commission and the member states should establish ways of estimating the marginal social costs of transport. Then, between 2001 and 2004, the principles would be put into effect by means of new legislation. After this the progress of the scheme would be reviewed.

It would be surprising if the proposed timetable were achieved, notwith-standing the promised collective gains. Despite the proposal to leave the level of charges to the member states, past history has shown that where the fiscal sovereignty is challenged, it can take a very long time to win even a minimum level of agreement. The proposals in the White Paper will bring about radical changes, which will be vigorously challenged by vested interests within the member states.

TRANS-EUROPEAN TRANSPORT NETWORK

In the past, member states tended to consider their own domestic transport needs rather than those of the overall European economy. This left areas of the European economy remote from the mainstream of economic development. At the same time, a mismatch within the transport provision led to inefficiencies. The Trans-European Transport Network (TEN-T) is intended to connect national transport networks, and to provide access to these networks. It is estimated that developing the TEN-T will cost at least ECU 400 billion by 2010. Most of this investment will come from member states and the private sector; however, the EU does provide some funding via the TEN-T budget line and the Structural and Cohesion Funds, and loans from the European Investment Bank (EIB).

The creation of the TEN-T is a major aspect of common transport policy, par-ticularly in the light of the need to ensure the proper functioning of the single market. It is an attempt to develop an integrated system that meets the needs of the total European economy. It is hoped that the TEN-T will ensure that competition is maintained throughout the European Union, that transport times are faster, and that capacity is more fully utilized. Also, it should help to avoid significant bottlenecks, such as those in the road network. This is normally achieved by the upgrading of roads, rather than the creation of new highways.

The TEN-T should promote economic growth, cohesion and integration within the European area, reaching well beyond the geographical limits of the present European Union. Not only should the volume passing through the network increase, but there will be efficiency gains via inter-operability and interconnectability.

There are a number of reasons why trans-European infrastructure (the basis of TEN-T) is important, including:

- Better and safer travel at lower cost.
- Effective planning in Europe in order to avoid a concentration of population.
- Bridge building towards Eastern Europe in order to step up investment and promote trade.

Originally TEN-T was seen as separate networks, but the EU began to see benefits from adopting an intermodal strategy. This would mean that the modes of transport would be interconnected, in the hope that this would lead to the creation of an integrated transport network with a door-to-door transport chain. The Commission believes that, by actively promoting intermodality, the TEN-T can assist with the process of moving towards a more environmentally friendly transport system (CEC 1997f). The most important aspect of this would be the linking of road and rail, so that long-distance haulage would be by rail (or inland waterway), and shorter distances by road. (Similar initiatives are required for passenger transport.) If this intermodality is achieved, not only will the spare capacity of the different transport modes be fully utilized, but also greater use will be made of more environmentally friendly modes.

The intermodal approach assumes that freight hauliers will willingly move towards this position, but this will only happen if the connections between the different transport modes are improved, and the progress on creating open information systems for transport is maintained. Those responsible for the movement of goods need to know how the market opportunities can best be exploited. It is the member states that have the responsibility of effecting the infrastructure changes, and the private sector that has the most important role in developing the information systems. There is also a danger that liberalization linked with privatization has created a device for competition between modes, rather than intermodality. The only way to be certain that this does not happen is to ensure that the rail system becomes more competitive, and the suggested way to achieve this is through greater liberalization, along with the provision of good infrastructure.

The Railway System

The rail network is a key element in developing a successful TEN-T. Although rail is a relatively environmentally friendly form of transport, it has failed to deliver on its potential. It might make an important contribution towards achieving the EU's goal of sustainable mobility sometime in the future, but only if the sector is expanded, and is able to compete with other modes of transport. The volume of passengers carried by rail increased by 25 per cent over the period 1970–95, but as the total number of passengers carried by all modes increased by 113 per cent, this is a poor performance. Over the same period, rail freight suffered an absolute decline, falling by 22 per cent from 283 billion tonne kilometres to 220 billion tonne kilometres, whilst total freight transport grew by 71.3 per cent (CEC 1997i: 39). If these trends continue, the Commission estimates that rail will carry only 4 per cent of the passengers and 9 per cent of the volume of freight (CEC 1996g: para. 12).

The reason for rail's decline is the rise in other more flexible and cheaper modes of transport. Rail has failed to improve its performance compared to other modes. Railways have not set out fully to meet the needs of their customers, and if they are to be revived, they must adopt a more market-oriented approach. It has been estimated that rail freight travels at an average of only 16 kilometres per hour (10 mph) (Kinnock 1998). If this speed could be doubled, costs might be reduced by a third.

A significant development has been the construction of the high-speed rail network, with trains able to travel at speeds between 160 and 300 kilometres per hour (ideally, between 250 and 300 km/h). This is having an impact on the carrying of passengers over longer distances, where it is an alternative to road and, in some cases, air travel. The Fifth Environmental Action Programme published in 1992 suggested that 9000 kilometres of new track might be constructed by 2020, along with the modernization of 15 000 kilometres of existing track (CEC 1992a: vol. III: 74). If the high-speed rail network develops to its potential, the share of passengers making journeys of over 80 kilometres by train could rise from 14 per cent in the mid-1990s to over 23 per cent by 2010. High-speed trains offer an environmentally friendly alternative to road transport, and to air travel for journeys of medium length. However, their threat to air traffic is unclear. Rail journeys of between two and three hours are highly competitive with air travel, but they also widen the catchment area of airports.

The construction of a high-speed rail network which stretches across borders is an immediate priority for the EU, but clearly any attractive and viable alternative to more polluting forms of travel within the member states is to be welcomed. The track requires only one third of the space of highways, and the trains are powered by electricity, which does not produce exhaust gases. However, the track is expensive to construct, and there are still problems with respect to the creation of the TEN-T in this area. Also, high-speed track requires more space compared to traditional track, especially when new track has to be constructed. The national technical specifications are not fully harmonized with respect to power supply and signalling, for example, which increases costs. Finally, as many travellers prefer to travel to stations in cars, stations (as with airports), require the construction of extensive car parks.

The Commission's view is that the greatest potential for improved performance in the rail sector is in the area of freight (CEC 1996f). Rail can only have a limited role in carrying the 85 per cent of freight that is transported less than 150 kilometres. Indeed, it is generally assumed that it does not offer significant cost advantages until journeys of over 300 kilometres are being considered. However, there is still a considerable market for long-distance freight that could be carried by rail. The important consideration here is the number of kilometres multiplied by the tonnage, which means that long-distance road haulage absorbs a huge amount of road space on certain key routes.[3] Many of these journeys are likely to cross national borders, so that there is a key role for the EU in encouraging the development of a system that will attract greater rail usage.

In order to combat the lack of competitiveness of railways compared to road haulage, in terms of price, speed, flexibility and reliability, the Commission proposed the creation of 'Trans-European Freight Freeways' (CEC 1996f). The national focus of the systems means that negotiating rail transport arrange-ments across borders remains a complex business for shippers, because the railway companies have to be dealt with on an individual basis. For example it took European Rail Shuttle (ERS), a consortium of shipping companies and the Dutch rail freight operators NS Cargo, between 18 months and four years to create a regular long-distance rail freight service from Rotterdam. The rail companies showed no sense of urgency in reaching agreements and generally were not particularly competitive in terms of price. Passenger traffic was considered to be the main focus of business. Even where a service is established, it is often slow. For example, the 260-kilometre journey between Rotterdam and Neuss in Germany takes ten hours for a freight train, and involves six changes of locomotive (Batchelor, 1997).

The Commission's proposal for Trans-European Freight Freeways is designed to counter the above problems, and it builds on the rights which rail operators have to access rail infrastructure in other member states under Directive 91/440/EEC.[4] Whilst this provided for the international grouping of railway companies and the right of transit, it did not provide for the loading or unloading of cargo and passengers in transit states. However, these rights did exist to a limited extent where combined transport modes were involved. The creation of a 'one-stop shop' for rail users was suggested in the White Paper, with open access to all operators and simplified use of the rail infrastructure across borders. The weakness of the proposal is that infrastructure managers would create the Trans-European Freight Freeways on a voluntary basis (CEC 1997aa). As a consequence, there will be a lack of a formal structure, which will inevitably reduce the impact of the proposal.

There is a need for awareness about the potential of railways to play a greater part in the future of EU transport policy. This implies continuing with high levels of investment, even where returns may be modest. However, the expansion of railways is not a panacea for the problems created by road transport. Even if there are substantial shifts of freight to rail, this would only absorb one or two years' growth in road traffic (House of Lords 1997b: para. 30). The enthusiasm for rail transport by environmentalists, if realized, would create demand far in excess of present capacity.

THE ALPINE AREAS

Most of the concerns of EU transport policy can be generalized. However, the member states that carry the greatest proportion of transit traffic through their national systems have a greater stake in the policy. The most environmentally sensitive aspect of this relates to the provision of facilities for transit across the Alps. The passes, which are a barrier between the industrial areas of Northern Europe and those of Northern Italy, cut through ecologically sensitive areas, where the emissions from trucks have significantly damaged forests and polluted soil. There have also been significant negative effects for the populations of the regions from transit traffic, including continuous noise and chemical pollution. Attempts to abate these nuisances in the member states are subject to the agreement of the EU.

Freight volumes have increased consistently with the development of the EU. The volume of freight carried by road through the Alps has grown from 29.3 million tonnes in 1985 to 51.1 million tonnes in 1998, whilst rail freight grew from 26.2 million tonnes to only 33.3 million tonnes over the same period (CEC 1998i). The annual percentage growth in road transport was 6.2 per cent over the period 1985–90 and 5.8 per cent over the period 1990–95. The growth of rail freight was more modest, at 3.2 per cent and 2.4 per cent respectively. In 1996 the road volume fell by 2.5 per cent and rail by 3.2 per cent.

The relative importance of the different modes of transport has changed over time. In 1965, 87 per cent of traffic was by rail; this had declined to 47.2 per cent in 1985, and to 39 per cent in 1996. The Swiss impose restrictions on the size and movement of trucks, and this has restricted the growth of road freight through their Alpine passes. Rail still maintains a significant share of transit freight traffic, accounting for 73 per cent in 1995.

The Swiss are not members of the EU, but nevertheless they negotiate with respect to transit rights. They have conflicting aspirations, in that they have a significant stake in the single market, and yet wish to avoid the negative environmental aspects of being a transit state. Under the 1992 Transit Agreement with the EU, strict controls were introduced over road freight travelling through Swiss territory. There was a 28-tonne laden weight limit on trucks travelling through the country and the ban on night and Sunday driving (CEC 1992g). Although the aim is to increase the use of rail transit, the restrictions have been criticized for causing trans-Alpine traffic to be deflected via Austria and France. Also the Swiss restrictions are unsophisticated in that they do not take into account the environmental performance of trucks. An annual quota of 40-tonne trucks has been agreed with the EU, to be phased in by 2005, once the current transit agreement has come to an end. The EU accepted that charges should discriminate against less environmentally friendly vehicles. The Swiss will impose charges per tonne and per kilometre of transit lorry traffic, set at a level which will cause traffic to be switched to rail. Two-thirds of the revenues from the charges will be used to improve the Swiss railway system, including two new tunnels through the Alps and connection with the high-speed rail network. The introduction of the heavy vehicle tax was supported in a referendum on 27 September 1998.

Austria, as a member of the EU, does not have the luxury of independent action. As early as 1980, negotiations started with respect to the regulation of traffic through the Tyrol. These were concluded with the signing of a treaty in 1992, which came fully into effect in 1993. The Austrian transit scheme attempts to limit the polluting effects of transport by reference to the emissions of nitrogen oxide (NO_x).[5] Eco-points are allocated to truckers according to the level of emissions generated by their vehicles. Each member state is allocated an agreed percentage of the points available.

Austria joined the EU in 1995, and was granted derogation from the common transport policy. This allowed for the maintenance of the Austrian transit scheme, initially until 1 January 1997, when quotas were to be eliminated. This deadline was not met, and as a consequence the transit scheme remained, and continued to apply to those trucks not starting or finishing their journeys in Austria.

Drivers of heavy goods vehicles travelling through Austria were required to carry documents indicating the level of NO_x emissions from the vehicle and an eco-point card. (The electronic technology to support this scheme was not, however, available at first, and monitoring was reduced to paper records.) Eco-points were deducted from the overall annual total number of points for each journey made. The scheme aimed to limit the number of vehicles in transit across Austria, so that a 60 per cent drop in NO_x is achieved over the period 1991–2003.[6] This implied a 60 per cent reduction in the number of journeys unless there is a significant improvement in the environmental performance of trucks, and could have meant a crisis with respect to the transit of goods. A system of reserve points was in place (within the overall quota), which had to be fully utilized once, in 1995. However, the performance of vehicles has improved, so that the volume of heavy goods vehicles actually increased by 36 per cent in the first four years of the scheme's operation.

The achievements with respect to the eco-points scheme appear at first sight to be remarkable, but the scheme does not take into account all the environmental aspects. It is narrowly applied to just one indicator of environmental degradation. The lower level of emissions does not guarantee that congestion has been reduced, or that there has not been a considerable nuisance caused by traffic noise. It may also be that the terms of the scheme may have been too generous, given the lack of any evidence of switching of transport modes (Humphreys 1997).

Few would argue that the Austrian Transit scheme should be extended across the EU, even if that were practical. It is an island in the middle of the common transport policy, designed to meet specific circumstances. The scheme does not appear to have reduced the free movement of goods. Indeed, as the volume of trade with the states of Central and Eastern Europe increases, there will be additional demands for transit through Austria. This is without any extra demands made by increased traffic from Italy and Greece to the rest of the EU. There will be further pressures from transit traffic when restrictions are placed upon traffic through Switzerland. The only really satisfactory solution to this would be to introduce a common set of charges for all routes through the Alps. However, attempts to raise charges for transit through the Brenner Pass were not seen as acceptable by the Commission, when they were pitched at a rate that was significantly higher than tolls throughout the rest of the EU. In 1998, the Commission threatened to take legal action against Austria.

CONCLUSIONS

The transition to sustainable mobility is unlikely to be realized in the short to medium term, because it would mean a substantial change in the lifestyle of EU citizens. In addition, it is unlikely that the member states would be prepared to meet the high cost of investment in infrastructure. Indeed, the total emissions from the transport sector are increasing rather than stabilizing or reducing, as in other sectors. It is unlikely that the level of transport demand within the EU will abate, and as a consequence there is a need to consider the extent to which environmental damage can be contained. Improving efficiency and promoting competitiveness within the framework of a pricing system which reflects environmental costs is a way forward, but this is an ideal which will be slow to be realized, because it implies utilizing fully the fiscal powers which are the prerogative of the member states.

Whilst the EU's role is restricted to one of encouraging activity at the member state level, progress has been made by ensuring that new initiatives are constantly debated. The linking of transport with the development of the TEN-T is a case in point. This is an initiative that is concerned with improving the efficiency of the transport system, but also helps to ensure that transport resources are not wasted. Agreeing EU-wide technical standards for emissions is another. These initiatives will not, however, change the public perception of what needs to be done. But if attitudes do change, the EU is well placed in terms of coordinating the actions required to make transport and environment policies effective.

NOTES

1. The European Auto–Oil Programme was established in 1992. This is an initiative to promote cooperation between the European automobile and oil industries to provide a technical base for new legislation. This involved the modelling of air quality to determine emission reduction needs, which involved establishing the cost and benefits of different technical and non-technical measures. (See Chapter 7.)
2. Council Directive 85/210/EEC of 20 March 1985 on the approximation of the laws of Member States concerning the lead content of petrol, OJL 096, 3 April 1985.
3. Statistics are not available for weight in tonne kilometres.
4. Council Directive 91/440/EEC of 29 July 1991 on the development of the Community's railways, OJL 237, 24 August 1991.
5. NO_x is seen as a benchmark for environmental degradation. If NO_x levels change, other pollutants will change to a similar extent.
6. The number of eco-points should diminish from 23 556 220 in 1991 to 9 422 488 in 2003.

11 Tourism and the environment

INTRODUCTION

Two of the most important problems facing the tourism industry are the destruction of the environment and pollution. For this reason it can be argued that any environmental protection measure will assist the tourism industry. The EU has in place a large number of measures designed to improve the environment, but few target the sector directly. The bathing water directive agreed in 1975[1] is an early exception to this. Since that time, most environmental measures directly related to the tourism industry have been on a small scale. This has been largely due to the reluctance of the member states to involve themselves in the sector.

The EU's concern relating to tourism and the environment is that the industry develops in a way that is sustainable and that its potential is not damaged. This concern comes about not only because the industry's activities can be damaging, but also because the industry's performance is enhanced by a clean environment. The tourism industry is of great economic importance to the European Union, in terms of both wealth creation and jobs. It contributes 5.5 per cent of gross domestic product (GDP), 6 per cent of employment, and one third of all trade in services (CEC 1997h). The 9 million jobs it has created offer particularly good employment opportunities to certain groups such as women and young people, and the industry has great potential to assist less developed and peripheral regions. It is estimated that, by 2010, there will be an additional 2 million travel and tourism jobs in the EU, a 9 per cent share of EU employment. Estimates of global growth are similarly buoyant. The World Tourism Organization estimates that the number of international tourists will increase from an estimated 595 million in 1996 to 1.6 billion in 2020 (World Tourism Organization 1997a).

Tourism encompasses both business and leisure activities, and can be defined as travel outside the place where the person lives, for a period of more than 24 hours. Shorter periods are normally considered as recreation (Stanners and Bourdeau 1995: 489). It is a heterogeneous industry, made up of a complex system of activities involving different functions and sectors in the economy. In a business sense the companies involved range from multinational corporations to medium and small family firms. It is also an industry that can have relatively low levels of individual productivity, despite its scale, because of demands for personal service.

Tourism activities are spread throughout each region of the EU, but tourist attractions are concentrated in a limited number of areas, leading to pressure on land resources. It is an area of growth, as incomes are rising and there is a greater amount of leisure time. The tourism industry operates throughout the world, but Europe has a major stake in it. In 1996 the 20 countries which form part of OECD Europe accounted for 65.5 per cent of international tourism receipts and 60.4 per cent of tourism expenditure within the OECD (OECD 1997c).

The industry is seasonal. The performance of the tourism industry depends on the competence, expertise and financial resources of its entrepreneurs, and on the availability of specific features such as city centres, monuments, museums, galleries, beaches, mountains and countryside. It is also highly dependent on transport infrastructure such as airports, roads and railways. Tourism affects society, culture, the environment and the economy; however, the threshold of capacity is likely to be reached at a uniform rate. The ecosystem may well be put under pressure long before there are adverse signs with respect to the economy, for example. The environment, in either its natural or man-made form, is an essential element of the tourism product. Tourism will change the environment, consequently it is important to ensure that these changes are not damaging and that, where feasible, the environment is made more resilient to damage. This suggests that the larger the scale of tourism, the more need there is to consider the planning of infrastructure and the management of the process. So, for example, as coastal resorts are developed, there is a need to ensure that adequate sewage systems are put in place and that waste is no longer just pumped into the sea. Also, where there are particularly ecologically sensitive coastlines, these should not be overexploited.

As travel costs fall, Europe's tourism industry faces more intense global competition, both to retain domestic tourists and to gain those from international sources. One of the main sources of competitive advantage for the industry is a reputation for good environmental standards. Consequently it is in the interest of the industry to reduce damaging pollution, whatever its source. This means that not only must the industry's activities be regulated, but also that the activities of other sectors, which may damage tourism assets, need to be controlled. The industry is under pressure to ensure that the environmental impacts of tourism are positive. The experience of the past has shown that unregulated development can lead to overdevelopment, and tourists moving on to new destinations. Policy makers have generally learnt that there is a close link between preserving and improving the environment related to tourism features, and the generation of long-term employment. This has led to campaigns to ensure that natural habitats and forests are preserved. National parks have been created, which has involved restricting harmful farming activities and quarrying. Generally, the threat of an adverse market reaction will help to ensure that the tourist sector will support the management of the natural environment and any steps taken to avoid overexploiting man-made features such as ancient monuments.

At first sight, tourism looks to be an ideal area for EU policy intervention. This is because of its strong international character, and its potential for affecting the environment. However, the complexity of the industry and the interaction between the different sectors means that it is difficult to achieve effective action, especially as the environment is one of a number of competing priorities. Despite enthusiastic support from the tourism industry for EU schemes, this is an area where little beyond policy rhetoric can be identified. The Commission has made frequent policy proposals, but they have failed because they have lacked the unanimous support of the Council of Ministers. (This is not a policy area where qualified majority voting (QMV) normally applies.) The Commission has long realized that the industry benefits from a good environmental performance, and it would be criticized if it did not attempt to limit the environmental impacts of the industry. This is not to suggest that there have not been policy successes, for example the bathing water directive. In addition to this, the Blue Flag logo (which the EU endorses) is one of the few European-wide industry standards which is generally recognizable to the public.

SUSTAINABLE TOURISM

The definition of sustainable tourism is the subject of very active debate. Tourism as an industry relies on the consumption of natural resources, and as such poses all the standard problems with respect to sustainability. The industry, to be sustainable, should not consume more environmental resources than can be replaced, and it should not damage the environment for future generations. It is therefore important that the industry and policy makers take a long-term view of the environment in order to ensure that tourism can be maintained.

Tourists need to visit a place to consume the product, and therefore they will have an impact. The extent of the impact will depend upon a number of factors, such as the volume of tourists, the structure of the host economy, the type of tourism activity taking place and the vulnerability of the local environment. There is a limit to the 'carrying capacity' of all tourist destinations, although the precise nature of this concept is debatable. Cooper et al. define 'carrying capacity' as 'that level of tourist presence which creates impacts on the host community, environment and economy that are acceptable to both tourist and hosts, and are sustainable over future time periods'[2] (Cooper et al. 1993: 95).

If the carrying capacity of tourism facilities is exceeded, the problems associated with overdevelopment start to become apparent.

The growth of mass tourism has posed problems for policy makers who wish to ensure that the environmental consequences of the industry are kept under control. Where there are problems related to overdevelopment, the industry is unlikely to respond adequately because of its disparate nature. In the past there have been far too many examples of the unregulated development of new resorts which has destroyed a local environment. Often the developers themselves realize this, but lack the mechanism to take collective action to ensure that the development will match the carrying capacity of the resort. They cannot prevent new developers coming into the area, as this is the essence of the free market mechanism. Controlling the number of new hotels and bed spaces is therefore a task which should fall to local and regional authorities. They should, in turn, take account of national tourism plans, as well as those subject to international agreement, such as those governing the Mediterranean. Whilst this is of course a highly rational prescription, it should be remembered that governments face a continuing conflict between the need to preserve the environment, the desire of the public for recreation, and the need to create jobs.

There are a number of perspectives as to whether mass tourism is a good thing or not. These can be categorized as follows:

- Mass tourism is the opposite of sustainable tourism. This view suggests that small groups of tourist are a good thing, but that mass tourism is environmentally damaging. The EU does not support this somewhat élitist view.
- There is a continuum between sustainable tourism and mass tourism. This view recognizes that sustainable tourism uses the infrastructure, transport and reservation systems of mass tourism. However, there is a danger that, if tourism is not managed, it will not be sustainable. The criticism of this view is that tourism is a complex and dynamic phenomenon and that it is not just a question of right or wrong or of scale. The impacts of tourism are not static, and the industry cannot be seen to serve an élite, as it did in the past. Indeed, the reality is that the scale of the industry has grown at least 20 times in the last 40 years.
- Mass tourism can contribute towards sustainable development. Where very sensitive natural resources are being exploited, it is important to aim for low-impact tourism, which preserves particular features. In this respect, social responsibilities are important in that local people should share in the benefits of tourism. Resources should be generated and made available to conserve the environment. Finally, there is a strong argument for having an educational aspect to tourism, so that eco-tourism has a more substantial purpose.

Sustainability is the goal that all tourism should seek to attain (Clarke 1997), but this does not mean that the industry should be confined to being a minority pursuit. The tourism industry is capable of being dynamic and responding to constraints. This includes innovations in which natural sources become part of the tourism product, for example eco-tours,[3] or specialized tours. The processes of the industry can be improved so that there is energy saving, better waste management and recycling. Finally, the managers of the industry should encourage employees and local inhabitants to act on environmental issues (Hjalager 1996).

From an EU perspective, mass tourism can be the source of significant social and economic benefit. It is dependent on a high quality of environment. Large-scale tourism operators are seeking to maintain the value of their product. Consumers interested in maintaining this environment can put pressure in a direct sense by not supporting environmentally damaging projects. Also, investments in ethical companies are a source of pressure: in 1991, British Airways was one of the first tourism companies to produce an environmental report.

THE EU'S TOURISM POLICY

Tourism policy is enmeshed in a wide span of EU policy initiatives, ranging across all those areas which cover the services sector. These include transport, competition, consumer protection, employment and social policy. Most EU documents that discuss the growth of tourism also refer to the environment. Linking the environmental cause with the success of the industry is one way of ensuring the cooperation of those involved in the industry.

The primary responsibility for the coordination of tourism policy lies with the Tourism Unit of DG XXIII. Actions with respect to the tourism sector pre-date any mention in the treaties. It only rates the briefest of mentions in the Treaty establishing the European Community. Originally, the EU's justi-fication for involving itself in tourism issues came from article 2 of the Treaty of Rome that gave the Community the task of promoting closer relations between the member states. It was believed that tourism could assist in achieving this by bringing the peoples of Europe together (CEC 1982). Article 2 of the Treaty establishing the European Community refers to sustainable growth which respects the environment, and article 3u refers to measures in the sphere of tourism. The First Environmental Action Programme mentions the link between tourism and the possible damage it might do to the quality of coastal waters (CoM 1973: 43). The Commission document 'Initial guidelines for a Community policy on tourism' (CEC 1982, section IV) noted that a large number of environmental measures which were of benefit to tourism had been introduced, but in its turn tourism should take environmental requirements into account.

The Council of Ministers declared that 1990 would be the European Year of Tourism, an initiative which dealt with a range of aspects of concern to the industry.[4] This initiative promoted the growth of the tourism sector and its cultural benefits for the citizens of the EU. In addition to this, it sought to promote a more even spatial distribution of tourists and use of facilities over a longer time span, while at the same time respecting the quality of the environment. This latter point can be seen as an attempt to extend the carrying capacity of the industry by making better use of existing facilities. The result should be reduced congestion in areas where there was pressure, and greater utilization of spare capacity. During the European Year of Tourism it is estimated that ECU 500 000 was given to 50 co-financed projects which were related to tourism and the environment. This was a very small amount in the total scheme of things, but it was significant in terms of establishing the EU's policy role.

In 1990 both the European Parliament and the Economic and Social Committee expressed concern that tourism should be developed in harmony with the environment. This was a theme which was then expanded on by the Commission in the document 'A Community action plan to assist tourism' (CEC 1991b: 11). The Fifth Environmental Action Programme put tourism for the first time on a level comparable with agriculture, energy, industry and transport. The Fifth EAP recognized that tourism is a big business, and capable of having a significant environmental impact. The reason for the selection of tourism for the mention of the process of environmental improvement is related to its overall importance and links with the service sector. However, it is an industry, which is private-sector-oriented, where the majority of government intervention is at the local and regional level. The EU's role is to ensure that environmental resources are fully protected.

Tourism is an industry that is growing within Europe, particularly in the Mediterranean region (although the trend in global tourism has been for even faster growth). Unlike the growth in energy use or the use of private cars, tourism does not come in for disapproval by the Commission. The individual has a legitimate right to enjoy tourism activities and tourism is of importance to European economic development, particularly in peripheral regions. However, along with the attendant benefits, there are potential conflicts. The Fifth EAP therefore calls for tourism activities to be well managed and organized on a sustainable basis (CEC 1992a, vol. II: 7). The EU is directly involved in the support of tourism by its contribution to tourism infrastructures, and less directly by its involvement in transport policy and the free movement of people.

Whilst the standards with respect to noise, air and water can be defined, and these can have a direct bearing on tourism activity, there is a degree of ambiguity attached to many tourism activities. The Fifth EAP recognized that tourism could be both a force for environmental improvement and a damaging pursuit. The impact of tourism depends on individuals' activities and how well they are managed. This is particularly the case where tourism activities are likely to grow, in mountain and coastal areas.

In the document 'A Community action plan to assist tourism' (CEC 1991b) a number of specific measures were suggested which link tourism development with environmental protection. The Tourism Action Plan 1992–95[5] was funded only very modestly by a budget of ECU 18 million. It aimed to ensure that the interaction between tourism and the environment was taken into account by supporting the following:

- Initiatives aimed at informing and increasing the awareness of tourists and suppliers of services about the interaction between tourism and the environment, in particular through the creation of a European environmental prize. The first award of the 'European Prize for Tourism and the Environment' was introduced in 1995, with 269 destinations competing. There was widespread interest in repeating the initiative. However, attempts to revive it by its incorporation into the PHILOXENIA Programme (see below) meant that it was caught in the stalemate associated with that programme.
- Innovative pilot projects to reconcile tourism and nature protection at local or regional level, in particular coastal and mountain areas, nature parks and reserves, for example by measures for the guidance of visitors.
- The development of networks involving transnational exchanges of experience, including experience of environmental problems and their possible solution through visitor management at tourist sites.
- Initiatives encouraging forms of environment-friendly tourism.

In line with the principle of subsidiarity, the EU has recognized that any strategy for tourism policy relies especially on the activities of the industry, and the national, regional and local authorities. The industry is best helped by appealing to the industry's own economic self-interest, in a combination of regulation and economic incentives. The actual impacts of tourism are likely to appear in different forms depending on the level at which they examined. At the local level, the problem is likely to be one of excessive competition for land and fresh water, along with pollution of air and water. At the regional level the problem of maintaining biodiversity and loss of habitats becomes important, whilst at the global level problems of excessive traffic and global warming become an issue (Stanners and Bourdeau 1995: 491).

The Fifth EAP listed proposed measures under the three categories shown in Table 11.1, while at the same time making clear that their implementation was likely to be carried out by different levels of government. The Fifth EAP did not propose radical strategies for the industry. Initiatives such as the introduction of a tourism levy, in line with the concept of the polluter pays principle, were considered, but they are not easily applied. The fragmentary nature of the industry makes any kind of taxation difficult to target.

The proposed successor to the Community Action Plan for Tourism was the PHILOXENIA Programme (Multi-annual programme to assist European tourism) (CEC 1996d). It might have been expected that PHILOXENIA would have taken further the strategies proposed by the Fifth EAP. However, it was a programme strongly oriented to the needs of the industry in general. It aimed to stimulate the quality and competitiveness of European tourism, in order to contribute to growth and employment, with a strategy for the environment only a small element within it. Under the heading 'Improving the quality of European tourism', the Commission proposed promoting sustainable development through support to local initiatives geared to sound management of visitor flows and the sharing of successful ideas. There was support for the implementation of environmentally friendly management systems in tourist accommodation, and the 'European Prize for Tourism and the Environment' (to be held every two years) was carried forward from the Community Action Plan for Tourism.

The programme had objectives and proposed specific measures to provide a coherent framework designed to assist the industry, via cooperation between the EU, the member states and regional authorities. It was proposed that the programme would be monitored on an annual basis. The general aims of PHILOXENIA were generally uncontroversial, and its proposed budget, of ECU 25 million over five years, was modest. However, the real issue was that of subsidiarity. The British and German governments believed that tourism was a matter for the member states (*European Report* 1997b). By 1998, it had become lost in the decision-making process.

The problem for EU tourism policy is that most of the actions are part of several programmes, many of which are not specifically targeted at the sector. This does not mean that their role with respect to tourism is not understood: the improvements in the free movement of people, consumer protection and facilities for the handicapped would all be examples of this. However, there is a need to coordinate these improvements and produce a clearer strategy in the light of the industry's growing economic importance. The current fragmentation is illustrated by the nature of the spending that takes place with respect to tourism and the environment.

In 1995 ECU 1.5 million was spent under the LIFE Programme to develop sustainable tourism projects.[6] (See Chapter 4 for further details of LIFE.) In 1996, ECU 4.4 million was made available for tourism projects in coastal zones,

Table 11.1   Tourism policy and the environment

Objective	Measures	Instruments
Type of tourism	• Better management of mass tourism • National and regional plans for coastal and mountain areas	• Improved control on land use • Strict rules on new constructions • Management of traffic flows in and out of tourist areas • Visitor management; exchange of expertise • Pilot models of sustainable tourism • Strict enforcement of environmental standards • Creation of buffer zones around sensitive areas
Behaviour of tourists	• Building environmental awareness • Liberalizing transport • Increasing the cost of private cars • Better dispersion of holidays • Diversification of tourism	• Developing codes of conduct • Completing the EU's transport policy • Economic incentives including an energy tax and road pricing • Tourism plans at the EU, national and regional levels • Use of the European Regional Development Fund • Creation of an EC Tourism Advisory Committee[1]
Quality of tourist services	• Promotion of new forms of environment friendly tourism • Building environmental awareness of those involved in tourist activity	• Brochures • Professional training • Pilot projects • Professional training and education of best practice

[1] This consists of representatives from the member states.

and ECU 1.5 million under the framework of the Environment and Climate Programme (CEC 1996d). The EU spends a significant amount of money to promote tourism-related projects in less developed areas via the Structural Funds (ECU 7.3 million was budgeted for the period 1994–99).

TOURISM AND BATHING WATER

A number of directives have been designed to reduce water pollution and are therefore of consequence to the tourism industry. These include a directive relating to detergents,[7] followed by a directive limiting the discharge of dangerous substances into the aquatic environment, which sought to prevent the deterioration of the quality of water by pollution by toxic substances on a 'black list' or a 'grey list'.[8] In 1978 a directive to reduce and eventually eliminate the pollution of the sea by waste from the titanium dioxide industry was published.[9]

Shipping has on occasion proved to be a major source of pollution, with some spectacular spillage resulting from accidents at sea. The pollution caused by the wreck of the supertanker *Amoco Cadiz* on the Breton coast early in 1978 led to an attempt to forestall such catastrophes in the future. In June 1978, the Council set up a Community action programme on the control and reduction of pollution caused by hydrocarbons discharged at sea.[10] This did not, of course, eliminate the problem: accidents still happen, although they are comparatively rare. What is still of concern is the deliberate discharge of oil-based waste from ships, which has from time to time caused devastation to colonies of sea birds, as well as making beaches unpleasant for holiday makers.

The main thrust of the EU's strategy with respect to its water policy and tourism has been to tackle the problem of bathing water. In the nineteenth century, bathing in sea water was seen as having great health-giving properties, but since we now know a great deal more about public health issues, it is clear that, where waters are polluted, they can be a significant source of health risk. In a number of coastal areas, untreated sewage had been discharged directly into the sea. The extent to which this sewage was screened for solid human waste varied, but the overall effect was, at times, very unpleasant. The contamination of bathing waters increased as a result of growing population. From the 1960s onwards this caused the Italian and French governments particular concern with respect to the Mediterranean.

In the First Environmental Action Programme of 1972, there was a specific request for the French, Italian and UK governments to supply information on the disposal of waste into sea water (CoM 1973: 17). In 1975, the EU set about the task of trying to raise the standard of bathing water to a minimal acceptable standard by adopting the bathing water directive.[11] The rationale for introducing the directive was concern about the impact of the discharge of raw sewage on human health, the biological effects of sewage, and the loss of amenity value caused by visual pollution. Environment Commissioner Bjerregard reasserted the rationale for continued EU involvement in the quality of bathing water in 1997. The Commissioner commented: 'It is not only the health aspect that attracts people to go to the beaches, also the aesthetic aspects of the water have to be taken into account' (Bjerregard 1997).

The directive, which came into force in 1977, laid down minimum quality standards for inland water and seawater where bathing was authorized or permitted, and it provided checks on bacteria which transmit infectious diseases. It was of particular importance to the tourism industry, because of concerns about the appearance of the water and its acceptability to bathers. The directive required the monitoring of substances giving taste, odour or an unpleasant colour to bathing water, such as hydrocarbons and phenols from oil refineries and chemical works situated on coasts or near rivers and canals. The justification for action at the EU level was that:

- it ensured that there were common standards of bathing water;
- action could be taken in cases where standards were deteriorating;
- comparable information could be provided to the general public;
- it contributed to the control of water pollution.

The need to take action varied between the Northern European and the Mediterranean states. As a consequence, a strong case could be made against the directive on the basis of subsidiarity. The Mediterranean is a closed sea, with a growing tourism potential. In contrast, the North Sea is open to the world's oceans. Therefore it could be argued that the process of dilution and dispersal, along with the effects of sunlight, gave Northern European states a greater capacity to absorb pollution. Also, the summers are cooler further north, and fewer people feel brave enough to enter the water. Consequently, the UK made little attempt to implement the spirit of the directive, arguing that there were special difficulties in determining the timing of the bathing season and the numbers actually bathing.

Whilst most member states had a system of designated bathing beaches, the UK and the Netherlands did not. The directive took account of this by including in its definition of bathing waters places where bathing is not prohibited, and is traditionally practised by a large number of bathers. However, this offered an ideal opportunity for the UK to avoid its commitment. The UK took until 1979 to identify 27 bathing waters in 16 resorts. This compared to 8000 in the rest of the EU, including 39 in Luxembourg, which has no sea coastline. Underlying these arguments is the enormous cost of introducing an adequate sewage disposal system for the coastal resorts of the UK, given the general decline in tourist appeal of British seaside resorts. An example of the UK's non-compliance was the premier seaside resort of Blackpool. The beaches were not declared to be bathing beaches. This eventually led to a 'reasoned opinion' being taken against the UK in 1981. In 1986, the Commission threatened to take the UK to the European Court of Justice over the same issue. The Commission has set great store by its legal actions against member states to ensure that standards are maintained. The waters are tested for faecal coliforms, phenols, surface-active substances and mineral oils.

Since the introduction of the directive, there has been widespread general support for these common standards. In 1996, the Commission's bathing water report covered 13 000 seaside beaches and 6000 fresh water areas. In that year almost 90 per cent of seaside beaches achieved the standard set by the bathing water directive, but only one third of inland sites were adequately monitored, or met the minimum quality standards. The picture was not, however, uniformly good. The actual standard of bathing water, even when it meets the standard of the EU's bathing water directive, is not particularly high, as the choice of a standard was the result of political compromise. Also it does not take into account more recent scientific developments.

Some member states have a much better record than others. By 1992, 92 UK beaches met the standard of the directive, and this had risen to 224 in 1996, but this was out of a possible 472 coastal bathing beaches. Blackpool's south beach still failed in 1997, with 25 times the permitted level of faecal coliforms laid down by the directive (Bond 1997). Beaches such as this are likely to continue to fail to meet bathing water standards, as long as the UK continues to pump raw sewage into the sea. The use of long sea-outfalls does not work in those circumstances where tides and the prevailing winds push the waste towards the shore. The only certain way of achieving an acceptable minimum standard is to process sewage in the same way as is done inland. However, the problem of costs and benefits of environmental improvement have to be taken into account. Whilst polluted bathing water is extremely unpleasant, the cost of improvements may be disproportionately high, especially where there are relatively few bathers. In this context the Commission's case is rather weak, because it does not give a cost–benefit analysis of this well-established policy.

Action taken to improve the position with respect to pumping sewage into the sea now comes under the urban waste treatment directive, which was adopted in 1991.[12] This required that all towns with a population of more than 10 000 should apply secondary treatment to sewage before it was discharged. By the end of 1998 the dumping of untreated sewage into the sea was to have ceased. The Commission believed that this measure would be beneficial for tourism, as it would improve the quality of bathing water at established resorts. It would also reduce public health costs as a result of people swimming in less polluted waters. As with the bathing water directive, there were problems with implementation of this directive. Greece did not even put it into force until

1997. In 1998, the Commission was so dissatisfied with the general performance of the member states that all but Sweden were faced with the prospect of infringement proceedings. Much to the embarrassment of all concerned, the city of Brussels was cited for discharging raw sewage into the River Senne (Boulton 1998).

The quality of bathing water was expected to meet the minimum standards laid down by the EU, but there are other inspection schemes. In the UK, the Marine Conservation Society's 1997 *Good Beach Guide* showed that only 136 out of 763 beaches met their water quality standards (*Yorkshire Post* 1997). Beyond this, there is an EU-sponsored 'Blue Flag' scheme. This scheme was started in France in 1985, when 11 beaches were given the award. By 1995, 18 countries were awarding the Blue Flag. Since 1987 (The European Year of the Environment), the Commission has fully endorsed the Blue Flag initiative. It was originally managed by the European Foundation for Education and the Environment (FEEE), an independent non-governmental body based in Copenhagen. The coverage of the award is far wider than just bathing water, and it is designed specifically to be a positive tourism feature. The criteria for the award include absence of oil pollution, absence of visible sewage, displays indicating the quality of the bathing water, availability of public toilets and first aid facilities.

In the spring of 1994, the Commission proposed a revised bathing water quality directive (CEC 1994a). Its view was that, as the original bathing water directive had led to significant improvements in the quality of life for European citizens a revised directive with technical amendments would be valuable. The Commission concluded that the bathing water directive made a distinct contribution to the integration of environment policy and tourism policy. As such it was desirable that it should have a separate identity (CEC 1997ee). Thus the revised directive would supplement the urban waste treatment directive.

The Commission's aim was to simplify and consolidate the original proposals, and to take account of scientific and technical progress (CEC 1994a). The new proposals maintained the scope of the existing ones. However, micro-biological research showed that certain parameters could be removed, and the Commission believed that certain definitions and obligations needed to be made more explicit. Proposals for extending the scope of the directive to include the testing of waters used for water sports came from the European Parliament. The Commission rejected these proposals. However, improving the quality of water used for all recreational purposes would appear to be a reasonable longer-term objective, which would have significant benefits for the tourism industry (*Europe Environment* 1997).

Not all the member states shared the Commission's enthusiasm for the revised bathing water directive, because they believed that the balance between the costs and benefits of complying with the 1975 bathing water directive had not been securely established. The UK government was to criticize the revised directive on the grounds that it would add between £1.6 and £4.2 billion to costs, over and above the existing directive and the urban waste water treatment directive (House of Commons 1998: vii). The UK has of course felt little enthusiasm for such measures in the past, but there can be little doubt that bathing water has improved as a result of EU intervention. However, the substantial gap between the UK and the Commission in terms of the real costs of environmental measures is a cause for concern.

EU INVOLVEMENT IN REGIONAL CONVENTIONS

The tourism industry has created a need for the EU to cooperate on environmental matters with non-member states on a regional basis. This is particularly the case with the Alps and the Mediterranean, which are not only popular, but also environmentally sensitive regions. It is on the borders of the EU that the problems related to environmental interdependence pose the greatest problem, because non-members are under no compulsion to participate in schemes to preserve valuable tourism resources. Whilst it may be logical for all those who share a resource to contribute towards its sustainability, participation will inevitably depend upon a shared perception of that need. In addition to this, non-member states often lack the resources to contribute fully.

About one third of the world's tourism takes place in the Mediterranean region. More than half the population is also concentrated on the coastline. This pressure of human activity has caused significant damage to the marine environment, the coastal ecosystems and landscapes. One response to this has been to involve the EU actively in regional conventions with non-member states. The Convention for the Protection of the Mediterranean Sea against Pollution (Barcelona Convention) was adopted in February 1976, but came into force on 12 February 1978. It called for regional cooperation to manage one of the world's most important tourism resources, the Mediterranean. It aimed to assist Mediterranean governments to collaborate in the control of marine pollution. By 1996, it involved 21 participants, including the EU.

Affiliated to the Barcelona Convention was the protocol for the prevention of pollution of the Mediterranean Sea by dumping from ships and aircraft, and the protocol concerning cooperation in combating pollution of the Mediterranean Sea by oil and other harmful substances in cases of emergency. These were also agreed in Barcelona in 1976, and came into force in 1978. In 1980 the protocol for the protection of the Mediterranean Sea against pollution from land-based sources was agreed in Athens, and came into force on 17 June 1983. The protocol concerning Mediterranean specially protected areas was agreed in Geneva in 1982 and came into force on 23 March 1986. All of these had the same participants as the Barcelona Convention.

A number of other protocols relating to the protection of the Mediterranean Sea from pollution were agreed in the mid-1990s, including that relating to exploration and exploitation of the Continental Shelf and the seabed and its sub-soil in 1994, the protocol concerning specially protected areas and biological diversity in the Mediterranean in 1995, and the protocol on the prevention of pollution of the Mediterranean Sea resulting from the trans-boundary movements of hazardous wastes and their disposal in 1996. In addition, amendments to the protocol for the protection of the Mediterranean Sea against pollution from land-based sources were adopted in 1996.

As part of its response to this the Euro-Mediterranean Conference held in November 1995 in Barcelona adopted a declaration. This established a new Partnership between the European Union and 12 Southern and Eastern Mediter-ranean states.[13] Whilst it is of vital importance that these 12 states are involved and, indeed, that others are added to the list, many are very poor, and as a consequence do not have the resources to contribute fully to the clean-up of the Mediterranean. The Euro-Mediterranean partnership built upon the Barcelona Convention and the Mediterranean Action Plan. Its objectives were both political and economic. An important objective integrated into the Euro-Mediterranean partnership was the promotion of sustainable development. The Conference had emphasized interdependence with respect to the environment, and the need for a regional cooperation and coordination of existing multilat-eral programmes. It was recognized that economic development and environmental protection should be recognized. Arising out of this, the EU was given the task of developing the short- and medium-term priority environ-mental action programme (SMAP). This is a framework programme of action for the protection of the Mediterranean environment, and was adopted unanimously by the Euro-Mediterranean Ministerial Conference on the Environment, held in Helsinki on 28 November 1997.

The SMAP was intended to help reverse the trend towards environmental degradation and to contribute to the sustainable development of the region. It was to become the common basis for the coordination of policy and funding in the Mediterranean region, responding to national and regional needs. In particular it offered the chance of better funding, particularly from EU sources. Thus whilst it was designed as a partnership arrangement, it was also designed to give the leadership of the initiative to the EU.

The SMAP developed five priorities:

- The evaluation and monitoring of the quantity and quality of water, including assessing potential new sources in areas such as tourism resorts that have a significant seasonal demand, and making drinking water safe.

- Promoting integrated waste management through a variety of initiatives. The pressure of population growth and the development of tourism have created a problem of waste disposal for the region, which threatens living conditions.
- Establishing strategies for tackling pollution 'hot spots', and places where biodiversity is threatened.
- The development of integrated coastal zone management. This involves planning of coastal zones compatible with the development of sustainable tourism.
- The combating of desertification by better agricultural management.

The development of the SMAP is of importance in creating a shared commitment to the environment for tourism in the Mediterranean region. The EU cannot dictate its policy to other Mediterranean entities, which remain outside its structure and have other priorities, especially in the light of differing levels of economic development. It is too early to say how successful the strategy will be, or indeed how much funding the programme will command. However, unless the EU and the member states are prepared to contribute significantly to the various projects, they will not be a success. Since the Mediterranean is a shared resource, any environmental improvement on the EU's side of the sea will be undermined elsewhere.

The programme included actions to assist the non-community partners and to create a link with the future, which involved promoting the use of environmental impact assessments, awareness enhancement (campaigns, information activities, documentation centres) and capacity building, including consolidation of the environmental agencies in the Mediterranean. Added to this there was to be transfer of appropriate and environmentally sound technologies and know-how, including maintenance. Cooperation was to take place at differing levels of government, and between non-governmental organizations.

The Alpine Convention, which was signed in 1991 and came into force in 1995, is an example of transborder cooperation which involves the EU and states that face common environmental problems. The signatories were Germany, France, Italy and Austria, along with Slovenia, Liechtenstein and Switzerland. Its development arose out of the first Alpine Conference of Environmental Ministers held in Berchtesgaden in 1989. The convention defines a series of principles for protecting Alpine ecosystems, and aims to preserve and protect the Alps through prudent and sustained use of resources. It calls for cooperation in research activities and scientific assessments, and contains a number of detailed objectives relating to population and culture, regional planning, prevention of air pollution, soil conservation, water management, conservation of nature and the countryside, mountain farming, forests, transport, energy and waste management. Whilst all of these can affect tourism, there is a specific objective which covers tourism and recreation. Article 2.2.10 calls for appropriate measures to restrict activities that are harmful to the environment, and to harmonize tourism and recreational activity. In particular it calls for the setting aside of quiet areas.

The provisions of the Convention do not imply a loss of national sovereignty, but they do call for the exchange of information, cooperation and the holding of regular meetings with the contracting parties. The Alpine Conference was established on a regular basis. It will take place every two years, and can make decisions that affect the rules of the Convention, but changes to it can only be made on a unanimous basis.

CONCLUSIONS

The development of mass tourism is a fairly recent phenomenon and has created an industry largely concerned with increasing the number of visitors. Now the consumers of tourism products are increasingly aware of environmental issues and their concern influences their overall satisfaction. There are therefore pressing commercial as well as ecological reasons for aiming to reduce the level of environmental degradation. This is a policy area where the EU could achieve a considerable level of public support for its intervention to improve the environment. But it has been consistently held back by a lack of support from those member states which believe the industry's activities are only of national concern. It is recognized that Europe's tourism assets need protecting and improving in order to allow for the inevitable expansion of the industry. But, unless environmental concerns are addressed, the industry will add further to environmental degradation, instead of contributing to its improvement.

The failure of the member states to agree fully to support the Commission's initiatives may result in less progress being made towards establishing higher environmental standards in some regions which are dependent upon the tourism industry. It will also give a competitive edge to those centres outside Europe where tourism is developing. With the fall in the cost of air travel, even long-haul destinations are becoming a viable alternative to the EU. High environmental standards could therefore be a source of competitive advantage.

Even without the unanimous support of the Council of Ministers, the EU can still assist the environmental performance of tourism by ensuring that funds for both urban and rural projects include an element of environmental improvement. This can be done by coordinating the EU's support both within the Commission and with the member states. The EU might also have a role in encouraging the staggering of holidays, which may help to reduce the pressure on tourism resources. However, public information campaigns tend to have only a limited impact.

NOTES

1. Council Directive 76/160/EEC of 8 December 1975 concerning the quality of bathing water, OJL 31, 5 February 1976, p. 1.
2. The term 'tourism presence' is used to take account of factors such as the length of stay, characteristics of the tourism, geographical concentration and seasonality.
3. The World Tourism Organization estimates that eco-tourism amounts to between 10 and 15 per cent of the world market (World Tourism Organization 1997b).
4. Council Decision 89/46/EEC of 21 December 1988 on an action programme for European Tourism Year (1990), OLJ 17, 21 January 1989, pp. 53–6.
5. Community Action Plan for Tourism, Council Decision of 13 July 1992, OJL 231, 13 August 1992.
6. The LIFE Programme called for the integration of environmental factors into land-use planning and management, and socioeconomic activities, including tourism.
7. Council Directive 73/404/EEC of 22 November 1973 on the approximation of the laws of the Member States relating to detergents, OJL 347, 17 December 1973, p. 51.
8. Council Directive 76/464/EEC of 4 May 1976 on pollution caused by certain dangerous substances discharged into the aquatic environment of the Community, OJL 129, 18 May 1976, p. 23.
9. Council Directive 78/176/EEC of 20 February 1978 on waste from the titanium dioxide industry, OJL 54, 25 February 1978, p. 19.
10. Council Resolution of 26 June 1978 setting up an action programme of the European Communities on the control and reduction of pollution caused by hydrocarbons discharged into the sea, OJC 162, 8 July 1978, p.1.
11. Council Directive 76/160/EEC of 8 December 1975 concerning the quality of bathing water, OJL 31, 5 February 1976, p. 1.
12. Council Directive of 21 May 1991 concerning urban waste water treatment, OJL 135, 30 May 1991.
13. Morocco, Algeria, Tunisia, Egypt, Turkey, Israel, Jordan, Lebanon, Syria, Cyprus, Malta and the Palestinian Authority.

12 The future for environmental policy within the EU

INTRODUCTION

Environmental policy has been slow to develop in the history of the European Union. The early policy action of the 1960s and 1970s was fragmented. It was based on reactive measures which concentrated on finding remedies for specific problems and harmonization of national policies to prevent distortion of trade. The EU's environmental policy at the beginning of the twenty-first century is part of the global search for policies which will achieve a balance between environmental protection, economic growth and more rational allocation of increasingly scarce natural resources. The treaty revisions made in Maastricht (1992) and Amsterdam (1997) have provided a firm basis for the policy which emerged in the late 1990s. It is a policy based on a wide-ranging body of legislation which has been augmented throughout the 1990s by the development of a number of other tools of policy, for example voluntary registration for schemes such as the eco-label initiative, advocacy of eco-taxation within the national policy structures and the enhanced funding opportunities for environmental policy. Funding is now available through the LIFE Programme established in 1991, the Cohesion Fund in 1993 and the revisions of the regulations for the Structural Funds in 1993 and 1999.

FROM ENVIRONMENTAL REGULATION TO ENVIRONMENTAL POLICY

The early history of environmental policy within the EU was characterized by a regulatory approach which was often considered to be too prescriptive and too rigid; as a result the policy failed to achieve its objectives. The bulk of the legislation adopted during the 1970s and the 1980s concentrated on responding in an *ad hoc* fashion to environmental problems identified as a result of growing environmental awareness among the populations of the member states (for example Directives 76/464/EC and 78/176/EC on freshwater and marine pollution). Directives of this type were mainly designed to deal with a specific target at an individual point of source emissions. Specific limit values were set or targets identified for a wide range of individual pollutant in the directives. In addition, measures were introduced that were intended to ensure that the market was not subject to distortion by differences in the developing national environmental policies (such as Directive 84/631/EC on the transfrontier movement of waste). However, in 1988 the ECJ did rule in the 'Danish bottles case' that environmental concerns could outweigh any trade concerns, when the Danish government introduced regulations requiring containers being used for beverages to be recyclable.

In the late 1980s and early 1990s the flow of legislation being adopted in the EU increased dramatically. It covered all areas of environmental protection – protection for wildlife and its natural habitats, measures which had an impact on human health, and controls on industrial and agricultural pollution. Some pieces of legislation dealt with very specific issues; others were much broader and more general in their impact. The result was that by the beginning of the 1990s more than 200 pieces of Community legislation had been adopted and approximately 200 other measures introduced. Some pieces of legislation dealt with very specific issues, others were much broader and more general in their effect. Despite the criticisms of the type of legislation which had been adopted, the EU's environmental policy had achieved a great deal by the early 1990s. However, these legislative developments continued to be undermined in the mid- and late 1990s by a lack of adequate implementation.

The Fifth Environmental Action Programme (1992) was intended to introduce a new approach to environmental policy which would set clear objectives. There were three main principles around which the programme was established. First, where possible, market-based mechanisms should be relied on. Second, there should be more flexibility in the implementation of the policy. Finally, policy measures should be based on environmental quality standards and general permitting requirements. The Fifth EAP was both a philosophical statement about the intention of the EU to commit to a strategy designed to develop sustainable development and an outline of what could be done on a sectoral basis. It was a major step forward for the future development of the EU's environmental policy. At the same time it was seen as desirable to view the Fifth EAP as the starting-point from which a wider-ranging and more detailed European plan for sustainable development in a Sixth Environmental Action Programme would be developed for the period from 2000 onwards.

Certain actions were necessary for such a sustainable development plan to be introduced. The legal basis was given in the Treaty of Amsterdam by the introduction of the explicit statement of commitment to sustainable development in article 2 TEU (2 TEU) and article 2EC (2 EEC). Despite this commitment, mobilization of the national governments to support the introduction of a sustainable development plan remains problematic. The European Commission reported on the disappointing lack of enthusiasm among the national governments for a policy to achieve sustainability (CEC 1996p). The support of the national governments is required to strengthen the mechanisms which will achieve a balance between the economy, equity and ecology. This is to ensure that the objectives of economic growth, employment creation and environmental protection are achieved within the EU. The integration of environmental requirements into the drafting of policy measures forms an early and crucial stage of the policy process. Changes will be required as a result to the level of consultation and the form of the legislation used.

The Fifth EAP concentrated on a sectoral approach to policy development, identifying areas of economic activity where the actual and potential levels of environmental degradation were high. The approach had its origins in what had been accomplished in environmental policy to that date. Coherence in policy and effectiveness of action is difficult to achieve if legislation deals with single issues. Concentrating on a particular sector may lead to duplication of effort if a measure specifically designed to affect water usage or air pollution in industry or agriculture has an unintentional effect on the aquatic or atmospheric ecosystem elsewhere. This reveals an underlying tension in environmental policy. The revisions of the Treaty undertaken in 1997 have given a legal basis to action for the future which will provide the EU with the opportunity to remedy this lack of coherence.

Other types of inconsistencies have also emerged. In the case of the directive on nitrates in water[1] (see Chapter 8) the national governments have consistently failed to comply with the directive and have been subject to action by the European Commission under Article 226 TEC (169 TEC). This effort by the European Commission has been taking place in a context in which the levels of nitrates in water have been falling in any case. The moves to ensure that the agricultural sector is open to the market have led in some areas to a fall in intensity of cropping and use of nitrate fertilizers which has in turn had an impact on the run-off into the watercourses from which drinking water supplies are obtained. This has been a trend evident since the closure of fertilizer factories began in the late 1980s. The case demonstrates the way in which the regulatory approach may become locked into bureaucratic and legal inefficiencies. On its own the approach is not sufficient to protect the environment. It is essential to coordinate actions across areas within the policy to ensure that the spillover effects (in this case advantageous!) do not hinder the development of an effective overall environmental policy.

The adoption of a sustainable development plan will help to overcome these problems by reinforcing a number of existing initiatives. Among the most important of these is the review of the current environmental legislation begun by the European Commission following the Council Summit held in Edinburgh in 1992. The objective of the review was to simplify, consolidate and update existing legislation, particularly in the areas of air and water quality. The review was necessary to remove many of the administrative and bureaucratic inefficiencies and duplications which were contributing to the failure of the effectiveness of the EU's environmental policy. As many of the directives dated from the 1970s, the review was also necessary to take into account the most recent scientific and technical progress. As a result of the review process, proposals were made for framework legislation for the two sectors. The objective of the legislation was to establish harmonized targets for water and air quality to be achieved at the national level with overall targets to be achieved by the EU. These proposals did not encompass all the issues covered by the existing legislation (see Chapter 2), but as they were based on a media-oriented approach rather than a sectoral approach they showed the way forward for future developments. The use of framework legislation provides the opportunity for a more holistic approach to environmental protection. Of necessity this type of legislation encourages greater participation of all those involved in the policy-making and implementation process.

Among the earliest of the directives introduced by the EU in the 1960s was legislation to control levels of noise (see Chapter 2). This legislation was, however, limited and piecemeal and did not build up to any comprehensive action by the EU to curb noise levels. In 1996 the European Commission published a consultative Green Paper as the first stage in the adoption of a framework directive on ambient noise pollution (CEC 1996k). There was wide consultation with industrial groups, non-governmental organizations, and research and academic institutions before the timetable was drawn up for the adoption of this legislation. The consultation process confirmed the need for supranational action to be taken, but the proposals contained in the Green Paper were generally considered not ambitious enough. Three areas were identified where further research and exchange of information was required: assessment of the existing methods of noise reduction; the fixing of national and local targets as well as those for the EU; and action to be taken if the targets were exceeded. During 1998, working groups were set up at national level to determine the common indices for action so that the framework directive proposal adopted during 1999 would be in force by 2002. The wide-ranging consultation process undertaken for this directive is an example of the application of the principles of shared responsibility and subsidiarity.

Framework directives provide an opportunity to resolve some of the more intransigent of the controversies which have been generated within the EU's environmental policy. In the early 1990s the European Commission proposed that common taxes should be introduced on carbon energy use. This proposal was unacceptable to the national governments and, despite different attempts through the 1990s, the issue remained a major area of controversy (see Chapter 5). In July 1998 the European Commission outlined two possible options which would resolve the problem. Both were based on the use of framework directives.

In the first option the national governments would agree to adopt a framework directive for the taxation of energy products and at the same time set positive minimum rates of excise duty on electricity, natural gas and coal. Exemptions could be permitted, or a transition period allowed. The second option would establish a framework directive to increase excise duties, where they already existed, on road fuels but to allow national governments to set a zero rate for coal, gas and electricity. This option was supported by the national governments which did not support the introduction of common energy taxes and also received the support of the European Parliament.

The use of framework legislation raises monitoring and management of environmental policy to a new priority within any future steps which are taken. The biggest single change that using directives in this form will bring will be to the role of DG XI of the European Commission (see Chapters 3 and 4). As the amount of legislation is scaled down, as existing legislation is reviewed and simplified and as the introduction of framework legislation becomes the norm, the role and work of DG XI will acquire a new orientation. It will become much more focused on the management and maintenance of the measures which will shape the policy as it develops in the twenty-first century. Among the essential elements of the work of DG XI will be the preparation of the reports required in the treaty articles and requested by the European Council on the progress being made on environmental policy. The provision of information to the national governments about developments, and close cooperation with the European Court of Justice to ensure that implementation of the policy is effective will have a higher priority for DG XI. The balance of the role which DG XI plays as a 'motor of integration' will therefore swing in favour of its role as the 'guardian of the Treaties' (see Chapter 3).

The Fifth Environmental Action Programme, begun in 1992, did not contain, as had the earlier action programmes, a date for the conclusion of its measures. The Fifth EAP was the beginning of a long-term strategy to put in place the foundations of an EU environmental policy based on the objectives of sustainable development. It proved to be problematic for the European Commission to bring forward a Sixth EAP incorporating any detailed proposals for a European plan for sustainable development before the appointment of the European Commission in the year 2000. Agreement has to be reached within the College of Commissioners on major new proposals before they are forwarded to the Council of Ministers. To reach a decision on any proposals for environmental policy required a coalition to be formed between the commissioner with responsibility for the environment and the commissioners responsible for areas such as agriculture, industry, trade and social affairs. Agreement amongst the commissioners with these responsibilities is often difficult and surrounded by controversy (see Chapter 3).

The resignation of the entire Santer Commission in March 1999 before they had completed their term of office introduced a great deal of confusion about what courses of action could be taken during the remainder of 1999. The new Commission, nominated in the autumn of 1999, was under pressure to introduce institutional and bureaucratic reforms so that the problems of financial mismanagement did not emerge again. In addition, at the end of the 1990s the European Union was occupied with the introduction of the single currency, the process of enlargement to Central and Eastern Europe and Cyprus, and attempts to curb unemployment. Future developments in the EU's environmental policy will take place within the constraints imposed by these issues.

THE EUROPEAN UNION AS AN INTERNATIONAL ENVIRONMENTAL ACTOR

The importance of global environmental action as a stimulus for the national governments of the member states to agree to the development of supranational action was clear in the 1970s. However, from the adoption of the First Environmental Action Programme in 1972 the EU has been able to develop its role as an international environmental actor, resulting in a reversal of the situation of the 1960s and 1970s. During the 1990s the national governments have adopted joint negotiating positions in international environmental agreements.[2] There has been agreement among them on the necessity and effectiveness of supranational action. The EU has been seen to take the lead globally on some issues. The approach adopted by the member states of the EU has been to support the introduction of binding agreements on national governments to meet the set objectives.

The United Nations Conference on Environment and Development which was held in Rio de Janeiro in June 1992 adopted a plan of action for sustainable development ('Agenda 21'). In 1997 the European Commission carried out a review of the progress which had been made in meeting the objectives of Agenda 21. The division of responsibilities between the national governments and the supranational tier of government were set out in the review and a structure for the role of the EU, through the European Commission, was provided.

> As a supranational entity encompassing 15 highly diverse Member States stretching from the Arctic Circle to the Mediterranean, the EU obviously cannot do everything itself. Some areas targeted by Agenda 21 are primarily the competence of the EU Member States, in other areas the Community can and does take the lead ... [and] even where it lacks legislative responsibility the Community seeks to support the actions by the Member States. (CEC 1997t: 5–6)

The main areas of action which were accepted by the governments meeting in Rio were the linkage of social and economic development, the conservation and management of resources, the strengthening of public participation in the policy-making process and the extension of the tools of sustainable development. As the discussion of the previous chapters has shown, the EU has made considerable progress with regard to the implementation of measures to ensure that the appropriate actions are begun and success has been achieved in some areas. The governments of the EU are now responding in a more proactive manner to the environmental issues than in the 1970s. However, in some areas the progress made has had only a marginal impact. In the wider context of the issues raised in the Rio Summit, the EU has responded to the pressure for global social justice which has grown since 1992. A chapter on development policy was included for the first time in the Maastricht Treaty Title XX TEC (XVII TEC). This provided an important legal basis for the EU and enabled it to extend its involvement in development cooperation. As a result the member states of the EU, working as a group, have supported the World Bank in its attempts to lighten the debt burden on the poorest states. This is not without its benefits for the EU, as 11 of the 13 poorest states are signatories to the Lomé Conventions with the EU.[3]

In order to implement some of the most important of the environmental commitments which were made in Agenda 21, the member states of the EU adopted a joint negotiating position at the UN Framework Convention on Climate Change (UNFCCC) held in Kyoto in 1997. This joint negotiating position covered three greenhouse gases (carbon dioxide, methane and nitrous oxide) (see Chapter 6). The most important of the three is carbon dioxide (CO_2), which is responsible for 80 per cent of the global warming potential of the three taken together, and, of the total emissions, produces those most difficult to curb. The EU concentrated on developing its joint position on measures which would result in an average reduction of the three together. Specific targets were not initially set for the three gases individually, although it was recognized that a higher relative weight would have to be given to CO_2 for this gas to reach the overall target.

The Dutch presidency of the Council in 1997 was responsible for brokering the agreement between the national governments which led to the joint position in Kyoto. It was based on a 'sharing of the burden' of cutting emissions among member states so that those states which would find it particularly difficult to introduce the necessary measures would have a longer period in which to introduce them. However, the fragility of holding joint positions in international agreements was shown in spring 1998, when the Dutch government itself appeared to undermine the agreement. The argument of the Dutch government was that as it had already introduced measures to curb emissions of greenhouse gases, any further reductions would impose a much greater burden on its industries than in those of other Member States. The German and Danish governments supported the Dutch calls for re-examination of the targets. The UK government also appeared to undermine the agreement, but for differing reasons, as the UK Labour government stated its intention to double the UK's agreed 10 per cent reduction in gas emissions. Whilst the environment ministers of the member states did sign the agreement negotiated at Kyoto in April 1998, in New York calls continued from some member states for flexibility to be exercised within the strategy adopted to meet the targets.

During the Cardiff Summit in June 1998 the UK government proposed an aggregate EU cut of 8.9 per cent between 1990 and the period 2002–12 in the gases addressed in the Kyoto Protocol. The overall cut outlined in this proposal was almost 1 per cent higher than the 8 per cent aggregate cut agreed in Kyoto. Changes were proposed in the way in which 'burden sharing' would take place to reach that target. Some states such as Portugal and Greece, which had been granted an allowance for emissions growth, had that allowance altered (Portugal 40 per cent reduced to 24 per cent, Greece 30 per cent to 23 per cent). On the other hand, countries which had accepted big cuts in emissions would have their targets relaxed (Germany from 25 per cent to 22.5 per cent, Austria and Denmark below the 25 per cent cuts agreed in Kyoto, and Belgium below its 10 per cent commitment). The UK was the only state which had its commitment strengthened in line with its national government policy. Finland and France retained the same percentage, but there was a 7 per cent cut for Italy and a 5 per cent increase for Sweden.

A number of other initiatives have been developed within the EU since the 1992 Rio Summit to meet the commitments made. They include the development of a strategy on acidification and air quality within the EU, the EU's Auto-Oil initiative, the sustainable cities campaign, the strategy on water quality, commitments on protection of biodiversity and the Natura Programme to establish sites for special conservation measures. The Natura Programme was also intended to fulfil the requirements of the directive on the conservation of natural habitats and of wild fauna and flora (Directive 92/43/EEC, amended 97/62/EC) and the directive on the conservation of wild birds (Directive 79/409/EEC, amended 97/49/EC).

SUPPORT FOR THE ENLARGEMENT OF THE EU

In the introductory chapter the challenges currently facing the EU's environmental policy were outlined. From an environmental point of view the prospects of enlargement to Central and Eastern Europe (CEE) would appear to present insurmountable problems to the future of the EU's environmental policy. In the early 1990s the euphoria surrounding the changes in Central and Eastern Europe was at its height. The prospect of enlargement appeared to enter the EU's agenda with little regard for the environmental concerns. As the EU began the process of negotiation with the states of Central and Eastern Europe for accession, it became apparent that there were serious problems of environmental degradation in many parts of the applicant states (CEC 1997o). The Dobris Assessment in 1995 (Stanners and Bourdeau 1995) and the follow-up 'Dobris + 3' Report in 1998 covered the whole of Europe, not just the EU, and highlighted the seriousness of the problem. The cost implications of the introduction of the EU's environmental policy into the states of Central and Eastern Europe therefore became a more prominent issue from the mid-1990s.

The first stage in the preparations for the CEE states, accession to the EU required the national governments to put the EU's environmental legislation in place. The European Commission prepared a structured framework for the Central and Eastern European states in order to enable approximation of the environmental legislation to take place. The view of the European Commission at the Environment Council meeting in September 1996 was that the associated countries should take over the whole of the environmental acquis before their accession (Mayhew 1998: 219). A considerable amount of work was accomplished and during 1996 some sectors were beginning to show evidence of completion of approximation of legislation (see Table 12.1). Overall, however, progress was slow. The transposition costs remained as a major financial burden on the applicant states. Implementation of the legislation once it was transposed remained very problematic.

Table 12.1   Progress on approximation of legislation (1996)

Category	Poland	Hungary	Czech Rep.	Slovak Rep.	Average, 4 CEE states	Average, 10 CEE states
General environmental policy regulation	63	87	77	72	75	57
Air	47	40	60	77	56	46
Chemicals, industrial risks, biotechnology	33	14	31	33	28	27
Nature conservation	100	67	67	100	84	65
Noise	50	50	17	50	42	32
Waste	26	18	56	78	45	33
Water	78	61	61	78	70	61

Source: Regional Environmental Centre for Central and Eastern Europe, Budapest, January 1996, quoted in Caddy (1996: 28).

By the time that the European Commission published its opinion on the applicant states in 1997 (CEC 1997o), it was recognized that it would not be possible for the candidate states to introduce the whole of the environmental acquis before accession and that a more pragmatic approach had to be adopted.[4] Derogations from legislation would have to be negotiated and more relaxed time scales would have to be applied for the introduction of the EU's environmental legislation into the CEE candidate states. It was also apparent that there were differences between the CEE states in the nature of their existing environmental legislation and differences in the scale of their national environmental problems. Allowances had to be made for each state on an individual basis and the phased introduction of some legislation determined. The precedent had been set in the arrangements made for unification of Germany. A staged approach to the introduction of the environmental acquis was agreed for the new *Länder* of the Federal Republic. When the Nordic states and Austria became members of the EU, derogations from legislation were negotiated with the states individually. However, in the case of the enlargement to include Central and Eastern Europe the number of states involved, their greater population size and the scale of the environmental degradation increased the number of issues requiring special arrangements. Environmental degradation was recognized as 'one of the more expensive, if not the most expensive, area involved in the enlargement process' (CEC 1998e: 2).

The total costs of environmental damage are difficult to estimate precisely. Studies which concentrate on gross costs may overestimate the true economic costs of environmental legislation by not taking into account the economic benefits of environmental improvement (CEC 1997w: 15). These benefits may include reduced health care costs, reduced costs of maintaining buildings and increased agricultural yields. Where rough assessments have been made which do take these factors into account the total environmental damage in Central and Eastern Europe was estimated to be in the range of 2–10 per cent of GDP. A World Bank report estimated the damage for Poland on its own to be between 3 and 4 per cent of GDP because of the effect on human health of environmental degradation (World Bank 1993, quoted in CEC 1997b: 15). The World Bank report further identified that the Polish government needed to invest a sum equivalent to around half of its GDP to meet EU environmental standards. Spending of between ECU 30 and 45 billion· was required to bring Polish industry up to date and deal with the most serious problems of air and water quality. The outdated nature of the agricultural sector was also seen as raising problems. The overall conclusion was that Poland, the largest of the candidate states, would require ten years to bring it into line with European environmental legislation (Turner 1997: 1). Table 12.2 shows the scale of the problem in Poland and the other candidate states.

Table 12.2　The cost of reaching environmental standards for accession (ECU billion)

	Water	Air	Waste (maximum)	Total investment (maximum)	Total per capita (ECU)
Poland	18.1	13.9	3.3	35.2	927
Hungary	6.6	2.7	4.4	13.7	1306
Czech Republic	3.3	6.4	3.8	13.4	1427
Slovak	1.9	1.9	1.6	5.4	760
Estonia	1.5	n.a	n.a	1.5	n.a
Slovenia	n.a	0.7	1.1	1.8	n.a

Source:　Financial Times, 3 March 1998, p. 3.

The European Commission presented an outline strategy for accession of the states of Central and Eastern Europe to the Cardiff Summit in 1998 (CEC 1998d). The starting-point of the proposed strategy was that the investments needed to meet the environmental acquis should come from the national governments of the CEE states with the EU making only a partial contribution. PHARE[5] was the main financial instrument to support the CEE states through the pre-accession process during 1998 and 1999. The Instrument for Structural Policies for Pre-Accession (ISPA) and the Pre-Accession Measures for Agriculture and Rural Development were introduced with increased funding for the period after the year 2000.

In addition, the European Commission also identified legislative and administrative weaknesses within the CEE states which could create serious obstacles in the approximation process in all cases. The lack of coordination between ministries was seen as an additional problem for the authorities charged with implementing and enforcing environmental legislation. There were also serious problems of air and water quality and waste management to be overcome. The overall conclusion reached by the European Commission in the 1998 strategy document was that none of the candidate states could be expected to comply fully with the environmental acquis by the time of accession. However, they were required to have in place long-term strategies to implement the acquis. The first stage in ensuring that this was done was to require that environmental strategy plans be submitted to the European Commission by March 1999. The details in the plans were to include how the candidate states would bring their air, water and waste disposal facilities up to EU standards.

In July 1998 the European Commission began a screening of EU legislation with the five applicant countries that had not begun accession negotiations: Bulgaria, Latvia, Lithuania, Romania and Slovakia. Environmental legislation was among the first 20 chapters of the EU legislation to be considered. The same problems were identified for these states as for candidate states. There were considerable problems for their governments in establishing and strengthening the structures required to implement the EU's environmental policy.

THE STRUCTURE OF FUTURE EU ENVIRONMENTAL POLICY

The structure of the EU's environmental policy for the future is given by the three main axes around which it has developed. The first is the commitment to a strategy of sustainable development. This has come into focus particularly since the Fifth Environmental Action Programme was adopted in 1992 to ensure that the EU makes an active contribution to the global agenda of changing environmental practices to reach sustainable development targets. The second is the sharing of responsibility for the protection of the environment and, in association with this, the application of the principle of subsidiarity. The third is the integration of environmental objectives into all areas of EU activity.

Sustainable Development

Sustainable development is a term that has come into common use since the World Commission on Environment and Development (WCED) published its report in 1987. The WCED was established in 1983 by the United Nations as an independent body with a three-part mandate:

1. To re-examine environmental and development issues which appeared to be becoming critical
2. To propose new forms of international cooperation on these issues
3. To raise levels of understanding and commitment at all levels of government and among groups as varied as industrialists, consumers, voluntary groups and individuals.

The first of the WCED's meetings was held in October 1984, chaired by Gro Harlem Brundtland, who was then the Norwegian Prime Minister. The report which was produced in 1987 has become generally known by her name – the Brundtland Report.

The Brundtland Report presented a more optimistic view than that which had been current during the 1960s and early 1970s. The influential Club of Rome report, *The Limits to Growth* was published in 1972 and carried a dire warning of overshoot and collapse of the world economic and environmental system if the rate of growth was not curtailed (Meadows et al. 1972). Its main conclusions raised the possibility of changing the activities that were producing the problem. The report emphasized the over-arching need for commitment to ensure that the necessary changes occurred. Even with increased commitment the Report warned that this would lead to ecological and economic stability, but not improvement. The 1992 follow-up report, *Beyond the Limits*, pointed to the fact that 'in spite of the world's improved technologies, the greater awareness, the stronger environment policies, many resource and pollution flows have grown beyond their sustainable limits' (Meadows et al. 1992: xiv). The solution found in 1972 to achieving sustainability had not altered. The technical and economic solutions may have changed, but are still possible to identify. It is the political and psychological changes which are still difficult to establish.

Other views supporting an Armageddon scenario had also been current during the 1960s. The view of many environmentalists was that all economic activity was harmful to the environment and should be severely curtailed. For those who accepted the logic of the market failure model, all economic activity that had a damaging impact on the environment could only be controlled by draconian regulation. These views did not appear to be tenable in Northern and Western modern industrialized society; nor were they acceptable in the developing economies of the Third World. Hence the search for alternative means of ensuring economic activity could continue, resources be equitably allocated and the environment be protected. The Brundtland Report was not to be 'a prediction of ever increasing environmental decay, poverty and hardship in an ever more polluted world', but instead foresaw 'the possibility for a new era of economic growth, based on policies that sustain and expand the environmental resource base' (WCED 1987: 1).

The concept of sustainable development as outlined in the Brundtland Report was 'development that meets the need of the present without compromising the ability of future generations to meet their own needs' (WCED 1987: 42). Since 1987 this apparently clear statement has become a major concern for researchers and policy makers alike. Investigation shows that there is considerable confusion and ambiguity about both the meaning and the achievement of sustainable development. There has also been change over time in the connotations of the term. Pearce identified more than 40 definitions of sustainable development (Pearce et al. 1989). The British Government Panel on Sustainable Development commented on this problem of definition: 'It is not so much an idea, as a convoy of ideas, and all single definitions have proved defective in one way or another' (DoE 1995: Preface).

Although there are so many definitions, it is possible to identify two underlying ideas on which the Brundtland statement was built: first, that there is a concept of needs and the policy makers' overriding priority should be to overcome poverty; and second, action is limited by the levels of technology which have been reached and by present forms of social organization. Other characteristics which also figure in all the definitions of sustainable development include futurity and public participation.

There are three main features common to all definitions of sustainable development which have implications for the EU's policy makers:

1. Environmental considerations must be incorporated into economic policy making
2. The concept contains a commitment to social equity both within countries and between the northern and southern hemispheres
3. Development does not simply mean growth. It must also include qualitative improvements (Dodds and Bigg 1995: 40).

The confusion within the EU and the length of time taken to adopt explicit mention of the concept of sustainable development in formulating the EU's environmental policy reflect a global uncertainty about what it involves for the policy makers. Sustainable development as the basis of action was implied in the First EAP (see Chapter 2). However, it was not until 1992 that the EU became explicitly committed to the pursuit of this goal in the European Union's Fifth EAP. The Maastricht Treaty was being negotiated and ratified at the same time. The confusion of ideas and the ambiguity inherent in the definition of sustainable development was reflected within the EAP and the Treaty. The title of the Fifth EAP is 'Towards Sustainability' and the Brundtland definition features in it. In the Maastricht Treaty, however, article 2 refers to 'non inflationary growth respecting the environment', as if the two were interchangeable. This is not the case, as Nigel Haigh (Haigh 1995) and David Pearce (Pearce et al. 1989) have demonstrated. In the Progress Report on the implementation of the Fifth EAP sustainable development is described as being 'seen for what it is, a development within the environmental limits of which we have the knowledge at a particular point in time' which 'will only come about when sustainable development is seen as the only model of economic development for the future and is fully accepted by every citizen' (CEC 1996p: 6).

The problems associated with the definition of sustainable development and its implications were recognized during the 1997 Intergovernmental Conference, where it formed one of the four crucial environmental questions raised for debate. (The others were the integration of environmental policy into other areas of policy, the decision-making process and the linkage between democracy and environmental rights.) The importance of using the phrase 'sustainable development' must not be undervalued, in spite of any problems of definition. In incorporating it into the Treaty, the European Union has provided the legal basis for, and a clear political commitment to, a change in the nature of the approach to policy actions which the member states will take together. This approach had already been incorporated by some of the national governments of the European Union into their environmental policy making (see Table 12.3).

Table 12.3   Examples of the common elements in national strategies for sustainable development

UK	Denmark	Finland	Netherlands
Introduction and principles	Introduction	Introduction and definition	Introduction
	State of the Danish environmental initiatives	Priorities and the means to achieve them	The strategy in outline
			International environmental policy
Environmental media and resources	Perspectives for the environmental initiative	The economy and its resources	Environmental themes
	Main themes of future initiatives		
Economic development and sustainability	Individual activities and environmental pressure	Sustainable development in main sectors	Target groups
Putting sustainabliity into practice	International nature and environmental assistance	Reducing degradation of the environment	Policy instruments and integration
		Means of implementing sustainable development	Economic and spatial implications
	Follow-up to Denmark's nature and environment policy		

Source: Green Alliance (1996: 10).

An effective policy to achieve sustainable development includes the active participation of national governments, local authorities, non-governmental organizations and individual citizens together in managing economic and environmental development. It provides the framework on which the sharing of the responsibility for environmental measures and public participation in the making and implementing of policy may be built. Within the European Union the desirability of and the means by which all these actors could become involved in the policy process was outlined in the Fifth Environmental Action Programme (see Chapters 2, 3 and 4).

Among the most important of the initiatives to enable the sharing of responsibility and participation in the policy process to become a reality was the introduction of the three dialogue groups proposed in the Fifth EAP. The European Consultative Forum on the Environment and Sustainable Development – 'the Green Forum' – brings together 32 senior representatives from business, trade unions, professional organizations, consumer organizations, and regional and local authorities. Their main objective is to discuss how to move towards the EU's goal of sustainable development. The effectiveness of this group was undermined in the first 18 months of its operation in 1994 and early 1995 as the group spent a great deal of time concentrating on identifying its own terms of reference. The mandate of the first appointees to the Forum was from 1993 to 1996, when the title of the group was 'the Consultative Forum on the Environment'. In replacing the original group in 1997 the European Commission made a number of changes, apart from the title, which strengthened the role of the Forum. Thorvald Stoltenberg (the former Norwegian Foreign Minister and UN envoy to Bosnia) was appointed as its independent chairman. There were other appointees from the members of the European economic area and the applicant countries of Central and Eastern Europe.

The second of the groups, Network for the Implementation and Enforcement of Community Law (IMPEL), targeted the authorities which had responsibility for the implementation and enforcing of the legislation within the national context. IMPEL is the informal network set up in Chester UK in 1992. Its intention was to allow the authorities with responsibility for the implementation and day-to-day operation of the policy to meet to share information about the best practices to adopt. The third group, the Environment Policy Review Group, targeted the policy makers. Of the three groups this one probably achieved the most success, as it enabled the views of the Environment Directors-General from the member states and the European Commission to discuss progress on meeting the targets set out in the Fifth EAP.

However, it is difficult to assess the extent of the success of the dialogue groups and the public participation in the process. Certainly in terms of the number of cases of infringement of EU legislation reported to the European Commission, the largest number of reports from the public are in the area of the environment. Directive 90/313/EEC on the freedom of access to information on the environment provides the basis for the public to participate in the implementation and enforcement of legislation. In early 1997 the work of the non-governmental organizations (NGOs) received additional support from the

EU with the adoption of a legal framework for funding (see Chapter 4). Both measures are crucial to ensuring that the public can contribute actively to the development of the EU's environmental policy.

The Application of the Principle of Subsidiarity

The second and more controversial of the axes around which the policy has developed is the principle of subsidiarity. This principle regulates the sharing of responsibility between the different tiers of government. It places the burden of proof on the European Union to show that there is a need to legislate and take action. It is also used to determine the intensity of the action to be taken: 'In essence, subsidiarity represents no more than a general principle of good governance: decisions should be taken as close as possible to the affected public, at the lowest level of jurisdiction encompassing all those affected' (Blackhurst et al. 1994: 24). However, 'it was not a concept capable of being a precise measure against which to judge legislation because the necessity and effectiveness of action at one level rather than at the other cannot be judged in a wholly objective and consistent manner' (House of Lords 1996: 12).

Decisions within the European Union about the appropriate level of action on environmental issues have always been taken on the basis of the application of the principle of subsidiarity (see Chapter 2). Subsidiarity is a political principle to do with the allocation of power to the appropriate level of governance. As such it is the basis on which federal constitutions are drafted (for example the United States of America). For the European Union the legitimacy of supranational action was conferred by the Treaty of Rome, an agreement made between a group of nation states whose political systems were based on the principles of liberal democracy. The Treaty established the European Economic Community, a grouping of nation states which agreed to a degree of pooling of sovereignty in order to achieve a number of shared objectives. The principle of subsidiarity is the means by which the member states of the EU decide if those shared objectives can be achieved as a result of action by the supranational or the national tiers of government. Unlike the US, however, the European Union remains short of being a federation and instead is often described as having a quasi-federal structure.

In the first major revision of the Treaty in 1987 (Single European Act) the political principle of subsidiarity was included in an explicit statement, but applying only to the chapter on the environment: 'The Community shall take action relating to the environment to the extent to which the objectives (to preserve, protect and improve the quality of the environment) can be attained better at the Community level than the level of the individual Member States' (article 174 TEC (130r SEA)). This wording appears to imply competence of the EU in all issues relating to the environment, as it emphasized Community action first of all. The opportunity for the European Court of Justice to present its view of this emphasis in a ruling based on article 174 TEC (130r SEA) did not occur during the period before the Treaty was again revised in Maastricht.

In the changes to the wording of the articles of the Maastricht Treaty the implication of emphasis on centralized action was altered. The principle of subsidiarity was removed from article 174 (130r SEA) and applied to the entirety of European Union actions, not just environmental ones: 'the Community shall take action, in accordance with the principle of subsidiarity, only if and in so far as the objectives of the proposed action cannot be sufficiently achieved by the Member States and can therefore be better achieved by the Community' (article 3 TEC (3b TEC)). The wording of the article appears to contain less certainty.

Lack of consensus about the definition of the principle underlined the debate about susbsidiarity before it was included in the Maastricht Treaty. Following the treaty changes, further controversy surrounded the application of the principle. The Edinburgh Summit in 1992 produced a series of general guidelines on the application of the principle in order to overcome some of the controversies. Some of the states of the EU clearly saw subsidiarity in a positive light in terms of the allocation of roles between the different tiers of government. In the case of the UK it was and continues to be seen as the means of preventing more powers being given to the supranational national tier of government. The concern that some national governments will attempt to use the subsidiarity principle inappropriately as an excuse for maintaining national environmental standards has continued. Jacques Santer began his presidency of the European Commission in January 1995 by pointing to the dangers of an abuse of the subsidiarity principle. 'It is important to remember that the worst enemy of subsidiarity is the lack of trust between the Member States' (Jacques Santer, Address to the European Parliament, 17 January 1995).

The application of the principle of subsidiarity requires clarity and a decision about a mechanism to measure the degree or extent of the appropriate action to be taken by the different tiers of government (the principle of proportionality). A number of rulings by the European Court of Justice have established the following criteria which identify this measure of proportionality:

- to fulfil a legitimate political objective;
- to approach this objective;
- to ensure that there is no measure that is less restrictive for the free circulation of goods.

However, many of the details of the proportionality principle remain open to question, particularly those relating to the environment (Kramer 1995: 114).

Subsidiarity implies that a great deal of discretion may exist at the national level about establishing environmental measures. However, it does not provide an adequate argument for the national governments to continue with differing environmental policies, for two reasons. It is inappropriate in cases where there are significant transborder implications and distortion of the market may occur. In the Sutherland Report (1992) on the operation of the single market, it was suggested that fragmentation of the internal market might result from the application of the subsidiarity principle. Consequently, consistency in environmental measures had to be seen as a key element in achieving the internal market (Sutherland 1992: 18). In May 1995 the European Commission Report for the IGC Reflection Group again highlighted the potential that differing views on subsidiarity might create an obstacle to the process of economic integration within the EU. Furthermore, there is no justification for allowing any discretion in the application of subsidiarity if any of the citizens of the EU feel that they are being disadvantaged because of national environmental conditions. In the case of environmental protection, the role of the European Union is crucial in deciding, given a range of viable and effective options, which form of action would achieve the objectives of the policy and leave the national governments, individuals and businesses concerned the greatest degree of freedom.

During the 1996/97 Intergovernmental Conference there was pressure from some national governments to ensure that the Treaty included a degree of clarification about the principle of subsidiarity. A number of states wanted to take further action and include a separate protocol based on the Edinburgh Summit declaration on the application of the principle. Of the five states that were most supportive of changes to article 5 TEC (3b TEC) the UK Conservative administration took a lead role. Only Denmark and Spain had strong reservations about the proposals. Additional concerns were expressed about the effective and systematic enforcement of the principle and the excess of detail with which much of the EU's legislation is encumbered. In highlighting the frustrations of excessive detail, the danger is that deregulation or complete return of environmental policy to the national level may be considered the only alternatives. The growing problems of environmental degradation within the EU and the environmental impact of future enlargement to Central and Eastern Europe require the effective operation of the mix of instruments which the EU has at its disposal, including legislation.

Article 5 TEC (3b TEC) was left unchanged in 1997 but to meet some of the concerns a protocol on subsidiarity was added to the Treaty of Amsterdam. A number of points highlighted in this protocol are of particular relevance to the developments taking place in environmental policy. These include:

1. The commitment to the preference for the use of directives over regulations, and framework directives over detailed directives (article 6).
2. The European Commission (article 9) is required to:

   - consult widely before proposing legislation except in the case of urgency or confidentiality;
   - publish the consultations in the form of consultation documents, ensuring that the principle of subsidiarity is respected at all times. In addition, an explanatory memorandum is to be included in the documentation giving details of where the principle is to be respected;
   - explain why the proposals are to be financed from the Community's budget and include the explanation in the documentation accompanying any proposals;
   - take into account the burden of finance or administration falling on the Community, the national governments, the local authorities, economic operators and citizens and find ways to minimize it and ensure that it is proportionate to the objective to be achieved;
   - present an annual report to the European Council, the Council of Ministers and the EP on the application of article 5 TEC (3b TEC) of the Treaty. These Reports are also to go to the Committee of the Regions and the Economic and Social Committee.

3. The Community measures should leave as much scope as possible for national decisions, consistent with the aim of the measure and observing the requirements of the Treaty. In addition, the measures should be as simple as possible to achieve those requirements (protocol number 30 on the application of subsidiarity and proportionality).

Integration of Environmental Requirements into EU Policies

The third axis of the EU's environmental policy, the necessity of integrating environmental requirements into other areas of policy, is a long-held commitment within the EU. The importance of integration was included in the Third Environmental Action Programme in 1982 (see Chapter 2). It was incorporated into the chapter on the environment in the Single European Act in 1987. The Fifth Environmental Action Programme identified a series of target sectors where the integration of environmental objectives was to be a priority. In the Progress Report on the Fifth Environmental Action Programme the European Commission concluded that: 'Integration of environmental considerations into the different target sectors has made progress, but at varying speeds ... [it] is generally most advanced in the manufacturing sector' (CEC 1996p: 3).

Progress in ensuring that there is integration of environmental requirements into policy has occurred in the manufacturing sector as a result of a number of pressures. The sector has been subject to increasingly stringent environmental legislation since the 1960s. Whilst this commitment is a vital element of any strategy intended to increase the efficiency and effectiveness of the operation of the policy, it has to be seen in the context of a series of measures. The biggest impact of the integration of environmental requirements into other areas of policy will occur if an opportunity is gained to avoid contradictions and inconsistencies in the policy-making process. Failure to ensure that inconsistencies are removed has led to the introduction of 'reactive' measures to counterbalance problems created as a consequence of EU action in other areas. The consequence of this approach has been to impose considerable economic and environmental costs on the European Union.

A three-pronged approach has to be adopted to integrate environmental requirements into other areas of EU policy. For the EU to adopt this commitment requires procedures and political and administrative mechanisms designed to protect the environment and the incorporation of these into other areas of policy. The objective of integration must:

1. become part of the strategic planning of the EU's approach to environmental protection which is set out in the Environmental Action Programmes;
2. be incorporated into the Treaty in order to ensure a firm legal basis;
3. be reinforced by procedural and institutional arrangements which give a practical framework to the commitment.

There are a number of sectors of economic activity which carry with them the potential for degradation of the environment on a massive scale. These include agriculture, manufacturing industry, energy generation, transport and tourism developments. Energy and transport are of particular concern because of adverse effects on human health and ecosystems. Agriculture and water use are important because inadequate land-use planning, poor water management and inappropriate technology may result in the degradation of the natural environment and make the production of food problematic. Management of marine resources must be addressed, as competition and overexploitation can damage the resource base, food supplies and the livelihood of the fishing communities as well as the environment. The integration of environmental objectives into these areas of policy at the policy formulation and the operational levels is necessary if the EU is to fulfil its commitment to sustainable development.

The integration of environmental requirements into policy was given legal basis when it was included in article 174 TEC (130r SEA) para. 2. This article was reaffirmed in the Maastricht Treaty in the last sentence of the paragraph:

'Environmental protection requirements must be integrated into the definition and implementation of other Community policies.' A great deal of criticism of this provision focused on the non-specific nature of the phrase 'other Community policies'. When the Irish presidency produced a draft treaty in December 1996, integration of environmental protection into all of the sectoral policies of the EU was proposed through a new treaty article 3d to replace the last sentence of article 174 TEC (130r SEA), para. 2: 'Environmental protection requirements must be integrated into the definition and implementation of Community policies and activities referred to in Article 3, in particular with a view to promoting sustainable development.' The policies listed in article 3 included agriculture, transport, energy and the single market. The final draft in June 1997 included the commitment to integration of environmental protection into all sectoral policies in the new article 6 TEC and activities referred to in article 3 TEC (3 TEC) with a view to promoting sustainable development.

Following the signing of the Treaty in October 1997 the Heads of Government asked the European Commission to prepare a strategy document for presentation at the Cardiff Summit which outlined how integration of environmental requirements was to be achieved (CEC 1998d). This was an important opportunity to bring coherence into environmental policy and may also help to overcome some of the problems which have emerged, in particular, the frequent accusation that the rhetoric of the policy has swamped the reality. The main conclusion of the European Commission was that commitment from the national governments would be crucial. Included in the strategy was a procedure to be adopted by the national governments demonstrating a firm commitment to the integration ideal. In addition, the European Commission's strategy emphasized the requirement to show that the integration of environmental objectives into policy would be given a high priority during the enlargement negotiations.

The European Union has a firmly established environmental policy. Since 1972 the dynamism of its development has been apparent. The actions which the EU has taken in this area are relatively defined and specific, but have wide-ranging implications across all spheres of the EU's activities. The policy involves a particular package of legislation, organization and activity as well as measures to facilitate the adoption and usage of market-based and other types of instruments. The role of the European Commission has been crucial in the formulation of the policy as a result of its programmatic nature. As the policy has evolved to encompass instruments other than legislation, the role of the European Commission will alter to concentrate on the monitoring and management of the policy rather than the introduction of new proposals. Indeed, if the integration of environmental requirements into other areas of policy functions effectively in the future, then the work of DG XI will have been achieved and its *raison d'être* may disappear!

The challenges to future developments in the policy area are, however, mounting in severity. These challenges come from the political, economic and social dimensions of EU action, but most of all from within the political system evolving within the EU. The difficulty of reconciling different national interests within the policy process has remained unchanged throughout the history of the development of the EU's environmental policy. Enlargement and the environmental guarantee of the Treaty are among the events that are reinforcing that dominance of national actions. There is a significant danger that the EU's environmental policy will become fragmented and unable to fulfil its twin objectives of environmental protection and support for a freely operating European market economy.

The Fifth Environmental Action Programme enabled a very different type of environmental policy to develop. Probably the biggest single change came from the advocacy of economic instruments and a more market-based approach. The commitment to sustainable development has laid the basis for a framework of action which incorporates more participation from the general public. Eco-labelling and eco-auditing are measures based on voluntary registration, and are therefore intended to encourage changes in behaviour which will have a beneficial impact on the environment. The discussion in this book has concentrated on evaluating the success of this new approach. The overall conclusion is that the lack of commitment of the national governments remains a problem which must be overcome. This is a somewhat disappointing conclusion. Much has been achieved, but the tension inherent in the policy's twin objectives of environmental protection and harmonization of national policies to avoid trade distortion remains.

At the end of the twentieth century the EU's environmental policy has the opportunity to enter a new phase of confidence and dynamism. It is a firmly established area of legitimate activity at the supranational level which is very different from the fragmented and rather tentative policy which began to emerge in the early 1970s. Three problems remain: first, how to continue to raise and maintain the interest of the national electorates of the member states of the EU in environmental issues; second the need to ensure the commitment of the national governments to measures to protect the environment; and third, the urgent requirement to find more effective mechanisms for the management of the policy measures that are in place.

The view presented in the introductory chapter was that the policy is not in need of radical change. The measures are in place and, whilst the Treaty of Amsterdam has made only minimal changes in terms of the actual text, the implications of those changes are wide-ranging. The EU has the opportunity to increase the range of measures and policy tools used to protect the environment and encourage economic growth within the EU. However, criticisms must continue of the way in which the European Union's environmental policy is undermined during the process of implementation and enforcement by the national governments and the designated national authorities.

NOTES

1. Council Directive 91/676/EEC on protection of waters against pollution caused by nitrates from agricultural sources, OJL 375, 31 December 1991.
2. The key international fora include the United Nations (UN), the World Trade Organization (WTO), the Organization for Economic Cooperation and Development (OECD), and the global and regional agreements on Climate Change, Biodiversity, Desertification, Forestry and Acidification.
3. Lomé Conventions are a series of trade and aid agreements reached between the EU and 71 states from the African, Caribbean and Pacific regions (collectively known by the abbreviation ACP states). These agreements have been criticized as neo-colonialist and predominantly favouring the EU rather than the ACP states.
4. The European Commission considered all the applicant states in its 1997 Opinion. These included Poland, Hungary, the Czech Republic, Slovakia, Bulgaria, Romania, Latvia, Lithuania, Estonia, Slovenia and Cyprus. As some of these states were not considered ready to begin negotiations for accession to the EU in the early part of the twenty-first century, the EU began the negotiations with Poland, Hungary, the Czech Republic, Slovenia, Estonia and Cyprus in March 1998. The reports on the costs of compliance with the environmental acquis which were prepared for the European Commission did, however, include all the CEE states which had concluded association agreements with the EU. Cyprus was considered in separate reports.
5. PHARE is the main vehicle through which the EU channels technical assistance, training, grant finance and investment in the states of Central and Eastern Europe. Its budget for the first five full years of its operation was ECU 4.3 billion. This was increased for the period 1995–99 to ECU 6.7 billion.

Bibliography

Aldous, A. (1986), 'The Environment has arrived', in R. Mayne (ed.), *Western Europe*, New York and Oxford: Muller, Blond and White.

Andersen, M.S. (1994), *Governance by Green Taxes: Making Pollution Prevention Pay*, Manchester and New York: Manchester University Press.

Andersen M.S. and D. Liefferink (eds) (1998), *Environmental Policy: the Pioneers*, Manchester and New York: Manchester University Press.

Andersen, S.S. and K.A. Eliassen (1993), *Making Policy in Europe*, London: Sage Publications.

Anderson, T.L. and D.R. Leal, (1991), *Free Market Environmentalism*, San Francisco: Pacific Research Institute for Public Policy.

Avery, G. and F. Cameron (1998), *The Enlargement of the European Union*, Sheffield: Sheffield Academic Press.

Barbier, E.B. (1989), *Economics, Natural Resource Scarcity and Development*, London: Earthscan.

Barde, J.-P. and D.W. Pearce (eds) (1991), *Valuing the Environment*, London: Earthscan.

Barnes, I.G. (1996), 'Agriculture, Fisheries and the 1995 Nordic Enlargement', in L. Miles (ed.), *The European Union and the Nordic Countries*, London and New York: Routledge.

Barnes, I.G. and P.M. Barnes (1995), *The Enlarged European Union*, London and New York: Longman.

Barnes, P.M. (1992), 'Environmental policy', in A. Griffiths (ed.), *European Community Survey*, London and New York: Longman.

Barnes P.M. (1994), 'The European Community's environmental management and audit regulation', in I.G. Barnes and L. Davison *European Business: Text and Cases*, Oxford and New York: Butterworth Heinemann.

Barnes, P.M. (1996a), 'Crisis or opportunity – environmental policy', Discussion Paper of the Jean Monnet Group of Experts, Hull UK: University of Hull, Representation of the European Commission and CEUS.

Barnes, P.M. (1996b), 'The Nordic countries and EU environmental policy', in L. Miles (ed.), *The European Union and the Nordic Countries*, London and New York: Routledge.

Batchelor, C. (1997), 'Rail groups obstruct European freight plans', *Financial Times*, 27 November, p. 5.

Bjerregaard, R. (1996a), 'The view of the Commission on environment and pesticides', speech to the Second Weed Control Congress, Copenhagen, 28 June.

Bjerregaard, R. (1996b), 'Environmental liability', speech at the Meeting of the Belgian Environmental Conference, Brussels, 13 June, Rapid Reports.

Bjerregaard, R. (1997), '1996 bathing water report', Press Release IP/97/419.

Bjerregaard, R. (1998), Speech by Commissioner, Graz, Austria, 18 July, Speech/98/160.

Blackhurst, R. et al. (1994), *Trade and Sustainable Development Principles*, London: International Institute for Sustainable Development.

Blackhurst, R. and A. Subramanian (1992), 'Promoting multilateral co-operation', in K. Anderson and R. Blackhurst (eds), *Greening World Trade Issues*, London and New York: Harvester Wheatsheaf, p. 249.

Boehmer-Christiansen, S. (1998), 'Environment friendly deindustrialisation and unification in East Germany' in A. Tickle and I. Welsh (eds), *Environment and Society in Eastern Europe*, London and New York: Longman.

Bond, R. (1997), 'Bathing water fails tests despite £500m clean-up', *Surveyor*, 27 November: 7.

Boulton, L. (1996a), 'Survey – energy efficiency', *Financial Times*, 11 November.

Boulton, L. (1996b), 'A trail blazer fizzles out', *Financial Times*, 4 December.

Boulton, L. (1997), 'Acceptable price of recovery', *Financial Times*, 20 January.

Boulton, L. (1998), 'Brussels hits snags over sewage curbs', *Financial Times*, 12 February.

Bowers, J. (1987), 'Set-aside and other stories', in D. Baldock and D. Conder (eds), *Removing Land from Agriculture: The Implications for Farming and the Environment*, London: Council for the Protection of Rural England and Institute for Environmental Policy.

Brack, D. (1995), 'Trade and the environment', in *Ethics, the environment and the changing international order*, special edition of *International Affairs*, **71** (3) July, pp. 479–514.

Brittan, L. (1998), 'Solving the trade and environment conundrum', speech to the Bellerive GLOBE International Conference, Geneva, 23 March, EU Press Release: Speech/98/51.

Caddy, J. (1996), 'Hollow harmonization', *Proceedings of Fifth Annual Conference on the Environment*, Leeds, September 1996, ERP.

Cairncross, F. (1995), *Green, Inc.*, London: Earthscan.

Carson, R. (1962), *Silent Spring*, London and New York: Penguin.

CEC (1982), 'Initial guidelines for a Community policy on tourism', Communication from the Commission to the Council, COM(82)385 final, Brussels.

CEC (1985), White Paper: 'Completing the Internal Market', COM(85)310 final, Brussels (The Cockfield Report).

CEC (1989), 'Proposals for a Council Directive on civil liability for damage caused by waste', COM(89)282 final, Brussels.

CEC (1990), '1992: The environmental dimension', Task Force Report, Brussels.

CEC (1991a), 'A Community strategy to limit carbon dioxide emissions and improve energy efficiency', Communication from the Commission to the Council, SEC(91)1744 final, Brussels.

CEC (1991b), 'A Community action plan to assist tourism' COM(91)97 final, Brussels.

CEC (1991c), 'The development and future of the CAP', *Bulletin of the European Communities*, Supplement 5/91, Brussels.

CEC (1992a), 'A Community programme of policy and action in relation to the environment and sustainable development – towards sustainability – Fifth Environmental Action Programme (5th EAP)', 3 vols, COM(92)23 final, Brussels.

CEC (1992b), 'The impact of transport on the environment: a community strategy for sustainable mobility', COM(92)46 final, Brussels.

CEC (1992c), 'Draft directive introducing a tax on carbon dioxide emissions and energy', COM(92)226 final, Brussels.

CEC (1992d), Green Paper, 'Industrial competitiveness and the protection of the environment', SEC(92)1986, Brussels.

CEC (1992e), 'The climate challenge: economic aspects of the Community's strategy on limiting CO_2 emissions', *European Economy*, no. 52, May, Brussels.

CEC (1992f), 'The environmental dimension', Task Force Report on the Environment and the Internal Market 1990, Brussels.

CEC (1992g), 'Agreement between the European Economic Community and the Swiss Confederation on the carriage of goods by road and rail', Declarations by the Delegations – Joint Declaration – Exchange of Letters, OJL 373, 21 December, Brussels, 28–46.

CEC (1993a), Green Paper, 'Remedying environmental damage', COM(93)47 final, Brussels.

CEC (1993b), 'Second Commission working document concerning RTD policy in the Community and the Fourth Framework Activities', COM(93)158 final, Brussels.

CEC (1993c), 'Report on reinforcing the effectiveness of the internal market', COM(93)256 final, Brussels.

CEC (1993d), 'Proposal on integrated pollution prevention and control', COM(93)423 final, Brussels.

CEC (1993e), 'Report on the adaptation of Community legislation to the subsidiarity principle', COM(93)545 final, Brussels.

CEC (1993f), Communication on 'Making the most of the internal market – Strategic programme', COM(93)632 final, Brussels.

CEC (1993g), White Paper: 'Growth, competitiveness and employment', COM(93)700 final, Brussels.

CEC (1993h), 'Impact of completion of the internal market on the tourism sector, DG XXIII.

CEC (1993i), 'Community guidelines on state aid for environmental protection', *Bulletin of the European Communities*, No. 12, Brussels.

CEC (1993j), 'Administrative structures for environmental management in the European Community', European Environment Agency Task Force, Brussels.

CEC (1994a), 'Proposal for a Council Directive concerning the quality of bathing water', COM(94)36 final, Brussels.

CEC (1994b), 'Economic growth and the environment: some implications for economic policy making', COM(94)465 final, Brussels.

CEC (1994c), 'Directions for the European Union on environmental indicators and green national accounting: integration of economic and environmental information systems', COM(94)670 final, Brussels.

CEC (1994d), 'A policy for the European Union on industrial competitiveness', Brussels.

CEC (1995a), 'Communication from the Commission concerning the promotion of energy efficiency in the European Union (SAVE II Programme), COM(95)225 final, Brussels.

CEC (1995b), 'Report of the group of independent experts on legislative and administrative simplification (the Molitor Report)', COM(95)288 final, Brussels.

CEC (1995c), 'European employment strategy: recent progress and prospects for the future', COM(95)465 final, Brussels.

CEC (1995d), 'Study on alternative strategies for the development of relations in the field of agriculture between the EU and the associated countries with a view to future accession of these countries (Agricultural Strategy Paper), a communication', presented by the Commission to the Madrid European Council in December 1995, COM(95)607 final, Brussels.

CEC (1995e), 'Proposal on the review of the Fifth Environmental Action Programme', COM(95)647 final, Brussels.

CEC (1995f), Green Paper: 'an EU energy policy', COM(94)659 final, Brussels.

CEC (1995g), 'An energy policy for the European Union', COM(95)682 final, Brussels.

CEC (1995h), Green Paper: 'Towards fair and efficient pricing in transport', COM(95)691 final, Brussels.

CEC (1996a), 'The Single European Market in 1995 – Report of the Commission to the Council and the European Parliament', COM(96)51 final, Brussels.

CEC (1996b), 'Trade and environment' COM(96)54 final, Brussels.

CEC (1996c), 'The demographic situation in the EU', COM(96)60 final, Brussels.

CEC (1996d), 'Proposal for a Council Decision on a first multiannual programme to assist European tourism (PHILOXENIA)', COM(96)168 final, Brussels.

CEC (1996e), 'Communication under the UN Convention on Climate Change', COM(96)217 final, Brussels.

CEC (1996f), 'Commission Annual Report on the Cohesion Fund', COM(96)388 final, Brussels.

CEC (1996g), White Paper: 'A strategy for revitalising the Community's railways', COM(96)421 final, Brussels.

CEC (1996h), 'Communication on the implementing of Community environmental law', COM(96)500 final, Brussels.

CEC (1996i), 'Proposal to amend Directive 85/337 on assessment of effects of certain public and private projects on the environment', COM(96)511 final, Brussels.

CEC (1996j), 'The impact and effectiveness of the Single Market', COM(96)520 final, Brussels.

CEC (1996k), 'Proposal for a framework directive on ambient noise pollution', COM(96)540 final, Brussels.

CEC (1996l), 'Guidelines for environmental agreements', COM(96)561 final, Brussels.

CEC (1996m), Green Paper: 'Energy for the future: renewable sources of energy', COM(96)576 final, Brussels.

CEC (1996n), 'Thirteenth report on the application of Community law (1995)', COM(96)600 final, Brussels.

CEC (1996o), 'Assessment of the Community eco-label scheme', COM(96)603 final, Brussels.

CEC (1996p), 'Progress report from the Commission on the implementation of the Community programme of policy and action in relation to the environment and sustainable development (Fifth EAP)', COM(95)624 final, Brussels.

CEC (1996q), 'Re-examining the proposal for the Council Decision concerning a multi-annual programme for the promotion of energy efficiency in the Community – SAVE II', COM(96)640 final, Brussels.

CEC (1996r), 'Benchmarking the competitiveness of European industry', Internet version, 9 October, Brussels.

CEC (1996s), 'The 1996 Single Market review – background information', Commission Staff Working Paper SEC(96)2378(1), Brussels.

CEC (1996t), 'Report on the operation of the Single Market – 1996', SEC(96)2378, Brussels.

CEC (1996u), 'Reinforcing political union preparing for enlargement', Commission opinion on the Intergovernmental Conference, 1996.

CEC (1997a), 'Environmental taxes and charges in the Single Market', COM(97)9 final, Brussels.

CEC (1997b), 'Report on the application of directives on waste management', COM(97)23 final, Brussels.

CEC (1997c), 'Proposal for an energy product tax', COM(97)30 final, Brussels.

CEC (1997d), 'A framework for water policy', COM(97)49 final. Published in *Europe*, 2 July, Brussels.

CEC (1997e), 'Trans European rail freight freeways', COM(97)242 final, Brussels.

CEC (1997f), 'Intermodality and intermodal freight transport in the European Union', COM(97)243 final, Brussels.

CEC (1997g), 'Fourteenth Report on the application of Community law (1996)', COM(97)299 final, Brussels.

CEC (1997h), 'Community measures affecting tourism (1995–1996)', COM(97)332 final, Brussels.

CEC (1997i), 'Proposal for a directive on end of life vehicles', COM(97)358 final, Brussels.

CEC (1997j), 'Employment in Europe – 1997', COM(97)479 final, Brussels.

CEC (1997k), 'Commission report on implementation of Council Directive 91/676/EEC concerning the protection of waters against pollution caused by nitrates from agricultural sources', COM(97)473 final, Brussels.

CEC (1997l), 'Communication on environment and employment', COM(97)592 final, Brussels.

CEC (1997m), 'Energy for the future: renewable sources of energy', COM(97)599 final, Brussels.

CEC (1997n), 'Proposal for a framework for action in the field of water policy', COM(97)614 final, Brussels.

CEC (1997o), 'Agenda 2000: communication for a wider and stronger Europe' (including the Commission Opinions on the applicant states from Central and Eastern Europe), COM(97)2000 final, Brussels.

CEC (1997p), *Agenda 2000 vol. 1: For a Stronger and Wider Union; Vol: 2: Challenge of Enlargement; vol. 3: Opinions of the European Commission on the Applications for Accession*, COM(97)2000.

CEC (1997q), *EU Transport in Figures* (2nd edn), Brussels.

CEC (1997r), 'Agriculture and the environment', CAP Working Notes, Brussels.

CEC (1997s), 'CAP 2000: Long-term prospects for grains, milk and meat markets', Working document DG VI, Brussels.

CEC (1997t), 'Agenda 21 – the first 5 years', report on the progress of implementation of Agenda 21, 1992–97, Brussels.

CEC (1997u), 'An estimate of eco-industries in the EU 1994', report prepared by ECOTEC Research UK, BIPE France and IFO Germany, May, Brussels.

CEC (1997v), 'Climate change – the EU's approach for Kyoto', communication by the Commission to the Council, the European Parliament, the Economic and Social Committee and the Committee of the Regions, Internet version, Brussels.

CEC (1997w), 'Compliance costing for approximation of EU environmental legislation in the CEEC', report published in April 1996 by Environment Policy Europe for DG XI, Brussels.

CEC (1997x), 'Newsletter on the EU eco-label issues', July 1997 and February 1998.

CEC (1997y), 'The European Commission approves the labelling of genetically modified organisms', Press Release Ref. IP/97/528 rev., 18 June, Brussels.

CEC (1997z), 'The future of North–South relations', Forward Studies Unit Paper no. 1, Brussels.

CEC (1997aa), 'Europeans and energy', a report for DG XVII in *Eurobarometer*, 46.0, Brussels.

CEC (1997bb), 'Case studies of job creation associated with the environment' report to DG XI, May, Brussels.

CEC (1997cc), 'Climate change – the EU approach for Kyoto', communication to the Council, the European Parliament, the Economic and Social Committee and the Committee of the Regions, Brussels.

CEC (1997dd), 'Single market: business survey reveals cautious optimism', press release, 19 November.

CEC (1997ee), 'Explanatory memorandum: Proposal for a Council Directive establishing a framework for water policy', COM(97)49 final, Brussels.

CEC (1998a), 'Amended Proposal for a framework for action in the field of water policy', COM(98)76 final, Brussels.

CEC (1998b), 'Amended Proposal for a Council Regulation on the establishment of the EEA', COM(98)191, final, Brussels.

CEC (1998c), 'Fifteenth annual report on the monitoring of the application of Community Law', COM(98)317 final, Brussels.

CEC (1998d), 'Partnership for integration', COM(98)333 final, Brussels.

CEC (1998e), 'Newsletter from Ritt Bjerregaard on the Agenda 2000', May, Brussels.

CEC (1998f), 'Commission proposes system to ensure fair payment for the use of transport infrastructure in Europe', Rapid Report IP/98/679, 22 July, Brussels.

CEC (1998g), 'Evaluation of the financial impact of the Commission Proposals concerning the reform of the Common Agricultural Policy: Agenda 2000: 2000–2006, Brussels.

CEC (1998h), *Transport Advance*, Brussels.

CEC (1998i), *Transport in Figures*, Brussels.

CEC (1998j), 'EU Research Ministers reach agreement on the Fifth Framework Programme (1998–2002)', press release, Brussels.

CEC (1998k), 'Accession strategies for the environment', Internet version.

CEC (1998l), *Single Market Scoreboard*, No. 2 May, Brussels.

CEC (1998m), 'Set-aside rate proposed for the 1999/2000 marketing year', Rapid Report DN: IP/98/517, 10 June, Brussels.

CEC (1999a), 'Agricultural Council: Political agreement on CAP reform', *Agricultural Newsletter*, special edition, 11 March.

CEC (1999b), 'Single Market Action Plan bears fruit', Internet version, 23 February.

CEC (1999c), *Transport in Figures*, Brussels: CEC.

CEC (1999d), Sixth Periodic Report on the Regions, Brussels.

CEC (1999e), 'June 1999 Single Market Scoreboard Underlines Further Efforts required by Member State', Internet Version, June.

CEC/European Parliament (1997), *Environment and Employment: Proceedings of Conference held 26/27th May 1997*, European Parliament, Brussels.

Chance, C. (1995), *European Environmental Law Guide*, London: Clifford Chance Associates.

Chemical Business News Base (1996), 'Environmental Taxes: Implementation and Environmental Effectiveness', 1, October.

Cini, M. (1996), *The European Commission*, Manchester and New York: Manchester University Press.

Clarke, Jackie (1997), 'A framework of approaches to sustainable tourism', *The Journal of Sustainable Tourism*, **5**(3).

Coase, R.H. (1960), 'The problem of social costs', *Journal of Law and Economics*, **III**, 1–44.

CoM (1973), 'Declaration of the Council on a programme of action of the European Communities on the Environment (First Environmental Action Programme', OJC 112, 20 December, pp. 1–53, Brussels.

CoM (1977), 'Resolution of the Council on the continuation of the implementation of the European Community policy and action programme on the environment (Second EAP)', OJC, **20** (139), 13 June, pp. 1–46, Brussels.

CoM (1983), 'Resolution of the Council on the continuation and implementation of a European Community policy and action programme on the environment (1982–1987) (Third EAP)', OJC, 46, 7 February, pp. 1–146, Brussels.

CoM (1987), 'Resolution of the Council on the continuation and implementation of a European Community policy and action programme on the environment (1987–1992) (Fourth EAP), OJC, 328, 7 December, pp. 1–44, Brussels.

CoM (1992), 'Community action plan for tourism', Council Decision of 13/7/1992, OJL 231, 13 July 1992, Brussels.

CoM (1999), 'Presidency conclusions: Berlin European Council 24 and 25 March 1999', SN 100/99 EN.

Cooper, C., J. Fletcher, D. Gilbert and S. Wanhill (1993), *Tourism: Principles and Practice*, London and New York: Longman.

Corbett, R. (1997), 'Governance and institutional developments', in N. Nugent (ed.) *The European Union 1996 – Annual Review of Activities*, Oxford and Boston, MA: Blackwell.

Corbett, R. et al. (1995), *The European Parliament* (3rd edn), London: Cartermill International.

Cremer, W. and A. Fisahn (1998), 'New environmental policy instruments in Germany', in J. Golub (ed.), *New Instruments in Environmental Protection in the EU*, London and New York: Routledge.

Dodds, F. and T. Bigg (1995), *Three Years since Rio*, London: UNED–UK Report.

DoE (Department of the Environment) and DTI (Department of Trade and Industry) (1994), *The UK Environment Industry: Succeeding in the Global Market*, London: HMSO.

DoE, British Government Panel on Sustainable Development (1995), *First Report*, London: DoE.

DoE, British Government Panel on Sustainable Development (1995), *Second Report*, London: DoE.

Duff, A. (ed.) (1997), *The Treaty of Amsterdam*, London: Sweet and Maxwell for the Federal Trust.

Economic and Social Committee (1993), 'Opinion on the Packaging Waste Proposed Directive', ECOSOC.

Economic and Social Committee (1994), 'Opinion on the Commission report on the functioning of the Single Market', ECOSOC.

Economist (1997a), 'Taxing matters', 5 April.

Economist (1997b), 'Europe: Wanted: a farming revolution', 6 September.

Esty, D.C. (1994), *Greening the GATT*, Washington, DC: Institute for International Economics.

Europe (1994), 'History, Contents and Timetable of the First Implementation Treaty of the European Energy Charter', 19 October.

Europe (1996a), 'Commission sets out guidelines on trade and environment, Rejecting 'eco-duties', advocating positive measures', 29 February.

Europe (1996b), 'Commission approves Swedish tax measures on CO_2 and Danish measures on waste water', 5 December.

Europe (1996c), 'Conclusions of the Turin Summit', 29 March.

Europe (1997a), 'EP Greens Group welcomes proposal on energy tax but considers it too limited. Criticisms and suggestions', 26 March.

Europe (1997b), 'Commission proposes tax regime for all energy products based on minimum rates to be respected by all member states – social environmental objectives, progressive implementation', 14 March.

Europe (1997c), 'Parliament calls for strict and more binding standards for fuel and motor vehicle emissions', 11 April.

Europe (1997d), 'While backing better use of renewable energy sources, Eurelectric considers the objective fixed by the Commission is too ambitious if not unrealistic', 1 April.

Europe (1998a), 'American report on European trade barriers denounces non-tariff barriers, agricultural export subsidies, state aid to Airbus, obstacles to services', 9 April.

Europe (1998b), 'Commission adopts communication on energy efficiency, first step towards adopting EU global strategy', 30 April.

Europe (1998c), 'Adoption of 1998/99 Renewable Energies Programme but without targets – other results', 11 May.

Europe (1998d), 'EU and US call for conference on link between environment and trade', 27 May.

Europe Environment (1997), 'Commission amends draft directive on bathing water quality', 9 December.

European Environmental Agency (1996), 'Environmental Taxes: Implementation and Environmental Effectiveness', Environmental Issues Series No. 1, Copenhagen: EEA.

European Environmental Agency (1998), *Second Report on the State of Europe's Environment – 'Dobris + 3'*, Copenhagen: EEA.

European Parliament (1992), Report of the Committee on Economic and Monetary Affairs and Industrial Policy, 'On the environment and industrial competitiveness', A3-0343/92.

European Parliament (1994a), Committee on the Environment, Public Health and Consumer Protection, 'Report on the environmental aspects of the enlargement of the Community to include Sweden, Austria, Finland and Norway' (The Bjornvig Report).

European Parliament (1994b), Committee on the Environment, Public Health and Consumer Protection, 'Report on the need to assess the true costs to the Community of the non-environment' (The Pimenta Report).

European Parliament (1997a), 'Fair and efficient transport pricing', press release, 29 January.

European Parliament (1997b), Environment Committee, 'Internal Working Document summarizing the work of the Committee during the period September 1994 to March 1997'.

European Parliament (1998), 'Parliament–Council Conciliation Committee: The "Auto-Oil" Programme is on the Road! Parliament and Council agree on cleaner fuels and pollution standards for cars', Press release 230, 7 July.

European Parliament (1999), 'First Report of the Committee of Independent Experts on allegations regarding fraud, mismanagement and nepotism in the European Commission', 15 March.

European Report (1996), 'CO$_2$ energy tax proposal to take a broader view', 9 October.

European Report (1997a), 'Commission sketches outlines of EU action on environmental liability', 30 January.

European Report (1997b), Germany and UK block Philonexia programme', 28 November.

European Voice (1997), 'In brief', 11–17 September, p. 9.

Eurostat (1996a), 'Energy economy of the European Union in 1995', from Frontier-free Europe, no. 10.

Eurostat (1996b), *Statistics in Focus: Environment*, no. 2.

Eurostat (1997a), 'Statistical aspects of the energy economy in 1996, *Statistics in Focus: Energy and Industry*, no. 16.

Eurostat (1997b), Press Release no. 8097, 27 November.

Eurostat (1998), 'Indicators of sustainable mobility', Press Release no. 5898, 31 July.

Field, B.C. (1994), *Environmental Economics: An Introduction*, New York: McGraw-Hill.

Freestone, D. (1992), 'The 1992 Maastricht Treaty – implications for European environmental law', *European Environmental Law Review*, 1, 23–6.

Gardner, B. (1996), *European Agriculture: policies, production and trade*, London and New York: Routledge.

Grant, C. (1994), *Delors: inside the House that Jacques built*, London: Nicholas Brearley Publishing.

Green Alliance (1996), *National Sustainable Strategies*, European Environment Bureau.

Haig, Simonian (1998), 'Clean air costs will fall on oil industry', *Financial Times*, 20 August.

Haigh, N. (1989), *EEC Environmental Policy and Britain* (2nd edn), London and New York: Longman.

Haigh, N. (1995), *The 1996 Intergovernmental Conference – Integrating the environment into other EU policies*, London: IEEP.

Hardin, G. (1968), 'The Tragedy of the Commons', *Science*, **162**, 1243–9.

Helm, D. (ed.) (1991), *Economic Policy Towards the Environment*, Oxford: Blackwell.

Heyes, A. (1997), 'Greening the law', *New Economy*, **IV** (2), Summer, 123–6.

Hildebrand, P.M. (1993), 'The EC's environmental policy, 1957 to 1992', in D. Judge (ed.), *A Green Dimension for the EC*, London and Portland, OR: Frank Cass.

Hjalager, Anne-Mette (1996), 'Tourism and the environment: the innovation connection, *The Journal of Sustainable Tourism*, **4** (4).

Hogwood, B. and L. Gunn (1984), *Policy Analysis for the Real World*, Oxford: Oxford University Press.

House of Commons (1998), Select Committee on European Legislation, Twelfth Report, Session 1997–98, HC 155–xii.

House of Lords (1989), Select Committee on the European Communities, Fifteenth Report, Session 1988–89, 'Habitats and species protection', HL Paper 72, London: HMSO.

House of Lords (1992a), Select Committee on the European Communities, Eighth Report, Session 1991–92, 'Carbon/energy tax', HL Paper 52, London: HMSO.

House of Lords (1992b), Select Committee on the European Communities, Ninth Report, Session 1991–92, 'Implementation and enforcement of legislation', HL Paper 53, London: HMSO.

House of Lords (1992c), Select Committee on the European Communities, Eighth Report, Session 1992–93, 'Fifth Environmental Action Programme: Integration of Community Policies', HL Paper 27, London: HMSO.

House of Lords (1992d), Select Committee on the European Communities, Fourteenth Report, Session 1992–93, 'Environmental aspects of the reform of the Common Agricultural Policy', HL Paper 45, London: HMSO.

House of Lords (1993a) Select Committee on the European Communities, Eighteenth Report, Session 1992–93, 'Industry and the environment', HL Paper 73, London: HMSO.

House of Lords (1993b), Select Committee on the European Communities, Third Report, Session 1993–94, 'Remedying environment damage', HL Paper 10, London: HMSO.

House of Lords (1994), Select Committee on Sustainable Development, Session 1993–94, 'Minutes of evidence', 7 March 1994, London: HMSO.

House of Lords (1995), Select Committee on the European Communities, Fifth Report, Session 1994–95, 'European Environment Agency', HL Paper 29, London: HMSO.

House of Lords (1996), Select Committee on the European Communities, Eleventh Report, Session 1995–96, 'An EMU of ins and outs', HL Paper 86, London: HMSO.

House of Lords (1997a), Select Committee on the European Communities, Second Report, Session 1997–98, 'Community environmental law: making it work', HL Paper 12, London: HMSO.

House of Lords (1997b), Select Committee on the European Communities, Seventh Report, Session 1997–98, 'Community railway strategy', HL Paper 46, London: HMSO.

Hoyer, K. (1993), 'Nordic and EC environmental policies: differences and similarities', unpublished paper presented to Third Annual European Environment Conference, Bristol, 20–21 September.

Humphreys, M. (1997), 'European integration and environment: a case study in Austrian transit traffic', Unpublished paper presented to the Second UACES Research Conference, Loughborough, 10–11 September.

Hurrell, A. and B. Kingsbury (1992), *The International Politics of the Environment*, Oxford and New York: Clarendon Press.

International Energy Agency (1991), *Energy Efficiency and the Environment*, Paris: OECD.

Jager, J. et al. (1995), *Global Environmental Change and Sustainable Development in Europe*, Commission of the European Communities.

Johnson, S.P. and G. Courcelle (1995), *The Environmental Policy of the European Communities* (2nd edn), London: Kluwer Law International.

Judge, D. (1993), 'The Environment Committee of the EP', in D. Judge (ed.) *A Green Dimension for the European Community*, London and Portland, OR: Frank Cass.

Judge, D. (ed.) (1993), *A Green Dimension for the European Community*, London and Portland, OR: Frank Cass.

Kågeson, P. (1996), 'Effects of internalisation on transport demand and modal split', in European Conference of Ministers of Transport, *Internalising the Social Costs of Transport*, Paris: OECD.

Kinnock, N. (1998), 'Trans European rail freight freeways', speech to the *Economist* Conference, Sheraton Hotel, Brussels, 16 January.

Kramer, L. (1993), 'Environmental protection and article 30 EEC Treaty', *Common Market Law Review*, **30**, 111–43.

Kramer, L. (1995), *EC Treaty and Environmental Law* (2nd edn), London: Sweet and Maxwell.

Laffan, B. (1996), in *Proceedings of the Jean Monnet Chairs Conference on the 1996 IGC*, Brussels, May.

Legg, W. and L. Portugal (1997), 'How agriculture benefits the environment', *OECD Observer*, no. 205 April/May, pp. 27–30, Paris: OECD.

Lévêque, F. (1996), *Environmental Policy in Europe*, Cheltenham, UK and Brookfield, US: Edward Elgar.

Liefferink, D. (1996), Environment and the Nation State – the Netherlands, the EU and Acid Rain, Manchester and New York: Manchester University Press.

Liefferink, D. et al. (1993), *European Integration and Environmental Policy*, London and New York: Belhaven.

Maitland, Alison (1997), 'Fertiliser groups see further decline: manufacturers predict fall in consumption as European farming practices change, *Financial Times*, 9 October, p. 37.

Mann, M. (1997), 'Green Scheme under attack by Big Three', *European Voice*, 9 January, p. 2.

Matláry, J.H. (1998), *Energy Policy in the European Union*, Basingstoke: Macmillan Press.

Mayhew, A. (1998), *Recreating Europe – the EU's Policy towards Central and Eastern Europe*, Cambridge and New York: Cambridge University Press.

Mazey, S. and J. Richardson (eds) (1993), *Lobbying in the EC*, Oxford: Oxford University Press.

Mazey, S. and J. Richardson (eds) (1996), *EU: Power and Policy Making*, London and New York: Routledge.

McLaughlin, A. et al. (1993), 'Corporate lobbying in the European Community', *Journal of Common Market Studies*, **31** (2), June.

Meadows, D.H. et al. (1972), *The Limits to Growth*, New York: Universe Books.

Meadows, D.H, D.L. Meadows and J. Randers (1992), *Beyond the Limits: Global Collapse or Sustainable Future*, London: Earthscan.

Mill, J.S. (1857), *Principles of Political Economy*, London: Parker.

Ministry of the Environment, Sweden (1995), *The Environment – Our Common Responsibility*, Stockholm, Sweden.

Murphy, J. and A. Gouldson (1995), 'The missing dimension in EU environmental technology policy', *European Environment*, **5**, Jan–Feb. pp. 20–26.

Nairn, G. (1996), 'This happy breeze', *Financial Times*, 17 July.

National Consumer Council (1996), *Shades of Green – Consumers' attitudes to green shopping*, London: NCC.

O'Riordan, T. and J. Jager (1996), *The Politics of Climate Change – a European Perspective*, London and New York: Routledge.

OECD (1989), *Economic Instruments for Environmental Protection*, Paris: OECD.

OECD (1993a), *Taxation and the Environment: Complementary Policies*, Paris: OECD.

OECD (1993b), *Environmental Performance Review: Norway*, Paris: OECD.

OECD (1993c), *Environmental Performance Review: Germany*, Paris: OECD.

OECD (1994a) *Environmental Performance Review: UK*, Paris: OECD.

OECD (1994b), *The Distributive Effects of Economic Instruments for Environmental Protection*, Paris: OECD.

OECD (1994c), 'Methodologies for environmental and trade reviews', ECD/GD(94)103, Paris: OECD.

OECD (1995a), *Urban Travel and Sustainable Development*, Paris: OECD.

OECD (1995b), *Global Warming: Economic Dimensions and Policy Responses*, Paris: OECD.

OECD (1995c), *Environmental Performance Review: Poland*, Paris: OECD.

OECD (1997a), *Transport and Environment*, Paris: OECD.

OECD (1997b), *Environmental Policies and Employment*, Paris: OECD.

OECD (1997c), *International Tourism in the OECD Area*, Paris: OECD.

OECD (1997d), 'Report of the High Level Advisory Group on the Environment – Guiding the transition to Sustainable Development: a critical role for the OECD' (Internet version).

OECD (1998a), *Agriculture and the Environment: Issues and Policies*, Paris: OECD.

OECD (1998b), *The Environmental Effects of Reforming Agricultural Policies*, Paris: OECD.

OECD (1998c), *Agricultural Policies in OECD Countries: Monitoring and Evaluation 1998*, Paris: OECD.

Oppenheimer, Wolff & Donnelly (1997), 'Possibilities for future EU environmental policy on plant protection products', report for the Commission of the EC, DG XI, Brussels.

Palmer, J. et al. (1996), 'Mapping out fuzzy buzzwords – who sits where on sustainability and sustainable development', *Proceedings of 1996 International Sustainable Development Research Conference*, ERP Environment, Leeds, UK.

Papoutsis, C. (1996), 'Community policy on renewable sources of energy and the World SOLAR Summit Process, World SOLAR Summit', Harare, Zimbabwe, 16–17 September, EU Rapid, 16 September.

Parkinson, A. (1997), 'Change in UK green attitudes pin-pointed', *Insurance Day*, 16 April.

Pearce, D.W. (1991), *Blueprint 2: Sustaining the World Economy*, London: Earthscan.

Pearce D.W. (1993), *Blueprint 3: Measuring Sustainable Development*, London: Earthscan.

Pearce, D.W. and R.K. Turner (1990), *Economics of Natural Resources and the Environment*, London: Harvester Wheatsheaf.

Pearce, D.W. et al. (1989), *Blueprint for a Green Economy (Blueprint 1)*, London: Earthscan.

Peterson, J. (1995a), 'Policy networks and European Union policy making', *West European Politics*, **18** (2), 389–407.

Peterson, J. (1995b), 'Decision-making in the EU: towards a framework for analysis', *Journal of European Public Policy*, **2** (1), 63–93.

Pigou, A.C. (1920), *The Economics of Welfare*, London: Macmillan.

Pinder, J. (1991), *The EU: Making of a Union*, Oxford: Oxford University Press.

Porter, G. and J. Welsh Brown (1991), *Global Environmental Politics*, Oxford and Boulder, CO: Westview Press.

Pressman, J.L. and A. Wildavsky (1974), *Implementation*, Berkeley: University of California Press.

Puchala, D. (1983), in H. Wallace et al. (eds) *Policy Making in the EC* (2nd edn), Chichester, UK: John Wiley and Sons.

Reuters News Service (1996), 'EU Commission re-iterates support for eco-taxes', 27 February.

Richardson, J. (ed.) (1996), *European Union – Policy and Policy-Making*, London and New York: Routledge.

Robins, N. (1996), 'Greening European foreign policy', unpublished paper presented to UACES Conference on Greening the IGC Agenda, Kings College London, 29 March.

Rogers, A. (1997), 'EC tax favours rail and water over roads', *International Freighting Weekly*, 17 March, p 2.

Sands, P. (1996), 'The European Court of Justice: an environmental tribunal?', in H. Somsen (ed.), *Protecting the European Environment, Enforcing EC Environmental Law*, London: Blackstone Press.

Sbragia, A. (1996), 'Environmental policy' in H. Wallace and W. Wallace (eds), *Policy Making in the European Union*, Oxford: Oxford University Press.

Self, P. (1993), *Government by the Market? The Politics of Public Choice*, Basingstoke: Macmillan.

Shan, S. (1996), 'Kerosene tax to cut flying', *Business Times* (Malaysia), 19 February.

Smith, F.L. (1996) 'Learning from the past: freeing up the future', IEA Briefing Paper.

Smith, Z.A. (1995), *The Environmental Policy Paradox*, Englewood Cliffs, NJ: Prentice-Hall.

Somsen, H. (ed.) (1996), *Protecting the European Environment: Enforcing EC Environmental Law*, London: Blackstone Press.

Southey, C. (1997), 'EU hard choices over grain set-aside', *Financial Times*, 6 March, p. 2.

Stanners, D. and P. Bourdeau (eds) (1995), *Europe's Environment – the Dobris Assessment*, Copenhagen, Denmark: European Environment Agency.

Strange, S. (1994), *States and Markets* (2nd edn), London: Pinter.

Sutherland, P. (1992), 'The internal market after 1992: meeting the challenge', Report to the EC Commission by the High Level Group on the Operation of the Internal Market, October, Brussels: CEC.

Suzman, M. (1998), 'Greenhouse gas treaty will cost US', *Financial Times*, 10 June.

Thunberg, B. and P. Hanneberg (eds) (1993), *Acidification and Air Pollution*, Stockholm, Sweden: Swedish Environmental Protection Agency.

Tindale, S. and G. Holtham (1996), *Green Tax Reform: Pollution Payments and Labour Tax Cuts*, London: Institute for Public Policy Research.

Turner, M. (1997), 'World Bank reveals the cost of EU accession', *European Voice*, 17–23 April.

Turner, R.K., D. Pearce and I. Bateman (1994), *Environmental Economics: An Elementary Introduction*, Hemel Hempstead: Harvester Wheatsheaf.

UNICE (1996), 'UNICE basic views on ways to promote better control of CO_2 emissions for the industrial sector', Document 15/3, 12 June.

UNICE (1997) 'Opinion on Regulation EEC No. 880/93 March 23rd 1992 on the Community award scheme for an eco-label', Brussels, Belgium: UNICE.

Van Vreckem, D. (1996), 'European Union policy on taxes and charges in the road transport sector', in European Conference of Ministers of Transport, *Internalising the Social Costs of Transport*, Paris: OECD.

Vaughan, D. and Craig Mickle (1993), *Environmental Profiles of European Business*, Royal Institute for International Affairs and Centre for Environmental Studies, London: Earthscan.

Wallace H. and W. Wallace (eds) (1996), *Policy Making in the EU* (3rd edn), Oxford: Oxford University Press.

Ward, B. and R. Dubos (1972), *Only One Earth – the Report on the Human Environment*, London and New York: Penguin.

Wates, J. (1996), *Access to Environmental Information and Public Participation in Environmental Decision Making*, Brussels, Belgium: European Environmental Bureau.

Weale, A. (1994), 'Environmental Protection, The Four Freedoms and Competition Among Rules', in M. Faure, J. Verveale and A. Weale (eds), *Environmental Standards in the European Union in an Interdisciplinary Framework*, Antwerp: Maklu.

Weale, A. (1996), 'Environmental rules and rule making in the European Union', *Journal of European Public Policy*, **3** (4), December, 594–611.

WCED (World Commission on Environment and Development) (1987), *Our Common Future (The Brundtland Report)*, Oxford: Oxford University Press.

Whitelegg, J. (1992), *Transport and Sustainable Development*, London: Belhaven Press.

Wieringa, K. (ed.) (1996), *Environment in the European Union 1995: Report for the Review of the Fifth Environmental Action Programme*, European Environment Agency and Eurostat, Copenhagen, Denmark.

Wolf, M. (1997), 'Licence to pollute', *Financial Times*, 2 December, p. 18.

Woolcock, S. (1995), *Single European Market: Centralisation or Competition Among National Rules?*, London: The Royal Institute of International Affairs.

World Energy Council (1994), *New Renewable Energy Resources: A Guide to the Future*, London: Kogan Page.

World Tourism Organization (1997a), 'Travel surge in the 21st century', *WTO News*, November.

World Tourism Organization (1997b), 'Eco-tourism rapidly growing niche market', *WTO News*, December/January.

World Trade Organization (1999), 'World trade growth slower in 1998 after unusually strong growth in 1997', Press Release, 16 April 1999.

Wurzel, R.K.W. (1996), 'The role of the EU presidency in the environmental field', *Journal of European Public Policy*, **3** (2), June, 272–91.

Yorkshire Post (1997), 'Pollution blackspots on tourist trail', 22 May, p. 11.

Index